101
GREATEST
ATHLETES
OF THE
CENTURY

THE OUTSTANDING

ALL-AROUND ATHLETES

OF THE 1900s

JIM THORPE

BABE DIDRIKSON ZAHARIAS

101 GREATEST ATHLETES OF THE CENTURY

by *WILL GRIMSLEY*

and The Associated Press Sports Staff

Supervising Editor: Ben Olan

BONANZA BOOKS, New York

PROJECT DIRECTOR: Dan Perkes

SUPERVISING EDITOR: Ben Olan

AUTHOR: Will Grimsley

OTHER EDITORIAL CONTRIBUTORS:

**Bill Bernard, Jim Donaghy, Bob Green, Bob Greene,
Mike Harris, Dick Joyce, John Kreiser, Charles Morey,
Ken Rappoport, Bert Rosenthal, Rick Warner, Barry Wilner**

ASSOCIATE EDITOR: **Norm Goldstein**

PHOTO EDITOR: **John Griffin**

BOOK DESIGN: **Philip Grushkin**

ART DIRECTOR: **Jack Elcik**

GRAPHIC ARTWORK: **Ed De Gasero**

*Pictures were made by staff photographers of
The Associated Press and its member newspapers.*

Printed and Bound in the United States of America
by Arcata Graphics

This 1987 edition is published by Bonanza Books,
distributed by Crown Publishers, Inc.,
225 Park Avenue South, New York, New York 10003.

ISBN 0-517-65579-9

h g f e d c b d

Library of Congress Cataloging-in-Publication Data
Grimsley, Will.
    101 greatest athletes of the century.

    1. Athletes—Biography—Dictionaries.   I. Olan,
Ben.   II. Associated Press.   III. Title.   IV. Title:
One hundred and one greatest athletes of the century.
GV697.A1G698   1987   796′.092′2 [B]   87-23827
ISBN 0-517-65579-9

CONTENTS

INTRODUCTION 9

HANK AARON *The All-Time Home Run King* 13

KAREEM ABDUL-JABBAR *The Sky Hook Is His Calling Card* 16

VASILY ALEXEYEV *"The World's Strongest Man"* 20

MUHAMMAD ALI *"Float Like a Butterfly, Sting Like a Bee"* 22

EDDIE ARCARO *Racing's Grand Slam King* 26

HENRY ARMSTRONG *The Human Buzzsaw* 29

DR. ROGER BANNISTER *Broke the Four-Minute Mile Barrier* 32

SAMMY BAUGH *The First Great Passer* 35

ELGIN BAYLOR *The Franchise-Saver* 37

YOGI BERRA *The Brilliant Buffoon* 40

LARRY BIRD *"He'll Cut Your Heart To Win"* 44

BJORN BORG *Sweden's Golden Boy of Tennis* 48

TERRY BRADSHAW *Country Bumpkin to Super Quarterback* 51

JIM BROWN *"Sheer Power and Desire"* 55

DON BUDGE *The Complete Tennis Player* 59

DICK BUTKUS *The Bruising, Battering Bear* 62

ROY CAMPANELLA *Tragedy Followed Triumphs* 66

WILT CHAMBERLAIN *Triggered the Seven-Foot Revolution* 70

TY COBB *The Fiery Georgia Peach* 74

NADIA COMANECI *Princess of the Bars and Beams* 77

MARGARET SMITH COURT *Queen of Grand Slam Tennis* 80

BOB COUSY *Houdini of the Hardwood* 82

JACK DEMPSEY *The Devastating Manassa Mauler* 86

JOE DIMAGGIO   *The Classy Yankee Clipper*   90

JULIUS ERVING   *A Fond Farewell To Dr. J*   94

CHRIS EVERT   *Ice Princess of the Court*   97

BOB FELLER   *The Blazing Fastballer*   100

A.J. FOYT   *Feared Demon of the Ovals*   102

LOU GEHRIG   *Pride of the Yankees*   105

OTTO GRAHAM   *A Versatile Winning Quarterback*   108

RED GRANGE   *The Galloping Ghost*   111

WAYNE GRETZKY   *"Great In Any Hockey Era"*   114

WALTER HAGEN   *The Brilliant "Climax Player"*   117

BILL HARTACK   *Sullen, Surly . . . But a Standout Jockey*   119

ERIC HEIDEN   *The Olympic Speed Skating Marvel*   122

SONJA HENIE   *"Pavlova" of the Silver Blades*   124

BEN HOGAN   *Golf's "Wee Ice Mon"*   127

ROGERS HORNSBY   *The Arrogant, Abrasive Rajah*   130

GORDIE HOWE   *The Greatest of the Hockey Greats*   132

BOBBY HULL   *The Powerful Golden Jet*   135

JACK JOHNSON   *A Man Without a Country*   138

MAGIC JOHNSON   *A Remarkable Court Wizard*   140

WALTER JOHNSON   *The Big Train Was Quick*   144

BOB JONES   *King of Golf's Grand Slam*   146

BILLIE JEAN KING   *The Court Crusader*   149

JACK KRAMER   *Refined the Serve-and-Volley Game*   152

ROD LAVER   *Tennis' First Millionaire*   154

SUZANNE LENGLEN   *France's Phenomenon*   157

SUGAR RAY LEONARD   *How Sweet It Was*   159

JOHNNY LONGDEN   *First Rider to Score 6,000 Victories*   163

JOE LOUIS   *The Destructive Brown Bomber*   166

MICKEY MANTLE   *The Most Powerful Switch-Hitter*   170

ROCKY MARCIANO   *The Brockton Blockbuster*   174

BOB MATHIAS   *The Decathlon's Schoolboy Phenom*   179

WILLIE MAYS   *The Dynamic "Say Hey Kid"*   182

GEORGE MIKAN   *Basketball's First Big Man*   186

HELEN WILLS MOODY   *"Little Miss Poker Face"*   188

STAN MUSIAL   *The Cards' "Mr. Nice Guy"*   190

BRONKO NAGURSKI   *Like a Runaway Freight Train*   194

JOE NAMATH   *A Genius and a Rascal*   196

MARTINA NAVRATILOVA   *Wimbledon's Perennial Power*   200

BYRON NELSON   *The Texan With a Textbook Swing*   203

JACK NICKLAUS   *The Golden Bear With a Golden Touch*   205

PAAVO NURMI   *The Flying Finn*   208

AL OERTER   *Iron Man of the Discus Throw*   210

BOBBY ORR   *The Grace of a Ballet Dancer*   212

JESSE OWENS   *Star of Hitler's Nazi Olympics*   215

SATCHEL PAIGE   *The Incomparable Ageless Wonder*   219

ARNOLD PALMER   *Charismatic Leader of "Arnie's Army"*   222

WALTER PAYTON   *A Standout, Durable Record-Breaker*   225

PELE   *The World's Most Famous Athlete*   228

WILLIE PEP   *"The Greatest Boxer I Ever Saw"*   231

RICHARD PETTY   *Stock Car Racing's Best*   233

JACQUES PLANTE   *The Masked Gambler*   235

GARY PLAYER   *The "Black Knight" of South Africa*   238

WILLIS REED   *The Ultimate Team Player*   240

MAURICE RICHARD   *... And the Rocket's Red Glare*   243

OSCAR ROBERTSON   *"He Could Beat You All By Himself"*   246

JACKIE ROBINSON   *Breaker of the Color Line*   249

SUGAR RAY ROBINSON   *"Pound For Pound, the Greatest"*   253

PETE ROSE   *The Hustling "Hit" Man*   256

WILMA RUDOLPH   *A Symphony of Speed and Grace*   260

BILL RUSSELL   *"Best Defensive Player of All Time"*   263

BABE RUTH   *Savior of Baseball*   266

GENE SARAZEN   *Maker of Golf's "Miracle Shot"*   270

TERRY SAWCHUK   *The Temperamental "Mr. Zero"*   273

WILLIE SHOEMAKER   *Ageless Sultan of the Saddle*   275

O.J. SIMPSON   *"The Juice" Was Loose*   278

SAM SNEAD   *The Slamming Mountaineer*   282

MARK SPITZ   *Conqueror of the Water World*   285

BART STARR   *Lombardi's Unflappable Leader*   287

ROGER STAUBACH   *The Cowboys' "Mr. Clutch"*   291

JIM THORPE   *The Greatest of Them All*   295

BILL TILDEN   *The Artistic Court Jouster*   297

JOHNNY UNITAS   *"Like Being in a Huddle With God"*   300

TOM WATSON   *The Perennial Golfer of the Year*   303

JOHNNY WEISSMULLER   *Tarzan of the Swim Lanes*   306

JERRY WEST   *The Lakers' "Mr. Clutch"*   308

TED WILLIAMS   *Last of the .400 Hitters*   311

BABE DIDRIKSON ZAHARIAS   *The Phenomenal Wonder Woman*   315

EMIL ZATOPEK   *The Indefatigable Czech*   319

INTRODUCTION

Sports have been a passion of men from time immemorial. There always has been a human instinct to achieve—to climb the unreachable mountain peak, pierce the impenetrable barrier, run faster, jump farther, throw greater distances and display greater skills than one's contemporaries. The reward: personal pride, adulation, gleaming trophies and, as the world has changed, financial security.

This is the stuff of which heroes are made. History and mythology are rich with references to men and women of great physical attributes and accomplishments. Atlas was the first premier weightlifter. He hoisted the world onto his shoulders. The Roman god Mercury had wings on his feet—the fleetest of the fleet. The Biblical Samson was the strongest of men, his muscles yanking the giant pillars of the temple and turning it into rubbish. David had to be the first successful underdog, felling the giant Goliath with a single pebble from his slingshot—a 1,000 to 1 upset.

Nations have measured their strength by the moral fiber and the physical prowess of their athletes. It was a famous Englishman of another century who said the seeds of the British Empire would be sown on the "playing fields of Eton."

Baron Pierre de Coubertin of France revived the Olympic Games because he sought to stimulate the dedication of his country which he feared was going soft. The Olympic credo: "Citius, Altius, Fortius." ("Higher, Faster, Braver.")

When, where and how did sports begin? It's a mystery shrouded in fog which has defied the research of our most persistent historians. The only certainty is that sports simply evolved. They have many fathers and mothers.

One might let his imagination run rampant and drift back to the Stone Age when primitive man was just beginning to fashion the wheel and sampling the first dregs of recreational pleasure.

You might picture a group of four or five men in the prehistoric Age returning to their caves after a day of hunting. One of the men grabs a stick and starts belting a rock down a path.

"Hey, let's play a game," one of them perhaps suggests.

"Okay, what do you want to do?" asks another.

"See that tree down yonder. I'll bet you I can hit it with fewer strokes than you guys can."

"You're on."

So the game is on. One of them wins. One loses. A stick and a rock. A stick and a ball. The rudiments of what may have evolved into the games of baseball, racquetball and tennis.

Once back at the cave, they see a pot boiling with the evening's dragon broth.

"I can put this rock in that pot with fewer swings than you can," insists one of our bearded ancestors.

"Got a bet," says another.

Thus golf is born.

Somewhere along the line, a caveman sees another making overtures to his mate.

A fight ensues. The first boxing match, the most primal of all sports. If they pick up tree limbs and start whaling at each other, that's the birth of ice hockey.

Then, over the centuries, ensued the metamorphoses of big time sports, as we have known them, sewing themselves into the social fabric of all nations, creating idols that have been perpetuated in story and song through the pens of great writers and lyricists.

The Olympics became—and, in the purest sense, remain—the epitome of sports competition although marked over the years by jealousies, national aggrandizement and commercialism which finally has threatened to turn them into a strictly professional show, stripped of their old and cherished values.

They began in 776 B.C. as religious festivals to honor Olympian Zeus, local in nature, staged in the sacred valley at Olympia in Elis near the western coast of Greece. Centuries later they became Pan-Hellenic. Every four years warring nations laid down their arms and went forth in peace to pay tribute to their manhood. The program was simple, consisting largely of competitors racing 200 yards—a "stade," or length of the site which became known as the "stadium."

Over the centuries the program was enlarged to include boxing, wrestling, the pentathlon, discus and spear-throwing. Victors were crowned with a wreath of olive branches.

Two of the greatest early heroes were Theagenes of Thasos, said to be the son of a god and a man who won as high as 1,400 crowns in the fourth century B.C., and Leonidas of Rhodes, a runner who scored three victories in each of four Olympics in 164-152 BC.

The Romans allowed the Games to continue after enslaving the Greeks in 146 B.C. but allowed the Olympic ideal to become so corrupted that they were discontinued in 393 A.D. not to be revived until Baron de Coubertin revived them as the Modern Olympic Games in 1896. Rome's Caesars continued to find sport in staging battles between the Christians and the lions in the Colosseum.

Sports flourished in the Middle Ages. They were closely akin to war. Knights on horseback dueled with lances. Archers tested their skill with bows and arrows and England once outlawed golf because it interfered with archery practice. England's Henry

VIII was playing his favorite sport—Real Tennis—in the catacombs of Hampton Court while having one of his wives, Anne Boleyn, beheaded. He later celebrated the occasion with a beer party for courtiers.

Nevertheless, organized sports as we know them are little more than 100 years old. The Baseball Encyclopedia, puts the first game in Hoboken, N.J., June 19, 1846. The National Association of Professional Baseball Players, the acorn from which the major leagues grew, was formed on March 17, 1871.

American football, an offshoot of the game of soccer originating in Britain, traces its formal birth to a weird game between Princeton and Rutgers Universities in 1869 in which there were 25 players on each side with a single player stationed at each opponent's goal.

The college game, slowly refined, was the premier fall attraction of the public until after World War II when the professional game, started on a shoestring by Chicago's George Halas and with an assist from the popularity of the great Red Grange, used the television screen to gain recognition. The first Super Bowl game was played January 15, 1967.

Meanwhile, soccer, a game spawned on the meadows and village streets of England, itself was growing into adulthood. The first professional league was formed in 1888. From its mob-like primitive youth it was to grow into the world's most widely played and popular sport although never getting a firm foothold in America.

Basketball was a strictly American sport originated by a Springfield, Mass., physical education teacher, who had his students shooting a big ball into a peach basket in 1891. Boxing's roots could be traced back to the Roman Empire but showed up in England in the 18th Century and spilled over into America where at first the sport, fought with bare knuckles, was banned but later developed into one of the country's and world's most practiced and most entertaining endeavors.

Tennis was the brainchild of a stuffy English major who conceived the game to delight lawn party guests in 1873. Wimbledon, the grandpappy of tennis tournaments, celebrated its 100th anniversary in 1986. References have been made to golf being played in Scotland in the 15th Century and the Low Countries before that but the big championship tournaments in Britain and the United States did not start until the 1880s and 1890s. Horse racing's first Kentucky Derby was run in 1875. Indianapolis' Indy 500-mile auto race was inaugurated in 1911.

Thus it's apparent that most of sports' greatest deeds and the men and women who performed them were products of the present century. Yet they occurred under vastly different circumstances.

In those early years baseball players used bats that looked like wagon tongues to hit balls loosely wound and with hand-sewn covers. Their gloves were small and primitive, sometimes with fingers cut out. They played on diamonds that were rough and bumpy, making every infield shot a risk of limb and lumps. The early footballs were fat as balloons, offering the quarterback a limited chance of accuracy.

Players, baseball and football alike, wore heavy, cumbersome uniforms of sweltering wool. Football players had wooden slats in their pants for protection and bulky shoulder pads. These have been replaced with skin-fitting fabrics. The modern baseball is like a bullet, the football a sleek missile.

Participants in both sports no longer perform on grounds that resemble corn fields. They have manicured turf and artificial surfaces.

Golf originally was played with hand-fashioned, wood-shafted clubs which carried such unique names as cleek, mid-iron, mashie, mashie-niblick and spoon. Today, the players have $1,000 bags filled with finely tuned tools numbered for the task required, shafts of honed steel, graphite and other modern materials which add to lightness, whip and strength. The gutta percha and old rubber golf balls have been replaced by pellets precision-made to cut into the wind.

Golf courses which once taunted par-seekers with natural hazards, fairways and greens of unpredictable texture were turned into magnificently cultured layouts by modern golf architects. Original tennis racquets were small, misshapen and a first cousin of the butterfly net. France's great champion, Rene Lacoste, introduced the all-steel frame in the 1960s and this was followed with a slew of weapons made of various alloys. The Prince racquet, with a hitting surface almost twice that of the old conventional model, added years to the careers of women and seniors while turning the established star into a more formidable player.

Equipment and playing conditions have not been the only factors favoring the latter day sports giants. Health and diet studies have added to the size and strength of the modern individual.

George Mikan of the old Minneapolis Lakers basketball team, 6 feet, 10½ inches tall and weighing 245 pounds, was considered an awesome giant back in the late 1940s and early 1950s. In the 1980s, he would have been dwarfed by such gargantuans as Kareem Abdul-Jabbar (7-2), Ralph Sampson, (7-4) and Manute Bol (7-6). A 6-foot-6 basketball player, a big man in Mikan's time, would need extraordinary speed to make him a valuable commodity in the 1980s.

Jack Dempsey, who weighed 187 pounds when he demolished the 245-pound Jess Willard for the heavyweight boxing championship in the sweltering Toledo heat July 4, 1919, would have been considered scrawny beside the heavyweights who came along later.

How would the Manassa Mauler have fared against the lightning-quick, nimble-footed Muhammad Ali? Could Bob Jones, golf's great Grand Slammer, have taken the measure of Jack Nicklaus, who has won almost twice as many major championships? How would you like to see a cleat-flying duel at second base between the tough Ty Cobb and gutsy Pete Rose? Could Big Bill Tilden have blunted the cannon-like services of Boris Becker or the left-handed wizardry of an inspired John McEnroe?

Who knows? They were stars of different eras, playing with different equipment and under varying circumstances. An athlete's greatness can be measured only by his performance against his contemporaries at the time. To do otherwise is unfair.

Golfer Bob Jones, speaking at a dinner honoring Ben Hogan

for his sweep of the Masters, British and U.S. Open golf titles in 1953, told an audience:

"People ask me how I would have fared against Ben Hogan," the late king of the fairways said. "I always tell them one thing. Athletes today are running faster, jumping higher and throwing things farther than ever before. It is only natural that they should be playing golf better, too.

"Ben will find himself answering the same question because there will come another who will outshine his deeds, just as some feel Ben has done mine."

Thirty-three years after that speech, Jack Nicklaus won the Masters golf crown at age 46 for his 20th national championship.

Jones was a product of the heady era in sports after World War I which historians of the period labeled "The Golden Twenties" and the "Age of Wonderful Nonsense."

Everybody was a hero. The nation froze during the period of baseball's World Series and big heavyweight fights such as the historic two duels between Jack Dempsey and Gene Tunney. Notre Dame's Coach Knute Rockne was more famous than the President and Babe Ruth was paid a higher salary than the nation's chief executive.

In those pre-TV days, a whole population hovered around their radios to hear famed announcers such as Graham McNamee reveal the details in a staccato, machine-gun style or they gathered at city squares—New York Times Square, among them—to watch the play-by-play flashed on a giant electronic screen. Crudely crayoned inning-by-inning baseball scores were flashed in shop windows.

The Associated Press assigned 16 reporters to cover the collegiate (Poughkeepsie) rowing regatta, stationed at key points to relate by walkie-talkie progress of the race and such minute details as the rowing beat of the crews. Others followed by train. The New York Times' Pulitzer Prize winning columnist, James B. Reston, was one of these leg men.

When the century passed the halfway mark in 1951, the AP conducted a poll of its hundreds of member papers asking a vote on the greatest athletes—broken down by sport—of the first 50 years.

The result was unique if not completely surprising. Although decades had passed and sports had continued an assembly line flow of great performances and performers, the "Golden Age gang" monopolized the honors.

Babe Ruth beat out Ty Cobb as baseball's greatest player. Dempsey, beaten twice by Gene Tunney, was the best of the boxers although the world was still acclaiming a remarkable black man, named Joe Louis (the Brown Bomber). Bill Tilden and Helen Wills Moody headed the tennis list. Bob Jones had no contender, not even from the emerging Ben Hogan, as the all-time golf king. Jim Thorpe was hailed as the greatest all-around male athlete and the phenomenal Babe Didrikson Zaharias best of the women. The movie Tarzan, Johnny Weissmuller, was sultan of all swimmers although teen-age schoolgirls were beginning to shatter his water records.

This would seem to have revealed a malfunction in Bob Jones' "bigger, stronger, quicker" theories but not necessarily.

It only tended to emphasize that great legends are not forged on feats of strength and skills alone preserved in record books but are governed in part on intangibles—an unexplainable charisma or magnetism that fires the imagination and fealty of their fans.

In all of sports history there is no more magical and enduring name than that of Babe Ruth. His home run records may be broken and rebroken but school kids for generations to come will not be allowed to forget the moon-faced, pot-bellied man who glamorized the sight of a baseball soaring out of the park in America's favorite pastime.

Ring analysts still measure their heavyweight champions by Jack Dempsey. Despite the brilliant performances of Martina Navratilova and Chris Evert, polls of latter day tennis writers persist on listing France's graceful Suzanne Lenglen and California's stoical Helen Wills Moody at the top of their rankings. No woman athlete has emerged to compare with the Texas tomboy, Babe Didrikson Zaharias, for all-around athletic prowess.

Some theorists have reckoned that voters in the AP's mid-century poll were mesmerized by the glamor of the so-called "Golden Age" and the tales passed down by their fathers and grandfathers. Others have contended that the legends of the 1920s and early 1930s were the products of the flamboyant prose of the sportswriting giants of the period—Grantland Rice, Ring Lardner, Westbrook Pegler, Damon Runyon and others. They covered the major sports events as people cover wars, painting word pictures of supermen performing super deeds. It was a mad, crazy age and infectious.

Then came World War II. Ernest Hemingway, a sports writer, donned battle fatigues. From its Rockefeller Plaza headquarters in New York, The Associated Press sent a directive to all its bureaus to tone down the euphoric rhetoric of their sports coverage.

The directive essentially said this: "When men are dying on the battlefields, it is improper to use words such as 'hero,' 'valiant' and 'courageous' in writing about games."

Sports writing underwent a marked change after World War II. Purplish prose and pressbox hysteria gave way to a more cynical, critical and probing form of reporting. The advent of network television forced the print media into an investigative in-depth, reaction mode in place of simply relating what happened.

The craft was swamped with so-called "chipmunks," aggressive young newcomers who zeroed on the "angle" and the "different approach." While some fine essayists such as the New York Times' Red Smith and masters of the metaphor such as the Los Angeles Times' Jim Murray prevailed, the trend veered toward a hard-hitting, no-holds-barred style of journalism.

While in the old days few dared speak of Babe Ruth's gluttonous and high-living escapades or the well-known homosexual proclivities of Big Bill Tilden, the new breed zealously peeked into every closet and searched out every wart of the nation's sports celebrities. Nobody was immune.

Yet athletes continued to grow bigger, stronger, faster with expanding natural skills. Their deeds kept overshadowing almost everything that had gone before. Still, there was no diminishing the luster of those earlier giants who had to be measured by the competition and conditions of their times.

There seems no set formula for establishing legendary status in sports. In assessing the "101 Greatest Athletes of the Century," we found no particular key that unlocked the door to immortality.

There were those who attained plateaus that appeared beyond the reach of all others—Lou Gehrig's streak of 2,130 games without a miss. Joe DiMaggio's 56-game hitting streak, Emil Zatopek's sweep of the three longest distance races in the 1952 Olympics at Helsinki and Mark Spitz's seven gold medals in the Olympic swimming pool at Munich in 1972.

Longevity, the ability to persevere on a winning scale over decades, marked the championship careers of others—notably the ageless jockey, Willie Shoemaker; golfer Gene Sarazen, whose career spanned four distinct eras of the game; discus thrower Al Oerter, who won gold medals in four Olympics and could have competed in three more; basketball's Kareem Abdul-Jabbar, and such baseball indestructibles as Rogers Hornsby, Ty Cobb and the latter day Pete Rose.

While the exploits of these titans were spread over decades, Zatopek, Spitz and speed skating's Eric Heiden carved their names in perpetual stone in the space of a fortnight or less—the length of an Olympic Games.

Bob Jones conquered all there was to conquer in the golf world and retired with 13 national titles and an unmatched Grand Slam at age 28. Ben Hogan was 37 before he won the first of his four U.S. Open crowns and was in his 41st year when he completed his professional Little Slam—the U.S. and Brit-

ish Opens and the Masters—in 1953. Jack Nicklaus appeared to have two separate careers, overshadowing both of his distinguished predecessors with 20 major championships.

Sports legends in some cases were enhanced by events. The four gold medals won by black Jesse Owens in Berlin's Olympics in 1936 shattered Hitler's boast of Aryan supremacy. Joe Louis' one round knockout of Max Schmeling came when national sentiment against Nazism was at a boil.

Both Owens and Louis paved the way for the arrival on stage of the Dodgers' Jackie Robinson, hand-picked as the wedge to crack baseball's color line. All three of these black men, outstanding in their professions, nevertheless will long be remembered for their roles in bringing better understanding between the races.

Arnold Palmer won only one U.S. Open golf championship and not a single PGA crown, yet perhaps no single golf figure had greater impact on the game. A colorful charger with a flair for dramatic comebacks, he became the sport's matinee idol in the late 1950s when television discovered the Masters. Arnie had his own private "army."

Still, personal popularity never became the barometer of public acclaim and acceptance. Palmer was a charmer. Stan Musial was baseball's "Mr. Nice Guy." Joe DiMaggio was revered. But Ty Cobb, one of baseball's greatest, was a belligerent bully. Rogers Hornsby feuded with teammates and rivals alike. Ben Hogan was golf's "Wee Ice Mon"—dour and reclusive.

It was on the playing field that all were judged—and there their places in history must be determined.

Will Grimsley

HANK AARON

The All-Time Home Run King

On the crisp evening of April 8, 1974, before the largest crowd ever to jam into Atlanta Stadium and millions watching on television, Henry Louis Aaron caught a fastball thrown by Al Downing of the Los Angeles Dodgers on the fat part of his bat and sent it soaring over the left field fence, triggering a wild celebration and at the same time a touch of remorse at the passing of one of baseball's cherished records.

Hail the new home run king, Hammerin' Hank, sultan of the game's premier thrill—the massive one shot blow out of the park, now with 715 homers. But no goodbyes for the great Babe Ruth, savior of the game whose place in baseball can never pale.

Aaron's erasing of a mark that most people felt would never be broken was a stark testament to changing times and an irony in the contrast of personality and lifestyles.

The Babe emerged in the wild, swinging era of the Golden Twenties and partook of the period to its fullest. He was big, lovable and outgoing, with a massive appetite for food, women

and song, and basked in the limelight of the biggest city and most glamorous team, the New York Yankees.

Aaron was a product of the Jim Crow South, born at the height of the Great Depression. He had to struggle through early want and racial indignities and spend most of his career in virtual obscurity with a team in the so-called hinterlands. Mild-mannered, dignified, unspectacular and determinedly private, he received relatively little media hype.

Most baseball followers felt that, if Ruth's record was to be challenged, Mickey Mantle and Willie Mays would be the ones to do it. So, while these two charismatic figures on popular teams pursued the goal, Aaron methodically kept smashing 25, 30 or 40 home runs a year with the shifting Braves, who moved from Boston to Milwaukee to Atlanta.

A strong body, powerful wrists and perseverance proved the determining factors, as Aaron's career spanned 23 years. During that time, he played for 12 managers, and not only broke

THERE IT GOES! Hank Aaron eyes flight of the ball after hitting his 715th career homer on April 8, 1974, eclipsing the mark set by Babe Ruth. Dodger lefty Al Downing was the victim of the blast.

Another one of Aaron's 755 major league home runs. This one was hit at Shea Stadium in New York in 1969. Jerry Grote is the catcher and the umpire is Ed Vargo.

Ruth's record, but extended his home run total to 755. He also set other baseball records which have become a lasting tribute to his conditioning, consistency and durability.

He played in the most games (3,298), had the most plate appearances (13,940), the most official times at bat (12,364) and the most runs batted in (2,297), 93 more than Ruth. All told, he set 11 major league and 18 National League records.

A notorious bad-ball hitter, Aaron developed into a record-breaker through hard work and intelligence. Many attributed his power to strong wrists, eight inches around, and ability to wait until the last fraction of a second to snap his bat into action. He wasn't easy to strike out.

Aaron's advice to young hitters always was succinct: "Just be quick with your hands." He prided himself on his ability to assess pitchers. "I never forget a pitcher," he said.

Aaron was born February 5, 1934, in Mobile, Alabama, the third child of Herbert and Estella Aaron. The father was an unskilled shipyards worker, the mother tended a vegetable garden to help feed the family in a $9-a-month shack in a black district known as Texas Hill.

When Aaron was six, the family moved to a larger house, with no electricity and primitive plumbing, but with a backyard big enough for the kids in the neighborhood to hit tin cans and rag balls in one-eyed-cat games.

At 11, he was the shortstop on a kids' team managed by his father, and at 16 he was playing semi-pro ball with the Mobile

Bears, collecting $10 a week. He was good enough in high school to be offered a college scholarship but his mind was made up, over objections of his mother, to play pro baseball.

He was 18 when, with two pairs of pants, $2 in his pockets and lunch in a paper bag, he caught a train to Indianapolis to join the Indianapolis Clowns, a black professional team whose manager had been impressed by the teen-age shortstop in an exhibition game against the Bears in Mobile. Aaron was paid $200 a month.

By this time, with Jackie Robinson the pioneer, blacks were being integrated into major league baseball and young Aaron was too fine a talent to be confined to the Negro League. In May 1952, the Braves outbid the New York Giants and signed the 18-year-old for $350. Aaron was assigned to the Braves' Class C farm club at Eau Claire, Wisconsin.

Aaron batted .336 and was named Rookie of the Year in the Northern League. From Eau Claire, he went to Jacksonville, Florida, in the Sally League, where he became the most valuable player despite insults and abuses of the biased fans in the South.

He couldn't stay in the hotel with his teammates but had to be hauled to a boarding house in the black end of town. He couldn't eat with them at restaurants. Despite his production, he was jeered on and off the field. Tragically, similar resentment surfaced two decades later when he began threatening the precious record of the immortal Ruth.

A loner by nature, Aaron took the indignities hard. Even on the field and in the clubhouse, he failed to join in the camaraderie. He never argued with an umpire. He stayed to himself and avoided confrontations.

He joined the Braves in spring training in March 1954, but was limited to pinch-hitting duties until outfielder Bobby Thomson suffered a broken leg in an exhibition game. Suddenly, Aaron was thrust into the lineup—a job he wasn't to relinquish until 23 years later. Ten days after the season opening, playing in St. Louis, he hit a Vic Raschi fastball over the left field fence for the first of his 755 home runs.

Divorced in 1971 from his first wife, mother of his four children, Aaron married a TV talk show hostess and assumed a $200,000-a-year front office post with the Braves.

Aaron (left) and another slugger, Frank Robinson, pose together after being voted into Baseball's Hall of Fame in 1982. Hank received 406 of a possible 415 votes.

KAREEM ABDUL-JABBAR

The Sky Hook Is His Calling Card

The towering figure with the bald spot on the back of his head and industrial goggles that made him look like a masked man from outer space took a stutter step, spun, rose in the air like a graceful dove in flight and, with a flick of one of his long arms, dropped the basketball—almost gently—through the iron hoop. Defenders could only gape.

Such was Kareem Abdul-Jabbar's renowned "sky hook," the virtually unstoppable and unmatchable maneuver that shall forever mark the legacy of one of the most overwhelming, magnetic and complex personalities ever to play the game.

The 7-foot-2, 230-pound Jabbar dominated his sport from the moment he first picked up a basketball as a tyke in a Harlem playground in New York until he signed a $2 million contract with the Los Angeles Lakers to play his 18th season in the National Basketball Association in 1986, the year of his 39th birthday.

No other man had endured that many years in the tough, run-and-shoot pro game. No one had ever run up and down as many thousand hardwood floors, scored as many points, grabbed as many rebounds or achieved as much success on every rung of his career ladder—high school, college and the big time. The sky hook was his calling card. And nobody could copy it.

"It's a matter of triangulation," he told Sports Illustrated after being named that magazine's Sportsman of the Year in 1985, sounding like a college professor lecturing a science class.

"A normal shot is easier to triangulate. The three corners of the triangle are your eyes, the ball and the rim, and most players shoot from near their eyes. But on the sky hook the ball is way up there and that... keeps most players from getting the coordination of it."

He added that teammate Magic Johnson had asked to be shown the shot but "was never able to get it right."

There it is...the hook shot that goes up to the sky and comes down for a two-pointer. In this 1974 photo, Kareem, then with Milwaukee, shoots over the Lakers' Elmore Smith to register a couple of his 31 points. Bucks won, 112-90.

The sky hook and a unique training regimen—swimming, jumping a heavy rope and especially yoga, hours of meditation at the Yoga College in Los Angeles—provided the somber, enigmatic giant a durability and longevity that defied the imagination of his peers. The normal career life of a pro basketball player is less than four years.

Jabbar, as a converted Muslim, didn't drink or eat red meats. He shunned social functions and informal parties. While he never shirked heavy practice, he learned to pace himself in a game and not exert unnecessary energy. His younger teammates treated him reverentially and went to extra lengths in the latter years to shield him from pressure by rolling up big leads so he wouldn't be forced to play more than 40 minutes a game.

Jabbar set NBA records for most seasons played, most games played and most minutes played. In 1985, he surpassed Wilt Chamberlain's NBA career record of 31,419 points, a mark that had stood for 12 years. And on Feb. 20, 1987, he became the first to reach 36,000 points. He held records also for most field goals and most blocked shots.

Six times he was voted the league's Most Valuable Player, 15 times selected for the NBA All-Star game, 10 as a starter.

At 18 years of age, Jabbar (then Lew Alcindor) starred for UCLA's freshman team. In this 1965 game, he led his squad to a victory over Orange Coast Junior College.

His legs, the first to go under basketball's constant pounding, stood up like stanchions of steel. He never suffered a serious injury although twice he broke a hand in an altercation with an opposing player—a reaction to the elbow liberties he felt referees gave to the smaller men.

Jabbar, who abandoned his Christian name while in college, appeared destined for a king-sized role in life—physically as well as athletically—from the moment he arrived. Ferdinand Lewis Alcindor was born in New York April 16, 1947, the only child of middle-class parents. Lew was big baby—22 1-2 inches long and 12 pounds at birth.

Entering kindergarten, he was head and shoulders taller than his classmates. By the time he reached the seventh grade he was 6-3 and upon entering high school 6-11. His size turned him into a shy, retiring kid who felt uncomfortable with others and he stayed largely to himself. For company, he turned to books and the be-bop and swing music of his times. His home life

didn't help bring him out of his shell. His mother, Cora, was very possessive, his father, Big Al, a transit cop and trombone player, was uncommunicative.

Because of his size and natural talent, young Lew could find some pride in his basketball ability. At Power Memorial High School, he led his team to a 95-6 record, a winning streak of 71 games, and three New York City championships.

Perhaps no high school player in history was more widely recruited. Lew chose UCLA and, as a three-time All-America, proceeded to lead the Bruins to three consecutive NCAA titles, losing only two of 90 games.

In 1969 he signed a $1.4 million contract with the Milwaukee Bucks of the NBA, who six years later sent him to the Lakers in a five-player trade. His salary rose from $500,000 to $2 million a year.

It was while a junior at UCLA that Jabbar adopted the Muslim faith, as Muhammad Ali had done earlier, although it was

18

not until 1971 that he made it public. It was a time of racial turmoil and Jabbar, studious and sensitive to the social injustices, became even more sullen and reclusive.

He criticized the people of Los Angeles as "phonies" and "hate-filled." He expressed resentment that he was accepted only as a jock and not a human being. He cold-shouldered the press and avoided people. He boycotted the 1968 Olympics. He distanced himself from his family. He broke up with his wife and mother of three of his children, taking another mate.

It was not until his Bel Air mansion and many of his prized possessions burned in a January, 1983 fire, that he seemed to mellow—touched by public response to his tragedy—and to rejoin the human race. The change was monumental.

He did TV commercials and bit parts in the movies, invested in Arabian horses in Texas and with friends set up a financial firm to build and restore hotels, clubs and spas.

HERE'S KAREEM! Abdul-Jabbar can jump nimbly off the court, too. Here, he skips rope with the host of the "Tonight Show," Johnny Carson. In this case, too, Kareem was the center of attraction.

VASILY ALEXEYEV

"The World's Strongest Man"

If the Russians wanted to choose an athlete to best symbolize the vast Soviet nation as a whole they would have to look no further than the obscure village of Shakhty and pluck the biggest and strongest man in town.

Vasily Alexeyev was a personification of "The Big Russian Bear."

In the 1970s, as both the world and Olympic super heavyweight weightlifting champion, he was recognized on all the seven continents as the "World's Strongest Man." A massive ham, he relished the title and played his role to the hilt. No other strong man in the 20th Century was more widely celebrated for his feats of strength, although his records subsequently went by the wayside.

Alexeyev was six feet, one inch tall and weighed 353 pounds. He had arms like wagon tongues and thighs like ham hocks but most of his muscle appeared concentrated in an ample belly which poured out over his belt-line. He called it his ballast.

A dark complexion, bushy black eyebrows and sideburns that grew heavy and thick over his ears and almost reached his chin gave him a sinister look. But there always was a puckish good humor behind his menacing facade and he delighted in playing to the audience as some more delicate artist might with the strings of a violin.

Before he would reach down to pick up a 500-pound bar of iron, he would stand immobile for a long time as if waiting for a signal from some unseen power. He would roll his eyes back

The massive Soviet weightlifter (center) won the Olympic super heavyweight crown in 1972. German competitors Rudolph Marg (left) and Gerd Bonk, placed second and third, respectively.

in his head and then slowly reach for the weight. A hush would come over the gallery.

Then, while sweat poured like a waterfall down his chest, he would emit a big grunt and—quick as a flash—thrust the weight over his head. Once held long enough to make the exercise official, he would drop the heavy barbell with a tremendous thud, turn quickly and stomp off the stage, the cheers of acclaim ringing in his ears.

Crowds loved him. American rivals respected but envied him and it wasn't unusual for them to complain, "I think he is taking some kind of drug to stimulate him. Look at his eyes. They are glassy."

Alexeyev chuckled at such accusations. Everybody knew that almost all weightlifters, Russians and Americans alike, gorged themselves with high protein powders and pills and were heavy into steroids. No single country had a lien on these strength-giving, nerve-settling and sometimes illegal stimulants.

The Russians dominated the sport and none was more dominating for his era than Vasily Alexeyev.

Vasily was the first man in history to break the 500-pound barrier in the clean and jerk. To the weightlifting buffs, the feat was every bit as dramatic as Roger Bannister's cracking of the four-minute mile in track. They had thought America's John Davis had reached the ultimate when he raised 400 pounds over his head in the 1952 Olympics at Helsinki.

Another American, Paul Anderson, five feet, 10 inches in height and 300 pounds, had set new standards when he lifted 1,102 pounds in three categories—press, snatch and clean and jerk—four years later in Melbourne, Australia. But the press was dropped after the 1972 Games, leaving the other two as basic lifts.

The snatch requires the lifter to pick up the weight with both hands in one continuous movement and hold it over the head motionless for a few brief seconds. In the clean and jerk, the lifter pulls the weight to his chest and then raises it above his head, arms extended. Both require extraordinary strength and concentration. Alexeyev was a master at both.

Alexeyev won his first world championship in 1970 and soon had the entire sport in the palm of his beefy hand. Every time he went to a meet, whether it be a Russian, European or World Championship, he would break a record. It became routine.

The big Russian won the super heavyweight gold medal in the 1972 Games at Munich with a combined (two events) total of 1,411 pounds. He continued his string of victories for the next four years but was 34 years old and perhaps softened a bit by easy living when the doves were unleashed at the Montreal Olympics in 1976.

Everybody thought that one of two younger men, Khristo Plachov of Bulgaria or Gerd Bonk of East Germany, would dethrone him. But Plachov became ill and failed to make the Games and Bonk seemed to have been psyched right out of his sweat socks.

Arrogantly, Alexeyev elected to sit and let all his 10 opponents finish their attempts in the snatch before lifting a single bar. Bonk's best lift was 375 pounds. Vasily lifted 386 pounds on his first effort, asked for more weight and raised his mark to

Alexeyev weighed 353 pounds. He had arms like long wagon tongues and thighs like ham hocks, but most of his muscle appeared concentrated in an ample belly.

408 pounds. Already he had a 33-pound edge over his 24-year-old rival.

In the clean and jerk, Bonk, who earlier in the year had lifted 557 pounds to break Alexeyev's record, could raise only 518 pounds. Alexeyev asked for 562 pounds. Tension in the big hall mounted.

The Soviet Samson stood over the bar momentarily, eyes closed. Then he took a quick breath, grabbed the weight, and hoisted it toward the roof while splitting and positioning his legs.

The crowd roared. Vasily was still the king. But that was his last hurrah.

He remained a cult hero. Soviet sports stars don't have to worry where their next dish of caviar is coming from.

In his native Shakhty, Alexeyev and his family were given a "state house" by the government and enjoyed the luxuries of a $10,000 automobile, two 21-inch color television sets and a bank account accruing from some 80 world records which brought bonuses of $750 to $1,500 each.

MUHAMMAD ALI

"Float Like a Butterfly, Sting Like a Bee"

"**A**li! Ali! Ali!"
It was a cry that started as a chant in the early 1960s and grew in volume over the next two decades, reverberating around the world from London to New York, Manila to Zaire to the accompaniment of flailing leather gloves.

Muhammad Ali won the heavyweight boxing championship an unprecedented three times. He fought monsters and push-overs, once compiling a winning streak of 31 straight fights, yet his greatest victory was scored outside the ring.

He beat Uncle Sam. He reversed public opinion. Down but not out, he struggled back to become one of the most popular and celebrated athletes of his time.

Refusing to take the step for military service when drafted in 1967, during the Vietnam War, he was stripped of his title,

indicted by the government and, while never jailed, was forced into professional exile for three years.

Although he became a symbol of resistance for fellow blacks and the oppressed people of the world, much of the American public slapped him with the label "slacker"—one of the most reprehensible of terms.

After three years, he was vindicated by the Supreme Court.

Spray flies from the head of challenger Joe Frazier as heavyweight king Muhammad Ali connects with a right in the ninth round of their title fight in Manila on Oct. 1, 1975. Ali retained the crown on a 14th round K.O.

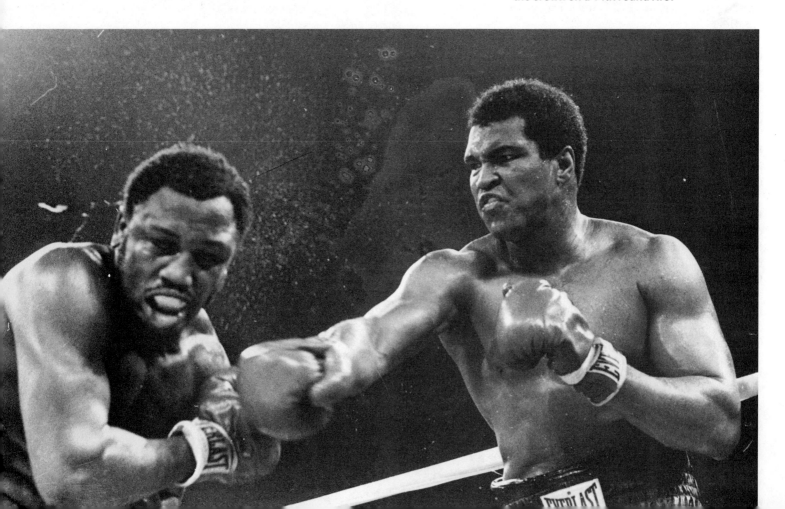

Referee Zack Clayton counts George Foreman out via an eighth round knockout by Muhammad Ali in the ring in Kinshasa, Zaire. The bout, in which Ali regained the heavyweight title, was fought on Oct. 30, 1974.

He returned to reclaim his crown dramatically, lose it, regain it a second time and then a third.

Ultimately, the outcast had become a hero—a world figure, admired and cheered everywhere he roamed, and his journeys had no boundaries.

After winning the heavyweight crown, the puckish son of a Kentucky sign painter adopted the Muslim faith, changing his name from Cassius Marcellus Clay—as he was christened—to Muhammad Ali. It was uncomfortable for the public to accept at first.

"I am 90 per cent preacher and 10 per cent fighter," he contended in Houston when he rejected the military draft on the grounds, upheld later by the highest court, that he was a conscientious objector.

The taint of the experience faded, and Ali's popularity soared.

He was a superb fighter, a sleek punching machine with quick hands, dancing feet and blows that carried the sting of a sabre thrust. More than that, he was a personality—brash and brassy at times, "The Mouth That Roared," they said, cocky almost to the point of arrogance, but rarely offensive.

He intrigued the masses and charmed potentates and kings, who courted his favors. There was no more recognizable personality in the world.

He gave the world some of its greatest ring battles—two knockouts of the fearsome Sonny Liston, his "Rope a Dope" tactics against George Foreman in Zaire, and three great slugfests with Smokin' Joe Frazier.

He was always on stage—boasting, chiding, philosophizing, spouting kindergarten poetry.

"They all must fall, in the round I call."

He told the veteran Archie Moore: "When you come to the fight, don't block the door. You will go home after round four."

His shortest poem: "Whee! Me!"

He was indeed a tremendous specimen—6 feet, 3 inches tall and 210 pounds at top fighting trim—with a blacksmith's shoulders and arms, but lean legs that moved like fleeting light.

"Float like a butterfly, sting like a bee," became his clarion call as he danced about the ring challenging his foes to land a damaging blow and then moving in with a left jab punctuated by a bone-rattling right.

Son of a house painter, the boy known as Cassius dropped out of school early, haunted the playgrounds, and boxed in the local gym. He piled up 108 victories as an amateur and battled his way onto the U.S. Olympic team at age 18, winning the light-heavyweight gold medal in Rome in 1960.

Returning home, he syndicated himself with a group of Louisville businessmen who gave him expenses and $500 cash each month plus 50 per cent of his earnings as a pro.

The Louisville youngster won 19 fights before he was considered ready for a shot at the heavyweight crown, held by an awesome bear of a man named Sonny Liston, who had twice battered Floyd Patterson into insensibility in the first round.

The fight was set for Miami February 25, 1964. Everybody considered Cassius a sacrificial lamb. When the challenger

Heavyweight champion Cassius Clay, before he announced his conversion to the Muslim faith, stands over fallen challenger Sonny Liston shouting and gesturing after knocking him down with a short right to the jaw in their title bout in Lewiston, Maine on May 25, 1965. The bout lasted only one minute and some observers called Clay's blow a "phantom punch."

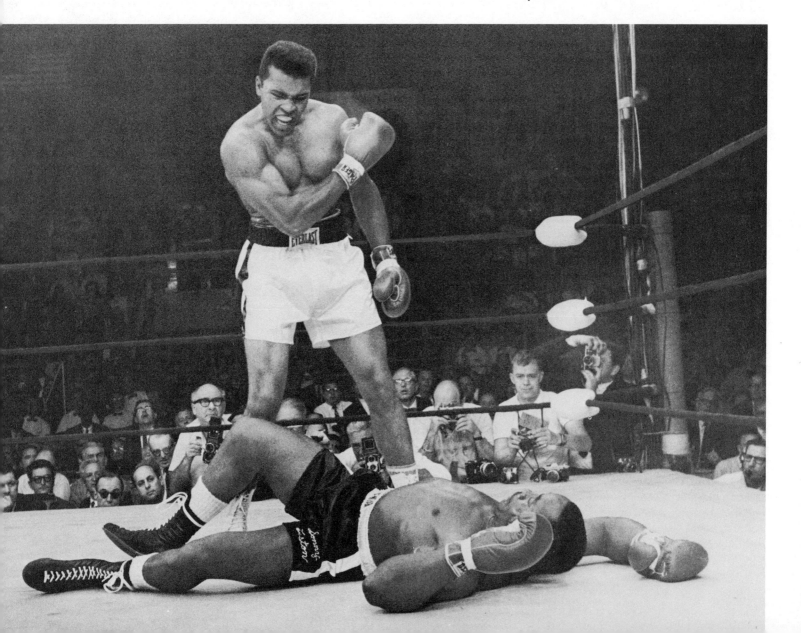

staged a wild tantrum at the weigh-in, doctors attributed it to fear and considered calling off the fight.

But the fight went on. A calm, methodical challenger danced and stabbed and made a monkey of the fearsome titleholder, who failed to come out for the seventh round. It was after this fight that Cassius announced his conversion to the Muslim faith and a new name: Muhammad Ali. In his first defense in May of the following year, Ali knocked out Liston with an historic "phantom punch" in the first round at Lewiston, Maine.

Then followed a series of victories, the draft tribulations, the three-year banishment from the game and finally vindication.

Wild excitement greeted his comeback October 26, 1970— a bout in a 5,000-seat Atlanta gym against brawling Jerry Quarry, who lasted only three rounds. But 300 million—live and on TV—reportedly witnessed the "Battle of the Century" in New York's Madison Square Garden against Smokin' Joe Frazier, the reigning champion, March 8, 1971.

It was a brutal fight, slugger against scientific boxer, won by the slugger Frazier, but a battle that left both gladiators so bat-

tered that they needed medical attention. It was Ali's first defeat after 31 straight victories.

Ali later scored a close decision over Frazier in a non-title bout, regained his title by stopping big George Foreman in Kinshasa, Zaire, in October, 1974. He kept the crown three years, winning a "rubber" battle over old rival Frazier in the bloody and brutal so-called "Thrilla in Manila," before losing lackadaisically to outsider Leon Spinks in 1978.

The great Ali defeated Spinks later in the year to become the only man ever to win the heavyweight title three times, but age and ring punishment had taken their toll. He announced his retirement in 1981 after losses to Larry Holmes and Trevor Berbick.

"I am still the greatest," he bellowed in a tired, almost inaudible voice. The world echoed agreement.

EDDIE ARCARO

Racing's Grand Slam King

"Eddie Arcaro," said Willie Shoemaker, "was the greatest rider I ever saw. He could do everything. I know he beat me more times than I beat him."

No greater tribute could befall a man than that delivered by a respected rival, particularly one of Shoemaker's stature, who over four decades won more races and more prize money than any jockey who ever lived.

"He could do everything," Shoemaker added. "He was a good gate boy, had the intelligence to make the right moves, and was in a good position when he needed it. And there was nobody like him for finishing on a horse."

If Shoemaker was thoroughbred racing's all-time winningest rider as records attest, then Eddie Arcaro must be judged the best ever in the big time events. He was once proclaimed, the "King of the Stakes Riders." He accumulated 554 stakes, a mark broken by Shoemaker. Arcaro was racing's Grand Slam King, however. In a career spanning 31 years between 1931 and 1961, Arcaro rode an unchallenged 17 winners in the three Triple Crown events—five Kentucky Derbys, six Preaknesses and six Belmont Stakes, holding or sharing records in all. He was the only rider to score a double in the Triple Crown races—aboard Whirlaway in 1941 and Citation in 1948.

He rode 4,779 winners and finished in the money on more than half of the 24,092 horses he rode and earned $30,039,543, a sum exceeded only by his friend and golfing companion, Shoemaker.

Although he had a hard time breaking in, Arcaro developed an artistry in his craft that earned him the sobriquet, "The Master," from his contemporaries while railbirds affectionately called him "Banana Nose," because of his elongated beak.

"A strong pair of hands and a sense of rhythm," was Eddie's own assessment of the requisites of a good jockey. "That and a good horse," he said. "You've got to make the horse think you are part of him."

Ben Jones, the Calumet Farm trainer for both Whirlaway and Citation, attributed Arcaro's success to a rare, sensitive touch. "It's like playing a piano," he said.

There was a confidence bordering on arrogance in the way Eddie sat on a horse, and he often drew "boos" from the fans in the parade to the post. Psychologists reasoned that this was the penalty of success.

"They never expect you to lose," Arcaro was once told.

"Oh, well," he said with a shrug, "it's their money."

Eddie had to conquer a once violent temper and a wild, neck-rising abandon to attain stardom. It was costly.

He was suspended for a year, starting in September 1942, when, after being bumped by jockey Vincent Nodarse coming

Arcaro rode an unchallenged 17 winners in the three Triple Crown events—five Kentucky Derbys, six Preaknesses and six Belmont Stakes.

out of the gate at New York's Aqueduct Race Track, he gave chase and tried to push the offender into the infield.

Summoned before the stewards for an explanation, Arcaro snapped: "I'd have killed that SOB if I could."

He drew a six-month suspension at Pimlico in 1936 for deliberately colliding with nearby horses, and was set down in 1941 for blocking. A fatalist who recognized the constant danger, Arcaro had dozens of spills but only two were serious.

In 1933, he suffered a fractured skull and punctured lung in a spill at Chicago's Washington Park, sidelining him for four months. In 1959, riding Black Hills in the Belmont Stakes and moving into the stretch, he was tossed violently into a mud puddle, where he lay motionless for minutes. He was out a month with a concussion and other injuries.

Born in February 1916, in Cincinnati, the son of an Italian immigrant taxi driver, and christened George Edward Arcaro, Eddie quit school at 13 to gallop horses at nearby Latonia. He would gallop as many as 20 horses in the morning for $20 a month, then ride other horses for free.

Trainers taunted him and told him he could never be a rider. Discouraged, Arcaro took off for California, where a gypsy trainer named Clarence Davison gave him his first chance, at Tanforan. His debut was unspectacular. He rode 45 losers before he scored his first victory on January 14, 1932.

He was the top apprentice at New Orleans in 1933, then moved to Chicago and got his first contract with Warren Wright of Calumet Farm. He rode Nellie Flag to a fourth-place finish in the Kentucky Derby, but came back to win on Lawrin in 1938.

Five feet, 2 inches and 114 pounds with powerful wrists and the touch of a violinist, Arcaro was on his way.

Arcaro always figured he should have won two or three more Kentucky Derbys.

"In 1942, I picked the wrong horse," he said. "I had my choice of Shut Out and Devil Diver and I took the Diver. Shut Out won. In 1947, I had Phalanx, the best horse in the race, but he hit a soft spot in the track at the sixteenth pole. In 1950, I should have won with Hill Prince but got behind Middleground, who won."

In the final stages of his career, Eddie called his own shots. He rode only quality horses and refused to shoot for a quantity of victories. He waited for the telephone to ring, then would answer "yes" or "no" to proffered assignments.

"I don't kid myself," he said. "I have won a lot of big races. Also I've been on many of the best horses. Sure, there sometimes are bad breaks, but take the best horse in any race and put one of a dozen riders on him and he will come through."

On April 4, 1962, he abruptly hung up his silks, explaining only, "I don't think anyone can pick out the day he is going to quit. It just happens."

He had handled his money well and retired as a millionaire, living at first in the affluent community of Garden City, Long Island, and later moving to Miami Beach.

He said he never bet on a race and dropped this pearl of wisdom to race goers: "Never bet anything you can't afford to lose—it's risky business."

In a career spanning 31 years, Arcaro covered considerable ground. Here, he speeds along on Taboo in the MRC International Stakes in Australia during December, 1961.

HENRY ARMSTRONG

The Human Buzzsaw

In winning the lightweight championship, one of an unprecedented three world titles he held simultaneously, Henry Armstrong epitomized the sum and substance of his boxing career.

This was on August 17, 1938 against Lou Ambers in Madison Square Garden and although Armstrong was ahead on points late in the fight, he had been taking a severe beating from his rugged opponent.

Along about the 11th round, referee Arthur Donovan wanted to stop the fight because Armstrong had been bleeding profusely.

"I told him I was ahead on points and why stop it?" Armstrong later remembered. "He said, 'Look at the ring, it's covered with blood—your blood.'

"I told him I'd stop bleeding, then, so I swallowed the blood."

Literally bloody but unbowed, Armstrong went on to a 15-round decision over Ambers, climaxing a spectacular flurry that gained him his third world title within the short space of 10 months. In October 1937 he had knocked out Petey Sarron for the featherweight championship, and in May 1938 had taken the welterweight title from Barney Ross.

Although he had to eventually relinquish the featherweight championship because of weight-making difficulties and later lost the lightweight title back to Ambers, Armstrong's place in ring history was secure. His achievement of three simultaneous major championships was a euphorious peak never scaled by other boxers.

And Armstrong was a true fighting champion—he participated in 26 title bouts, more than any other boxer in modern times except Joe Louis, who fought in 27.

By the time he retired in 1945, Armstrong had participated in 175 professional fights in 15 years, winning 97 by knockouts and 47 by decisions. He had eight draws, one no-decision, and only 22 losses, most of them early in his career when he hadn't yet developed the princely skills that would take him to the top of the boxing world. In 1937 alone, he engaged in 27 fights, 26 of which he won by knockouts, and from 1937 to 1939 he compiled a resounding 46-fight victory streak.

Armstrong's hand is raised in victory after adding the lightweight crown to two others by defeating Lou Ambers in August, 1938.

Remarkably, he narrowly missed winning a fourth championship, falling short when he battled middleweight titleholder Ceferino Garcia to a 10-round draw and the title was retained by the champion.

To say that Armstrong was a hungry fighter could almost be taken literally. One of 15 children in a poverty-ravaged St. Louis family, he had to fight for virtually everything while growing up and observers believe this was the main motivational force of his career. Said one writer: "He was a merciless meat-chopper (in the ring) because ambition, along with the fear that he might slip back to the poverty he had known most of his life, rode him hard."

Armstrong remembered living on a failing farm near Columbus, Mississippi, before being forced to leave for St. Louis, where his father took a job in a meat-packing plant.

Because many of his brothers and sisters died when he was young, Armstrong remembered only a handful of them.

"Life killed them," Armstrong declared.

These tragedies, however, only made Armstrong more determined to live a full life.

"I was very ambitious," he said. "I wanted to be something. I wanted to be a doctor. I wanted to be a great runner."

One of boxing's greats was born Henry Jackson of a father of mixed Negro-Caucasian parentage ("My grandmother married her former slave owner") and a Cherokee mother named "America." The young Henry Jackson conditioned his body by running every morning before classes at Vashon High School and working out in a gym he built himself. He also worked on a railroad construction gang to build up his muscles. One day while on the job he read a newspaper story about a fighter named Kid Chocolate who had earned $75,000 in a fight at Madison Square Garden.

He decided right then and there to be a fighter.

In a YMCA gym, he met Harry Armstrong, an instructor whose last name he would one day enshrine in Boxing's Hall of Fame. He personally showed the older Armstrong his knockout punch in one of their sessions together. "I flattened him," Armstrong recalled. "I called that punch my overhead right. I knocked out 27 guys in one year with that one punch."

However, his professional boxing debut was less than auspicious. Fighting in Pittsburgh under the name of "Melody Jackson" (because he used to sing in the gym), he was knocked out by Al Ivino. Armstrong said he had only eaten bread and water before the July 27, 1931 fight and he was so weak when he entered the ring, he couldn't remember the punch that decked him. The important thing, though, was that Armstrong made $30 from that fight. "I ate steak the week before my next fight and won," he said.

Before turning pro, Armstrong had engaged in 67 amateur bouts, winning 52 by knockouts and 10 by decision. After turning pro, he kept on winning and changed his name to "Henry Armstrong" when he began building a reputation in Los Angeles. He "arrived" as a fighter of major status when he

By the time he retired in 1945, Hammerin' Henry had participated in 175 pro fights in 15 years, losing only 22, most of them early in his career.

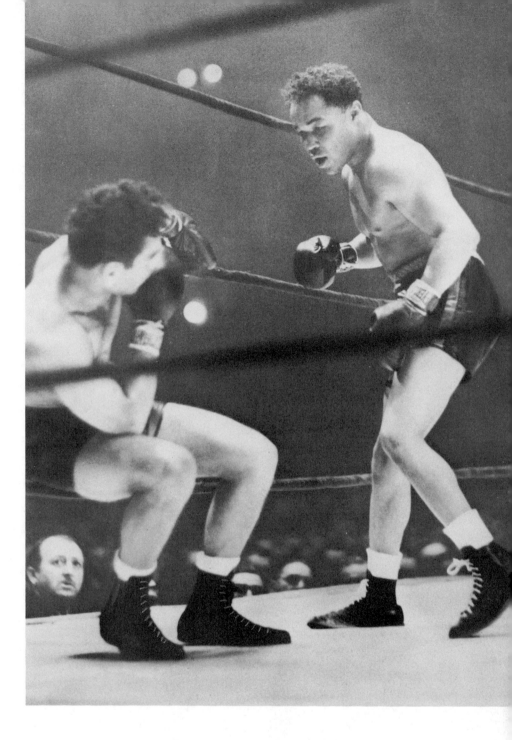

The perpetual fighting machine staggers challenger Pedro Montanez during their welterweight title bout in January, 1940. The champ won on a TKO in the ninth round.

defeated former featherweight champion Baby Arizmendi in 1936.

For a period of 28 months and 20 successful defenses, Armstrong was the dominant figure in the welterweight division, his preferred weight class after flings in the featherweight and lightweight classes. It wasn't until Fritzie Zivic decisioned him in October 4, 1940 that Armstrong relinquished his welterweight crown and not until early 1941 when he was knocked out by Zivic that his great talents began to desert him. Armstrong finally quit the ring in 1945 after losing a 10-round decision to Chester Slider in Oakland.

He admittedly had a drinking problem near the end of his career, but turned to religion to cure it. He was ordained a Baptist minister in 1951 and then became an evangelist who, in his words, "turned a $5,000 bar in my home into a pulpit."

As a boxer, though, there were few like him. Boxing great Jack Dempsey once described Armstrong's fights as "a million punches thrown as fast and as hard as he could let them go." The 5-foot-5 Armstrong was the quintessential human buzzsaw in perpetual motion in the ring, his head bobbing constantly and his body in a semi-crouch.

In short, he was just too much for most to handle.

DR. ROGER BANNISTER

Broke the Four-Minute Mile Barrier

The doctor concocted a prescription for the "miracle mile" and filled it himself, making both medical and sports history.

Until Roger Bannister, a gaunt English medical student, shattered the four-minute mile barrier that bleak, blustery spring evening in 1954, both medical and athletic authorities had deemed it a physical impossibility. For generations, starting with Thomas Conneff in the previous century and continuing with Jack Lovelock, Gundar Haegg, John Landy and Wes Santee, it had been the impossible dream to run the distance in less than that magic figure.

Throughout the world men trained for the endeavor. They

In the first mile race in history in which two runners finished under 4 minutes, Bannister (329) defeated John Landy of Australia in August, 1954.

built up their chests and lung power. They ran up hills and over sandy beaches. They sought means to preserve oxygen and strengthen the heart. But time after time as they completed the ordeal, chiseling off seconds and fractions of seconds, they would collapse in a heap, puffing for breath. Often it would take hours to fully recover.

Bannister, in his Oxford studies, determined that the torture and anguish of the mile run had become largely psychological and no limit could be placed on human effort. "The human spirit is indominatable," he said.

He promptly set about the task of proving it. It was a scientific venture. It was Edmund Hillary clawing his way to the peak of Mount Everest and Neil Armstrong's first footsteps on the moon. It had similar dramatic impact.

Bannister was born in 1929 in Harrow, 10 miles from London. His father was an auditor for the British Exchequer (Treasury Department). He had an older sister who became a biologist and curator of the Bristol Museum.

Roger attended University College School, one of England's best prep institutions, graduated from Oxford in 1951 and took his internship at St. Mary's Hospital, where Sir Alexander Fleming discovered penicillin. Although he described himself as "an industrious student, if not a good one," he managed to get scholarships from every school he attended, reducing the financial load on his family.

While at Oxford he helped Professor C. G. Douglas on a research project dealing with the effects of lack of oxygen on the respiratory system and shared in the findings which were published in British medical journals. This helped create his interest in the possibility of a sub-four-minute mile.

Rowing was his principal sport. He had illusions of some day rowing with the Oxford crew against Cambridge on the Thames River and perhaps competing in the Henley Regatta.

Analyzing his physical equipment, the young medical student decided he was too light to be a good oarsman and should transfer his sports emphasis elsewhere. He chose track. At 6-foot-1 and 154 pounds, he found he was suited for distance running. He had a smooth, flowing style which covered 7 1-2 feet in a single stride. Five feet is average for milers. The mile became his obsession.

The gangling Englishman won a berth on the Oxford track team and for four straight years won the intervarsity mile race although his best time of 4:16.2 was far from excitable. Invited to join the British team for the 1948 Olympics in London, he declined, saying, "I'm too young."

He toured the United States with a combined Oxford-Cambridge team in 1949 and impressed track officials with his elegant form and strong finishing kick. He clocked 4:11.9 and 4:11.1 in races against Ivy League opponents.

By this time, Bannister—as both an athlete and a doctor—had begun to think seriously about the possibility of a four-minute mile. He turned himself into a veritable machine. Blessed with a barrel chest and large rib cage, he began boosting his chest measurements even more. He altered the structure of his heart, blood vessels and muscles through training methods. All the while he kept a close, scientific chart of himself and his progress. His problem was improving the oxygen supply from his lungs to his legs.

In 1952, he clocked a disappointing 4:10.6 in his only competitive race and finished fourth behind Luxembourg's Josef Barthel in the Olympic Games at Helsinki. While his supporters began to lose faith, Bannister went confidently about his campaign, working with a fellow British miler and friend, Chris Chataway, who served as his trial horse and pacesetter. Working in private, Bannister saw his game plan bearing fruit. He didn't like big, public events.

That's the reason Bannister chose the informal track and field meet on May 6, 1954 at the Iffley Sports Ground on the outskirts of Oxford for his shot at history. Only a few hundred people were on hand. British track officials were present with timekeepers to authenticate the occasion.

Chris Brasher and Chris Chataway acted as pacemakers. Bannister, who had gauged his physical potential to the finest degree, asked that times be announced over the loudspeaker at 220 instead of the usual 440-yard intervals.

Brasher led through the first quarter lap with 57.4 seconds and at the half with 1:58.0. Bannister was two-tenths of a second behind. On the third leg, according to plan, Chataway sprang into the lead while Brasher dropped back. At the bell, Chataway was timed in 3:00.4, Bannister 3:00.

Then Bannister unleashed his devastating kick. As he crossed the finish line, he heard the formal announcement, "R. G. Bannister, three minutes..." the rest lost in the roar of the crowd. The time was 3:59.4. A longtime barrier had at last crumbled. It was headline news around the world.

The psychological barrier also had fallen. Seven weeks later John Landy of Australia lowered the record to 3:58.0 at Turku, Finland. Then came a rash of sub-four-minute miles.

But Bannister's place in history remained secure. Late in 1954 he retired as an athlete and took a post at the London Hospital with the valedictory: "The man who can drive himself further, once the effort gets painful, is the man who will win."

Thirty years after becoming the first runner to crack the 4-minute mile, Sir Roger Bannister relaxes at his home in Lyminster, Sussex in England. Photo was taken May 2, 1984.

SAMMY BAUGH

The First Great Passer

The first forward pass in football reportedly was thrown around 1913, its perpetrator still a source of debate among historians. But it flowered as an offensive weapon with the wild "aerial circus" maneuvers of the Southwest Conference in the 1930s and found its greatest exponent in a skinny, slingshot-armed Texan named Sammy Baugh.

For decades this American game, a combination of rugby and soccer, had been a dull head-butting, body-slamming exercise fought on the ground with little or no scoring. It remained for a few daring, imaginative coaches in the cowboy country—Ray Morrison, Matty Bell and Dutch Meyer—to introduce a new "razzle dazzle" attack, fill the sky with spirals and prove that—in football as in traveling—one can get there more quickly through the air.

Baugh, a kicker as well as a passer, became the symbol of this revolution in the sport. A gifted all-around athlete courted by baseball's major leagues, Slingin' Sammy, as he was called, became a ball-tossing Houdini first at Texas Christian University and later with the Washington Redskins, where he played for 16 seasons before retiring at age 38.

He spanned two generations and two eras of the sport. When

he hung up his No. 33 jersey after an emotional game against the Chicago Cardinals in 1952, he left a long string of collegiate and professional records. He was elected to the College Football Hall of Fame in 1951 and the Pro Football Hall of Fame in 1963.

Baugh, trained in the skills by Meyer at Texas Christian, could throw the ball like a bullet and with the ease and accuracy of a man flipping a baseball. He could nail a running target half the length of the field away.

It was at TCU that Slingin' Sammy, at first a one dimensional player, was taught to punt—he became one of the game's greatest kickers—and to use the punt as an occasional double threat to catch opponents off guard. Also he was drilled in hooks, comebacks, posts, crossovers and other passing moves later popularized in the pro game.

He was a college All-America in 1935 and 1936, completing 109 passes for 1,371 yards the latter year, upsetting previously unbeaten-untied Santa Clara in the season's final game and leading TCU to a 16-6 triumph over Marquette in Dallas' Cotton Bowl.

With the Redskins, he led the National Football League in

Slingin' Sammy Baugh, who made the forward pass a standard weapon in pro football, looks for a receiver in 1942 NFL game against the powerful Chicago Bears.

passing six times and set records which were to last for years—such as most seasons played, 16; most passes thrown, 3,016; most passes completed, 1,709 and most yards gained, 22,085. He had 187 touchdown passes with a completion percentage of 56.6 and average gain of 12.5 yards. He once punted a ball 85 yards and in 1942 averaged a record-setting 48.9 yards with his kicks.

Sid Luckman of the Chicago Bears, Baugh's principal rival at the time, said: "I like to just sit and watch him."

"In his worst games," wrote historian Roger Treat, "Baugh is as good as most quarterbacks on their best days."

Another, Kevin Roberts, said, "He is to passing what Lindbergh was to the airplane."

Samuel Adrien Baugh was born in Temple, Texas, March 17, 1914, the son of a railroad man. He was 16 when the family moved to Sweetwater, Texas, where Sammy attended high school and developed a strange but profitable hobby. He hung an old automobile tire by a rope from a tree limb and spent hours throwing a football through its hole. After he was able to hit his target consistently while the tire was still, he practiced throwing through it as it swung back and forth.

He was equally adept at throwing a baseball. He had a natural snap-wrist motion. In high school, he was the best player on three teams—basketball, football and baseball—but he seemed to like baseball best.

When he was 18, Sammy played summer baseball in Abilene and was seriously considering bypassing college for a professional career on the diamond. He was a fine infielder but when he discovered he couldn't hit the curve ball he opted for a scholarship at Texas Christian.

Meyer, who became an institution at TCU, feared that the gaunt, skinny tailback—6 feet, 3 inches and 175 pounds—might have trouble standing the punishment. But he knew Sammy had the arm, and he planned to utilize it.

"Throw the ball, throw the ball!" he said. Sammy did.

After leading Texas Christian to victory over Marquette in the Cotton Bowl, Baugh was drafted by owner George Marshall of the Boston Redskins, who already was scheming to move his franchise to Griffith Stadium in Washington, D.C. Sammy also was considering a contract offer from baseball's St. Louis Cardinals.

Marshall prevailed on the widely acclaimed Texan to come to Washington to talk about it—"and don't forget to wear a 10-gallon hat and cowboy boots." Baugh signed for $8,000 a year, three times the salary of the next highest paid player.

Sammy made his pro debut against the Green Bay Packers in the 1937 All-Star game in Chicago, hitting Gaynell Tinsley for the only score, then went on to lead the Redskins to the NFL championship his rookie year, beating the Chicago Bears in the title game.

Sammy went home, got married, took a fling at the St. Louis Cardinals' spring training camp and finally returned to Washington to play 15 more years of football. As he aged, young quarterbacks came and went but, in the clutch, the Redskins still called on Sammy's rifle arm.

He played his final game in 1952 against the Chicago Cardinals at Comiskey Park. The lanky old pro, playing with an injured right hand, completed 11 straight passes before getting in a fight with Cardinal tackle Don Joyce and being ejected from the game. It was his last hurrah.

He did some coaching, then retired to his Texas ranch.

Here's Baugh as a College All-America at Texas Christian University. He paced his team to a 16-6 triumph over Marquette in the 1936 Cotton Bowl game in Dallas.

ELGIN BAYLOR

The Franchise-Saver

The term "franchise player"is loosely applied to an individual who can singularly take a team to a higher plane, usually transforming a loser into a winner and in some cases, into a world champion. In the case of charismatic Elgin Baylor, it was more literal than most.

The Minneapolis Lakers were down on their luck when Baylor signed with them out of Seattle University in 1958. "All I know is that he saved my franchise when it appeared that I was going to die," said Robert Short, owner of the Lakers then. "If I had moved to Los Angeles, nobody would have come out to see us play. He was the salvation of us all."

Baylor became an instant star in Minneapolis, in his first season establishing himself as one of the league's premier players at forward. He averaged 24.9 points, 15 rebounds and 4.1 assists, and was named to the all-National Basketball Association first team for the first of seven consecutive seasons. More importantly, the Lakers improved dramatically as a team. The previous season, they had finished last in the Western Division with the worst record in the NBA. In Baylor's first season, 1958-59, they finished second in their division and went all the way to the championship round of the NBA playoffs before losing to the powerful Boston Celtics.

Baylor's presence alone made the Lakers a more valuable commodity and Short, who bought the team for $200,000, eventually sold it for $5.1 million to Jack Kent Cooke, who moved it to Los Angeles.

"If Baylor had turned me down," Short recalled, "I'd have gone out of business. The club would have gone bankrupt."

Baylor not only made teams richer, but players around him better.

"Elgin was a great, great competitor," said Jerry West, his long-time teammate who combined with Baylor to give the Lakers one of the greatest 1-2 scoring punches in NBA history. "In all my years in the league, I don't think I've seen a player quite like him."

Statistically, Baylor ranks with the top scorers and rebounders in NBA history. When he retired shortly after the start of the 1971-72 season, Baylor was the Lakers' all-time leading scorer with 23,149 points, a 27.4 average, and ranked third in the league overall at that point. He once scored 71 points in a game, the NBA record for a forward. He also completed his career with 11,463 rebounds, an average of 13.5 per game.

Considering he was only 6-foot-5 and dwarfed by many of his front-court opponents, it is his rebound total that stands out particularly. In his second year, he finished fourth in the league

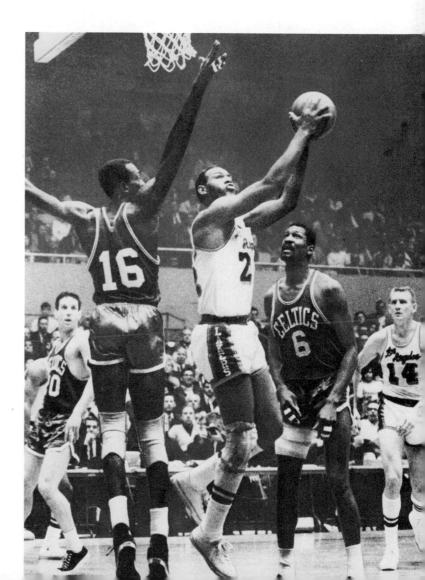

Elgin Baylor fires the ball back over his shoulder for two points for the L.A. Lakers in a 1967 game against the Boston Celtics. Number 6 for Boston is player-coach Bill Russell.

Baylor, named to the Basketball Hall of Fame in Springfield, Mass. in 1977, visits his plaque there in May of that year.

in rebounding with a 19.8 average, and in his first six years in the NBA, when his legs were still relatively springy, he averaged 15.7 and ranked in the top ten in rebounding each year.

As a collegian, Baylor had also played taller than his height. One year at Seattle University, he led the nation in rebounding.

"It was always instilled in me that rebounding was a key part of the game," Baylor said. "It was satisfying to go in there with the big guys, a real challenge."

In reaching his levels of the game, Baylor developed a style that was all his own. This powerful, 6-5, 225-pounder could hang in the air as if he were space-walking and get off a shot from the most outlandish of positions. It wasn't just that Baylor could score, West said, "it was the way he could do it."

Mostly because of Baylor, such terms as "hang time" and "body control" became a permanent part of the basketball lexicon.

Another of his trademarks was a nervous twitch which actually worked to his advantage on the court. It simulated a head fake and left more than one defender shaking his own head after Baylor left him in the proverbial dust.

"I'd go like this," Baylor said, snapping his head downwards, "and the defensive player would look down, too. He must have thought I was looking for money on the floor. Then I'd go by him."

One neurologist who evaluated Baylor's condition felt it was his way of responding to the pressures of the court.

"It made him tougher to guard when he was dribbling," remembered Dr. Robert Kerlan, the Lakers' team physician.

Baylor first drew attention to himself as a top scholastic player at Springarn High School in Washington, D.C. However, his schoolwork left a lot to be desired and he even dropped out for a while to work as a checker in a furniture store and play basketball in recreational leagues.

A friend arranged for Baylor to get a scholarship at the College of Idaho, where he was expected to play football as well as basketball. After one season, the school fired the coach and restricted the scholarships, leaving Baylor out in the cold. It was then that a Seattle car dealer named Ralph Malone interested Baylor in playing for Seattle University. While Baylor was sitting out the year needed for the transfer, he played for an amateur team sponsored by Malone.

At Seattle, Baylor helped make the Chieftains a national power. They went all the way to the NCAA finals before losing to Kentucky in the national championship game. Although Baylor still had a year of college eligibility left, he was available for the NBA draft, and was snapped up by the Lakers, who needed a franchise-saver.

But even Short couldn't know at the time how much Baylor would be worth to the Lakers in the coming years. By and large, the multi-dimensional Baylor became the fulcrum of the team. In the 1962-63 season, he became the first NBA player ever to finish in the top five in four different statistical categories: scoring, rebounding, assists and free throw accuracy. One month he played with a steel plate on the finger of his shooting hand and still managed to average 30 points a game for the season, one of three times he hit the 30-point level in his career.

His consistency in playoff games, where he averaged 27.0 points, was just as irrefutable as the regular season, even though knee troubles began plaguing him in 1963-64. During the 1965 playoffs, Baylor took a nasty spill and ripped off part of his left kneecap. During his career, he also suffered from stretched tendons in the right knee and calcium deposits in both knees. "It was like watching Citation run on spavined legs," Chick Hearn, the Lakers' broadcaster, said.

But a determined Baylor continued to work on strengthening his knees and despite the pain and problems brought on by injuries, managed to string together season after season of quality performances that vaulted him to the All-NBA First Team 10 times and eventually the NBA's 35th Anniversary All-Time Team and the Basketball Hall of Fame.

opposite:

Baylor (with ball) helped make Seattle University a national power. Here, he leaps between two Hawaii University players and scores with a one-hander in a December, 1956 game.

YOGI BERRA

The Brilliant Buffoon

Yogi Berra was like the man in those old magazine and newspaper ads... "They laughed when he sat down at the piano, but..." Only in Yogi's case they chuckled when he picked a bat and wobbled to the plate to take his cuts, and they were amused when he opened his mouth to speak.

One of the game's finest catchers on one of baseball's all-time greatest teams, the New York Yankees, who played in 14 World Series and later managed pennant winners in both major leagues, Yogi will also be remembered as a person who read comic books and a malaprop who kept people in stitches.

He craved to be accepted and admired for his lusty hitting and catching skills. However, some fans loved him as a cuddly

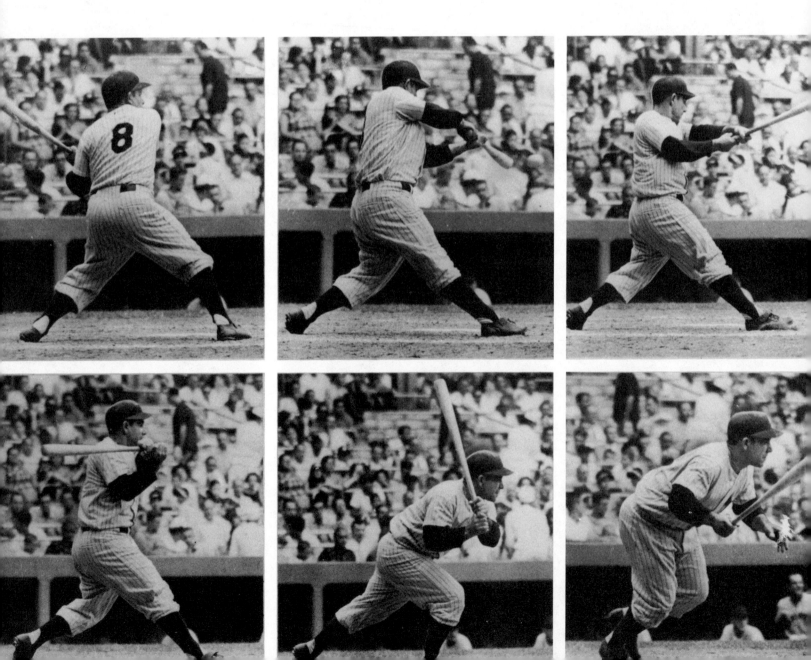

Berra was the first to acknowledge that he was no Mr. America in appearance. Yogi was 24 years old when this photo was taken in 1949.

Yogi's tendency to chase bad pitches worked to his advantage and made him one of the game's toughest hitters. He would lunge out for the ball and drive it over the wall. The Yankee star does just that shown in these sequence photos in 1955.

comic character who sometimes seemed misplaced in the pinstripes of the haughty Yankees and for all the absurd statements he may or may not have said.

Shy and self-conscious, this raw, naive native of St. Louis became embittered and unsocial at first, avoiding fans and reporters. But as he gained in maturity and confidence, he not only accepted his role but good humoredly helped embellish it.

After all, what other sports buffoon is quoted by the President on national radio and gets invited to the White House?

Yogi was the first to acknowledge that he was no Mr. America in appearance. A dumpy, gnome-like fellow, 5 feet eight

Yogi leaps into the arms of Don Larsen after the veteran Yankee right-hander became the first to pitch a perfect game in World Series history. The date was Oct. 8, 1956...the victims were the Brooklyn Dodgers.

ing skills and before long the game had no better receiver at pouncing in front of the plate on a bunt and throwing the runner out. His proclivity for chasing bad pitches worked to his advantage and made him one of the game's toughest hitters.

A pitcher would try to waste a pitch and Berra would suddenly lunge out for the ball and drive it over the wall. He had five seasons with 100 or more runs batted in. Pitcher Hal Newhouser once said, "I defy anyone to throw him a good pitch." Another, Early Wynn, called him "the toughest hitter in the league to pitch to."

Another canard—originated and perpetuated by a press corps inspired by a deep-seated fondness rather than malice—was that Yogi was as stupid as he looked. Thus the malapropisms were just too juicy to pass up.

Once he said of a restaurant: "Nobody goes there any more. It's always too crowded."

Honored at Yankee Stadium, he said, "Thanks for making this day necessary."

"Me in a slump? I ain't in a slump. I'm just not hitting."

"We'll come to the bridge when we cross it."

And his most famous line, repeated by President Ronald Reagan in a radio address: "It ain't over 'til it's over."

Manager Casey Stengel had a special fondness for Yogi, because he saw in the catcher some of himself, and referred to him as "my assistant manager."

Teammates credited Berra with a remarkable memory, a faculty for going back 10 years or more and recalling what a pitcher threw to a batter on a specific occasion. He was a veritable encyclopedia of sports trivia—all sports, not just baseball—and was the locker room whiz at card games such as hearts, pinochle and gin. In contract negotiations, he had few peers.

Born Lawrence Peter Berra in the Italian section of St. Louis, son of a bricklayer, Yogi grew up with Joe Garagiola, who became a catcher for the St. Louis Cardinals but later won more renown as a broadcaster.

It was Garagiola and other pals who gave Yogi his nickname because "he walked like a Yogi," something they'd all seen in a movie about India.

Yogi, a good all-around athlete, was 18, a star lefthanded-hitting catcher of the local American Legion baseball team when the Yankees signed him in 1943 for a $500 bonus.

Berra played with Norfolk for the season, joined the Navy and served on a rocket launcher in the Normandy invasion. After leaving the service, he played a season with Newark before moving up to the parent club at the end of 1946. Then followed a career, not as funny as it was historic.

inches tall and almost 200 pounds, he had thick shoulders, short legs, an over-sized head and a face that only some mothers could admire.

He did not look like a baseball player and, early in his career, he didn't act like one. He was embarrassed in the 1947 World Series when Jackie Robinson and his Brooklyn Dodger teammates ran wild on the bases, although the Yankees finally won. He had a reputation of being a notoriously bad ball hitter.

Bill Dickey, a former Yankee great, helped refine his catch-

Although some may remember him as a cuddly comic character, Yogi is a sound baseball man who twice managed the Yankees and once piloted the Mets. That's Yankee owner George Steinbrenner patting Berra on the back after naming him manager in Dec. 1983.

He was the American League's most valuable player three times. He was on the mid-season All-Star team 15 times. He played in 14 World Series, a record 75 games, and participated in seven others as a coach or manager. He hit 358 home runs, 313 of them as a catcher, second only to Johnny Bench. He set World Series records for games played, at bats, hits, singles, and consecutive errorless games, among others.

He managed the Yankees to a pennant in 1964, only to be fired for supposed inability to control players and later moved to the New York Mets where the same fate befell him two years after winning the pennant in 1973. He got another shot with the Yankees in 1984 only to be fired again in the spring of 1985. In 1986, Yogi was named a coach of the Houston Astros. He helped them win the National League Western Division pennant.

LARRY BIRD

"He'll Cut Your Heart Out To Win"

In 1986, after Larry Bird had played only seven years with the Boston Celtics, a Dallas Morning News poll of 60 leading professional basketball authorities selected him as the greatest forward ever to play the game. The hand-picked panel chose Bird over Elgin Baylor, Julius Erving, Rick Barry and the old St. Louis Hawks' floor wizard, Bob Pettit.

There have been others ready to acclaim—without the further proof that comes with aging—the cotton-haired, ball-handling Houdini from French Lick, Indiana, to be the most complete player in the sport's history.

While admittedly debatable, it was a remarkable tribute at this early stage of the gifted Hoosier's career and ironic since it became a story-book saga that almost didn't happen.

At Springs Valley High School, Bird, thin and gawky, played

The greatest forward ever to play the game? Here, Boston's Larry Bird drives around Rodney McCray of the Houston Rockets in 1986 NBA contest.

Bird flips a behind the back pass to a teammate. "I maintain the title was won when Larry Bird was born," said teammate Bill Walton after the Celtics took the crown in 1986.

the first two years in the shadow of a more highly regarded teammate, Steve Land, and, although later a state all-star, he failed to impress college scouts.

Indiana University's Bobby Knight watched him play and said, "The kid must learn to shoot a jump shot." Bird wanted to play at the University of Kentucky but Coach Joe B. Hall, after looking him over, said he was too slow to fit into the Wildcats' fast-break, fire engine style of basketball.

Larry became so discouraged that he was prepared to give up a college education altogether. "Larry really didn't want to go to college anywhere," his widowed mother said. "He feels he should get a job so I won't have to work so hard."

Larry's father had died in 1961 after separating from his mother and going to Tucson, Arizona, in hopes that a drier climate would help his emphysema. Larry's mother sold the fam-

ily farm and took her flock—three boys and one girl—to live with her own widowed mother. Times were hard.

Larry finally was persuaded to enter Indiana University but left after six weeks because he was used so sparingly in basketball practice. Coming from a small town and small school, he felt smothered by the size of the university.

He enrolled in a 200-student junior college, Northwood in West Baden, Indiana, but dropped out when he learned that he would have to stay two years before applying to a four-year college. His cage career appeared doomed.

Larry maneuvers around Kent Benson of the Detroit Pistons in a 1984 NBA tilt. Boston won the game in Hartford, Conn., 131-130, on Bird's shot at the final buzzer.

He drove a garbage truck and played AAU basketball on the side with a construction company, getting occasional headlines in state tournaments. He had an unsuccessful six-month marriage. His life appeared to be drifting until, out of the blue, he was recruited by Indiana State University.

Red-shirted for a year at the rather obscure Terre Haute institution, he played three seasons climaxed in 1978-79 when he gained All-America recognition for the second year, led his team to the NCAA Championship finals against Magic Johnson's Michigan State powerhouse and won the NCAA Player of the Year award. He was the first round draft choice of the Boston Celtics.

Quickly the sports world became aware of Larry Bird.

Bird's professional career was meteoric. He was the National Basketball Association's Rookie of the Year in 1980 and a member of the league's All-Rookie team. He proceeded to win a place on the All-NBA team and qualify for the mid-season All-Star Game for seven straight seasons, being named Most Valuable Player in the latter in 1982 and playoff MVP in 1984 and 1986. He joined Wilt Chamberlain and Bill Russell as the only players in league history to win MVP honors for three consecutive seasons. He did it in 1984, 1985 and 1986.

One of the game's most durable athletes, he missed only 13 games in regular season competition while leading the Celtics in minutes played, defensive rebounds, steals, points and scoring average each of his seven years. Prior to the 1986-87 season, he had gone 205 straight games scoring 10 points or more. He hadn't fouled out of a game since his second year in the league and never in a playoff game.

Although having filled out his once bony, 6-foot-9 frame with 220 solid pounds, Bird was not the biggest nor the strongest player in the league. He lacked the raw speed of some of his contemporaries and couldn't jump as high as many, yet he managed to dominate the floor with his intense competitiveness and instinctive skills.

He compensated for his lack of jumping ability by perfecting the three-point field goal, setting an NBA career record for that specialty with 267 through the 1985-86 campaign.

The three-point goal is a climactic art, which pulled out many close games for the Celtics, and Bird insisted that it was not a gift but the product of hard work. He built a special court at his home to practice hours at a time.

"If you go to the gym with the other guys, you may get 100 shots," he said. "By yourself you get 1,000."

"Larry's just a player who continues to grow," Celtics' assistant coach Jimmy Rodgers said. "When you think you've seen everything, he comes up with another gimmick, another approach."

Added Pete Newell, Golden State's director of player personnel: "He rebounds, scores, passes, picks up the tough guy on defense, can play inside or outside and is as good as any guard handling the break and hitting the open man. He's as skilled a forward as I've ever seen."

Matt Guokas, coach of the Philadelphia 76ers, said, "Bird's approach to the game is unparalleled. He will cut your heart out to win."

"I maintain the championship was won when Larry Bird was born," commented teammate Bill Walton after a Celtics' title in 1985-86.

Larry was born December 7, 1956, and he never forgot his roots, maintaining always that he was "just the Hick from French Lick," a resort town of about 1,800 where he'd go back to see old buddies and even mow the lawn. He showed up for black-tie dinners in a sport shirt and blue jeans, admitting:

"I eat, drink and sleep basketball 24 hours a day."

Two of today's stars. Bird loses rebound to Magic Johnson of the Los Angeles Lakers (32) during the first half of an NBA game in the West Coast city.

BJORN BORG

Sweden's Golden Boy Of Tennis

Bjorn Borg burst upon the tennis scene at age 15, a golden-haired "Wonder Child" with a suspect fighting heart, and retired at the age of 26 with a great sigh of relief as if he had just been freed from some dreadful dungeon.

In those intervening years, from 1971 through 1982, this somber, steely Swede with his devastating top-spin shots and thundering serve, provided audiences with the most gripping drama ever unfolded within those white rectangles that make up the arena of the sport.

His principal stage was the ancient turf of historic Wimbledon although he kept so-called "teeny-boppers" (youthful worshipers) squealing with delight from Paris' Roland Garros to Melbourne's Kooyong and New York's Madison Square Garden throughout his self-shortened career.

Wimbledon is the oldest and most prestigious of the world's tennis tournaments and it is on Wimbledon's archaic but storied Center Court turf that tennis heroes are forged, and none stood taller than the Scandinavian golden child.

Starting in 1976, at the age of 20, he stormed to five consecutive singles championships, an unbelievable feat that escaped such greats as Big Bill Tilden, Fred Perry, Don Budge, Jack Kramer and Rod Laver. It was Bjorn's one great badge of grandeur although he also won an unprecedented six French Opens, the Italian twice, the Masters in New York and World Championship of Tennis in Dallas. Strangely, his Achilles heel was the U.S. Open, which repeatedly escaped his grasp.

Borg never won the U.S. Open although he was runner-up four times, twice to Jimmy Connors and twice to John McEnroe, his chief rivals for world supremacy. A moody, private person, the young Swede never seemed comfortable in the teeming, fast-paced atmosphere he found in America and thus his performances suffered as a result. Five times he qualified for the WCT Finals in Dallas, winning only in 1976.

His battles with Connors and McEnroe, both lefthanders, became classics—duels matching markedly contrasting personalities and game styles. Connors was a feisty, alley fighter, a constant attacker who played every point as if it might be his last. McEnroe was a sulking, spoiled racket genius with tremendous natural talent and instincts.

Connors and McEnroe were given to court tantrums, con-

Borg raises his trophy over his head after winning the French Open title for a record fifth time in 1980 with a straight set conquest of Vitas Gerulaitis.

At the age of 20 in 1976, the Swedish ace reaches for a shot fired by Guillermo Vilas in the finals of the WCT Tournament in Dallas. Borg won first prize money of $50,000.

stant bickering with umpires and linesmen, and frequent antagonism toward fans and the press.

Both became natural villains in the scenarios that featured Borg as the good guy. A handsome athlete, close to six feet tall and slender at 160 pounds, Borg was a sphinx on the court. His strong, Viking features never showed any emotion. He never argued a point. He typified controlled strength as he literally pounded his adversaries into submission from the backcourt with his rocket-like two-fisted backhand and accentuated top-spin forehand. Although a foreigner facing Americans, he was the idol of American fans.

Borg was born June 6, 1956 in the small community of Sod-ertlage, just outside Stockholm. He took up tennis at an early age, playing on slow clay courts, and while still in elementary school caught the eye of Lennart Bergelin, a former member of the Swedish Davis Cup team. In a land of snow and ice, where skiing and hockey vie with soccer for the attention of youths, tennis was largely an orphan sport.

Bjorn was a court prodigy. Even before he got into his teens he could beat top men in his community. At 14, he was an internationalist, traveling to Miami to win the first of his two junior titles in the Orange Bowl. At 15, he captured the junior crown at Wimbledon and made the Swedish Davis Cup team, the youngest ever to compete for the famous trophy.

In 1974, a scrawny kid of 17, he won the Italian National, and captured the first of his six French crowns, beating Manuel Orantes after dropping the first two sets. A year later he led Sweden to its first Davis Cup victory.

By this time Borg was the toast of the tennis world although the huge Swedish press corps which followed him around the globe was creating negative vibes because of his continued frustrations in the United States, particularly in the Open and WCT Finals in Dallas.

The knock: "No heart. Can't win the big one."

They began asking: "Is Sweden's Golden Boy just a mechanical robot? Is what we took for tremendous calm merely a lack of fire and spirit?"

The doubts were soon shattered on the taut tension strings of Borg's familiar wooden racket.

Bjorn, twice beaten in the quarter-finals as a teen-ager, won his first Wimbledon in 1976 after just turning 20. He crushed flashy Ilie Nastase in the final 6-4, 6-2, 9-7, causing the Romanian to wonder if the kid was human.

"He's a robot from outer space," said Ilie, not questioning his rival's courage. "A Martian."

In 1978, the young Swede became the first man since Rod Laver in 1962 to win the Italian, French and Wimbledon titles in the same year. He didn't lose a match over a seven-month period, finally bowing to Connors in the U.S. Open.

Borg saved his greatest Wimbledon effort for his last in 1980—a knockdown, drag-out slugfest against McEnroe in the final. After dropping a heart-breaking tie-breaker 18-16 in the fourth set, he allowed McEnroe only three points against his service in the decisive set, winning it 8-6.

That was the year also that Borg was married to his longtime fiance, Mariana Simionescu, whom he divorced 2½ years later, and began contemplating retirement.

A wealthy man, who had earned $8 million a year in prize money and endorsements with vast business interests, Borg retired to the life of a jet setter on the French Riviera.

"I'm happy to be away from tennis," he said. "The practice. The crowds. The demands. The constant pressure. You can never relax your mind. It's good to feel free."

Bjorn typified controlled strength on the court as he pounded his foes into submission from the backcourt with his rocket-like two-fisted backhand.

TERRY BRADSHAW

Country Bumpkin to Super Quarterback

He was—by his own admission—a country bumpkin from a small school in a small bayou community. Rough hewn, naive and no mental Einstein, he came to the big town and showed the city slickers that not just brains but grit, guts and a strong right arm could turn a struggling football team into a national champion.

They called Terry Bradshaw "a Bible totin' Lil Abner." They said he lacked the savvy to be a No. 1 quarterback on a National Football League team. The big, blond dude from Louisiana weathered the early taunts, endless broken bones and bruises, to achieve what no other pro quarterback had ever done—win four Super Bowls in the space of six years.

Bradshaw achieved what no other quarterback had ever done—win four Super Bowls in six years. Here he fires pass against Dallas in Super Bowl XIII in 1979.

The Steelers' field general could run, too. "You could beat Terry half to death," said former coach George Allen, "but there'd still be enough life in him to kill you."

Playing with the Pittsburgh Steelers, he set additional Super Bowl records for most touchdown passes (nine) and most passing yards (932) and twice was the game's Most Valuable Player. He became a "cover boy" for Sports Illustrated and in 1979 shared the honor of that magazine's prestigious Sportsman of the Year Award with the Pittsburgh Pirates' Willie Stargell.

Old Art Rooney, the Steelers' owner who helped rock the cradle of professional football, called Bradshaw the equal of any quarterback who ever played the game.

"Anybody who ranks somebody over him," said Rooney, "well, I just don't know where their handicapping is."

Former coach George Allen said, "You could beat Bradshaw half to death, but there'd still be enough life in him to kill you."

Allen, who coached both the Los Angeles Rams and Washington Redskins, in his book, "Pro Footballs's 100 Greatest Players," called Bradshaw "the modern mold for a quarterback... tall, powerful," adding: "He had a great arm and great legs. He's been a better runner then most quarterbacks. And a stronger thrower."

Bradshaw, 6 feet, 3 inches in height and 215 pounds, played 14 seasons for Pittsburgh, completing 2,025 passes for 27,989 yards, a 51.9 percentage and 212 touchdowns. He rushed for 444 yards and 32 touchdowns.

He was born September 2, 1948 in Shreveport, Louisiana. He wasn't good enough to make the junior high school football team. Frustrated, he played pick-up games in his back yard. For hours at a time, he would practice throwing a football over the roof of his house, between clotheslines and into buckets.

In high school, he didn't make the team until his final year when he quarterbacked it to the state final. "I was a clumsy and awkward kid, growing fast," he said.

When time came to go to college, Terry had some feelers from bigger schools but chose little Louisiana Tech.

"I was scared of the competition at the bigger colleges," he said. "I didn't want to sit on the bench for three years before I got a chance."

Even at Louisiana Tech, although he worked harder than most, he was overlooked until his junior year. He set school passing and offensive records.

Bradshaw's excellent record in his two last years at Louisiana Tech, a 52.5 percent completion average, earned him an invitation to the post-season Senior Bowl game in Mobile, Ala., a showcase event for college seniors to impress the pro scouts. Although uneasy at having to play with the "big boys," Terry was the game's Most Valuable Player.

In the 1970 professional draft, the Steelers, having won a coin-toss with Chicago for the lead-off pick, chose Bradshaw. "I had quit growing and started filling out," Bradshaw said. "All the gears fell into place."

His confidence buoyed, Terry was impressive in pre-season training but, once the campaign started, he apparently became over-anxious to perform well and was an early disappointment.

His acquisition had been heavily publicized. He was supposed to be the Moses leading the Steelers out of the wilderness. When Terry failed to measure up to expectations, press criticism became biting, the fans hostile.

The "Lil Abner" label became a fixture. Critics insisted that Bradshaw's only use was to hand off to running backs Franco

The big, blond dude from Louisiana, once called, "a Bible totin' Lil Abner," displays his Most Valuable Player trophy after leading Pittsburgh to a 31-19 triumph over the Rams in Super Bowl XIV in 1980.

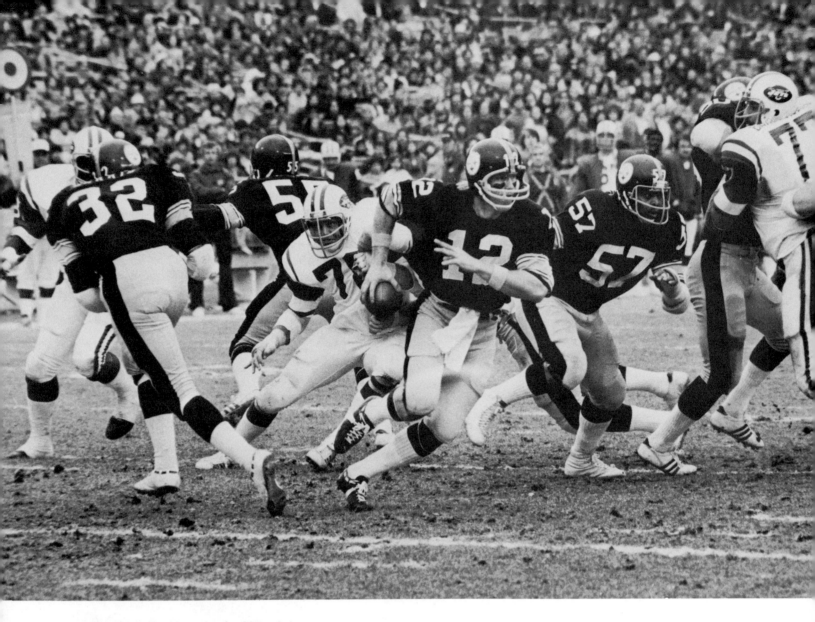

Bradshaw is off and running for 26 yards in a 1975 game against the New York Jets. He retired in 1984, becoming a television analyst and broadcaster.

Harris and Rocky Bleier while the Steelers' Steel Curtain did the rest.

"My rookie year was a disaster," Terry acknowledged later. "I was unprepared. I had no schooling on reading defenses. I never had looked at films. I'd never been on a team with another quarterback and never benched before."

Coach Chuck Noll called it "a case of inexperience."

The turning point in Bradshaw's career came in 1974, a year after a separated shoulder had kept him out of four games. Joe Gilliam had won the starting quarterback job in training while Bradshaw and other veterans were on strike.

Restored to the No. 1 position after six games, Terry proceeded to lead the Steelers to consecutive AFC championships which produced two straight Super Bowl victories—the first over Minnesota and the second over Dallas.

He clinched the triumph over the Cowboys with a 64-yard pass to Lynn Swann but suffered a concussion, one of many injuries to plague him over the ensuing years. There were neck and wrist injuries in 1975. In 1977, he broke his left wrist against Houston and played the final 11 games with his hand in a cast. In 1979 he had back spasms and ankle and arm injuries but refused to leave a game.

Record-setting seasons in 1978 and 1979 by Bradshaw brought the Steelers their third and fourth Super Bowl victories. The first of these produced a shootout between Bradshaw and Dallas' Roger Staubach, with Terry completing 17 of 30 passes for 318 yards and three touchdowns. The next year, he hit on 14 of 21 passes for 309 yards to beat the Los Angeles Rams. He was the Most Valuable Player on both occasions.

Twice married and twice divorced, Bradshaw retired—a genuine football hero—in July 1984, to his 400-acre ranch in Grand Cane, Louisiana, his Bible, guitar and newest career as a television football analyst and broadcaster.

JIM BROWN

"Sheer Power and Desire"

Jim Brown was considered a villain on and off the football field—a Tarzan-like and complex black man who shredded tacklers, allegedly beat up women, carried on a running feud with the law, starred in more than a dozen movies, yet spent much of his latter life trying to provide jobs, milk and bread for the less fortunate members of his race.

He never denied that he was tough, sometimes downright mean and basically a brooding loner, but he strongly resented the figure he often was publicly portrayed.

"There is the image and the man," he said. "The image is what the public thinks he is. The man is what he is. I am no angel. If I was a goody-goody, I'd be a psychological wreck—in a straight jacket."

Succeeding generations will remember him as neither devil nor angel but as one of the greatest athletes of all time, potentially another Jim Thorpe, who excelled in many athletic activities but chose football.

In high school, he won 13 letters in five sports—baseball, football, basketball, track and lacrosse. Recruited by Syracuse University for lacrosse, he turned to football and proceeded to run for 2,091 yards and 25 touchdowns as a slashing, almost unstoppable halfback and fullback.

His exploits made him the first round draft choice of the Cleveland Browns, with whom over nine seasons he stormed over would-be tacklers like a tornado, leaving shattered records in his wake.

Brown runs for a first down in a 1960 game against the Dallas Cowboys. The Cleveland star rushed for 12,312 yards during his brilliant NFL career.

He led the National Football League in rushing in eight of the nine seasons he played from 1957 through 1965. This constituted a league record, as did his lifetime carries, 2,359; yards gained, 12,312; career average per carry, 5.22 yards, and touchdowns rushing, 128. These were marks destined to last for years.

Magnificently built, 6 feet, 2 inches and 230 pounds, with broad shoulders, a 32-inch waist and narrow hips, he ran close to the ground, spinning and dodging and brutally stampeding over frustrated would-be tacklers.

"He was most dangerous when you thought you had him," said Sam Huff, the New York Giants' great linebacker. "He'd gather himself up and you'd find yourself empty-handed."

"Superhuman," acknowledged the Philadelphia Eagles' Chuck Bednarik. "He had finesse, ability, power—sheer power and desire."

Defensive back Henry Carr said, "He ran like he had a halo over his head saying you can't touch."

Brown disdained the suggestion that he had some extraordinary power. "There were a lot of running backs as good as me," he said. "The real difference was that I could focus. I never laid back and relied on natural ability."

Born in 1936, James Nathaniel Brown spent the first nine

Brown's decision to quit football came while he was in London making his second movie, "The Dirty Dozen." The picture grossed $63 million, the most successful of the 17 films he was to make over the next 15 years.

years of his life in the care of a great grandmother on a small island off the coast of southern Georgia after being deserted by a philandering father and a mother who moved North.

When Brown was nine, he joined his mother, a housemaid, and took up residence in the home of his mother's employer, in the affluent community of Manhasset, Long Island. The home owner saw that the boy had the best clothes and went to the best schools.

At Manhasset High School, Brown became an outstanding all-around athlete, particularly gifted in football and lacrosse. In his senior year, he averaged 14.9 yards a carry in football, 38 points a game in basketball and was a standout high jumper. Recruited by close to 50 colleges, Brown chose Syracuse, where at first the coaches sought to make him into a tackle. Later he found his proper position, running back, and won All-America honors his senior year.

Signed by Cleveland at the end of the 1956 season, he immediately turned around the Browns' fortunes. Having finished with a 5-7 record in 1956, the Browns won the Eastern Conference title with a 9-2-1 record in 1957, with Brown rushing for 942 yards.

Brown led a players' revolt in 1962 which resulted in the removal of Paul Brown as coach and followed that with his finest season in 1963 when he ran for 1,863 yards and 12 touchdowns. The Browns won the NFL crown in 1964 and another Eastern title in 1965, with Brown rushing for 1,544 yards.

He had been voted the National Football League's Most Val-

uable Player when he retired July 14, 1966, at the age of 30. He estimated he had six top-flight seasons remaining.

Brown's decision to quit football came while he was in London making his second movie, "The Dirty Dozen," with Lee Marvin. The picture grossed $63 million, the most successful of the 17 films he was to make over the next 15 years.

Although football's highest paid star at $75,000 a year, he had decided it was time to strike out on a new course.

"The money was more than I ever dreamed of," he said about his shift in careers. "I was still young. The movies gave me dignity and a chance to do something for my race."

Brown had earlier married a childhood sweetheart, the former Sue Jones, "a country girl out of Columbus, Georgia," who bore him three children before she finally found it impossible to adjust to the great football star's lifestyle.

Over a period of years, Brown was hit with paternity suits, charges of tossing a model from a second-floor balcony, assaulting a cop and leaving the scene of an accident after a collision on a Los Angeles thruway.

"Harassment," Brown charged. "They couldn't make any of the charges stick. They have made me a target."

Brown did some broadcasting, became a strident black activist and founded the Black Economic Union, designed to set up blacks in business. Few of his enterprises succeeded.

In 1971, his first year of eligibility, he was elected to the Pro Football Hall of Fame. He took his trophy to his retreat in the Hollywood Hills. "I am a loner," he said.

DON BUDGE

The Complete Tennis Player

"**P**laying tennis against Don Budge was like playing against a concrete wall—there was nothing to attack," said former Wimbledon champion Sidney Wood, a contemporary.

"Budge had to be the greatest player of all time—the records prove it," insisted Walter Pate, a player of the Bill Tilden era and for 11 years captain of the U.S. Davis Cup team.

Neither got an argument from Bobby Riggs, the feisty court hustler, himself a onetime champion whose career touched six decades from Tilden to Jack Kramer to Billie Jean King and who faced Budge as both an amateur and a pro.

"Tilden toyed with opponents—he teased them by letting them get close," said the redoubtable Riggs. "Ellsworth Vines was inconsistent. Kramer was troubled with a bad back. Budge wasn't just steady. He was explosive. He blew you off the court."

Don Budge, who played in the shadow of a developing World War II, had a comparatively brief career and thus from a public appreciation standpoint found himself sandwiched between the euphoria of Tilden's "Golden Twenties" and the emergence of a post-war breed of tough young professionals who hit the ball at 120 miles an hour and competed for purses that soared into millions of dollars.

Yet none of the widely acclaimed international stars who preceded him nor the lightning quick, hard-hitting champions who followed managed to cram as much success and dominance into such a small package.

In 1937 Budge won both the Wimbledon and the U.S. men's singles championships. In 1938 he repeated those two triumphs and added the Australian and French crowns to score the first Grand Slam sweep of the sport's major titles. It was a feat that escaped such greats as Tilden, Vines, Kramer, and Pancho Gonzales but was duplicated in the 1960s by Rod Laver.

Such credentials may appear trivial when measured by the plethora of victories compiled by the pros after the game went open in 1968. But it is significant that in that two-year period, 1937-38, Budge never lost a single competitive match. It was an achievement of which none other could boast.

A powerful server with a steady, effective forehand, Budge's greatest weapon—one for which he was renowned—was a whiplash backhand.

A gaunt, long-limbed Californian, who grew up in a city park rather than country club atmosphere, the red-haired Budge played with an exceptionally heavy racket, a veritable war club, 16½ ounces, heavier than those used by Tilden and Kramer. They called him the complete player, one without a technical flaw.

A powerful server with a steady, effective forehand, Don's greatest weapon—one for which he was renowned—was a whiplash backhand, a carryover from his baseball-playing days as a kid. Playing with his brother's heavier racket, he would bring it back with a two-fisted baseball grip, his left hand merely a steadying device, and then release it, providing an action similar to an uncoiling spring.

It wasn't a pure two-handed shot as popularized by Chris Evert Lloyd and Jimmy Connors. But it was deadly.

Don came by his competitive instincts naturally. His father was a Scotsman who played soccer for the Glasgow Rangers but who, after an injury and a bout with pneumonia, immigrated to Oakland, California, where he married an Irish coleen. She bore him two athletic sons. The older, Lloyd, also was a top-flight tennis player.

As a youth, Don played football and baseball in school and neighborhood lots. His first love was baseball. The story is told that once, after both had become famous in their respective fields, Budge met Joe DiMaggio in Toots Shor's restaurant in New York.

"You know, Don," said DiMaggio, "I always envied you. As a kid I dreamed of becoming a tennis champion."

"That's funny," replied Budge. "I always wanted to be a baseball player."

Budge didn't get interested in tennis until he was 15. Lloyd began hitting with him and one day prevailed on him to enter a local junior tournament. Playing in corduroy pants and high-top basketball shoes, Don won easily. He was on his way.

A stringy, gawky-looking kid, Budge won the Pacific Coast junior title in 1932 and, a year later, at age 18, captured the state senior event, beating Bobby Riggs. Later that year, he won his first national crown—the U.S. junior. His victim in the final was Gene Mako, who became his regular doubles partner.

Budge, after experimenting with an inconsistent forehand, made the U.S. Davis Cup squad in 1935 and earned his first voyage overseas where, for the next two years, he beat almost every good player in the world except Britain's Fred Perry, who dominated Wimbledon from 1934 through 1936.

After the 1936 season, Perry turned professional, leaving Budge and Germany's Gottfried von Cramm to battle for the world's No. 1 ranking. It also set up one of the technically greatest and most dramatic matches in tennis history.

The scene was the Davis Cup Inter-Zone final between the United States and Germany on Wimbledon's Center Court. The two teams had split the first four matches and the outcome hung on the final between Budge and von Cramm.

War fever was sweeping Europe. Shortly before the deciding match, von Cramm received a call from Adolf Hitler, exhorting him to "win for the Fatherland." Tension was thick.

Von Cramm won the first two sets and led 4-1 in the fifth, but Budge rallied to capture the blood-draining marathon which ended in semi-darkness. It was a slam-bang struggle with a minimum of unforced errors. Budge went on to lead the Americans over the British, ending a 10-year United States Davis Cup drought.

Tennis' "Big Red" turned pro in 1938, beating Ellsworth Vines, Perry, Riggs and an aging Bill Tilden in a series of cross-country tours that kept his tennis throne secure.

DICK BUTKUS

The Bruising, Battering Bear

In the memory of the oldest living naturalist, no grizzly bear has ever been spotted prowling the streets of Chicago.

Except one: Dick Butkus, who was 245 pounds of snarling, seething muscle at a middle linebacker post for the Chicago Bears from 1965 to 1973. He was Rambo without automatic weapons, using only his hands, shoulders, legs, feet and—it was charged—his teeth.

"The Animal" was the nickname fastened on Dick by the teams he terrorized. His teammates thought it was the right word. Butkus didn't seem to appreciate that handle but neither did he overly resent it. "I guess people think the Bears keep me

"The Animal" was the nickname fastened on Butkus by the teams he terrorized. "I guess people think the Bears keep me in a cage and only let me out on Sundays to play football," he growled.

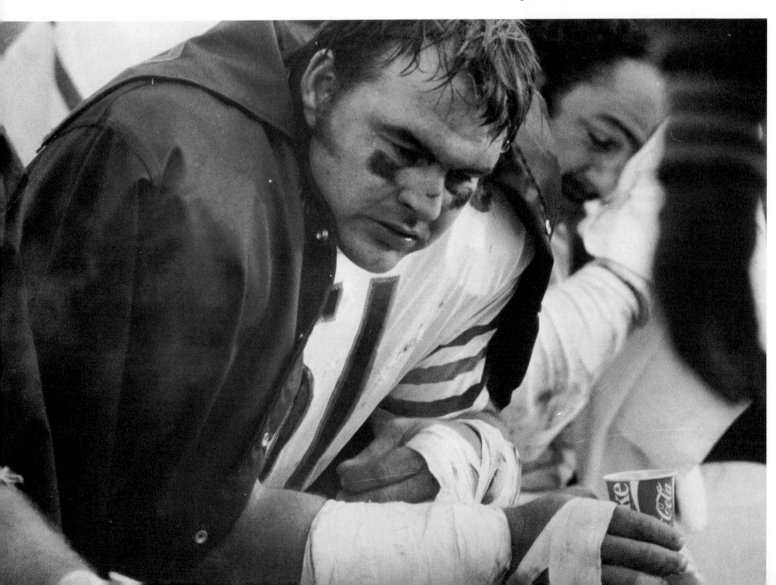

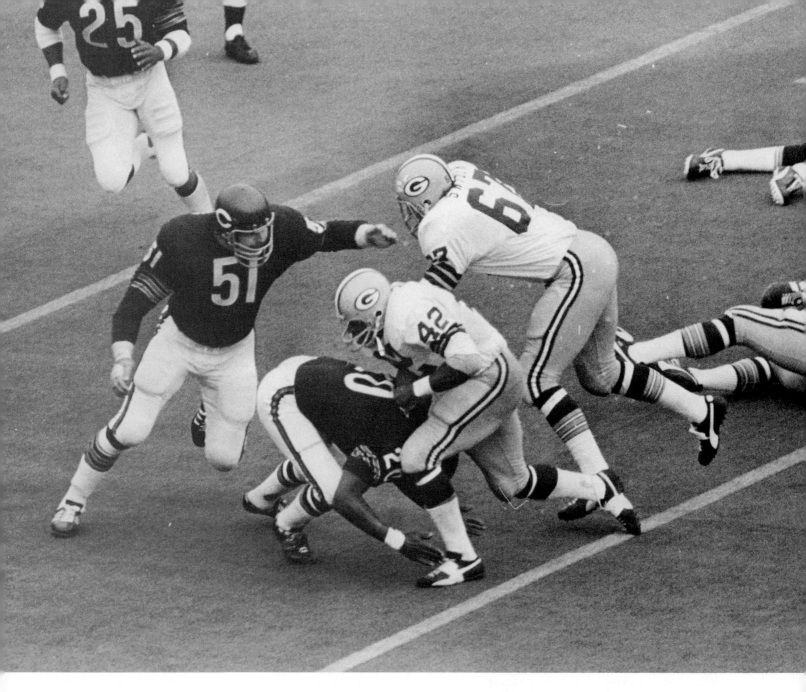

in a cage and only let me out on Sundays to play football," he growled. "Nobody thinks I can talk, much less write my own name."

Butkus roamed a football field sideline to sideline. There were no sophisticated defenses in his day which gave him areas to guard. No offensive keys to read. He went where the ball went and when he found it, he tried to knock the helmet off the guy who had it into the 20th row.

"Dick rattles your brains when he tackles you," was the comment of Bart Starr, the quarterback in the glory days of the Green Bay Packers.

"Butkus is so physical he puts the fear of God into you," observed Greg Landry, who played quarterback for the Detroit Lions and other teams.

"He plays the middle like a piranha," was the succinct summation of Joe Walton, a scout during Dick's playing days and later coach of the New York Jets.

About that business of using his teeth: Accused a couple of times of biting another player in the heat of battle, Butkus drew himself to his full height of 6-3 and replied reproachfully: "I'm a football player, not a gourmet."

Dick was an All-Pro seven times in his nine NFL seasons but never realized a pro football player's dream of taking the field in a Super Bowl game or even a league title game. In most of his

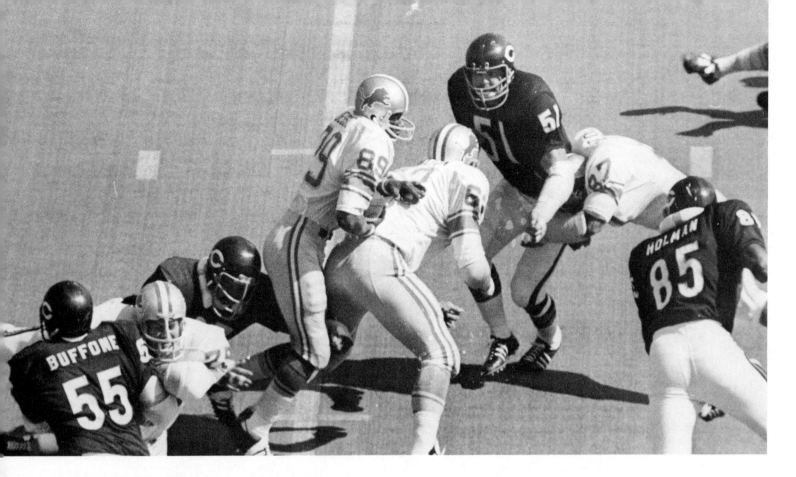

The Bears' standout linebacker (51) gets set to move in on Ron Jessie (89) of the Detroit Lions in October, 1972 game in Chicago.

seasons with the Bears, they had a losing record. There were times when he seemed to be a lone defender. There wasn't much he could do about a mediocre Chicago offense, except to catch a wobbly pass for a point-after-touchdown on a botched-up kick. That he did.

If he gave rival teams—especially quarterbacks—sleepless nights before a game, he did nothing to soothe the nerves of his own teammates. On one occasion he got the blame—deserved or not—for knocking out a window in an airliner before take-off, allegedly because he wanted more air.

Two linebackers who flanked him in the Chicago defense, Doug Buffone and Ross Brupbacher, charged that he set their dormitory door in training camp on fire late one night and was heard in the hall chuckling over the ensuing panic.

Once again Butkus pleaded innocent, "It was purely circumstantial evidence," he said. "They suspected me because I used to go around with placekicker Mirro Roder and he would do anything I asked. Yes, there was one night when I walked around spraying lighter fluid on the doors. Mirro followed me, dropping matches in the fluid. But that was a different night."

Butkus, Lithuanian by ancestry but Spartan by temperament, played in excruciating pain in his final two seasons with the Bears. He required several intricate knee operations. At the end of his career, it appeared a surgeon had been playing tic-tac-toe with a scalpel on his knee.

The knee problem and his inability to play brought on a suit for $1.6 million against the Bears. Dick settled for $600,000. It was then that he began to look around for other ways of making a living. Any further work for the Chicago club went down the litigation tube. There was even a prognosis that at some future date an artificial replacement or aid of some kind would be necessary for the knee.

There was another side to Butkus and it bubbled to the surface during the ceremonies in which he was inducted into the Pro Football Hall of Fame in Canton, Ohio, in 1979. He cried. This bruising, battering brute of a man had tears in his eyes throughout most of his acceptance speech. He choked visibly when he talked about his family and friends.

"I'm glad my mother is here," he said. "My parents were always sensitive to my needs as a player and a son. And I have to give the biggest thank you to my wife, Helen. Through the lonely years when I played, she was always there with welcome and love. She is my greatest fan and best friend, as well as a wonderful wife."

Helen, whom he met when he was 14, was the reason he did not go to Notre Dame after finishing high school in Chicago, where he attracted notice as a rampaging fullback. Before entering college, Dick wanted to take the nuptial vow and was told Notre Dame did not permit players to be married. A scout for the University of Illinois told him there was a "beautiful married facility" on the campus at Champaign.

As a linebacker at Illinois, he was the star of a team that went to the Rose Bowl in 1964 and whipped the Washington Huskies, 17-7. It was the only championship team he ever played on.

There is life after pro football and Butkus discovered it after leaving the Bears. He turned to acting and is still at it. He did some work as a commentator and then joined the elite squad of former sports greats doing beer commercials.

An inspired bit of casting teamed him with Bubba Smith, the hulking ex-defensive end for the Baltimore Colts. The scripts which pictured them as bruisers with a minus IQ were popular and the two former NFL greats read their lines with something close to professional smoothness.

Butkus continued to pile up TV and movie credits and, in his words, "anytime they needed a heavy, in more ways than one, they sent for me." But producers found a new image for the big boomer early in 1987. NBC came up with a pilot film for a new series called "Kowalski Loves Ya." The film looked like a natural for Butkus. He played a former linebacker, who has to manage a household of three children and a mother-in-law.

One of the finest tributes Dick ever received was unofficial. In a 1970 poll of National Football League coaches, Butkus was named by nine of them as the first player they would select if they were starting a team from scratch. His nine votes were three more than any other star, including quarterback Joe Namath, then at his peak.

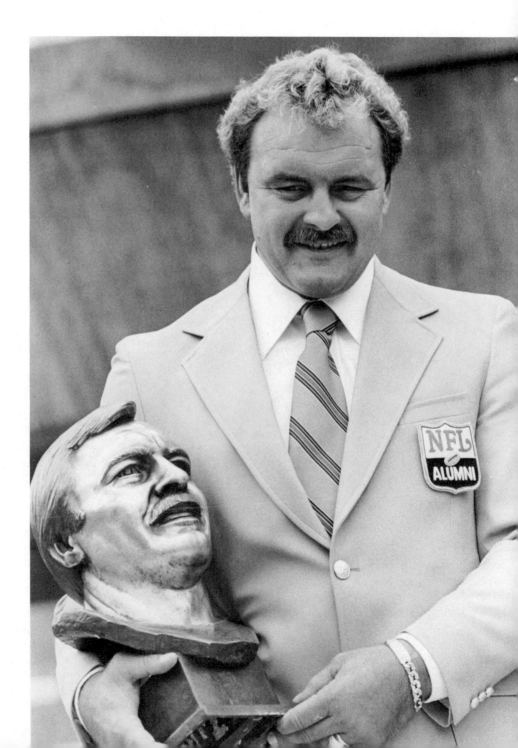

An All-Pro seven times in his nine NFL seasons although he never played in a Super Bowl or league title game, Butkus was voted into the Pro Football Hall of Fame in 1979.

ROY CAMPANELLA

Tragedy Followed Triumphs

On a cold, wintry night in January, 1958, an automobile careened off an ice-slick Long Island highway and crashed into a utility pole. The vehicle was almost totaled and from its wreckage was pulled the battered driver, miraculously but barely alive. He had been driving home late from a dinner in New York City.

Thus tragically ended the illustrious and historic baseball career of Roy Campanella, the black catcher on the famous Brooklyn Dodger teams of the late 1940s and 1950s immortalized in Roger Kahn's sensitive opus, "The Boys of Summer."

If Jackie Robinson was General Manager Branch Rickey's instrument for cracking the color line in major league baseball then Campanella, paralyzed by the accident, was the ointment to soothe the deep ruptures resulting from the prejudices of the period.

Joining the Dodgers a year after Robinson's controversial breakthrough in 1947, the chubby, hard-hitting receiver brought to the touchy situation an outgoing "hail-fellow-well-met" attitude which, aside from his contributions as a great player, pro-

Roy Campanella tags out New York Giant Daryl Spencer at the plate during 1953 game at Ebbets Field, Brooklyn. The Dodgers won, 8-4.

Campy, a National League three-time MVP, makes another putout, tagging Philadelphia's Richie Ashburn in a 1950 game. Roy put the ball on Ashburn after getting a rifle-like throw from right fielder Carl Furillo.

vided a leadership quality and solidifying influence on the club for 10 years.

He and Jackie had contrasting personalities. Robinson, well-educated and intensely proud, exercised remarkable restraint but often displayed quick anger when he felt demeaned. To Campanella, the kid from the ghetto, baseball was a huge playpen. Every day was recess.

Campanella frequently chided Jackie about having a persecution complex and a chip on his shoulder. Jackie countered by inferring that Campy was an Uncle Tom. The two were never close friends although respectful of each other's talents and contributions. They had different upbringings.

Born November 19, 1921, son of a black mother and an Italian father, Campanella grew up in a black neighborhood of Philadelphia known as Nicetown. He had a good home life. As a kid, he was fun-loving, athletic and a practical joker.

He was playing baseball with grown men when he was 12 years old. At 15, he quit school to join the Baltimore Elite Giants of the Negro National League, making $15 a week. He spent nine years with the club, moving to the Caribbean for winter baseball when the season was over. His salary was $3,000 a year.

He was indefatigable. In one day, he played four games—a daytime doubleheader in Cincinnati followed by a twi-night doubleheader in Middletown, Ohio.

It wasn't long before he caught the eye of Branch Rickey, who helped mold the St. Louis Cardinals' "Gas House Gang" and

A policeman stands beside automobile which Roy Campanella was driving early on Jan. 28, 1958 when it skidded and crashed into a utility pole at Glen Cove, N.Y. The accident left the 37-year-old Campanella a quadriplegic, immobilized from the chest down.

who, upon moving to the Brooklyn Dodgers, harbored the secret notion of opening the door for Negroes in organized baseball.

Campanella, in fact, came close to being the first black to play in the majors. Rickey acknowledged that he had debated between Campy and Jackie Robinson.

In 1945, before signing Robinson to a contract, Rickey approached Campanella. "I'd like for you to play for me," the Dodger boss said. Campanella, unaware of Rickey's secret plans, thought the offer was for a new Negro league which Rickey was rumored to be planning, and showed little interest.

Rickey subsequently signed Robinson in a move that revolutionized the game. The next season Rickey signed Campanella and pitcher Don Newcombe and sent them to the Dodgers' Class B New England League farm club in Nashua, New Hampshire. Robinson, meanwhile, was breaking into organized ball with Montreal, a Triple-A team.

Campanella and Newcombe became instant stars at Nashua, where the maximum salary was less than $200 a week. Local fans showered them with chickens—as many as 1,300 at a time—when the team won. Campanella was named the league's most valuable player.

From Nashua, Campanella moved to Montreal, where he hit 13 home runs and batted .273 in 1947. Although Brooklyn Manager Leo Durocher wanted Campanella immediately, Rickey thought the catcher needed more seasoning and shipped him to the Dodgers' farm team in St. Paul, Minnesota.

It was a temporary move. Batting .325, Campy was summoned to Ebbets Field in 1948 where he joined Robinson, Pee Wee Reese, Gil Hodges, Duke Snider, Carl Furillo and others for one of the most exciting eras in the game.

Campanella was a master at handling pitchers. He had a rifle throwing arm and batted for both percentage and power. He and the Yankees' Yogi Berra became objects of debates over who was the best catcher of the day.

Campanella batted .287 and hit 22 home runs his first full season in 1949. He was selected the National League's most valuable player three times—first in 1951 when he batted .325 with 108 runs batted in and 33 homers, again in 1953 and 1955.

His 41 home runs and 142 RBIs in 1953 both set major league records for a catcher. In his last big year, 1955, he had a .318 average, 107 RBIs and 32 home runs. He led the National League catchers in double plays with 12 in 1948. He played in five World Series. In 1969 he became the second black player to be enshrined in baseball's Hall of Fame.

Campanella was a robust 37 years old and looking forward to several more spring trainings when the terrible accident occurred. His spinal column severed, he was left a quadriplegic, immobilized from the chest down.

Confined to a wheelchair, he spent 10 months in a hospital, courageously undergoing therapy that restored some use of his arms and hands. He remained active in the game, doing radio and TV shows, attending special events, coaching kids and holding clinics. "I loved the game," he said. "I wish I could have played longer."

Campanella poses happily in January, 1969 after being named to the Baseball Hall of Fame. Others in the photo, left to right, are Monte Irvin, former Giants' outfielder, Baseball Commissioner William Eckert and Elston Howard, former Yankee catcher.

WILT CHAMBERLAIN

Triggered the Seven-Foot Revolution

If George Mikan was the first of the big men in basketball then Wilt Chamberlain was the first of the agile giants, triggering the "Seven-Foot Revolution" for muscular beanstalks who could move with the grace of ballerinas, fake, pass, shoot and slam dunk.

At 7 feet, 1 inch and 275 pounds, Wilt the Stilt emerged as the Goliath by whom all future titans—and they proliferated—had to be measured. He wrote the book. He copyrighted the slam dunk, broke the dam that unleashed capitalistic six-figure salaries and set records in such abundance that it took two pages of five-point type to record them all in the National Basketball Association Register.

It was Chamberlain who erased the words "klutz" and "ox" from the basketball dictionary and relegated to oblivion the notion that all big men had to be dumb, awkward stumble-bums. Chamberlain was an athlete of superb potential who might have been a champion in any athletic field he chose.

One of his early ambitions was to be a decathlon competitor in the Olympic Games. As a schoolboy, he was a good runner and high jumper and, because of his unusual strength, was out-

left:

THE RIVALS. Chamberlain (13) is determined to get the ball down the court, and defensive ace Bill Russell of the Celtics is just as determined to stop him, in this 1969 NBA playoff game.

opposite:

The 7-foot-1, 275-pound Wilt outjumps three members of the Detroit Pistons in December, 1959 NBA game in Detroit. Chamberlain led Philadelphia to a 124-112 triumph.

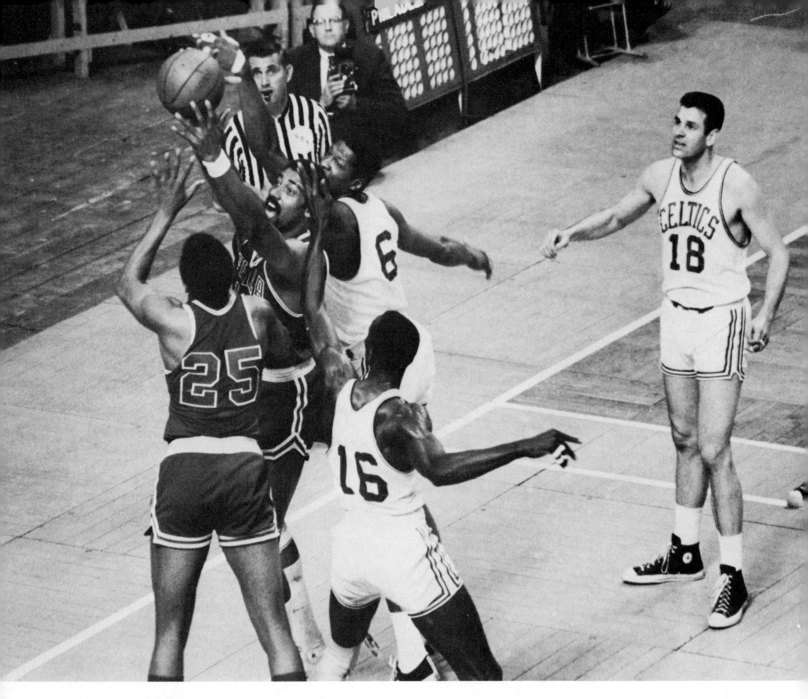

*Outstretching teammate Chet Walker (25) and
Boston's Bill Russell (6), Chamberlain controls
a rebound in 1968 playoff game won by
Philadelphia, 110-105.*

standing in such field events as the javelin, shotput and discus. "One of my regrets," he said later, "was that I never pursued this dream."

He raced boats and learned to water ski, reaching speeds of 85 miles an hour. He took up volleyball and even tried his hand at polo although he never found a big enough pony.

Reflective of the range of his talents, he both played tennis and boxed. After retirement, he once seriously considered challenging Muhammad Ali for the heavyweight championship but later abandoned the idea for which Ali was most thankful. "Only one man in this whole world might beat me,"

Ali said, "and that's that big, tough dude, the Stilt. It scares me just to think about getting in the ring with him."

So Wilt the Stilt—a label he abhorred—confined himself to busting basketball records instead of beaks and no one in the game did it on such an overwhelming scale.

In his 14 years as a professional, from 1959 through 1973, he twice scored more than 3,000 points in a season and once went over the 4,000 mark—plateaus no other player ever reached. Playing with Philadelphia's Warriors and 76ers, the San Francisco Warriors and Los Angeles Lakers, he accumulated a career total of 31,419 points, a record that lasted until Kareem Abdul-Jabbar, playing in his 16th season, broke it in 1985.

He led the league in rebounding in 11 of his 14 years and in field goal percentage in nine. Seven times he was the NBA's leading scorer. His one crowning season—one that should be recorded on marble and preserved for posterity—was 1961-62 when he scored a total of 4,029 points and averaged 50.4 points a game. It was climaxed when he rammed in 100 points—seemingly an untouchable mark—against the New York Knicks in Hershey, Pennsylvania, on March 2, 1962.

His various records ranged from career rebounds, totaling 2,075, to consecutive field goals, minutes played and other statistics. He was four times the league's Most Valuable Player and seven times a starter in the All-Star Game. He gained basketball's Hall of Fame in 1978.

Wilt was born in Philadelphia on August 21, 1936, the son of a handyman and one of nine children. Growing up, he was always taller than his schoolmates, a condition that made him self-conscious and unsocial. Young friends dubbed him "The Dipper," "Dippy" and "Dip."

By the time he reached Overbrook High School, Wilt was 6 feet, 11 inches tall, a torso on pipestem legs. Yet he had good coordination and became the star of the team, sometimes scoring 70 to 90 points a game. Courted by more than 200 colleges, he chose the University of Kansas where he led the Jayhawks to the NCAA finals in 1957, losing a four-overtime thriller to North Carolina in Kansas City.

He quit college after his junior year to join the Harlem Globetrotters for a salary of $65,000. On May 30, 1959, Owner Eddie Gottlieb of the Philadelphia Warriors signed the prize prospect for $30,000 plus fringe benefits. An immediate sensation, Wilt scored 43 points and grabbed 28 rebounds in his debut against the Knicks. Gottlieb began dreaming of a championship.

Unfortunately, Wilt was unable to deliver titles as easily as he could stuff basketballs through the hoop.

In his 14 years in the NBA, Chamberlain had the satisfaction of playing on only two championship teams—Philadelphia in 1967 and Los Angeles in 1972. This gave rise to comparisons with Bill Russell, the 6-foot-10 ball-handling wizard of the Boston Celtics, who had come directly from the Olympic Games into the league in 1956.

Great fanfare greeted their first confrontation February 23, 1960, in New York's old Madison Square Garden. Before a sellout crowd, Wilt drew first blood, scoring 53 points to 22 for Russell and leading the Warriors to a 126-108 victory.

Subsequently, the Celtics and Russell proved Wilt's nemesis, beating his teams twice in the NBA championship series and five times in conference finals. In all, the Celtics won 11 titles behind Russell, nine in the 10 years the two giant stars clashed—a source of pain for Wilt.

"I scored more points against the Celtics than anybody else," Chamberlain argued. "I outscored Russell in head-to-head meetings 440 to 212—two to one."

A contemporary said the difference in the two men was that Russell made the talent around him play better while Chamberlain was a more individual star. Some critics accused Wilt of being lazy and often guilty of loafing.

Elvin Hayes, who played against both men, said Chamberlain was the only player he ever saw who was unstoppable. "If he got stopped," said the former Houston and Washington star, "it was because he stopped himself."

One of Wilt's early ambitions was to be a decathlon competitor in the Olympic Games. Here, while attending the University of Kansas, he prepares to take off in the high jump of the Kansas Relays on April 20, 1957. He placed second in the high jump.

TY COBB

The Fiery Georgia Peach

In 1951, when The Associated Press released the results of a sports writers' poll naming the greatest athletes by sport of the first half-century, the telephone rang on the desk of Joe Reichler, the AP's baseball editor. The call came from Atlanta, and there was a raspy, agitated voice at the other end.

The caller was Ty Cobb. He was livid, having read in the Atlanta Journal that Babe Ruth had been chosen over him as the greatest baseball player of the past 50 years. In angry, no uncertain terms, Cobb made it known that the poll was a farce. Baseball's greatest player, Ty Cobb insisted, was Ty Cobb.

Such was the nature of the man—fiery, arrogant, egotistical, combative, outspoken. Yet there were many of his contemporaries who conceded that, love him or hate him (and most were in the latter category), the crusty old "Georgia Peach" may have been correct. He may well have been the greatest all-around ballplayer, if not the most popular, of all time. There were statistics to support the theory.

Playing 22 years with the Detroit Tigers and two with the Philadelphia Athletics, the rock-hard redneck from the red clay country, compiled records that endured for generations. In the 1936 voting for original inductees into baseball's Hall of Fame, Cobb led them all, including the great Ruth, with 222 of 226 votes.

He had a lifetime batting average of .367, the game's highest, with three seasons of better than .400. He won 12 batting titles, nine in a row, and never fell below .368 from 1909 through 1919. He was the first to get more than 4,000 hits. He scored 2,245 runs and stole 892 bases. It was not until more than a half century later that Pete Rose surpassed his mark of 4,191 hits and Lou Brock bettered his career stolen base record.

Cobb was not a slugger, in the sense of a Ruth, a Mickey Mantle or a Hank Aaron, who thrilled crowds later. He was a slashing left-handed hitter whose line drives rocketed over the heads of infielders. Once on base, he was a scheming strategist who drove defenders to nervous distraction with his speed and daring.

The "Georgia Peach" played in the "dead ball era," when runs were scarce and had to be milked around the bases. He had the tools for the times. He was leather tough, lightning quick and meaner than a bed of rattlesnakes. He treasured his reputation as a diamond villain—generally heckled by fans, resented by teammates, detested and feared by opponents.

In the 1936 voting for the original inductees into Baseball's Hall of Fame, Cobb led them all, including the great Babe Ruth, garnering 222 of 226 votes.

A lifetime .367 batter, Ty was also known for his tenacity and aggressiveness on the base paths. He went into a base with spikes flying.

Stories that he filed the spikes of his shoes in the locker room are probably untrue, but there is nothing fictional about his aggressiveness and tenacity on the base paths. He shunned the head-on slide and preferred to go into a base full-tilt, spikes flying, unmindful of the opposing player.

To Cobb, baseball wasn't a game, it was a war. And his animosity wasn't confined to the playing field. Contemporaries attributed it to an early tragedy in his life.

Cobb was born December 18, 1886, in the small north Georgia village of Narrows. His father was a man of local esteem— a teacher, farmer, weekly newspaper publisher, later mayor and state senator. Tyrus was the first child, named for the ancient city of Tyre. The elder Cobb wanted his son to go to college and be a lawyer or doctor. Athletically inclined and very competitive, the boy demurred.

At 17, he was a star of the local team in Royston, Georgia, played briefly with Augusta in the South Atlantic League and some semi-pro ball in Anniston, Alabama, before getting a chance with the Detroit Tigers in 1905. He was a scrawny, gristly kid of 18, 5 feet, 11 inches and 155 pounds.

This break coincided with news that his father had been killed—shot by his mother upon returning home late at night from a business trip. The mother claimed she had mistaken him for a burglar, but there were reports of a secret lover.

Cobb became bitter and the rage continued to manifest itself as he sought to gain a spot with the team. He was five years

This is Ty Cobb playing in his first big league game for Detroit in 1905. He played 22 years for the Tigers and two for the Philadelphia Athletics.

younger than any of the other Tigers' regulars and the only Southerner—a firebrand generally disliked by his teammates because of his temper and aggressiveness.

"He was still fighting the Civil War," said Sam Crawford, a contemporary. "We were all damn Yankees."

Cobb's first years with the Tigers were turbulent. Because of his cockiness, he was ostracized and hazed by his fellow players. His bats were sawed in half. He got into fights with teammates. Catcher Charlie Smith broke his nose. He knocked down and kicked a pitcher named Ed Siever. He had to be separated from a fellow outfielder, Matty McIntyre.

As Cobb got older, he got bigger (6-1, 175 pounds), more audacious and meaner. He taunted pitchers and kept rival infielders in a tizzy by getting caught between bases and dodging back and forth to force a mistake.

In 1912, he leaped into the stands in New York and punched and kicked a fan who was badgering him. There was a celebrated hotel brawl with Buck Herzog of the Giants in 1917. In 1921, he challenged umpire Billy Evans under the stands. He was constantly having scrapes with blacks off the field—a street worker, an elevator operator, a watchman.

At age 34, he became playing manager of the Tigers and had six years of moderate success. He played his final two years, 1927 and 1928, with the Philadelphia Athletics.

Even after retiring, Cobb became involved in many public scrapes. A friend sued him for $50,000. He was barred from some golf courses in California. Nevertheless, he was a shrewd businessman, investing in firms such as General Motors and Coca-Cola. Twice married and twice divorced, he died July 17, 1961, a multi-millionaire, angry at the world.

NADIA COMANECI

Princess of the Bars and Beams

She was just a sprite of a child, a brooding, dark-eyed girl of 14, a little more than four feet tall and less than 80 pounds—seemingly a windup toy on a stick, spinning, leaping, somersaulting with a cold, mechanical precision while millions, watching in the flesh and on television, cheered.

Her name was Nadia Comaneci, the icicle princess of the bars and beams in the 1976 Olympics who became the first gymnast in history to score a perfect "10"—she did it seven times and turned her once neglected and cult discipline into an exact science.

The world fell in love with her, but the little girl from behind Romania's Communist curtain refused to respond with even a smile. Her aloof reserve remained impenetrable.

"In 1976," said Gordon Maddux, a gymnastics authority who did TV commentary on the Olympics' gymnastic competi-

Fourteen-year-old Nadia Comaneci flies herself out of the uneven bars during the 1976 Olympic Games in Montreal to score the first perfect 10 in Olympic history.

"Nadia was extremely stoic, a robot," said the coach of the American team, Don Peters, about the Olympic standout. "But she was in a class by herself."

tion, "Nadia was the best athlete in the world, all sports included."

Nadia and her cordon of teammates, all looking like cub girl scouts as they marched in unison through Montreal's Olympic Village, came to the Games in the shadow of the Soviets' celebrated Olga Korbut, the cute, outgoing heroine of the 1972 Games in Munich, Germany.

It was actually Olga, 84 pounds of personality and flying pigtails, who made the world conscious of her sport, a dizzying routine of swinging on bars, staging daring loops on narrow beams and doing barefoot exercises to music much in the fashion of figure skaters on ice.

A TV reporter had noticed Korbut doing a difficult back somersault on the uneven bars and persuaded the American Broadcasting Company to alter its program and include a segment of Korbut's routine in its broadcast. The network was

hooked. Before it had finished, its cameras were giving special attention to the 17-year-old Russian girl and, before long, it had its viewers joining the live chorus of "Olga! Olga! Olga!"

Olga won the balance beam and free exercises—only two gold medals—but television made her a world personality and she relished the role. A natural "ham," she was the star of the Russian team that toured the United States in 1976.

She dressed up in jeans and monogrammed shirts and, when someone asked her what she liked best about America, she replied:

"I enjoyed meeting the President at the White House but I liked Disneyland the best."

The ever-smiling, effervescent Olga, although then a maturing 21, was still the main attraction on the stage when the gymnastics competition began in Montreal in 1976. Few paid much attention to Comaneci until the Romanian schoolgirl began whizzing through her routines, her supple body performing like a metronome on the platforms, bars and beams.

Nadia was not a complete unknown. She was one of an underaged brood, look-alike miniatures in their white leotards with a bold stripe down the side ostensibly being groomed by Romanian coach Bela Karolyi for some future Games. A year earlier Nadia had scored an upset over the Soviet Union's veteran European champion Ludmilla Turischeva.

But interest was quickened when Nadia scored her first "10"—an unheard of achievement in 80 years of the sport—and soon fans began flocking to the big hall and fighting for tickets to get a look at the newest sports phenomenon.

Flawlessly, Comaneci swept to gold medals in the balance beam and uneven parallel bars and captured all-around individual honors while Korbut, a forlorn and distraught figure, slipped from the limelight, finally winning the free exercises to the delight of her faithful followers.

While Nadia inspired admiration and wonderment among specialists and ordinary spectators alike, she never was able to engender the warmth and personal attachment that had marked the reign of her Russian rival.

"Nadia was extremely stoic, a robot," said the coach of the American team, Don Peters. "But she was in a class by herself—head and shoulders above the rest."

Whereas Olga had been bouncy and ebullient, Nadia was as cold as the blade of a rapier. She never showed emotion—not even to the crowd that was constantly bursting into wild applause. She swept through her routines as if pushed by some unseen button, then, having finished, she sought quick refuge in the privacy of the Village.

Some of her aloofness was accountable. The daughter of an auto mechanic, she was discovered by Karolyi when she was six years old doing flip-flops in a schoolyard. Karolyi immediately enrolled her in a training class. She never had a childhood as such. All she knew were rings, bars and beams.

At 14, she was unprepared for the public and media attention which poured down on her at Montreal. She was timid and half-scared. But under that schoolgirl facade was a competitive drive as cold and sharp as steel.

Her and Olga's impact on their sport was dramatic. Gymnastics interest mushroomed throughout the world. In the United States alone, the gymnastics pool grew from 15,000 in 1972 to 150,000.

Olga drifted into oblivion behind the Iron Curtain. She gained weight, married and had a baby. Nadia had a nervous breakdown, tried to commit suicide but righted her life and showed up at the 1984 Olympics in Los Angeles—a bright, mature young woman no longer scared of the public. Karolyi, distressed over the Romanian government's attempt to exploit his prize pupil, moved to America and began turning out a new class of champions, particularly Mary Lou Retton, the star of the Los Angeles Games.

Four years after her sensational performance in Montreal, 18-year-old Nadia wins a gold medal while performing on the balance beam in the 1980 Olympics in Moscow.

MARGARET SMITH COURT

Queen of Grand Slam Tennis

They called her "Maggie." She was a scrawny, skinny-legged lass of 11, living in the country town of Albury, Australia, when she first heard mention of the term "Grand Slam" in tennis.

Margaret Smith had been playing the game for two years and was showing great promise as a junior in a land where tennis was more than a sport—it was a religion. Every day the train would arrive with newspapers from Sydney and Maggie would scan the sports pages zealously for reports of the Australian National Championships then in progress.

She was particularly interested in the widely acclaimed American star named Maureen "Little Mo" Connolly, a back-court precisionist. The court experts had tabbed "Little Mo" the world's best prospect for sweeping all the major titles—the Australian, Wimbledon, U.S. and French championships—for a Grand Slam no woman player had ever achieved.

The country girl was thrilled when Little Mo won and went on to fulfill her destiny in 1953. She never dreamed that 17 years later she would duplicate the feat, far exceeding Connolly's collection of titles and establish herself as the undisputed queen of the courts, one of the game's immortals.

"Whenever you talk of great women tennis players, you have to start with Margaret," said Marty Riessen, who shared many mixed doubles titles with the Australian. "She should go down as the finest woman player of all time."

Seven years almost to the day after Maggie had thrilled to Maureen Connolly's successful invasion of her country, she found herself in center court receiving the trophy as the youngest woman—at 17 years, six months—ever to win the Australian championship. It was merely the beginning of a long reign that saw her not only capture the Grand Slam but amass a cache of worldwide crowns, unmatched by any other player, before or after.

Margaret Smith, later playing under her married name of Court, won 26 Grand Slam tournament singles titles alone and 66 overall, including women's doubles and mixed doubles. Her total almost doubled those of her closest challengers, Billie Jean King (retired with 38) and Martina Navratilova, building on an

left:

"Whenever you talk of great women tennis players, you have to start with Margaret," said America's Marty Riessen. "She should go down as the finest woman player of all time." Here she's in the process of winning the Wimbledon singles title in 1970.

opposite, left:

Margaret holds trophy aloft after winning the 1973 U.S. women's singles crown at Forest Hills by defeating Evonne Goolagong in the final match.

opposite, right:

Between 1960 and 1973 Margaret won the Australian singles crown a record 11 times. She took the American crown seven times, the French five and Wimbledon on three occasions.

active list that reached 43 in January, 1987. In Grand Slam singles titles, Margaret boasted seven more than Helen Wills Moody, with 19, and eight more than Chris Evert Lloyd, with 18. Only Navratilova, with 15 through 1986, posed a serious threat.

Margaret won the Australian singles championship a record 11 times between 1960 and 1973. She captured the American crown seven times, the French five and Wimbledon on three occasions. An excellent doubles player, her trophies in these specialties would fill a gymnasium.

She was at home on all surfaces. Daughter of a cheese factory foreman, she learned to play on a public clay court across the road from her family's modest two-bedroom house. Her game was refined on Australia's big stadium grass.

In those formative years, Margaret was very skinny and awkward, appearing to be all arms and legs. Her father feared she would never be strong enough to play tournament tennis. Yet at 15 she could beat every boy her age in Albury and, as a junior, she won more than 50 trophies.

Discovered by the always alert Australian tennis hierarchy, the young girl was placed under the wing of Frank Sedgman, Wimbledon champion and Davis Cup star of the early 1950s. Sedgman and his wife took her into their home.

"You're going to have to get some muscle on those bones," counseled Sedgman, ordering a heavy build-up regimen. Margaret exercised on bars and trampolines, jumped rope and lifted weights.

By the time she reached maturity, she was a powerful woman, 5 feet, 9 inches tall and weighing 157 pounds. She remained a strikingly feminine figure—trim and graceful. Her long legs could cover a court in one bound and it seemed impossible to hit a ball out of the reach of her long arms.

Prior to the 1970 Wimbledon tournament, Dr. Reginal Whitney conducted a series of physical tests on her to compare with tests made on other famous athletes and concluded she was an athletic phenomenon. His report ranked her alongside Babe Didrikson Zaharias and Holland's Fanny Blankers-Koen of Olympic fame as among the outstanding sportswomen of the century.

Dr. Whitney found her "greatly above average." She was 2½ inches taller and 11 pounds heavier than the top 10 other women athletes in the program. Her right hand grip strength was found to be superior.

"These characteristics undoubtedly have a pronounced effect on her opponents," his report said. "They feel dwarfed by her size and strength. She has the advantage of serving from a greater height and from being able to kill smashes at the net. She made the highest jump of all the women we tested."

Margaret won seven consecutive Australian championships after her triumph as a teen-ager in 1960 and dominated the female segment of the game until her second and final retirement in the mid-1970s.

In 1966 she packed away her rackets, saying she was tired of traveling. She met and married a tall wool broker and yachtsman named Barry Court. It was Court who encouraged her to return and shoot for the Grand Slam. Thwarted three times previously one short of her goal, Margaret finally pulled off the coup in 1970. She won the Australian and French titles easily but was pressed to beat Billie Jean King at Wimbledon and Rosie Casals in three sets at Forest Hills.

BOB COUSY

Houdini of the Hardwood

When Bob Cousy joined the Boston Celtics in 1950, they were a struggling franchise in a city where basketball was overshadowed by baseball and hockey. By the time he retired in 1963, the Celtics had won six NBA championships and Cousy was the most popular athlete in town.

His spectacular passing and ballhandling dazzled crowds that were accustomed to seeing slow, methodical players and earned him the nickname, "The Houdini of the Hardwood."

"He could do more with a basketball—shoot, pass, dribble, anything—than anyone I ever saw," the late St. John's and New York Knicks' Coach Joe Lapchick said.

Coaches weren't the only ones awed by Cousy's skills.

"Some day," a referee said, "somebody's going to tell me that Cousy has just swallowed the ball, and I'm simply going to go over to the bench and get a new one."

Cousy never swallowed a ball during his 13-year pro career, but the 6-foot-1 playmaker did just about everything else.

He made the NBA All-Star team every year he played, led the league in assists for eight straight seasons and scored nearly 17,000 points. But statistics were not a true measure of his greatness. In addition to his considerable athletic skills, Cousy was an intense competitor.

"A lot of athletes, when they get into an agitated state, lose their cool and they can't function," he said. "I always looked for that feeling."

Cousy's climb to the top wasn't easy. He was born in a poor

Cousy (14) gets off a shot for the Boston Celtics in a 1959 game against the St. Louis Hawks. On defense are Bob Pettit (9) and John McCarthy (15).

A magician on the court, Bob was once referred to by an NBA game official with this comment: "Some day, somebody's going to tell me that Cousy has just swallowed the ball, and I'm simply going to go over to the bench and get a new one."

section of New York in 1928, and didn't begin playing basketball until his French-speaking parents moved to the suburbs when he was 12.

Although he worked hard in the playgrounds to improve his game, Cousy failed to make his high school team as a sophomore. However, he eventually became a prep star and earned a scholarship to Holy Cross.

Holy Cross won the NCAA championship during Cousy's freshman year, but he clashed with Coach Doggie Julian over his lack of playing time. Their relationship became so stormy that Cousy considered transferring to St. John's, but he stayed and led the Crusaders to a 26-game winning streak in his senior year.

Despite Cousy's fame in New England, the Celtics passed up an opportunity to draft him. Asked to explain the team's decision, first-year Coach Red Auerbach was characteristically blunt.

"We need a big man," he said. "Little men are a dime a dozen. I'm supposed to win, not go after local yokels."

Cousy was drafted by the Tri-Cities Hawks, who then traded him to the Chicago Stags. But the Stags folded before the season started, and their players were dispersed throughout the league.

The last players to be assigned were Cousy and two proven stars, Max Zaslofsky and Andy Phillip. One would go to New York, another to Boston and the third to Philadelphia. Not surprisingly, all three teams wanted Zaslofsky, the NBA's leading scorer. Phillip was the second choice and Cousy the last.

To settle the matter, the names of the players were drawn from a hat. Boston went first, and ended up with Cousy.

At that time, the Celtics were extremely disappointed. But years later, Auerbach would concede: "We got stuck with the greatest player in the league when we drew his name out of a hat."

Cousy had many great moments in the NBA, but his most memorable performance may have come in a four-overtime victory over Syracuse in an Eastern Division playoff game in 1953. He scored 17 of the Celtics' final 21 points and finished with 50 points, hitting 30 of 32 free throw attempts.

The following year, in the NBA All-Star game, Cousy scored 10 points in overtime, made several great passes and killed the clock with his dribbling, leading the East to a victory over the West. Before the overtime, the media had chosen Minneapolis' Jim Pollard as the game's most valuable player.

But they were so impressed with Cousy's overtime performance that they took another vote and gave him the trophy.

Despite Cousy's contributions, the Celtics couldn't win an NBA championship until they got a great big man, Bill Russell,

in the 1956-57 season. Still, the playmaker was an integral part of the Celtics' teams that captured six championships in his last seven seasons as a full-time player.

Cousy coached Boston College for six seasons after leaving the NBA, but returned to the league in 1969 to coach the Cincinnati Royals. He even played in seven games that season in an attempt to bolster the team's sagging attendance and provide backcourt help.

But the aging Cousy was a shadow of the player who had thrilled fans for so many years.

As one writer said, "People in Boston have little doubt that while Dr. Naismith may have invented the game, Cousy made it as close to an art form as possible."

JACK DEMPSEY

The Devastating Manassa Mauler

Of all a nation's sports heroes, traditionally none is more revered than the heavyweight boxing champion of the world. He stimulates a pride and near idolatry that traces back to the gladiators of Ancient Rome and the knights of the Middle Ages—a passion fed by the symbol of great strength and survival in raw, primitive, man-to-man combat.

Of America's unending parade of fighting greats, dating back a century or more, none has so captivated the people's fancy as the pug-faced, beetle-browed onetime hobo out of Montana's mine country whom they called "The Manassa Mauler."

One can visualize gray-haired fathers and grandfathers decades in the future, discussing some current champion with their offsprings, saying, "Well, son, let me tell you about a man named Jack Dempsey."

Jack Dempsey, a tough, fierce, devastating ring brawler, emerging just after World War I when the strife-weary nation was thirsting for some emotional relief, became the measuring rod by which all future champions would be judged.

He held the title for seven years. He eschewed the classic style. A crouching, weaving, bobbing aggressor with the kick of a mule in each hand, he battered opponents into pulps. He popularized the knockout punch and became the sport's first "Ring Killer."

Having smashed titleholder Gene Tunney to the canvas in the seventh round of their 1927 return fight, Dempsey wasted valuable seconds before going to a neutral corner. Tunney, with the benefit of the "long count," recovered to win.

The Manassa Mauler connects with a left to the face of challenger Tommy Gibbons during their title bout in Shelby, Montana on July 4, 1923. Dempsey retained the crown on a 15-round decision.

When he fought, commerce stopped. Families gathered around their radios for details. Thousands stood in town squares to see the round-by-round flashed on giant screens.

He introduced the "Million Dollar Gate." In 1950 a nation-wide poll of sportswriters and sportscasters by The Associated Press named him the greatest fighter of the first half of the 20th Century.

Ironically, Dempsey's greatest popularity came not while he was battering opponents into unconsciousness but after he had lost his title to a handsome ex-Marine, Gene Tunney, and failed to regain it in two of boxing's most historic fights.

During his career the Manassa Mauler had been the object of much negative publicity. Some sportswriters referred to him as "an animal hypnotized by his own ferocity." He was labelled a "slacker" because he failed to don a uniform while America's young men were sailing off to war in Europe. He was even accused of sneaking plaster of paris into his gloves, giving him a rock-hard substance for his punishing knockouts.

He not only weathered these barbs but saw his popularity mushroom in his final years and upon retirement when he became a prominent restaurateur on New York's Broadway, always sitting in a corner ready to sign autographs and to converse with tourists.

In Sept. 1923, Jack Dempsey stands in a corner as the referee counts out a flying Luis Firpo in the second round of their heavyweight title fight at New York's Polo Grounds. Dempsey had been sent reeling out of the ropes by the Argentine brawler in the opening round.

He remained forever "The Champ." The public never forgave Tunney, who wrested the title from him in 1926 and repeated the victory in 1927 in the famous "long count" battle that will be a source of debate as long as men pull on padded gloves. Dempsey praised Tunney and never complained.

The legend that grew around this dark-visaged, head-bashing warrior stemmed from the rags-to-riches nature of his early life. He was born in the small mining town of Manassa, Montana, June 24, 1895, the ninth of 11 children, and was given the presidential name of William Harrison Dempsey.

The family, seeking to scrub out an existence, moved from place to place—Denver, Provo, Salt Lake City and finally a farm near Utah Lake. Dempsey shined shoes, grudgingly farmed and finally began fighting in a chicken coop gym along with an older brother, Jack, whose name he adopted while substituting on a local fight card.

Jack left home at 16 and took up the life of a hobo, riding in freight cars and fighting in saloons until he fell under the influence of a wily manager named Jack Kearns.

Kearns brought his protege along judiciously and finally got him a shot at the heavyweight title against Jess Willard on a sizzling afternoon, July 4, 1919 in Toledo, Ohio. Willard was an awesome hulk of a man, 6 feet, 6½ inches tall and 230 pounds, who had wrested the crown from Jack Johnson. Dempsey looked overmatched at 6-1 and 187 pounds.

However, Dempsey, lightning fast and attacking like an enraged panther, hammered the gigantic champion into submission in three rounds, knocking out six teeth, breaking Willard's jaw and leaving him a helpless, bleeding mass.

Dempsey's reputation was made. "A killer," wrote Grantland Rice. "A superhuman wild man."

The Manassa Mauler's reputation as a brutal ring assassin was enhanced in two of his most famous title defenses and boxing, with the aid of Promoter Tex Rickard, was thrust into the era of its first million-dollar gates.

Fans paid $1,789,238 to witness Dempsey's title defense against classy Georges Carpentier, the idol of France, in 1921. The Frenchman was demolished in three rounds. In September of 1923 Dempsey flattened Luis Firpo, "the Wild Bull of the Pampas," in 68 seconds of the second after having been sent reeling out of the ropes by the Argentine brawler in the opening round. It, too, grossed more than $1 million.

Now a national hero and with no worthy challengers, Dempsey drifted into the free-swinging high life of society and Hollywood. Both his brine-hardened fists and competitive fire had become soft when Gene Tunney burst on the scene as a contender three years after the Firpo fight.

Fighting in the rain in Philadelphia September 23, 1926, the former Marine, dancing and jabbing, outboxed Dempsey for 10 rounds to take the title. A year later Dempsey, seeking revenge before 100,000 in Chicago's Soldier Field, smashed Tunney to the canvas in the seventh round but failed to go to a neutral corner. Tunney, with the benefit of a 17-second "long count," recovered to win the controversial bout.

Dempsey ultimately retired to his Broadway restaurant, took his fourth wife, Deanna Piattelli, and lived to the ripe old age of 87—a growing legend. He died on May 31, 1983.

Dempsey is shown in a 1972 photo in front of his restaurant, north of Times Square in New York. He lived to the ripe old age of 87—a growing legend.

JOE DIMAGGIO

The Classy Yankee Clipper

Joe DiMaggio will be remembered by baseball buffs as the majestic outfielder of the New York Yankees who set what appeared to be an unreachable record of hitting in 56 consecutive games. To the general populace he will be forever viewed as the sports hero who married Marilyn Monroe and, in his latter years, advertised coffee on television.

The man they admiringly called "The Yankee Clipper" transcended the single cold statistic—as tremendous as it was—and the tabloid headlines of his marriages to two Hollywood beauties, first Dorothy Arnold and then the tragic Miss Monroe.

Nominal successor to the great Babe Ruth, he epitomized dignity, class and polished skills on a team that dominated the sport from the mid-1930s until he retired after the 1951 season, saying, "I want people to remember me as I was."

left:

At age 56 in 1971, DiMag celebrated the 30th anniversary of his 56-game hitting streak. The top photo, taken on July 16, 1941, shows the Yankee Clipper singling in the first inning of the game between the Yankees and the Cleveland Indians, the 56th game of the streak. Below, DiMaggio shows he hasn't forgotten how to swing—he singles in a 1971 Old Timers Game.

opposite:

Charlie Silvera (29), Phil Rizzuto (10) and Tommy Henrich (15) greet DiMaggio after the first of his two home runs in a 9-7 triumph over the Boston Red Sox in 1949.

Author-historian Maury Allen said, "There never was a more stylish-looking, self-disciplined and controlled baseball player."

In a nationwide poll, conducted in 1969, DiMaggio was voted "Baseball's Greatest Living Player."

An impressive athlete, 6 feet, 1½ inches tall and 190 pounds, he moved like flowing water in the outfield, making the most difficult catches look easy. He was ever alert, and never threw to the wrong base. He hit for both average and power. He was a symphony in action. Quiet and retiring, he nevertheless was a tireless player and an inspiring leader among his teammates.

During the 13 years DiMaggio played with the Yankees, starting in 1936 with three years out for service in World War II, the club won 10 pennants and nine World Series. Joe had a career batting average of .325, hit 361 home runs, knocked in 1,537 runs and scored 1,390. He forged his 56-game hitting streak—a record regarded as least likely ever to be broken—from May 15 to July 17 in 1941, hitting at a .408 mark during that stretch. He was selected for the All-Star game in all the 13 seasons he played.

The marks are all the more remarkable because they were made in the original Yankee Stadium with its awesome "Death Valley" in spacious left-center and centerfield, where Joe's righthanded pull power was normally aimed. The distances were later shortened.

DiMaggio had a classic upright batting stance with feet planted far apart. He waited until the last instant to unleash his swing, whipping the ball with powerful wrists. He refused to change tactics and try hitting to the opposite field.

"I get paid to hit the long ball," he said. "If I started trying to punch the ball to right, I would lose my rhythm and not hit anything." He hit eight World Series home runs—tying a record for a righthanded hitter.

Born November 25, 1914 in Martinez, Calif., Joe was the most famous of three ball-playing brothers, sons of an Italian fisherman. Since no one spoke English in his home, Joe became self-conscious about his speaking ability in school and developed a timidity that he never lost.

Joe began his professional career with the San Francisco Seals of the Pacific Coast League in 1932, following his older brother Vince. He had his contract purchased by the Yankees after the 1934 season but, because of an injury in an automobile accident, didn't see major league action until 1936. He batted .323 as a rookie.

He was an instantaneous diamond hero.

His remarkable aura of greatness and mystique, celebrated in prose and song while he was a player, seemed to expand after he retired although baseball, the game he had honored so nobly for 13 years, was derelict in never recognizing his hold on the public and capitalizing on his image.

"When he walked into the clubhouse," former teammate Billy Martin said, "it was like some senator or president walking in there."

DiMaggio was strictly a loner. Always pleasant and soft-spoken, he never participated in locker room high jinx. Off the field, he had his own small circle of close friends. He defended his privacy fiercely. Friends always said he was basically shy.

He retained his athletic figure, paying close attention to diet and exercise. He loved golf. He was flat-bellied, straight as a poker, never more than 10 pounds over his playing weight. Silver-gray hair, which he was too proud to dye, softened his strong Italian features. His face remained deeply tanned, virtually free of lines.

Alan Courtney and Ben Homer wrote a song about him called "Joltin' Joe DiMaggio." The nation also tapped its toes to the beat of Paul Simon's song, "Mrs. Robinson," which had the catchy line, "Where Have You Gone, Joe DiMaggio?"

DiMaggio, after leaving baseball, seemed to grope for a security base in the game he loved. It never came. Charlie Finley of the Kansas City and Oakland A's hired him largely to hang

Glamorous Marilyn Monroe holds out her lips to receive a kiss from DiMaggio as they waited in the judge's chambers for the marriage ceremony which united them in San Francisco in 1954.

DiMaggio as a rookie. Joltin' Joe displays his batting style during spring training in St. Petersburg, Fla. in his first year with the Yankees in 1936.

around, perhaps hoping some of his lustre would fall off on the players. The baseball commissioner once offered him $10,000 a year to serve as a public relations representative on the Pacific Coast—"I leave that much for tips," Joe scoffed.

Joe remained in the public eye with a network commercial for Mr. Coffee, a special brewing process, and helped what started as a small enterprise into a multi-million-dollar business. He also did a local commercial for a bank in the New York area.

Even after passing his 70th birthday, the Clipper was constantly on the road, much in demand, playing in celebrity golf tournaments, attending Little League and Boy Scout affairs, even sponsoring such events as a boccie tournament in Las Vegas.

He would show up at Old Timer baseball games but was often too proud to play. He shunned interviews. Asked on one occasion what was his greatest thrill, he replied tartly: "Pulling on a Yankee uniform every day."

JULIUS ERVING

A Fond Farewell to Dr. J

In the spring of 1986, the year of the nation's mid-term elections with politicians laying the base for a shot at Ronald Reagan's job in 1988, Dave Berry, a columnist with only half a tongue in cheek, proposed basketball's Julius Erving as a candidate for President of the United States.

"He is a smart, decent and articulate person and a very sharp dresser," wrote Berry, adding that the Philadelphia 76ers' ball hawk was better known that most early candidates and could intimidate Mikhail Gorbachev with a handshake.

Less in jest, others found in the 6-foot-7, 205-pound forward, the renowned Dr. J, qualities exceeding his magical, almost ethereal exploits on the basketball court.

"Julius is an American treasure for the world to look at and admire," said Pat Williams, the 76ers' general manager. "He's

Erving goes high over John Lucas of the Houston Rockets to score in a 1977 NBA game. "Julius is an American treasure," said a general manager about the player who retired after last season.

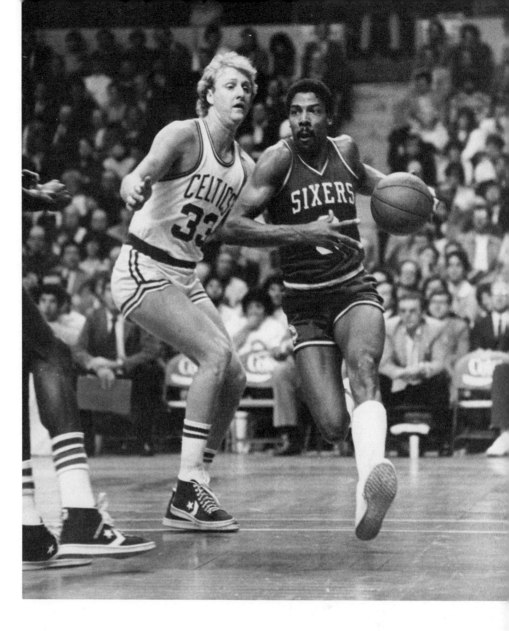

"For years the fans went to see Dr. J glean that one unforgettable moment," said Pat Williams, the 76ers G.M., "and he always seemed to offer it." Here, Erving moves the ball past Larry Bird.

on a plateau that's never been attained before, with style and grace and humility and patience."

Super athlete, successful businessman, humanitarian, philosopher, Dr. J found his forum on the hardwood floor of a gym and saw it as a springboard to a future career for reaching people, possibly as an international ambassador.

"It's not something you can chart," he said. "All things I do have to fit under my spiritual umbrella."

Erving, who returned after 15 years to get his diploma from the University of Massachusetts, was awarded an Honorary Doctor of Arts degree in 1983 by Temple University, which cited his career as providing "a new dimension of fine art."

Artistry indeed was the proper description for Dr. J's handiwork. If gargantuan Wilt Chamberlain was the true father of the dunk shot and was responsible for turning it into a normal basketball commodity, then it was Erving, the nice kid from Long Island, who refined it and made it pure theater. The slam dunk was Dr. J's private domain. Until he came along, no other one ever executed it with such flair and flamboyance.

Sometimes it appeared Erving was going to shoot right out of the roof. Other times he flew through the air like Peter Pan's Tinker Bell—sky walking, the sports writers called it. He was Nureyev and Barishnikov in short pants and sneakers instead of leotards. He would take a ball in full flight, sweep down the floor in long, flowing strides and, cradling the ball in one of his massive hands, suddenly project himself at the hoop and slam the ball home.

It was decisive. It was exciting. And it was raw drama. Dr. J made it no patented maneuver. He improvised. Besides those soaring dunks, he could finesse the ball with soft bank shots and delicate finger rolls. He could go backwards and sideways, twist his body like a contortionist, fake defenders out of their socks and score with a flair. There's no telling how many tickets were sold to admirers who came to the games to enjoy the Dr. J show. He left them breathless.

"For years the fans went to see Dr. J glean that one unforgettable moment," said Pat Williams, "and he always seemed to offer it."

Dr. J rides through throngs of cheering fans in a downtown Philadelphia parade in his honor last April 20, the day after the close of his final regular NBA season. At his right is his wife, Turquoise.

Dr. J was more than a showman. He was a producer and a motivator, serving as captain of his team. Only two players in history, Kareem Abdul-Jabbar and Wilt Chamberlain, scored more career points. Erving, seven times an NBA All-Star and twice Most Valuable Player in the All-Star game, was one of only seven men to average more than 20 points and more than 20 rebounds in their careers.

Dr. J's full name was Julius Winfield Erving II. Born February 2, 1950, in Roosevelt, New York, on Long Island, he grew up in a broken home. His father was killed in an automobile accident when he was 11 years old and eight years later he was to lose his older brother, whom he idolized, to a disease that destroyed immunization.

Young Julius, then called "Junior," was always big for his age, 5 feet, 6 inches tall at age 12, when he began playing with a neighborhood Salvation Army team. He attended Roosevelt High School where he showed remarkable ability but got little playing time until his senior year. Not highly recruited, he chose to attend the University of Massachusetts where he gained national prominence by averaging 26 points and 20 rebounds a game.

It was this attention plus his sparkling one-man shows in the summer Rucker League on Harlem playgrounds that attracted the eyes of the emerging new pro league, the American Basketball Association. He quit college after his junior year to join the ABA Virginia Squires for $500,000.

Starting in 1971, he played five years in the ABA, two with the Squires and three with the New York Nets, spearheading the latter to two league championships. Averaging 26.3 points a game and thrilling audiences with his slam dunk heroics, he helped keep the league alive.

He entered the National Basketball Association with the Nets when the NBA absorbed the ABA in 1976. Later that year he was sold to Philadelphia for $6 million. He was advertised as the Sixers' ticket to a long-sought league championship.

Frustration instead of immediate success greeted the Sixers and their "Six-Million-Dollar Man." While Dr. J played brilliantly and dazzled patrons with his acrobatics and sleight-of-hand, the Sixers couldn't find the proper formula. They lost to Boston in the Eastern Conference finals and to Portland and Los Angeles in championship showdowns.

It wasn't until 1983, after the Sixers had obtained a dominating center named Moses Malone for $13.2 million, that Dr. J got his championship ring. He scored seven straight points in a rally that overcame a 16-point Los Angeles lead. They let him hold aloft the title trophy for photographers.

By the time he had reached his 36th birthday, the durable doctor of dunk had moved from forward to guard and was talking about "one more year" and other priorities—a wife and four children; his Coca-Cola bottling company in Philadelphia, holding and management companies, endorsement contracts, a budding TV career and various charities.

In 1986 he announced that he would retire as a player after the 1986-87 season. He did quit after a most successful career, becoming only the third player in big league pro basketball to score 30,000 or more career points.

CHRIS EVERT

Ice Princess of the Court

"They keep calling me 'Little Miss Metronome,'" the attractive young lady complained one time. "At first I didn't know what it meant. I hated it. It sounded like a disease or something."

If a metronome were indeed a disease, with its steady, sleep-inducing pendulum measuring the exact tempo in music, then there's been nobody more afflicted than tennis' ice princess, Chris Evert.

From the moment she stepped on the center grass court at Forest Hills in the autumn of 1972—a fetching, pig-tailed lass of 17 who had stormed her way into the semifinals—right to 1987, Chris enthralled tennis galleries with her feminine charm, relentless patience and deadly killer instinct.

No power player such as Australia's giant Margaret Smith Court, lacking the ever-attacking verve of Billie Jean King, the effortless ease of Evonne Goolagong and the physical assets of Martina Navratilova, Chris nevertheless managed a dominant role in the game for more than a decade.

She did it the way her father, Jimmy Evert, had told her to do it back when she was a six-year-old, skinny tyke in Fort Lauderdale, Florida, swinging a racket she couldn't hold with one hand. Her strategy: run every ball down and hit it back. Don't whale away. Don't gamble. Just keep the ball in play and wait for the opponent to make a mistake. Simple? Dull? Maybe, but it worked. And Chris never varied.

Chris popularized the two-fisted backhand, which she had been forced to use as a matter of necessity. Shortly after she burst upon the tennis scene, the world's courts were teeming with teen-age sprites slashing at the ball in the same way as she did it.

The serve and volley game in tennis surfaced with Jack Kramer after World War II. It became the vogue. With both men and women, the feeling was that one could not survive without this new weapon. Chris proved it a fallacy.

Chris never mastered an overwhelming service, although she

Chris displays in 1985 the award given to her for being the "Greatest Woman Athlete of the Last 25 Years."

became very effective with spin and placement as she matured. She felt uncomfortable at the net and rarely moved into volleying range. Yet she managed to wear down more aggressive foes with backcourt steadiness.

She won close to 150 women's singles titles—18 of them Grand Slam majors, Wimbledon, Australian, French and U.S. Open. When she defeated Martina Navratilova for her sixth French crown in 1986, it marked the 13th year she had won at least one of the Grand Slam events.

She won her 1,000th career match in the 1984 Australian Open. In 1974 she wove a streak of 55 consecutive victories, a record which lasted until Navratilova bettered it 10 years later with 74. She ran up a total of 125 straight triumphs on clay— her native surface—between August, 1973, and May, 1979, a mark unchallenged. She was the first woman to win $1 million in prize money. Her career total neared $6 million.

At first, it was assumed that Chris and the buoyant aborigine from Australia's outback, Goolagong, were the players of the future and probably would dominate the women's game through the 1970s and 1980s. Fans looked forward to their first meeting.

It occurred at Wimbledon in 1971. Chris was 16 and Goolagong 19, the latter a happy youngster who just floated around a court like a ballerina, every movement a thing of artistic beauty. Chris was the antithesis—the grim machine, working for every point. Goolagong won the semifinal match and the championship but later surrendered to injury and the life of a housewife. Three years later, at age 19, Chris arrived at the top, winning the Wimbledon, French and Italian titles.

Evert's competition was to come from a native Czechoslovakian, Navratilova, who defected to the United States shortly afterward as a plump teenager two years Chris' junior. Theirs was a long-running series staged on the courts of the world— grass, clay, hardwood and artificial surface.

Chris ran up a decided edge in the early meetings but Martina, shaking off periodic attacks of nerves, evened the rivalry and pushed ahead in the mid-1980s. Chris maintained a lead in Grand Slam singles titles but Martina, a powerful lefthan-

Chris popularized the two-fisted backhand. Here, she prepares her return in an early round match of the 1984 U.S. Open. Chris went on to down Terry Holladay, 6-1, 6-1.

Friendly Rivals. Chris and Martina Navratilova (right) shake hands after Navratilova emerged as the 1985 Wimbledon women's singles titleholder.

der, soared to more than $9 million—almost twice that of Evert—in official prize money.

Martina could never rest on her newly gained laurels. Chris always was lurking up in the wings.

"I can beat her, and she knows it," Chris said after passing her 30th birthday, "but I have to be at my best. I have to hang tough and crack her confidence."

They gave the world some great matches—these two ladies of opposite personalities. Martina was the superb athlete, big and strong, a net-rusher but always tense. Then there was Chris, demure, very feminine, the epitome of decorum, yet on the court a cold and calculating retriever—a veritable backboard of steadiness. The British press dubbed her "The Ice Lolly," for popsickle.

Twice Chris almost quit the game, insisting she was con-

cerned about missing the normal life. Each time she returned to her racket. "It was in my blood," she said.

Chris met fiery Jimmy Connors at Wimbledon in 1972 and they fell in love. They announced their engagement and started making wedding plans. Then the wedding was suddenly cancelled. "I started having doubts about my permanent commitment," she said, "but not about Jimmy."

Six years later Chris married a handsome British Davis Cup player named John Lloyd. However, their marriage broke up in 1987.

BOB FELLER

The Blazing Fastballer

Bob Feller, the Iowa farm boy who became one of baseball's greatest right-handed pitchers, liked to do things with a flourish. So, instead of scribbling his autograph on an 8x10 photograph or a traditional loose baseball, he presented selected persons with a bronzed replica of his pitching hand, gripping a signed ball in the familiar two-fingered grasp of his blazing fastball.

It was an exact duplication of his big, strong hand, toughened by years of chopping corn. It was made of plaster of paris, gilded and set on a small round stand. Like something out of the old "Addams Family" TV series, it was attention-grabbing. Yet it was markedly significant.

This was the hand that threw perhaps the fastest ball in baseball history. There always will be debate on this subject, followers in the Walter Johnson era giving the honor to the Big Train, and later generations checking in with Tom Seaver, Sandy Koufax and Nolan Ryan.

Before the radar gun became a scientific baseball fixture, Feller insisted that his fastball was measured up to 107 miles per hour. Irrespective of the speed, Rapid Robert, as he was called, left credentials to prove that some of the game's finest hitters rarely saw the ball and, even if they did, often swung in futility and frustration.

His head-to-head confrontations with such hitters as Ted Williams and Joe DiMaggio filled ball parks to capacity.

"He was awfully fast, but his curve ball was the best I've ever seen," said DiMaggio.

"Best I ever faced," said Williams, the Splendid Splinter of the Red Sox.

The Cleveland Indians normally arranged their pitching rotation so that Feller would pitch on Sundays, particularly in New York and Boston, where the pitcher-hitter drama had special impact. Dollars cascaded at the turnstiles.

Besides his blazing fastball, Feller had a big, wicked curve and a baffling change of pace. A powerfully built six-footer at 185 pounds, he took a full pump, his unusually long arms moving in unison, unleashed a high kick and then let the ball fly. The ball often was past batters before they saw it.

He pitched 18 seasons with the Indians, winning 266 games and losing 162. He had an earned run average of 3.25. Conceivably, he could have won close to 350 games had he not lost nearly four years while serving in the Navy in World War II. His most miraculous feat was his record of three no-hitters and 12 one-hitters, giving him an unprecedented total of 15 games in which the opposition had one hit or none.

Rapid Robert posts the record 12th one-hit game of his career on May 2, 1955 against the Boston Red Sox. He also pitched three no-hitters and, during his heyday, his fastball was measured up to 107 miles per hour.

Feller pitching against the Detroit Tigers in a game on Sept. 22, 1946. He struck out 348 batters that year, a mark that endured for 19 seasons.

He struck out 18 batters in one game, a major league record that lasted for 31 years, and forged 348 strikeouts in a single season, 1946, a mark that endured for 19 years. In all, he struck out 2,581 batters. He led the American League in victories five times, tied a sixth, led in innings pitched five times, and seven times was the league strikeout king.

Feller was born November 3, 1918 on a farm in Van Meter, Iowa, which was corn country, and saddled with a full name that wouldn't fit on a two-column headline: Robert William Andrew Feller. He helped his father all day in the field and, during breaks, the two of them played catch behind the barn in an improvised area marked off with chicken wire. Young Bobby threw the ball to his dad hours at a time.

He was playing baseball with grown-ups at the age of 13. At 16, he signed a contract with the Cleveland Indians, and a year later made his pitching debut in an exhibition game against the St. Louis Cardinals. He struck out eight Cardinals in the first three innings, producing an anecdote that has become sports legend.

Frankie Frisch, the crusty St. Louis manager, had planned to insert himself into the starting lineup, but, after looking at Feller's fastball, decided against it, saying: "Face that kid? Are you crazy? The old Flash (Fordham Flash) may be dumb but he ain't that dumb."

Although hailed as a teen-age wonder, Feller was brought along slowly in 1936 and 1937, winning a total of only 14 games, but, in 1938, still two years short of voting age, he compiled a 17-11 record and was off on his meteoric career. During his next five full seasons—with time out for Navy duty from 1942 through 1945 (he got out in time to pitch in only 9 games in 1945), then at his physical peak—he reeled off seasons of 24, 27, 25, 24 and 20 victories to lead the American League each time in almost every category.

Feller won 26 games in 1946, the first full year after he got out of the service, one of them a no-hitter against the New York Yankees, which he called "my greatest thrill."

"I had been away for years and people said I was washed up," he said. "This game proved to me that I was still able to pitch." That season he struck out his high of 348 batters.

He held Williams, baseball's last .400 hitter, to an average of .270. He struck out 10 or more batters 55 times. Some say had he not spent those four years in the Navy he might have erased almost every pitching record in the book.

But Feller had no regrets. "You just can't saw sawdust," he said. "I came out healthy." And rich.

The Iowa farm boy was no slouch when it came to capitalizing on his talents. Next to Babe Ruth, he earned more money than any player in baseball prior to the advent of free agency and million dollar contracts. His earnings, from baseball and endorsements, ran into six figures for six straight years, 1946 through 1951, $148,000 in 1946 alone.

His baseball contracts had numerous bonus clauses based on attendance, victories, strikeouts and awards. He got into the insurance and real estate business in Cleveland, did public relations for a hotel chain, plugged a hair darkener, gave clinics for kids, and barnstormed around the country promoting the game and various products. He rarely missed a big baseball event. And in 1962, he was inducted into baseball's Hall of Fame.

A.J. FOYT

Feared Demon of the Ovals

AJ. Foyt was born with the scent of gas fumes stinging his nostrils and his ears pounding with the roar of racing engines. Son of a mechanic and parttime midget racer, his cradle was an oil bin and he teethed on a monkey wrench. Grease and grime were his heritage and his blood raced with the mad, frenzied excitement of Gasoline Alley.

From the very beginning, this auto racing prodigy was pointed for greatness. He took the wheel of his own hand-made car at the age of five and won his first race against an adult before entering kindergarten. He quit school in the 10th grade to become a full-time racer. Since then he almost indisputedly has driven more miles on more different tracks in more different cities and in more different types of racing machines than any man who ever lived.

Foyt gets the checkered flag as he crosses the finish line in 1977 to become the first man ever to win the Indianapolis 500-mile race four times.

"There's never been a driver with such an urge to excel," an associate said about Foyt, shown here waving and holding the plaque he won for victories at Ontario, Calif. Motor Speedway.

In three decades of competing in the prestigious Indianapolis 500 alone, a race he won four times, he once estimated that he had driven more than 10,000 miles around the 2½ mile oval. He raced midgets, sprints, hot-rods, stock cars and even motorcycles in addition to those low-slung, million-dollar turbo machines that zip around the track at better than 200 miles per hour.

At the peak of his career he even took a stab at the Grand Prix road circuit, the pride of Europeans, teaming with Dan Gurney to win the 1967 24 Hours of LeMans race in France in his first try. Foyt became the first man ever to win both the Indy and LeMans classics.

He earned more prize money than any other driver in history, reportedly close to $3 million with probably as much again from endorsements. But money and security were not the driving force behind this rugged Texan who continued to challenge racing's young daredevils past his 50th birthday.

"There never has been a driver with such an absolute urge to excel, the absolute necessity to win," said one associate. Author Bill Libby wrote, "His cars seem to challenge him. He drives them so hard they sometimes fall apart." A rival, Mario Andretti, said, "He thinks himself such a superior being that he can't think of himself fighting anyone. It's got to be a breeze or nothing."

Crew members rush through the gates of the winner's circle as they follow Foyt in his winning car after his victory in the first race of the 1974 Twin 100 at the Ontario Speedway.

Fiercely independent, sometimes arrogant, a loner who refused to run with the racing crowd, Foyt often provoked jealousy among rivals while earning their fear and respect.

Bloys Britt, automobile writer for The Associated Press during Foyt's heyday, wrote of him:

"Hard-nosed, sometimes violent, often truculent, always intense, sometimes boisterous, many times gentle, impetuous, rough, forceful, self-made, never vengeful.

"He would laugh with you one minute, completely ignore you the next. He could be moody, surly, taut as a banjo string under stress, a model of charm when things were going 'according to Foyt.'"

"Racing is the only thing I've ever known," A.J. said. "I'll admit—I get moody when I don't win."

A.J. was born January 16, 1935, in Houston, Texas, and given the name of his father, Anthony Joseph Foyt. The senior Foyt was not only a midget car racer but a genius with tools. From the time he could walk, A.J., Jr., was at his side, watching his dad take engines apart and put them together again. At five A.J. Jr., had his own scaled-down machine replete with engine. No soap box derby for this kid.

By the time he was 18, A.J., Jr.—a rugged, round-faced, handsome man 5 feet, 11 inches tall and 185 pounds—was winning with midgets, stocks and hot-rods throughout Texas. He became known as "Super Tex" and "Tough Tony."

He joined the United States Auto Club and at age 21 made his first official start in a midget race across the street from the Indianapolis Speedway, finishing 13th and earning $68.

Two years later he was able to make his debut in the Indy 500, qualifying 12th in the field, barely escaping a 14-car crash that killed Pat O'Connor and finally finishing 16th for $2,962 in prize money. Three years later, in 1961, Foyt breezed past front-running Eddie Sachs, the pole-sitting favorite, on the final three laps for the first of his Indianapolis triumphs.

Thirteen years later, in 1974, Foyt became the first driver to win four of the Indy 500 classics. By the mid-1980s, he had won more than 70 races in championship cars, and almost as many in stock cars, sprints and midgets. He was the U.S. Automobile Club dirt track champion in 1972.

While he relished any kind of racing, whether it be the Indy-types or hot rods, on dirt or on concrete, A.J. got his biggest thrill from driving the big cars. "It takes precision to run in a circle," he said. "You're always on edge. Somebody's always breathing down your neck."

He never underestimated the danger, the constant flirtation with death but took a philosophical approach, contending: "When your time comes, it can come anywhere. The scaredest I've ever been was driving on an expressway."

One of Foyt's closest calls came in a 500-mile race at Riverside, California, in 1964. Early in the race, his car lost its brakes going into a sharp turn and, seeking to avoid two cars ahead, he sent his car hurtling over a 35-foot embankment. He was pulled from the wreckage with vertebrae smashed and other injuries that sidelined him for months.

He had another bad spill in 1966 in Milwaukee, suffering second and third-degree burns. In July, 1981, at the Michigan International Speedway, his car careened into a wall, leaving him battered and unconscious.

"I'll never forget seeing that wall rushing closer," he said. "The next thing I could remember was lying in the ambulance on the way to the hospital. I didn't know whether I'd ever be able to drive again."

But he did. "Sometimes," Foyt said, "I think I live a charmed life."

LOU GEHRIG

Pride of the Yankees

His story was the kind that was read by millions in those 10-cent paperbacks featuring Frank Merriwell and the rags-to-riches dramas of Horatio Alger. It had all the ingredients—the poor kid, son of a janitor, who waited tables to pay his way through college. The superb athlete, shy and of impeccable character, plucked from a college campus by the greatest team in baseball to play in the shadow of the great Babe Ruth. Wonderful deeds on the playing field, home run power and a record for durability, climaxed by a debilitating illness and premature death.

It was a story that only Gary Cooper could play in the movies and people by the millions would turn out, thrilling to the moments of glory but dabbing their eyes with handkerchiefs at the film's tragic ending.

"Today, I consider myself the luckiest man on the face of the earth," a paralysis-stricken Gehrig told a Yankee Stadium crowd in 1939. He died two years later at the age of 38.

Larrupin' Lou slashes a single to right field in the first inning of a 1938 exhibition game against Boston's N.L. team in St. Petersburg, Fla. The catcher is Al Lopez.

Such was the true odyssey of Lou Gehrig, the fabled "Iron Horse," "Larrupin' Lou," who had to play the role of secondary Crown Prince to the King of Swat and, even when the king's reign ended with Ruth's retirement, had to share his star with an emerging new hero named Joe DiMaggio.

It was Lou Gehrig's unfortunate lot to bridge the two most successful eras of the New York Yankees' history and to dress in the same locker room with a couple of the most charismatic and popular players who ever lived. Yet he never complained. He quietly went about the business of hitting the ball out of the park and winning ball games.

"I'm not a headline guy," he once apologized.

While Ruth and DiMaggio may have dominated the headlines, Gehrig was a powerful contributing force to a Yankee dynasty that won nine American League pennants and eight World Series during his 15-year career, scoring four-game sweeps in five of the post-season showdowns.

Lou batted .300 or better in 13 of those years, dropping off the pace only when his ailment began taking its toll on his strength in his final two years. He hit 493 home runs and had a lifetime batting average of .340. He led the league in home runs twice and a third time, in 1931, tied Ruth with 46.

That was the year he had 184 runs batted, the league record topped in baseball only by Hack Wilson's National League mark of 190. On June 3, 1932, he hit four consecutive homers in a game. In 1934, he recorded the prestigious Triple Crown in batting with a .363 average, 49 home runs and 165 RBIs. He repeatedly battled the great Ruth for the home run lead and batting honors in the World Series. He was named the league's Most Valuable Player in 1927 and 1936.

Certainly his greatest achievement—the one for which he will be forever remembered—was that of playing in 2,130 consecutive games, a record which baseball buffs agree probably will never be challenged.

On June 1, 1925, he was sent to the plate as a pinch-hitter. The next day he replaced Wally Pipp at first base in the lineup. He didn't miss a game for the next 14 years. With Ruth, he formed the muscle of the Yankees' dreaded "Murderers Row."

Henry Louis Gehrig was born June 19, 1903 in Manhattan, the only child of German immigrant parents. His father worked as a janitor in a fraternity house. His mother was a cleaning woman. Lou was a big, strapping boy who starred in both football and baseball at Commerce High School and who, as a combination pitcher-outfielder, was regarded as the best high school baseball prospect in the New York area. It was only natural that he would attract the interest of both pro scouts and college recruiters.

Because of his talent, he was awarded a scholarship to Columbia University. But, before he began his studies as a freshman, he naively accepted an offer from John McGraw, the New York Giants' manager, to play minor league baseball during the summer with Hartford in the Eastern League under an assumed name. He played only a few games before Columbia officials learned of the situation and had his contract abrogated on the grounds he was under age.

Gehrig, 6-foot-1 and 212 pounds, was a hard-running football fullback as a sophomore in 1922. In the spring of 1923 he played baseball. As in the case of Ruth, he started out as a pitcher but, because of his batting power, was quickly converted into a daily player.

He was in his second year of college when Paul Krichell, the famous Yankee scout, offered him a cash bonus of $1,500 and a $3,000 salary for the remainder of the season to play pro baseball. It seemed like a fortune. Lou signed.

Ironically, Hartford by this time had become a Yankee farm club and Gehrig was sent there for seasoning. Although a bit awkward around first base, he demonstrated enough hitting power to be recalled by the parent club in the final weeks of the 1923 and 1924 seasons.

Manager Miller Huggins placed the big slugger on his roster in 1925 but used him only periodically as a pinch-hitter. Wally Pipp complained of a headache. Gehrig was sent in as a replacement. Pipp never got his job back.

Gehrig and Ruth were teammates but never close friends. They were men of contrasting personalities—the Babe, a big, outgoing man with a thirst for fun and a flair for the dramatic; Lou, the straight arrow, low key, shy, and allergic to the limelight.

Yet Lou always presented a challenge to the Babe, both in the home run races and in World Series batting honors. In 1927, when Ruth hit his record 60, Gehrig had 47. The Babe hit the ball for great distances. Gehrig overpowered it. "No man ever hit the ball harder," said teammate Bill Dickey.

Gehrig began slowing down in 1938 and later examination showed he was dying of a nerve-destroying type of paralysis which now carries his name. He took himself out of the lineup on May 2, 1939. The Yankees staged a day for him at Yankee Stadium. A crowd of 61,808 attended and heard a tearful Gehrig say, "Today, I consider myself the luckiest man on the face of the earth." He died June 2, 1941 at the age of 38.

The "Iron Man" had a career total of 493 homers and a lifetime batting average of .340. He paced the American League in home runs twice and tied for it a third time.

OTTO GRAHAM

A Versatile Winning Quarterback

For one sublime decade, from 1946 to 1955, no professional football team has ever been as accomplished as the phenomenally successful Cleveland Browns. Playing the first four years in the old All-America Football Conference and the next six in the National Football League, the Browns won a conference title each of those 10 years and a league title during seven of the 10.

A major contributor to this success was Otto Graham, probably the most dominant quarterback of his day.

Paul Brown, the owner and coach of the Browns, had built his powerful team around this artistic player from Northwestern and Graham became one of the brightest stars of his league and one of the most successful football players of all time.

"The test of a quarterback is where his team finishes," Brown said. "By that standard, Otto Graham was the best of all time."

Almost from the time he began organizing the Browns for the AAFC, Brown had ticketed Graham for his team, which opened operations with the new league in 1946. Graham had been a star at Northwestern as a single-wing tailback who specialized in the run-pass option play. He passed as much as he ran, however, setting Big Ten records for completions, attempts and yards, and this led Brown to believe that Graham could be a good T-Formation quarterback in the pros. He was even more impressed with Graham after the quarterback, while in military service, led the powerful North Carolina Pre-Flight eleven at Chapel Hill to an upset of Navy during World War II in 1945.

As soon as the war was over, Graham took over the controls of the Browns, who featured such talented players as fullback Marion Motley and Dante Lavelli, Graham's favorite pass receiver, among others.

If there were any doubts that Graham, the ex-tailback, could become a pure quarterback in the pros, these were quickly dispelled in the Browns' first victory, a 44-0 rout of the Miami Seahawks. In his years with the Browns, Graham completed 1,464 passes in 2,626 attempts and accounted for 23,584 yards and 174 touchdowns. His passes were directly responsible for one-third of the 2,990 points the high-powered Browns scored in his time, and his completion percentage of 55.7 for six years in the NFL ranks among the highest in league history.

More importantly, Graham was a "winner" in every sense of the word. Including 10 championships and playoff games, Graham had a brilliant 94-15-3 record. Another remarkable statistic: The Browns played for either the conference or league championship in every one of the years that Graham was at the helm.

Graham had a remarkable 94-15-3 record with the Browns, including 10 championship and playoff games. His passes were responsible for one-third of the 2,990 points the Browns scored in his time.

Graham's inestimable value to the Browns was no more apparent than in 1954, when he announced his retirement after Cleveland's rousing 56-10 victory over the Detroit Lions in the NFL championship game. The Browns struggled in the early part of the 1955 season without their long-time leader until Brown prevailed upon Graham to come out of retirement. Once Graham readjusted, he led the Browns to another league championship, capping the year with two touchdown runs and two TD passes in a 38-14 victory over the Los Angeles Rams in the title game.

Graham was especially adept at the sideline pass. Few quarterbacks could equal his proficiency in this regard. He would send a receiver down the sidelines on a down-and-out pattern and hit him just a few feet before he would step out of bounds.

Another of his trademarks was the long pass—though he arched the ball high, only a small percentage of his passes were intercepted.

"He had a natural ability to throw a pass that was straight, soft and easy to catch," Brown recalled. "He seemed to pull the string on the ball and set it down right over the receiver's head."

At 6-foot-1, 195 pounds, Graham was a strong, solid quarterback loaded with confidence. In the era of two-way football, he did more than his share on the field. Not only was he the Browns' quarterback, but Graham also played defense, ran back punts and returned kickoffs.

That Graham could perform in such diversified roles was no

Graham poses at his desk in his office at the U.S. Coast Guard Academy in New London, Conn. in 1978. He was athletic director at the academy at the time.

surprise to anyone. After all, he had been a multiple sports star at Waukegan (Ill.) High School, where his favorite sport was actually basketball. In fact, it was basketball that got him a scholarship to Northwestern, where he won honors as the Big Ten's most valuable player in his first year on the varsity. His football potential at this point was completely overlooked.

He literally played football for the fun of it, on intramural teams at Northwestern, until his brilliance finally became known to the varsity coaches. Basketball-minded for the most part, Graham didn't feel any sense of tragedy when he wasn't invited out for football in his freshman year, although he had also made his mark in this sport in high school.

"We had four or five all All-Staters on our intramural team, and we had a lot of fun," Graham remembered. "We just walked through everybody."

Finally somebody noticed, and Graham also became a star in football. When Graham finally got going, so did Northwestern. In his senior year, he filled many roles, as a passer, runner, defender and punter, to help the Wildcats rise from last to second place in the Big Ten, and Graham was named the league's most valuable player in a second sport.

Except for the Second World War, Graham might have wound up playing professional football with the Detroit Lions. But fate intervened, in the person of Brown, who was coaching the Great Lakes Naval Air Station powerhouse while Graham, a naval flying cadet, was playing for North Carolina Pre-Flight.

Graham had been drafted by the Lions, but instead of going to the NFL, he went directly to his naval pre-flight training in North Carolina. There, he caught the attention of Brown, who was looking for players for his Cleveland team in the new AAFC. It was at Glenview, Ill. another of Graham's Navy stops, that Brown caught up with him and signed him to a contract in the very shadow of the NFL. (The Rams, who would eventually move to Los Angeles, also had a team in Cleveland at the time.)

"The Browns even began to pay me while I was still in the service," Graham recalled. "And that sure came in handy. Cadets only made $75 a month."

Graham actually was the first person that Brown signed, as the coach was hoping to build a powerhouse around this gifted, young quarterback. Graham did not disappoint him, rallying a group of personalities ranging from West Virginia mountaineers to talented black players like Motley, Jim Brown and Len Ford who would accompany him to many a championship and eventually, in some cases, to the Pro Football Hall of Fame.

RED GRANGE

The Galloping Ghost

Back in the so-called "Golden Twenties," a zany age when the nation was obsessed with speakeasies, flappers and sports heroes, it's said that a letter simply addressed to the number "77" would find its way into the hands of a ball-carrying demon named Harold "Red" Grange.

Dubbed the "Galloping Ghost" by the flamboyant phrase-makers of the period, Grange was the gridiron wonder in a cast of sports giants accorded almost superhuman stature by writers and an adoring public—a group including Babe Ruth, the "Bambino of Swat," Jack Dempsey, the "Manassa Mauler," Helen Wills, "Little Miss Poker Face," and the incomparable Mildred Didrikson, known only as "The Babe."

The "77," Grange's jersey number first at the University of Illinois and later as a member of the professional Chicago Bears, and the feats the number represented have been passed down from generation to generation and ingrained in the country's consciousness.

Great football ball-carriers have come and gone but there are

Grange (left) starts for the goal line for another touchdown in historic 39-14 victory for Illinois over Michigan in 1924. He reeled off four TDs in the opening quarter in what was probably the finest display of ball-carrying in college football history.

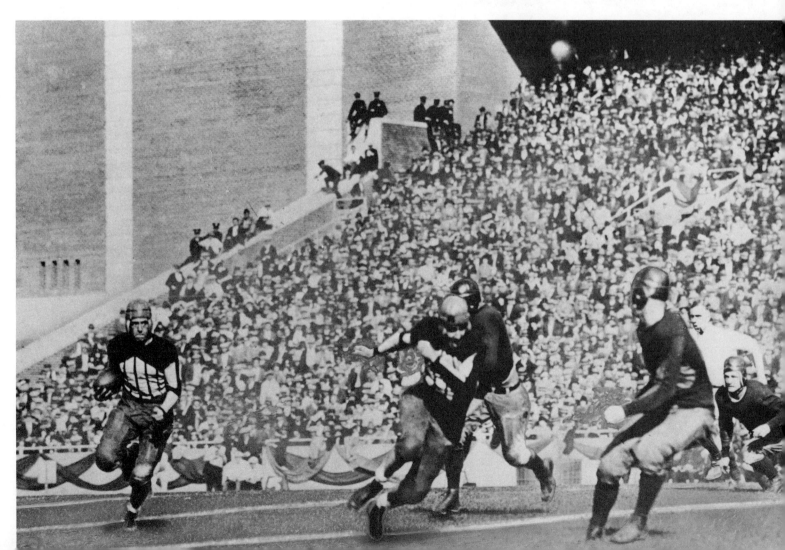

not very many enthusiasts of the sport who don't know that Grange wore "77" and that he made it a permanent part of American lore.

Red Grange was football's first dazzling breakaway runner who scored touchdowns in clusters and, if not the greatest, certainly was the one against whom succeeding whirling dervishes and line-cracking thunderbolts such as Jim Brown, O.J. Simpson, Gale Sayers, Walter Payton and Eric Dickerson had to be measured.

It was Grange's magnetism which, when he turned pro upon his graduation from college against the advice of his coaches and friends, catapulted the professional game from an impoverished, ragtag operation into a marketable enterprise that was destined to spawn the National Football League. He became the game's foremost celebrity, the first $100,000 player and the first to capitalize on his commercial value. He endorsed everything from meat loaf to ginger ale, candy bars to haberdashery.

When he played, both in college and as a professional, peo-ple hugged their radios and devoured their sports pages to absorb every ounce of the drama he generated.

Born June 13, 1903, Grange grew up in Wheaton, Illinois, a small town near Chicago where his father was chief of police. As a youngster, nicknamed "Red" because of his flame-colored hair, he excelled in basketball and track as well as football but his heart belonged to the gridiron. He scored 74 touchdowns at Wheaton High School and attracted the attention of college scouts. Long an admirer of Coach Bob Zuppke, he gravitated naturally to Illinois.

On October 18, 1924, Grange was a halfback on the Illinois team that met the awesome University of Michigan in a game dedicating Illinois' Memorial Stadium. The Wolverines, under Fielding H. "Hurry Up" Yost, had been unbeaten in three years and was the most feared power in college football.

Grange received the opening kickoff and—slashing, whirling, dodging, weaving, shedding tacklers—scampered 95 yards to a touchdown. Within the next 10 minutes, throwing phan-

The star of the Fighting Illini took the opening kickoff and raced 95 yards for a score in what developed into a rout of the rival Wolverines, in that 1924 contest.

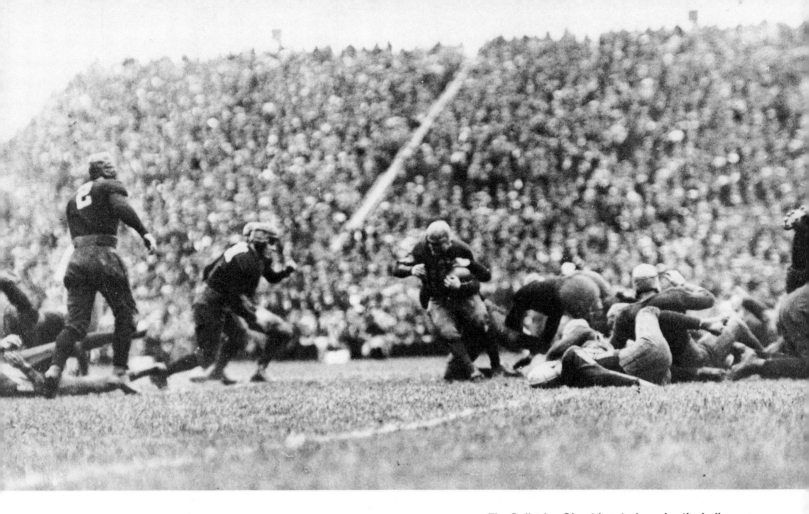

tom hips at frustrated defenders, he reeled off runs of 67, 56 and 44 yards before being given a rest with three minutes remaining in the first quarter.

Sports writer Grantland Rice compared Grange's moves with those of ring champ Dempsey, adding, "He moves almost with no effort as a shadow flits and drifts and darts." Others called the performance "the most fabulous 12 minutes in college gridiron history." Grange scored a fifth touchdown in the second half from 12 yards away and then passed 20 yards for another touchdown, as Illinois popped the Michigan bubble of invincibility 39-14.

The next year Grange was introduced to the skeptical East, the nerve center of mass communication, when Illinois played Pennsylvania before a crowd of 63,000. Was the "Galloping Ghost" for real or a Midwest myth?

Grange swivel-hipped for a 60-yard touchdown the first time he got the ball, leaving his closest pursuer 25 yards behind, and added two more on a slippery, muddy field that brought a standing ovation from the partisan spectators.

In an era of defensive football, when scoreless ties were more a norm than a rarity, Grange had a three-season total of 31 touchdowns, 3,637 rushing yards and 643 yards passing. The Air Game still was young. He helped draw 738,555 to Illinois games.

The day after he completed his Illinois career against Ohio State, November 21, 1925, Grange signed a contract with Promoter C.C. "Cash and Carry" Pyle, guaranteeing him $100,000 to play football for George Halas' professional Chicago Bears. Zuppke pleaded with him not to make the move.

Pro football was a dirty word at the time. College games were drawing 40,000 to 60,000 into the big stadiums. Pro games were lucky to attract 10,000 even with an aging Jim Thorpe as a drawing card.

Thirty-six thousand fans braved a snowstorm to watch Grange make his debut with the Bears before a capacity crowd of 36,000 at Wrigley Field on Thanksgiving Day, 1925. Then followed a whirlwind tour in which the team played 10 games in as many cities in 18 days, traveling 3,000 miles and giving the South and East a first look at the relatively new game. The tour drew more than 400,000.

Grange and Pyle formed a maverick league in 1927 but it was short-lived. Grange rejoined the Bears in 1929 and took part in the NFL's first title playoff game in 1933, as Chicago beat the New York Giants 23-21. He was a four-time all-NFL halfback.

The handsome, 6-foot, 185-pound star retired in 1935, became a charter member of pro football's Hall of Fame in 1963 and settled down to a peaceful life of boating and fishing from his lakeside ranch house in Florida.

WAYNE GRETZKY

"Great in Any Hockey Era"

Wayne Gretzky looks anything but like a player who has completely devastated the National Hockey League's scoring record book.

He's skinny (barely 6 feet and barely 170 pounds). He doesn't skate like a blur, he moves with an awkward, elbow-waving style, and his shot is not the hardest among NHL players.

Even youngsters, who have watched Gretzky play from afar—either on television or from a seat in an NHL arena—can't believe that the baby-faced center of the Edmonton Oilers is the greatest scorer in the league's history when they meet him close up.

A perfect example occurred once when Gretzky visited the Edmonton Children's Hospital. As he signed autographs with his uniform number "99" beneath his name, one youngster with thick glasses gave him a quizzical stare. Finally, the boy said courageously: "No way you're Wayne Gretzky."

"I can't believe you're the one who's got all those goals," another youngster said.

"I know what you mean," Gretzky said. "Sometimes, I can't believe it either."

Believe it!

It is no dream that Gretzky is living. He is continually surpassing scoring feats established by the game's most revered players, such as Gordie Howe, Bobby Hull, Maurice "The Rocket" Richard, Phil Esposito and Bobby Orr.

For example, Gretzky owns the fourth highest single-season total point output in the league's history, including four years with more than 200 points (his record is 215 points, in the 1985-86 season). He holds the NHL record for most goals in a season (92, in 1981-82). His 163 assists in 1985-86 is another league record—and surpassed the point total of the next highest single-season record not set by him, Esposito's mark of 152 points in 1970-71.

Gretzky's other league records—the total exceeds 40—include the longest consecutive point-scoring streak (51 games in 1983-84), most assists one game (7), most goals one period

The Great One (99) reaches out to handle the puck in front of St. Louis goalie Greg Millen (29) and set up a scoring attempt for Edmonton in a 1986 NHL game.

Gretzky poses with award given by an alcoholic beverage company which named him the outstanding NHL player in 1985-86. He helped Oilers win another Stanley Cup in 1986-87.

(4), highest points-per-game average, career (nearly 2½ per game), and the fastest to score 500 career goals (which he reached during the 1986-87 season, in only his 575th NHL game; the previous mark was 647 games, by Mike Bossy of the New York Islanders).

Some oldtimers contend that Gretzky is playing in an over-expanded league partially stocked with inept players who never would have made the NHL before expansion in 1967. However, former greats appreciate his talents.

"I have now seen Gretzky enough to say that in whatever decade he played, he would be scoring champion," Rocket Richard said about the player who tied for the scoring title in his rookie season in the NHL in 1979-80 and won the championship outright each of the next seven years.

"He's a born, natural scorer—just like I was," Richard added. "He's moving all the time, and it seems like the players trying to check him can't catch him."

"He plays more like the old days—the way he handles the puck, the way he handles himself," said Howe, whose pro career spanned five decades, from 1946-80. "When he has to hurry, he hurries; otherwise, he thinks it through. He would have been just as great in any day."

Gretzky's hockey instincts were instilled in him at an early age by his father, Walter.

When Gretzky was only 3, his father, who never advanced beyond Junior B hockey, had his son skating on a rink in the family backyard in Brantford, Ontario, a town about 60 miles southwest of Toronto.

Gretzky's father placed tin cans on the ice for him to swirl between. He dropped sticks for the boy to hop over as he received passes—as if in heavy traffic in front of the goal. He strung up lights so Wayne could practice at night. And he made the targets smaller and smaller—so his son's shots became more accurate.

Later, he would throw the puck into a corner and tell his son to get it. After young Wayne had chased several pucks around the boards, his father would say: "Watch me."

He would throw it again and skate to a spot, where he could intercept the puck as it caromed around the boards.

"I always told him, 'Skate to where the puck is going to be, not to where it has been,' " the elder Gretzky said. "The thing that I drilled into Wayne most was concentration. That's what gives him his edge today. He puts so much thought into what he's doing. He doesn't just chase the puck around."

By age 6, Gretzky was playing in a league with 10-year-olds. When he was 10, he scored 378 goals in 68 games, an average of 5½ goals per game. At 15, he had an agent. By 17, he was a pro, signing a four-year, $875,000 contract with the Indianapolis Racers of the now-defunct World Hockey Association.

After Gretzky had played only eight games with the Racers,

owner Nelson Skalbania, who was strapped for cash, sold his contract to the Oilers.

Edmonton owner Peter Pocklington reworked Gretzky's contract into a landmark deal that ran through 1999. The contract, however, paid Gretzky only $280,000 a year, a small sum for the game's greatest player. So, in January 1982, Pocklington renegotiated the contract, giving "The Great Gretzky" more than $1 million a year.

Despite all the money he makes, including hundreds of thousands of dollars in endorsements, and all the fame he has accumulated, Gretzky has remained very humble.

"When I'm compared with the greats of the past, it's an honor and a pleasure," he said. "But nobody will ever duplicate Howe, Orr, Esposito, Richard, Jean Beliveau—any of them. Nobody can play like those guys played. I am me.

"The really great players play at the same level year after year. That's why Gordie Howe is the greatest player in the history of the game. The year after year consistency, the records he set, the Stanley Cups he won... The important thing to me now is consistency.

"I don't consider myself different from the other 420 players in the league," the modest Gretzky continued. "I consider myself one player among 420 who has to do a job to help promote this game, help set an example, an image for the youngsters to want to be NHL players, or at least lead a good style of life. So I just try to live up to my one-420th of the responsibility."

Everyone in the NHL—and all those connected with the game—agree that Gretzky has more than lived up to his end of the bargain. His skills, combined with his personality, make him the game's No. 1 ambassador.

The Oilers' star gets ready to score his first of four goals in the 1983 NHL All-Star game played in the Nassau Coliseum, home of the New York Islanders. Ron Langway (6) is the defender.

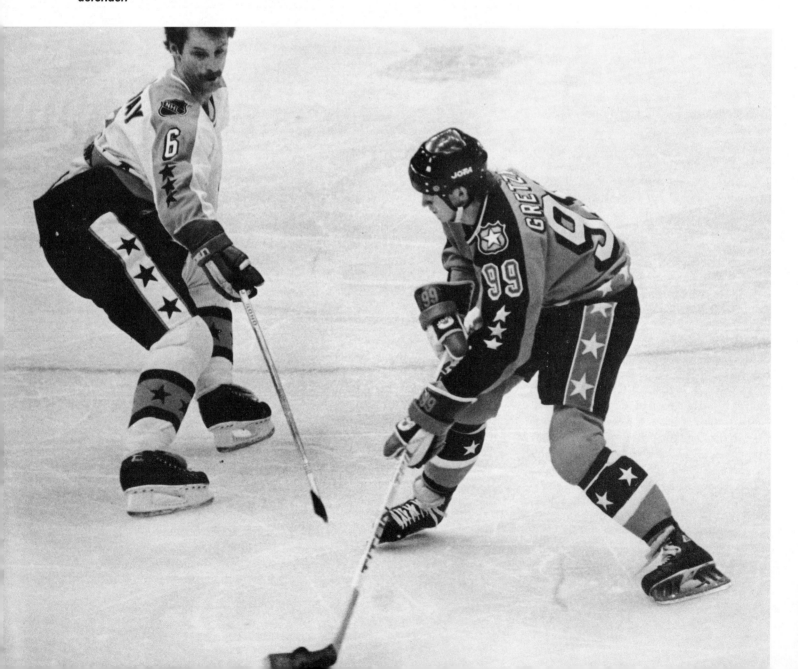

WALTER HAGEN

The Brilliant "Climax Player"

Once while playing a golf exhibition in the British Isles, Walter Hagen astonished his staid gallery by yelling to one of its members, "Hey, Eddie, hold the flag, would you please?"

The request might have gone unnoticed had it not been addressed to one of Hagen's friends and admirers, the Prince of Wales, destined to become King Edward VIII before abandoning the throne to marry an American commoner.

Walter Charles Hagen was a lowly ex-caddie out of Rochester, New York, schooled on the fairways rather than in the classrooms. He became a member of golf royalty, a king in his own right who personally tore down many of the game's stuffiest and snobbiest traditions.

He was monarch of the professionals when the great Bob Jones was amateur emperor of the Golden Era following World War I. Cocky, flamboyant, individualistic, he played with caddies and kings and treated them all with equal courtesy and disdain. Commoners and royalty alike, he called them by their first names. Nobody was ever offended.

Hagen played on five continents and captivated and enchanted everyone. He won 11 national championships, including the Professional Golfers Association crown five times, four times in a row, starting in 1924. He won the U.S. Open twice, followed with four British Open titles and the national championships of France, Belgium and Canada. Seven times he captained the U.S. Ryder Cup team against British professionals.

A fierce and often wily competitor, he was the supreme match player in the days that the PGA and other events were head-to-head battles. In marathon matches billed as "the official championship of the world," he scored one-sided victories over Cyril Walker in 1924, Bob Jones in 1926, Gene Sarazen in 1927 and Johnny Farrell in 1928.

His most satisfying triumph was scored over Jones, Atlanta's Boy Wonder who later was to score the game's only Grand Slam, a sweep of the U.S. and British Amateur and Open Championships in 1930.

In 1927, Jones, the young amateur, was universally hailed the world's greatest. Hagen was the undisputed best of the pros. At Hagen's insistence, a promoter, Bob Harlow, drummed up a "dream match" to determine who really was king of the hill.

Thirty-six holes were to be played over Jones' favorite course in Sarasota, Florida, another 36 over Hagen's stomping grounds in St. Petersburg.

Hagen led by eight holes after the first 36 and closed out the match on his home course, 12 holes up with 11 to play. It was the worst beating ever absorbed by Jones.

The match was doubly intriguing because it presented starkly contrasting lifestyles. Jones was the "gentleman golfer," epitomizing Southern charm and social graces. Hagen, something of a charmer himself, was a maverick who lived the high life and burned the candle at both ends.

"You're only here for a short visit," Hagen once said. "Don't

Hagen won 11 national championships, including the PGA crown five times. He captured the U.S. Open title twice and the British Open championship four times.

Hagen (right) poses with amateur champion Bob Jones (left) and an official after Walter, a pro titleholder, beat Jones in a 1927 72-hole match in Florida.

hurry. Don't worry. And be sure to smell the flowers along the way."

It was his credo. They said he made $1 million playing golf, a princely fortune in those days. He blew the bundle as fast as he collected it. After winning a tournament, he would often go to the nearest bar and spend his check downing toasts with his cronies.

He revolutionized wearing apparel on the golf course. His shirts were the silkiest, his cashmeres the fleeciest and his shoes the swankiest money could buy. He played in knickers, two-tone shoes, sweaters and ties. He gave out $20 tips as if they were chicken feed.

He frequently showed up on the first tee without sleep after an all-night party. Once, barely making his starting time, he teed off wearing a tuxedo, white tie and patent leather shoes.

The ladies considered him a handsome man—tall, a bit plumpish, coal black hair impeccably brilliantined. He had a quick wit and an outgoing personality. As a golfer, he wasn't much of a stylist. Critics said he threw too much of his body into his drives and was erratic off the tee.

Yet he was a precisionist with his irons and had a wonderful touch around the greens. A gambler, supremely confident and pirate bold, he became known as a "climax player."

Son of a blacksmith and a caddie at age nine, Hagen showed up for his first U.S. Open in 1913 flashily attired in a striped silk shirt, red bandanna, white flannel trousers and red-soled buckskin shoes and cockily announced:

"I'm W.C. Hagen from Rochester. I've come to help you boys take care of Vardon and Ray," the reference being to the two great English players who were favored.

The incident brought clubhouse titters at the time but the laughter shortly turned to awe and respect.

When the Haig showed up for the British Open at Deal in 1920, he was denied entrance to the clubhouse by a stiff-shirted secretary who advised him that club facilities were accessible to "gentlemen (amateurs) only" and that the professionals, whom the British regarded as hired help, had to dress in the golf shop.

Hagen found the golf shop small and dingy. He ordered his big, black limousine, replete with chauffeur and footman, driven daily to the front door of the clubhouse where he underwent his change of clothes.

The British brass was chagrined but found no way to prevent it. The gesture led to the ultimate abandonment of the stuffy British tradition.

Hagen, nearing 50, tried a comeback in 1940 in the PGA Championship. The old skills were gone. "I couldn't stand the thought of shooting 80," he said. Then, he retired.

BILL HARTACK

Sullen, Surly... But a Standout Jockey

During Bill Hartack's career of close to a quarter of a century riding race horses in the United States he was tagged with a lot of uncomplimentary names.

The news media referred to Bill as sullen, surly, silent beyond endurance, calculating and cold-eyed. But no member of the media, whether printed, video or audio, ever called him anything less than brilliant.

In one of his typical one-word verbal ripostes, Hartack blanketed the entire media as "stupid." Any newsman who called him Willie instead of Bill had Hartack on the verge of acute apoplexy.

Paradoxically, he was blunt and rapier-sharp. Bill talked back to trainers, the race track version of a lawyer sassing a judge in a court of law. He barked at track officials. He'd tell an owner or trainer what was wrong with his horse and if that brought on an attack of instant umbrage, Hartack would refuse to ride the animal.

With all of that, his career was just plain magnificent. In 22 years of riding, from 1952 to 1974, Hartack accumulated 4,272 winners. His mounts earned $26,466,758 and most of that came during the years when big stake purses had not mounted to the astronomical sums of the 1980s. He won with almost one-fifth of his mounts. A rough translation of that into baseball terms would have made him a .400 hitter. It's harder to win a horse race than it is to get a base hit.

Hartack tied Eddie Arcaro for most Kentucky Derby winners at five when Majestic Prince raced for the roses in 1969. Bill rode three Preakness winners, Fabius in 1956, Northern Dancer in 1964 and Majestic Prince in '69. He won one Belmont, aboard Celtic Ash in 1960.

Bill left the United States in 1974 to ride at the felicitously named Happy Valley course in Hong Kong. His American farewell, as ever, was succinct. The stupid American news media and weight problems had forced him to fly across the wide Pacific, he maintained. The scale of weights for riders is higher in Hong Kong than in the U.S.

With Bill Hartack aboard, Idun leads field home in the 1958 Mother Goose Stakes at New York's Belmont Park. In 22 years of riding, from 1952 to 1974, Hartack rode 4,272 winners.

Hartack stayed in the exciting and exotic Asian city for about six years and was a popular rider. He was cheered by Oriental railbirds and British sportsmen alike and had no problems with any section of the press.

Bill returned to the U.S. in 1980 and plunged into several new careers. He worked as an expert color man for the American Broadcasting Company on big races, the Kentucky Derby, Preakness and others. He managed a thoroughbred boarding center in California and then became a patrol judge at Hollywood Park.

Although Hartack once made Arcaro's eyes almost pop out of his head by referring to the Kentucky Derby as "just another horse race," right after winning a renewal, he was a grim student of how to ride in the madcap mile and one quarter "fastest two minutes in sports" on the first Saturday in May.

"You make your move where you have to in order to win," Bill said. "It depends on the horse you are riding and the situation. It's silly to think you have to wait until the head of the stretch. You can move at the half-mile pole and have the race won at the eighth pole."

His first Derby victory was on Iron Liege in 1957. He laid off the pace, had the devil's red and blue of Calumet in front at the furlong pole, and then held off the late-running Gallant Man with Willie Shoemaker up. That was the blighted Derby in which The Shoe misjudged the finish line, stopped riding for a fraction of a second at the 16th pole and then couldn't catch Hartack, losing by a nose.

Hartack had a laugher on Venetian Way in 1960, winning by three and one-half lengths. In 1962 Bill came from the rear guard with Decidedly to blow by the field at the eighth pole and grab the money by two and one-quarter lengths.

His handling of Northern Dancer in 1964 was right out of the textbook of jockeys but with two added ingredients, daring and trigger-quick thinking. He beat Shoemaker on the favorite, Hill Rise, to an opening on the backstretch and got enough daylight at the turn for home to hold the betting choice off by a diminishing neck.

Hartack's last Derby victory in 1969 on Majestic Prince was another virtuoso performance. He drove the Prince with hand, heel and whip to a photo decision over the stout-hearted Arts and Letters, who had the brilliant Braulio Baeza in the saddle.

Bill did not have a riding master's seat, something just about every other great rider has had. He seemed to bounce in the saddle. "Too much motion" was a frequent criticism. But he had the sensitive hands of a concert pianist, the wrists of an arm wrestler and the guts of a free-falling parachutist.

He feuded with other riders, especially the Cowboy from Panama, Manuel Ycaza. Veterans of the New York pressbox still remember a seven-furlong race at Aqueduct in 1960 when Ycaza pinned Bill on the rail the whole trip.

There was a definite threat of Hartack being tossed into the infield. Most riders would have taken up. Not the tough cookie from the Pennsylvania coal mines. He hung in there, refusing to yield, and right at the wire dropped his horse's head in front to get the verdict.

About those coal mines: Bill never worked in them but his father did for 30 years. Bill was born in Ebensburg, Pa. He grew up in a house without a furnace, no central heating, no phone, no electricity, no bathroom. In Bill's words, "no nothing."

He won his first race at Waterford Park in West Virginia aboard a horse named Nickleby on Oct. 14, 1952 at the age of 20. It was only his third mount. Seven years later, in 1959, he was elected to racing's hallowed Hall of Fame at Saratoga. It was the quickest any rider ever got there.

In his usual style, he made his move early to get there first. He didn't have to wait for the stretch run of his career to reach the place where only the all-time greats gain admittance.

This is Hartack in 1955, three years after he started his brilliant career, Bill rode five Kentucky Derby winners, sharing the record with Eddie Arcaro.

ERIC HEIDEN

The Olympic Speed Skating Marvel

Eric Heiden, a zephyr on silver skates, streaked to five gold medals in the 1980 Winter Olympics at Lake Placid, New York, in a dazzling one-man performance that marked him as one of the premier athletes of the age.

Participating in a sport with very little recognition in the United States, although popular in Europe, he did on an oval ice rink what Czechoslovakia's Emil Zatopek did on Helsinki's red clay running track in 1952 by sweeping the three long distance races and almost what Mark Spitz accomplished with seven swimming golds two decades later in Munich.

Before Heiden, no one had ever won five gold medals in the Winter Games. At age 21, the handsome Wisconsin collegian established himself as the unquestioned king of speed skating while sister, Beth, a year younger, also won a medal and turned the Games into a royal family affair.

By coincidence the Heidens had to share their moments of glory with a group of countrymen who also wore skates—the scrappy, gutsy U.S. hockey team which beat the Russians and won the gold medal, triggering a wave of unharnessed nationalistic fervor.

Prior to the Olympic hysteria, the Heidens, as a record-setting world championship brother-sister team, had monopolized the publicity spotlight, courted by TV and the slick magazines and fawned over by fans. After the Games, adulation for the hockey kids intensified while the Heidens, largely by personal choice, slid into virtual obscurity.

The 21-year-old handsome Wisconsin collegian races for and wins an unprecedented fifth gold medal in the 10,000-meter men's speedskating competition in the 1980 Winter Olympics in Lake Placid, N.Y.

The Heidens flashed on the sports scene like a meteor—just before and during the Olympics—and just as quickly faded from sight. They could walk down the main streets of any American city without being recognized. Part of that was due to their own desire for privacy. Mainly the reason was that theirs was a sport of which Americans had little knowledge or interest.

Before the 1980 Games the only facility for training in the United States was a poorly equipped rink in West Allis, Wisconsin, where skaters had to contend with an obsolete cooling system and dust drifting onto the track from a nearby cement factory. There were few dedicated devotees of the sport and fewer qualified instructors. Speed skating suffered from a lack of general interest and financial support.

In Europe the opposite was true, particularly in countries such as Norway and the Netherlands where the sport is a mania. Speed skaters, who perform before tens of thousands in huge arenas, are treated like rock stars. The difference in conditions and opportunities made Eric Heiden's record—and, to a lesser degree, that of sister Beth—all the more remarkable.

It was at West Allis that the Heiden kids first became interested in speed skating, tagging along with their parents. Their father was a well-to-do Madison, Wisconsin, physician. Both youngsters were athletically inclined and took up competitive cycling as a second activity.

By the time they had entered the University of Wisconsin—Eric as a pre-med student and Beth a year behind majoring in civil engineering—both had begun to gain world recognition in cycling and speed skating without creating any great stir in their own country.

Eric was a handsome young man, an inch over six feet tall and weighing 185 pounds. Beth was just a sprite of a girl, a full foot shorter than her brother and weighing only 99 pounds. But she was a whippet on skates.

With the Olympics approaching, the Heiden name began creeping onto the sports pages and their pictures appearing on the covers of sports and news magazines. They were establishing themselves as definite gold medal prospects.

In the winter of 1979 Beth won the all-around title in the Women's World Speed Skating Championships at The Hague by winning all four events at distances from 500 to 3,000 meters. About the same time brother Eric was duplicating her performance at the Men's World Championships in Oslo, winning the 500, 1,500, 5,000 and 10,000 meters.

It marked the third straight year that Eric had captured overall world honors. In the World Sprint Championships in Inzell, West Germany, Eric crushed the opposition with impressive victories in the 500 and 1,000 meters for the third time. Beth lost out to Leah Poulos Mueller.

Both Heidens were swarmed by admirers. In Oslo, U.S. Ambassador Louis Lerner appointed Eric honorary ambassador to Norway.

Norwegians adopted Eric as a folk hero. He had to be sneaked in and out of his hotel through garages to avoid admirers. His picture appeared on milk cartons. Songs and books were written about him.

By the time the Olympics arrived, Eric was in top form. In dramatic succession, he won his first four gold medals—in the 500, 1,000, 1,500 and 5,000 meters, surpassing the 1972 record of Holland's sensational Ard Schenk—and then had a rest before the draining 10,000 meter finals. He watched the U.S. hockey team upset the Russians.

Inspired, he went out the next day and won the 10,000 meter race in record time with a 7.9 second gap over his nearest pursuer, Piet Kleine of the Netherlands.

While both The Associated Press and Sports Illustrated magazine chose the hockey team for "Athlete of the Year" honors, European sports writers voted that award to Heiden. Eric also was presented the Sullivan Award as America's top amateur athlete for 1980.

A deeply sensitive, private person, young Heiden refused to capitalize on his newly gained fame, spurning thousands of dollars in commercial offers. "Put my face on a cereal box? No thanks," he said. "I didn't get into skating to be famous. If I had, I would have played hockey."

Eric retired, did some cycling and resumed pointing to a medical career. Beth, who won a bronze medal in the Olympics in the women's 3,000 meter race, later won the world championship in road cycling.

Eric and Beth Heiden, the brother and sister speedskating pair, wave to fans after Beth placed third in the 3,000-meter event in the 1980 Winter Olympic Games.

SONJA HENIE

"Pavlova" of the Silver Blades

In the 1930s, with the nation climbing out of a terrible Depression and seeking to bury its problems in the exciting exploits of sports idols such as Joe DiMaggio and Joe Louis, families would crowd into the neighborhood theater to watch a petite Nordic beauty glide and pirouette through romantic scenes in a setting of a winter wonderland.

Those in larger metropolitan areas would pour into arenas such as New York's Madison Square Garden and the indoor forums of Los Angeles, Chicago and Dallas to watch the same ice ballerina, in lavish costumes, spin through similar routines in a Ziegfeld-style follies.

Mothers sighed. They rushed out to buy their daughters ice skates. If they lived in the colder climes of the North, they sought out the nearest frozen pond. Others subscribed to ice rinks wherever available. Their purpose was the same:

"My daughter is going to be another Sonja Henie."

The impact on American culture was monumental. Little girls found Sonja Henie dolls and silver skates under their Christmas trees. Ice rinks mushroomed all over the country. In Canada, a little girl named Barbara Ann Scott laced on her first skates. In Boston, the parents of Tenley Albright put her on ice to combat a slight case of polio. A mother in Los Angeles sewed dresses for daughter Peggy Fleming. A humble baker in Queens, New York, hocked his shop to finance ice skating lessons for his daughter, Carol Heiss. Similar sacrifices were made for New England's Dorothy Hamill.

All became figure skating champions, giving the Americans dominance in a sport that previously had been reserved for those Alpine and Scandinavian countries with a heritage of ice and snow. All unquestionably could trace this ascendancy to the swan-like Norwegian described by a New York Times critic as "a transfigured Degas ballerina" and those old movies of winter chill and romance.

Sonja Henie was a real, live doll—only 5 feet, 2 inches, blonde, with a round, dimpled face that seemed to glow in the sparkle of lights and glistening ice.

Unlike the skaters who came along in later years, with their acrobatic leaps and triple spins in mid-air, Sonja was a symphony on ice—smooth, graceful, flowing, with never a hitch in

left:

Pretty Sonja Henie practices her spins and jumps on the Rockefeller Plaza ice rink prior to a professional appearance in Madison Square Garden that night in February, 1937.

opposite:

Sonja competes with an unidentified partner in the World Fancy Skate Championships in Oslo, Norway in 1927. Henie was only 15 years old at the time.

daughter and started giving her ballet and snow-skiing lessons when she was four years old.

She started collecting trophies almost immediately. At five, she won a copper medal for capturing a 40-meter foot race while the family was vacationing in Grenen, Denmark. She won a junior skiing trophy when she was seven.

A year later, she was disappointed when she opened her Christmas gifts and found only a doll and a kitchen stove, while her brother, Leif, received a pair of racing skates. When the elder Henies saw tears in their daughter's eyes, they rushed out, persuaded a merchant to open his closed store and bought some junior skates. Sonja was ecstatic. She hurried to join Leif on the frozen pond.

Sonja lived on the ice, getting counsel from her parents. She was only nine years old, a mere strip of a lass of 79 pounds, when she won the Oslo junior and senior ladies' figure skating crowns and only 10 when she captured the first of her 11 Norwegian national championships.

At only 12, Sonja found herself competing in the 1924 Olympic Games. It was immaterial that she finished last. She was hailed as "Das Wunderkind," the "Wonder Child," and she was never to lose on the ice again.

Shortly afterward, Sonja saw a performance by the famous Russian ballerina, Anna Pavlova, in London and acknowledged that the experience had a significant influence on her skating routines.

The Norwegian teen-ager easily won her first Olympic title at St. Moritz, Switzerland, in 1928, and in 1932 repeated at Lake Placid, New York, her first visit to the United States. She was intrigued by the country and admittedly smitten by "the movie bug."

In 1936, Sonja swept overwhelmingly to her third Olympic gold at Garmish-Partenkirchen, Germany, moved on to Paris for her 10th world championship, then launched her professional career in the United States. Billed as "Pavlova of the Silver Blades," she drew 90,000 in four shows at Madison Square Garden and later had tea with President and Mrs. Roosevelt at the White House.

She made numerous movies for 20th Century Fox, including "One in a Million," which grossed $25 million. She became a naturalized U.S. citizen in 1941 and married the first of her three husbands—Dan Topping, owner of the New York Yankees. Divorcing Topping in 1947, she married wealthy Winthrop Gardiner Jr., a merger dissolved in 1956. The same year she was wed to Niels Onstadt, a Norwegian shipping magnate. She had no children.

In 1969, Sonja collapsed on a Paris holiday and died at age 57, leaving a legacy on ice that may never be duplicated.

her routines. No one ever recalls seeing her take a spill. She performed before royalty—England's King George and Queen Mary, as well as the ruling monarchs of Sweden, Belgium and Norway—and thrilled them all.

A child prodigy, she won 10 consecutive world ladies' figure skating championships, starting in 1927, and Olympic gold medals in 1928, 1932 and 1936. No one else has won more than one. After the 1936 Games, she turned professional and organized the first of her extravagant ice spectaculars, the Hollywood Ice Revue, with which she toured leading American cities and Europe.

They said she became the richest athlete of all time.

Sonja was born April 8, 1912, in Oslo, daughter of a well-to-do wool merchant who had won trophies in cycling. Both Wilhelm Henie and his wife recognized artistic talents in their

BEN HOGAN

Golf's "Wee Ice Mon"

Ben Hogan battled early adversity, critics who advised him to give up the game, a crippling automobile accident and dire predictions he would never swing a club again to become the greatest golfer of his day—the period spanning and following World War II.

"People were always telling me what I couldn't do," he related years later after his putting nerves had failed him and he transferred his golf interests into the successful manufacture of clubs and balls bearing his name. "I found myself always having to prove they were wrong."

It was an inner battle that left lasting scars more damaging to his personal image than the physical ones he carried after his broken body was pulled from the wreckage of his car on a lonely Texas highway in the winter of 1949.

Always a grim competitor, a dour man who eschewed social contact and defended his privacy with a deep passion, he mel-

lowed only slightly in his retiring years and maintained a crusty, do-not-disturb exterior. He rarely attended a tournament. He became the only Masters winner to shun the gathering of the exclusive green-coat clan at the Masters' "Champions Dinner" on the eve of this great tournament. He avoided personal interviews and steadfastly refused efforts to cooperate in a biography.

Introverted and impenetrable as he was in private life, he was a dramatic and imposing figure on the golf course as he trod the fairways, a white cap pulled low over chiseled features, his lips a vise of determination, hitting the ball with machine-like precision and dropping half-smoked cigarettes and deadly putts on every green.

Scots, who adored him as they did the pleasant, gentlemanly Bob Jones, dubbed him "The Wee Ice Mon" after he won the only British Open in which he competed at Carnoustie in 1953.

Hogan's icy, defensive personality was understandable when

A dramatic and imposing figure on the golf course, Ben Hogan blasts out of a sand trap in a Chicago tournament in 1947. He shot a 14-under-par 270 to win it.

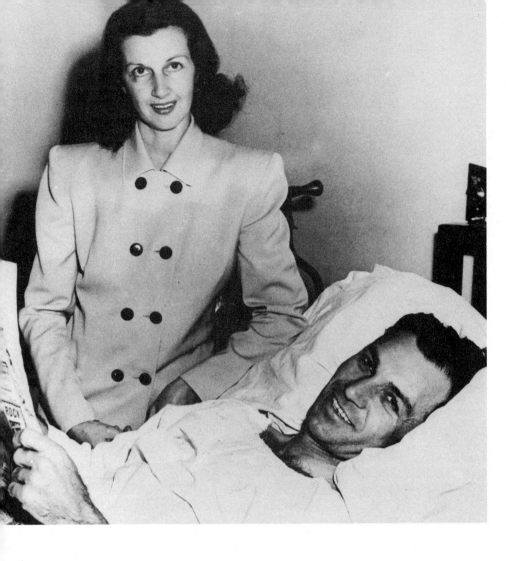

Medical men warned that Ben might never walk after he was seriously injured in an automobile crash in February, 1949. His wife, Valerie, (left) suffered minor injuries.

one considers the barriers he had to overcome to win all four of the major professional championships—a feat accomplished by only three other players, Gene Sarazen, Gary Player and Jack Nicklaus—and establish the late 1940s and the early 1950s as definitely "The Hogan Era."

He was born August 13, 1912 in the little town of Dublin, Texas, son of the village blacksmith who moved the family to Fort Worth when Ben was 10 years old. The boy sold papers on street corners to help provide food for the family. At the age of 12, he became a caddie at Fort Worth's Glen Garden Country Club for 65 cents a round. A fellow caddie was Byron Nelson, later one of his strongest rivals.

Ben was 15 when he won his first title, a Christmas caddie tournament at Glen Garden. At 19, he turned pro and, with $100 in his pocket, headed to the West Coast to join the pro tour. He lasted a month. He had to return to Fort Worth and save additional money before setting out again in 1933 at age 20. Again he failed, returning home with his confidence shaken by the well-meaning pros.

A converted lefthander, Hogan was plagued by an atrocious hook. "Look, son," the pros said to him, "why don't you go home and get a good job working in a store? With a hook like yours, you'll starve to death on the tour."

Hogan was not so easily deterred. He spent three years slav-

ing to refine his game and received encouragement when he qualified for the 1936 U.S. Open at Baltusrol in Springfield, N.J., although he failed to make the cut.

In 1937, newly married to a demure sweetheart named Valerie Fox and with $1,400 as a stake, he headed West again. "I know I can make it," he assured friends. The stake began to dwindle as Hogan moved from Pasadena to Los Angeles to Sacramento. He was down to $85 when he and Valerie reached Oakland for the next stop. Meanwhile, adding to their misery, a thief jacked up their second-hand car and made off with the two rear wheels.

Hogan acknowledged that at this point he was at rope's end. It was live or die. Ben and Valerie decided that if their fortunes did not turn at Oakland they would return to Texas and he would seek another career.

The tide turned. Ben shot an opening round 66, ultimately tied for third and collected $385. He never looked back. He won $4,150 in 1938 and $5,600 in 1939—enough to keep his head above water. He won his first tour title in the North and South at Pinehurst in 1940, was leading money winner in 1941 and 1942, finished third in the Open in 1941 and tied Byron Nelson for the Masters crown in 1942 before losing in a playoff.

World War II intervened at the time Hogan reached his peak. Hogan joined the Army's Special Services program and played sporadically in tour events which were being dominated by Byron Nelson, who was unable to enter the military because of medical reasons, but won 19 tournaments in 1945.

Hogan captured his first U.S. Open in 1948 at Los Angeles' Riviera Club, which became known as "Hogan's Alley." His future seemed now assured.

But on February 2, 1949, while he and Valerie were driving on a lonely Texas highway en route to Phoenix, Arizona, a huge trans-continental truck lunged out of the haze and skidded into their car. Instinctively, Hogan flung himself over to Valerie's side to protect her just as the impact drove the steering wheel through the driver's seat.

Valerie sustained minor injuries. Hogan suffered a double fracture of the pelvis, a broken collarbone, a fractured left ankle and a smashed rib. Hogan's life hung in the balance. Medical men saved the plucky golfer's life but warned that he might never walk, much less, swing a club again. The golf world thought it was the end of an era. But they reckoned without the grit and determination from the man they called "Little Ben."

Fiercely determined, Hogan not only walked but played again and went on to his greatest triumphs in 1953 when he won the Masters, U.S. Open and British Open and missed adding the match-play PGA perhaps because he chose not to play in it.

From Britain, he returned home to a ticker tape parade up New York's Broadway. As Hogan stood on a platform with thousands lining the streets and leaning out skyscraper windows, the world saw the icicle melt for the first time—even if only temporarily.

"I owe it all to Valerie and to God," he said, wiping a tear from his eye.

It's comeback time for Bantam Ben. In April, 1953 he tees off in the first round of the Masters Tournament. He not only won the Augusta tourney that year, but the U.S. and British Opens as well.

ROGERS HORNSBY

The Arrogant, Abrasive Rajah

Rogers Hornsby may have been the greatest righthanded hitter of all time—oldtimers insist he was—as well as the worst manager and one of the most fascinating and controversial characters baseball has ever known.

He was a veritable Dr. Jekyll and Mr. Hyde—at bat, a bold, grooved swinger who hit rocket-like line drives but who also could propel the ball out of the park; on the field, a slick, poised performer who played shortstop, second or third base; a fierce competitor respected but only tolerated by teammates, feared and disliked by his rivals. Off the field, he was an independent person who marched to his own drummer—arrogant, abrasive, often downright nasty.

A man's man, close to six feet and 175 pounds with good looks, he nevertheless became the idol of women. Debutantes bought seats near the dugout in order to catch his eye. He had an unusual lifestyle, frankly admitting he never cared for books, music or social activities. He couldn't dance or make speeches. He abhorred parties.

In his advancing years, he advised young players, "If you want to be a great hitter, don't go to the movies. It ruins your eyes."

He was an inveterate gambler, with a strong fetish for cards and race tracks, and those vices led to his repeated failures as a manager. He had difficulty relating to aspiring young players because he thought everyone should be as good as he was. He demanded perfection.

Hornsby played for five clubs and managed five in a volatile major league career that spanned 23 years. He earned close to a half-million dollars and blew most of it at the gambling tables and parimutuel windows before he was 45 years old.

He had a lifetime major league batting average of .358. He collected 3,030 hits in 8,173 times at bat and hit 303 home runs. Three times he batted over .400, setting a modern record in 1924 with .424. Between 1920 and 1925, he reeled off averages of .370, .397, .401, .384, .424 and .403 to lead the National League in batting for six consecutive years. He added a seventh batting title in 1928 with a .387 average. Twice he was the most valuable player in the National League.

Born on a farm in western Texas on April 27, 1896, he was the youngest of five children and given his mother's maiden name. He was six years old when the family moved to Fort Worth, Texas. By the time he was eight, he could handle ground balls with great skill and showed a good arm.

At age 10, he began working after school at the Fort Worth Stockyards and shortly earned a position on the stockyards' baseball team. He had everybody around the place talking about the "kid sensation."

Hornsby batted over .400 three times, setting a modern record in 1924 with .424. He played for five big league clubs, including the New York Giants, here, in 1927.

Purchased by the Chicago Cubs from the Boston Braves for $250,000 in 1929, the Rajah powers a tape-measure home run with Kiki Cuyler on base.

He was only 16, a scrawny 130 pounds, when he got his first professional chance in the Texas-Oklahoma League. The book on him was that he could hit but lacked power. Young Hornsby quickly remedied that.

He launched a rigorous training program to acquire more strength. He exercised and went on a heavy meat and potatoes diet. He reported to spring training the next year weighing 160 pounds. He batted over .300 and rekindled the interest of scouts who had seen him as a good fielder but weak hitter. In 1915, the St. Louis Cardinals bought his contract for $750.

Although he batted only .246 in 18 games in his rookie year, Hornsby was destined to dominate the team for the next 11 years, serving as manager in 1925 and 1926 when the Cardinals launched their "Gas House Gang" era. He contributed to the club's reputation as a free-swinging, base-stealing, go-for-broke aggregation, starting at second base and shifting to short-stop. He was acclaimed "one of baseball's greatest double-play middlemen."

In 1927, Hornsby—called "The Rajah" by the press—moved to the New York Giants for a season, then to the Boston Braves for a year before going to the Chicago Cubs in 1929 where he played until he returned to the Cardinals for a quick stopover in 1933. Before the 1933 season ended, he had donned the uniform of the St. Louis Browns of the American League. He managed the Cards, Braves, Cubs and Browns and—a couple of decades later—briefly the Cincinnati Reds.

This gypsy life was reflective of Hornsby's overbearing, abu-sive personality. He was constantly alienating his bosses and teammates, and irritating Baseball Commissioner Kenesaw Mountain Landis.

The Cardinals dropped him after the 1926 season at the height of his career after he spurned a $50,000 contract. He was traded to the Giants for Frankie Frisch. The Braves picked him up as manager in 1928 but decided they couldn't pay his $36,000 salary and traded him to the Cubs the following year in one of baseball's biggest deals. The Cubs gave up $250,000 and five players for him.

After the Cubs cut him in 1932, the commissioner had Hornsby on the carpet for allegedly borrowing money from his players, but he was exonerated. The Browns fired him for "actions off the ball field."

Blacklisted by major league teams, Hornsby refused to retire from baseball. He hooked on with several minor league teams, including Chattanooga, Baltimore, Oklahoma City and Fort Worth—an embittered, unhappy man.

Throughout his wanderings in his latter years, Hornsby maintained that he was misjudged. "The funny part is they're saying I went broke on the horses," he said. "What killed me was the stock market. I put $100,000 in one lump in a broker's hand and lost it quick."

Baseball author-historian Maury Allen reported that, during spring training in 1962, Hornsby, at 65 serving as a coach with the New York Mets, was asked by a photographer to pose with home run king Roger Maris of the Yankees. "If he wants to come over here," Hornsby snapped, "I'll pose with the busher."

On January 5, 1963, Hornsby, recovering from cataract surgery, died of a heart attack in a Chicago hospital.

GORDIE HOWE

The Greatest of the Hockey Greats

The great Gordie Howe.

How else could one describe a player who lasted through 32 professional hockey seasons, skated on the same team as his sons, led the world in goals, assists, points, games and respect when he retired, and has become one of the sport's finest ambassadors?

When Wayne Gretzky, now the most prolific scorer in hockey, speaks of Howe, it is with a reverential tone. Gretzky has met Howe dozens of times, yet he still feels in awe in Gordie's presence.

"If people someday compare me to Gordie Howe, it will be the biggest compliment they could pay me," Gretzky says. "If you ask me about my idol, there has been just one, Gordie."

Howe's Hall of Fame career began inauspiciously in 1946-47, when he scored only seven goals and 22 points in 58 games

Still playing at 49 years of age in 1977, Howe is thwarted in scoring attempt by goalie Richard Brodeur and defenseman Jean Bernier of the Quebec Nordiques of the World Hockey Association.

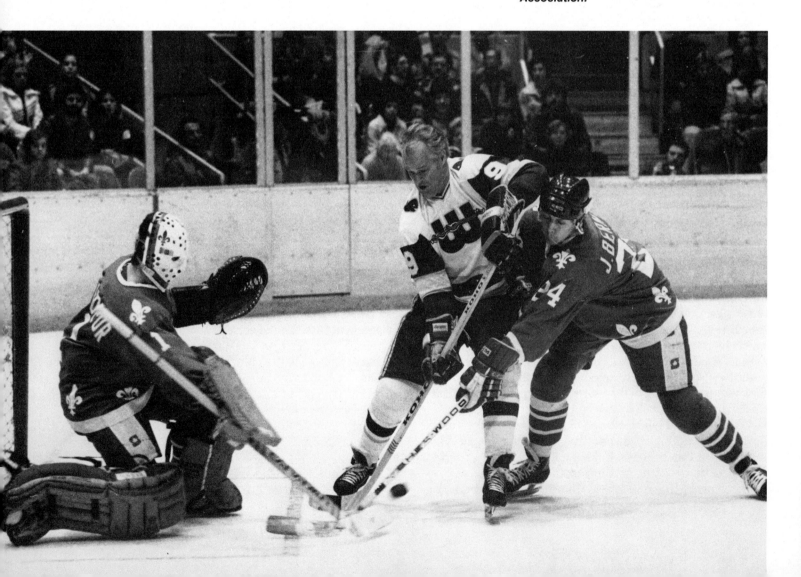

Gordie is flanked by sons Marty (left) and Mark as they wear their new Houston Aeros uniforms for the first time. The trio signed for a reported $1.8 million in 1973.

for the Detroit Red Wings. He did, however, quickly establish a reputation for toughness that he would hold onto.

"No one in their right mind ever wanted to tangle with him," said Red Wings' teammate Ted Lindsay, a fellow Hall of Fame member and one of the most rugged players in National Hockey League history. "Gordie had a lethal pair of elbows, was strong as a moose and knew every angle. He never let himself get into a bad position."

Phil Esposito, yet another Hall of Famer who idolized Howe, recalled the first time he lined up alongside Gordie.

"I was with the Chicago Blackhawks and we were getting ready for a faceoff," Esposito said. "I looked up at him and he said something like, 'Hi, kid.' I felt like a million."

Then, after the puck was dropped, Howe planted an elbow in Esposito that cost the rookie several teeth.

"I learned my lesson right away," Esposito said.

The lesson that Howe taught was that age never should mat-

ter as long as you have the drive and desire to succeed. Howe already was one of hockey's all-time greatest stars in 1971, when he retired after 25 years with the Red Wings. He had 786 goals, 1,809 points and six MVP awards. Howe also won the scoring title six times, including four straight from 1950-51 through 1953-54.

He still was performing well as a 43-year-old when he left the Red Wings following a 23-goal, 52-point campaign.

"I didn't feel I couldn't play any more," he said. "I felt I didn't *want* to play any more."

What more could the man do? He had been on four Stanley Cup winners, collecting 68 playoff goals and 160 points. He made a dozen All-Star teams. Offensively, he was the most productive player in history.

"I felt fulfilled as a player," he admitted. "I never would have come back if not for the chance to skate with the boys."

The boys, sons Mark and Marty, signed with the Houston

Howe scored 786 NHL goals when he retired after 25 years with Detroit. Here, he registers Goal No. 500, beating Gump Worsley of the New York Rangers in a March, 1962 game.

Aeros of the World Hockey Association in 1973. At first, convincing Gordie to return to play with them seemed like a publicity stunt. But the youngsters, particularly Mark, proved themselves immediately and Gordie still was Gordie. He averaged 30 goals a year for four seasons in Houston, scoring 100, 99, 102 and 68 points.

When the Aeros folded, the Howes moved to New England and Gordie scored 34 goals and 96 points in his first season with the Whalers.

"It was good, high quality hockey," Howe said. "There was nothing to be ashamed about in the WHA."

In 1979, four WHA teams entered the NHL. The Whalers, then representing Hartford, were one of them and, at 51, Howe again was playing in the league he once dominated. He scored 15 goals that season, lifting his NHL career total to 801.

"Playing with my sons is something I'll always remember," he said. "Returning to the NHL for that one season was just another dream come true—the three Howes playing together in the NHL."

Howe's marvelous NHL tenure nearly ended before it began, then almost ended in tragedy. When he was 14, Howe was sent to a New York Rangers' tryout camp in Winnipeg, 500 miles from his Saskatchewan home. But Howe was so homesick that he left the camp. Two years later, a more mature Howe made it through a similar camp run by the Red Wings in Windsor and became Detroit property.

In a 1950 playoff game, a collision with Ted Kennedy of Toronto sent Howe reeling head-first into the sideboards. He fell unconscious and emergency brain surgery was performed hours later.

"It looked pretty bad," Red Wings' boss Jack Adams said. "When they got him into bed, he started to bleed from the nose and mouth."

"I did awake and realize something was going on," Howe recalled. "Then they started shaving my head and I thought, 'Hell, no.' Then I remember the drilling to relieve the pressure."

The 90-minute operation saved Howe's life. He was allowed to attend the seventh game of the Stanley Cup finals, which the Red Wings won in double overtime. When the Cup was being presented to the Wings, the home crowd shouted for Howe, who came on the ice and accepted the trophy.

He would do so three more times.

Even in retirement, Howe has carried an aura of being special. At All-Star games and league meetings, he is swamped by fans seeking autographs, and by players anxious to meet the great man, talk hockey with him or just stand nearby in admiration.

Perhaps Mark Howe best summed up his father's contributions and stature.

"When I was younger," the All-Star defenseman of the Philadelphia Flyers said, "I always was called, 'Gordie's son.' To me, that was a great honor.

"Then, getting to play on the same team with my father was as great a thrill as any athlete could have. I can understand why people have been in awe of him. I was too."

BOBBY HULL

The Powerful Golden Jet

Has anyone ever fit a nickname better than Bobby Hull? The Golden Jet, indeed.

Hull had the power, the speed and the majesty of a jet. He soared above the opposition. Or he went through it with his strength. The blistering slapshot, launched from the prototype curved stick, made goalies shudder. The flowing blond hair made female fans swoon.

He made 50-goal seasons commonplace. His ability to change the flow of a game with one burst made other teams seek out one-dimensional skaters whose only job was to try to prevent Hull from scoring.

Few athletes have had the impact on their sport that Hull had on hockey in the early 1960s. The slapshot still was an oddity that only a few players, notably Montreal's Bernie Geoffrion, were using. Hull not only changed the way the slapshot was regarded by coaches and players, he changed the way it was used.

"His shot once paralyzed my arm for five minutes," Hall of Fame goalie Jacques Plante once said.

"The first time I saw that thing," added Glenn Hall, the star goalie for the Chicago Blackhawks and, luckily, a teammate of Hull's, "I said a prayer of thanks that I didn't have to worry about it."

Perhaps the incident with the most impact regarding Hull's howitzer came in 1966, at the height of his superb career. The opposing netminder was Eddie Giacomin of the New York Rangers.

"He was flying down the wing and started winding up at the red line," Giacomin said. "There was no way I was going to see the shot. You hardly ever did. I just hoped he was off-target."

Hull wasn't. His rising bullet struck Giacomin in the midsection. The force of the shot carried the goaltender backward into the net. With the puck.

Putting pucks into the net was a habit for Hull, who was named the Player of the Decade in the '60s. In 1966, he became the first player to break the 50-goal barrier, scoring 54. Two seasons later, he hit for 58.

A three-time NHL point-scoring champion, Hull also took league MVP honors twice. For many of his years in Chicago, he and Stan Mikita carried an inordinate load, skating as much as 40 minutes a game and working on all special teams.

"I was only 18 when I came to the Hawks, so anything they wanted me to do was fine by me," Hull said. "I sort of got used to playing a lot of time and I liked it."

What the fans liked most was seeing Hull come streaming down left wing, ready to unleash the fury of his 100-plus mph slapshot. But there was more to his game.

A three-time NHL point-scoring champion, Hull also was twice named the league's MVP. Fans liked to see him come streaming down left wing, ready to unload his 100 miles-per-hour slapshot.

"People forget that Bobby was one of the most physical players in hockey," John Ferguson, once a tough Montreal forward, said. "He wouldn't back away from anyone and he knew how to hurt you."

Hull and Ferguson were involved in one of the bloodiest fights in NHL history, a battle which made its way into Life Magazine, complete with photos of both players dripping red.

At 5-10, 195, Hull had a body that looked like it was sculpted from granite. His muscles bulging beneath the Indian on his jersey, Hull in full flight was a special sight.

"When I was eight years old, I started going out into the

Hull gets his stick on the puck before firing it past goalie Fern Rivard of the Minnesota North Stars in Chicago Stadium on March 3, 1969.

woods with my grandfather," he said. "I chopped down trees with an ax and that helped develop my arm and back muscles. I also walked to and from school four miles a day, and during the winter, I shoveled snow from morning until night."

When Hull was 14, the Blackhawks found him playing outdoor hockey in Belleville, Ontario, and signed him to their organization. By 1957, Hull had been invited to the Blackhawks' training camp.

"I don't think they expected me to make the team then," he said. "But they also realized when I got there that I was ready."

Ready to make history. But not immediately.

"I had a lot to learn about the game," he said. "I really was a raw player. I had the skills but I didn't really know how to use them. It took me a few years to get going."

In his third full season as a Blackhawk, Hull scored 39 goals

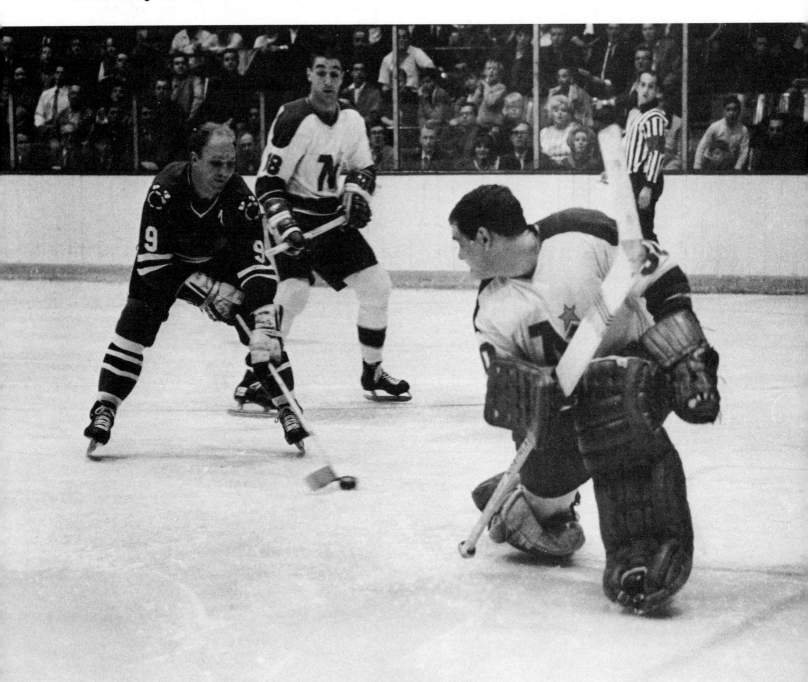

The Blackhawks' star holds pucks numbered to indicate his NHL career goals which moved him into second place in February, 1971. He had been tied for the runnerup position with Maurice Richard at 544.

and had 81 points, leading the league. He was a perennial All-Star the rest of his career and one of the most feared scorers the game had known.

For Hull, life on the ice never was without company.

"I made Bryan Watson famous," Hull once joked of the man who was called 'Super Pest' for his ability to shadow the Golden Jet. "I can't remember a game where there wasn't one guy assigned to check me. Even if he had a chance for a breakaway, he might forget it and just stick with me."

How did Hull handle such treatment?

"I tried to ignore those guys, not let them get to me," he said. "You couldn't show them they were getting to you. That would just give them confidence in what they were doing."

What was Hull's best way to frustrate the frustrators?

"With a goal or two," he said. "Scoring goals always did the trick."

Hull didn't limit his contributions to the ice. In 1972, he became the cornerstone of the World Hockey Association. The new league, seeking someone to give it instant credibility, found, in Hull, a willing pioneer. The Blackhawks haggled with Hull about his salary and the length of a new contract for several years, with Hull twice threatening to retire.

When the Winnipeg Jets of the WHA offered him a $2.5 million contract as a player-coach at the age of 33, Hull flew from the Blackhawks' coop. A sticky lawsuit couldn't halt him from playing in the WHA, where he scored a then-record 77 goals in 1974-75.

Perhaps more importantly, Hull's move meant other NHL stars would consider the new league. The WHA-NHL bidding war didn't help the sport, but the players' salaries skyrocketed.

Almost every player in the game today can thank Bobby Hull for that.

JACK JOHNSON

A Man Without a Country

Jack Johnson, the son of a schoolhouse janitor in Galveston, Texas, made Page One of the New York Times when he died at the age of 68 in an auto crash in 1946. Had he known, he certainly would have flashed one of his ear-to-ear smiles, featuring a dental keyboard of gold teeth.

Jack was the heavyweight boxing champion for almost seven years, from Dec. 26, 1908, to April 5, 1915. From 1913 to 1920 he was a "man without a country," living outside the United States to stay out of jail.

As a fighter, Johnson was decades before his time. Boxing historian Nat Fleischer, a founder of Ring Magazine, rated him No. 1 in a ranking of all-time heavyweight champions. More than four decades after his death on June 10, 1946, any consensus of boxing experts still put him in the Top Five.

Slightly over six feet in height and with weight that fluctuated between 195 and 220 pounds, Jack had dancing feet, quick hands, numbing power, and reflexes that would have looked good on a fighter pilot. He also had what seemed to be a bottomless pool of stamina.

The man known as L'il Arthur, a spinoff from his full name of John Arthur Johnson, won the heavyweight crown in Sydney, Australia. He knocked out the champion, Tommy Burns, in 14 rounds. It looked like a mismatch—and proved to be—when the fighters entered the ring. Burns was 5-7 and 175 pounds.

Johnson made five successful title defenses before losing to hulking Jess Willard on a knockout in 26 rounds in Havana. The bout is still the subject of endless forensic discussions among veteran ring fans. Was it a dump? A photo of the referee tolling 10 over the horizontal Johnson shows Jack seemingly shading his eyes against the searing, white Caribbean sun. It was an afternoon fight.

A long time afterward, in fact until the day of his death, Johnson insisted he threw the fight. At least one of his handlers differed with that. He said Jack was fat and way out of shape from too much rich food and everything that went with it.

Johnson died the way he lived, going too fast and then spinning out of control. He was at the wheel of a big, shiny car which somehow got away from him and rammed into a light pole near Franklinton, N.C., not too far from Raleigh. The car was "totaled." Jack and a passenger were thrown from the auto. Johnson died a few hours later of multiple injuries. Fred Scott, the passenger, survived.

Jack was the first black heavyweight champion of the 20th Century. He also was the last until Joe Louis wiped out the game Jim Braddock in 1937. In what was first suspected to be a touch

Johnson was the first black heavyweight titleholder of the 20th Century. He won the crown in 1908 by knocking out Tommy Burns in the 14th round.

of jealousy, Johnson predicted that Max Schmeling would knock out Louis in their first bout in 1936. Max did just that. Johnson was silent the second time around when Louis savaged Schmeling in one round.

Jack was so flamboyant he made it a weak word. He loved the high life and women by the dozen. Many among the latter were white. At one time, when only one family in 10,000 owned an automobile, Jack had six, all fast and flashy. He laughed at the conventions of his times, shook hands with European kings and queens, and was the epitome of arrogance.

When he whipped Jim Jeffries in a title defense in Reno on July 4, 1910, he not only had to win but humiliate the bulky ex-champ. Johnson laughed and sneered at Jim, taunting him with phrases like, "Mr. Jeff, come on, show me what you got." Jack carried Jim for 14 rounds until the bout was stopped. Jeffries was sadly out of shape after six years in retirement.

Johnson's decisive victory and boastfulness brought on a clamor for a "White Hope." The cumbersome Willard proved to be the man, whether by design or his ox-like strength. About a half century later, a Broadway play and later a movie called "The Great White Hope" sought to capture Jack's story.

In 1909 Jack fought Stanley Ketchel in a championship bout in Colina, Calif., that would not have been sanctioned in later years. Ketchel was the middleweight champ—and white—and feared nothing on two feet and probably few things on four.

Hopelessly outweighed, Stanislaus (his real name) pitched into L'il Arthur and was holding his own until he made a fatal faux pas. He dumped the great man on the deck. Johnson, enraged, got to his feet and all but dismembered Ketchel. He knocked Stanley out in the 12th round and also knocked out all of Ketchel's front teeth.

Johnson, in his prime, always traveled first-class and was never without an entourage. He toured Europe, after jumping bail following his 1913 conviction on a Mann Act charge. His sizable coterie of aides mirrored what he considered his station in life.

Inevitably, he went broke. The entourage vanished. In low spirits and weary of foreign lands, he stepped across the border between Mexico and the United States voluntarily in 1920. He was arrested by waiting Federal agents and whisked away to Leavenworth Prison where he served the one-year sentence from the 1913 conviction.

Upon his release, certainly in no shape to fight as a professional at age 43, he was still desperate for some form of celebrity status. From 1921 to 1933—he was then 55—he engaged in a string of meaningless bouts, which only proved that the once great champion was a hapless has-been.

He searched about frantically for other starring roles. How about this one: Jack Johnson, evangelist? Or Jack Johnson, a spear carrier in an opera? He made personal appearances for any kind of a fee for anyone who would pay it.

From 1937 to 1946, he periodically showed up doing some form of an act at a Times Square arcade in New York, where his co-stars were the tiny performers in a "Flea Circus."

The Ring Record Book lists his full career record as 113 bouts, 44 victories by a knockout, 30 triumphs on a decision, four wins

At age 54 in 1932, Johnson, broke and obviously out of shape, still engaged in meaningless exhibition fights.

on a foul, 14 draws, one losing decision, one defeat by foul, five times knocked out and 14 no decisions.

He once unintentionally launched a movie career. He fought a tough guy named Victor McLaglen in a six-rounder in 1909. It was a no decision bout but Jack's cruel gloves convinced even a hard-case like McLaglen to try something else. He did and became a Hollywood leading man and character actor for almost 40 years, winning an Academy Award as Best Actor for his performance in "The Informer" in 1935.

MAGIC JOHNSON

A Remarkable Court Wizard

When her son was given the flashy nickname of "Magic" in high school, Christine Johnson was the first to consider its practical consequences.

"When you say 'Magic,' people expect so much," she said. "I was afraid that it would give him a lot to live up to at some point."

However, few basketball players have matched their nickname with more expression and panache than the ebullient Earvin "Magic" Johnson, perhaps the most remarkable athlete of his generation in the National Basketball Association.

Johnson's improvisational skills inspire not only applause from fans, but acclaim from contemporaries.

"I'd pay to see Magic play," says Boston's Larry Bird, who along with Johnson are considered the top two players in the current game. "I think he's the best player in the league. Magic plays the game the way I like to see it played."

Like Bird, Johnson is a player around whom a game usually flows. With the Los Angeles Lakers, Johnson has been the motivating force, virtually from the time he came into the NBA in the 1979-80 season.

With ball-handling and passing abilities rarely seen in a player of his height, 6-foot-9, Johnson made an auspicious debut in the NBA when he triggered the Lakers to the league championship.

The success of the Lakers with Johnson should have surprised no one, however. He had always had a habit of turning teams into champions, as far back as high school.

In Johnson's senior year at Everett High in Lansing, Mich., 1976-77, the team won the state championship with a 27-1 record.

In his first year at Michigan State, Johnson helped the Spartans win the Big Ten title after a losing season, and in his sophomore year, he led them to the NCAA championship with a rousing victory over no less an opponent than Larry Bird's undefeated Indiana State team.

It would not be until his later years in the pros that his latent

left:

Magic Johnson (32) goes over Butch Carter of the Indiana Pacers to score for the Los Angeles Lakers in 1984 game. Magic was named league's MVP in 1986-87.

opposite:

The Lakers' Magic Man leaps for a rebound with Rolando Blackman (22) of the Dallas Mavericks in 1986 game. Johnson scored 21 points and collected nine assists in 117-113 L.A. victory.

Johnson starred in college at Michigan State. He led the Spartans to the NCAA crown in his sophomore year. In this semifinal game of the 1979 NCAA title competition, Magic (33) scored 29 points in a 101-69 triumph over Penn.

scoring abilities would blossom; it was, rather, as a playmaker that Johnson first expressed his genius on a basketball court: his flair for ball-handling and those fabulous, no-look, thread-the-needle passes that inspired applause. Not only did they make Johnson look good, but others as well.

Johnson's abilities, when first recognized on a national level at Michigan State, began changing the face of basketball in America, according to Spartan Coach Jud Heathcote. Johnson not only had a great impact on Michigan State, he said, but on basketball in general. Heathcote saw Johnson's imprint on high school players who made the pass prologue. "If these kids growing up have their sports idols and they can identify with them and emulate what they do best, that's how they'll play," Heathcote said. "If it's Earvin, they'll start thinking 'pass.'"

However, when the Lakers needed Johnson to score, he did that, too. A three-time assist leader before the 1986-87 season, Johnson was leading the league in that department again, but he had increased his scoring average by five points over the career-high of 19 the season before. Practically everyone jumped on the bandwagon to make him the league MVP, heretofore Bird's unchallenged domain for three years.

Furthermore, Johnson is not only a player who makes head-lines and the front covers of national magazines for his exploits, but is a neon advertisement for basketball. Ever eager, bristling with enthusiasm and wreathed in smiles, Johnson plays the sport as if he is having a ball every minute. And, actually, he is.

"One thing I'm always going to do is have fun," he says. "There is a time for business and a time for fun. Basketball is fun."

Johnson just wouldn't be what he is without the emotional touch. Bursting with glee after doing one of his specialities on the court, Johnson is apt to slap skin, raise his fist or break into a victory dance.

"I've seen Earvin Johnson dance the whole length of the floor after his group had won a shooting contest in a vacant arena during a road trip," said one writer. "The guy is consistent—he's always emotional. It doesn't matter whether he's doing his thing in front of 10,000 fans or playing a game of 'horse.' He reacts vividly to every shot."

And he's constantly chattering on the court—talking to teammates and opponents alike, waving his muscular arms dramatically while giving his teammates directions, like a traffic cop.

"I do try to run the team when I'm out there," Johnson says.

"I try to keep everybody cool, yet keep them fired up at the same time. I feel that's my job—to quarterback the team."

It is a role that Johnson had just naturally fit into all his life, starting with his frenetic approach to basketball in Lansing, where he would wake up especially before school to go out and practice on the schoolyards.

"People thought I was crazy," he says. "They really, seriously did. It would be 7:30 and they'd be going to work and they'd say, 'There's that crazy June Bug, hoopin.'"

"June Bug," however, soon turned into "Magic."

Good as he was in high school and college, Johnson became even better in the pros. In 1980, he was the first rookie to win the playoff MVP award, which he repeated in 1982. He became a perennial leader in steals and assists, as well as an all-NBA First Team player.

When Johnson is in tune with a game's rhythm, there are few players his equal. This was evident in a performance one night in Kansas City.

On a fast break in the first quarter, Johnson was met at the free throw line by a defender, but he dribbled behind his back and without breaking stride, passed off to a teammate. A few minutes later, he made a pass through traffic to another teammate while looking at the arena's ceiling. In the fourth quarter on another break, he was met at the foul line by a defender once again. This time, Johnson pirouetted 360 degrees and made a bee-line for the basket without missing a step.

"He's one of the few players I've seen who can adjust his game to whatever needs to be done," says Boston center Robert Parish of Johnson. "Larry (Bird) is like that, too. Stop him? You try to contain him. You try not to let him have those outrageous nights. You give him his 20 assists and hope he doesn't go crazy in other areas."

This is Magic as an NBA rookie in the fall of 1979, passing behind his back to a teammate over the head of Dudley Bradley of Indiana. The Lakers won, 127-120.

WALTER JOHNSON

The Big Train Was Quick

On December 10, 1946, the obituaries of two of America's most prominent personalities passed across the desks of the nation's newspapers—that of Walter Johnson, the great right-handed pitcher, and Damon Runyon, a sports writer turned author whose colorful characters were to be immortalized in books and the movies.

How should the two stories be played—on Page 1 or back in the sports sections?

The answer was both intriguing and significant. Johnson's death was played prominently on Page 1 by most newspapers while that of Runyon was relegated to the inside.

The big, raw-boned farmer's son out of Humboldt, Kansas, christened "The Big Train" by sports writer Grantland Rice in comparing the pitcher's fastball to the whine of a locomotive passing over the countryside, had grown into a legend, more popular than presidents, movie stars and industrial tycoons.

He was indeed "King of the Hill"—that small hump of dirt comprising the pitcher's mound—in the swinging, pre-Depression era when defense and the dead ball predominated and the game was a national fever.

For the entire 21 years of his career, Johnson pitched for one of the sorriest teams in baseball—the Washington Senators, chided as "first in war, first in peace and last in the American League"—yet compiled records that were to endure for generations.

Johnson won 416 games, a total exceeded only by Cy Young; completed 531 of the 666 games he started; hurled 113 shutouts; struck out 3,508 batters, and once had a string of 56 consecutive scoreless innings. He had a dozen seasons with 20 or more victories, 10 in a row. His career earned run average was 2.17.

A big man at 6 feet, 1 inch and 200 pounds, he never resorted to subtlety or tried to confuse opposing batters with a repertoire of breaking pitches and off-speed stuff. Utilizing a sidearm delivery, he reared back and fired.

His speed was awesome, perhaps the fastest of all time. In his thick, leathery hands, the ball became a weapon that was feared by every hitter who faced him, even the dauntless Ty Cobb.

"You always knew what was coming—always just raw speed, blinding speed," Cobb said. "You were lucky to see it."

Umpire Billy Evans liked to relate an ironic anecdote involving Cleveland's Ray Chapman, who was killed by a pitch from

Johnson won 416 major league games, pitched 113 shutouts and struck out 3,508 batters. He also had a dozen seasons with 20 or more victories for the usually lowly Washington Senators. This photo was taken in Johnson's final big league year in 1927.

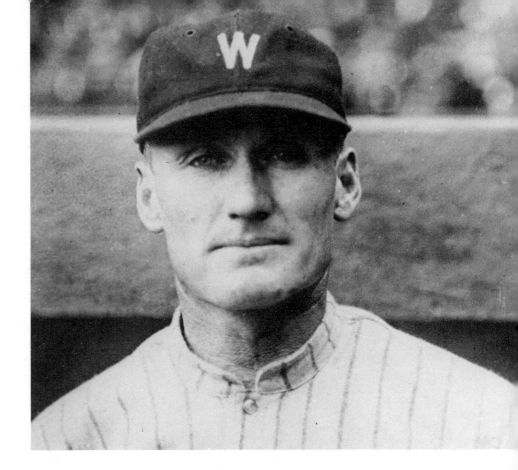

"You always knew what was coming—always just raw speed, blinding speed," the great Ty Cobb said about the Big Train. "You were lucky to see it."

Carl Mays of the New York Yankees in 1920—the only such baseball fatality.

It was five years before this tragedy that Chapman came to bat against Johnson in a game at Cleveland. Johnson fired a pitch over the plate.

"Strike one!" Evans, blinking, barked.

Johnson unleashed another sizzler.

"Strike two!" Evans boomed.

Whereupon Chapman wheeled and headed for the bench.

"Hey." the umpire yelled, "that's only strike two."

"I know it," a dazed Chapman shot back. "You can have the next one. It won't do me any good."

Born November 6, 1887, Johnson was of Swedish stock. His father quit farming wheat and corn in Humboldt in 1901 and headed for California in hopes of striking oil. Unsuccessful, the family wound up in Idaho.

Young Walter got a job with the telephone company and played semi-pro ball. In Weiser, Idaho, Johnson was discovered by a traveling cigar salesman who first recommended his sensational find to the disinterested Detroit Tigers and finally to the Senators.

Cliff Blankenship, an injured catcher on the Washington club, was dispatched on a Western scouting mission with the suggestion that he look in on this "19-year-old kid in Idaho." Blankenship was amazed.

"He throws a ball so fast nobody can see it," Blankenship wrote his bosses after watching Johnson. "His control is so good that the catcher just holds up his glove, shuts his eyes, then picks the ball, which comes to him looking like a little white bullet, out of the pocket."

Johnson was given a $100 bonus and offered $350 a month to join the Senators for the rest of the 1907 season. Thus began the major league saga of "The Big Train."

Johnson was a soft-spoken, easy-going man described by Washington columnist Shirley Povich as "everybody's country cousin, a big, handsome, modest hick." He didn't drink, smoke or swear. He purposely avoided brushback pitches for fear he might hurt someone.

He started with three losing seasons, although in 1908 he pitched three shutouts in four days against the New York Highlanders, the future Yankees. However, during the next 10 campaigns, starting in 1910 and playing with a mediocre club, he consecutively won 25, 25, 32, 36, 28, 27, 25, 23, 23 and 20 games.

In 1913, he fashioned 12 shutouts and five one-hitters and recorded an earned run average of 1.14, the best ever in baseball until Bob Gibson of the St. Louis Cardinals broke it with 1.12 in 1968.

Johnson's only no-hitter came on July 1, 1920, in Boston's Fenway Park, an error by second baseman Bucky Harris preventing it from being a perfect game. Johnson finally made it to the World Series in 1924 and 1925, posting a 3-3 record for the two Series.

After retiring, he managed the Newark club, the Senators and Cleveland Indians. In 1936, he was one of the five original inductees into baseball's Hall of Fame.

BOB JONES

King of Golf's Grand Slam

Bob Jones made the term "Grand Slam" a part of the lexicon of golf. An expression originating with the card game of bridge, it meant taking all the tricks. Baseball borrowed it to describe a home run with the bases loaded. It carried the same connotation in golf—a sweep, winning all of the big ones, clearing the board.

Jones became its symbol. In 1930, he scored the first and only Grand Slam in golf history, winning the U.S. and British Amateur, and the U.S. and British Open championships in a single season. Not only has the feat never been equaled, it has not been seriously challenged. Nor will it ever be, in the judgment of the game's finest minds.

The achievement is all the more remarkable because it was fashioned by a young amateur who proved himself master not only of his amateur contemporaries but of the sport's greatest professionals. No more worlds to conquer, Jones retired from competition at age 28, leaving an unattainable goal for generations that followed.

Jones' departure marked a change in the character of the game. There was a sharp shift from the amateurs, the blue ribbon competitors in sports' Golden Age, to the professional tour with its mushrooming purses and television exposure. One man who made the changeover was Jack Nicklaus, a two-time U.S. amateur champion who turned pro in 1961 and went on to win 20 major championships, seven more than Jones, and establish himself as the all-time monarch of professional golf.

The pros set up their own version of the Grand Slam, bracketing the Masters, U.S. and British Opens and the American PGA as the four major events, but none has packaged them neatly in a single year. Ben Hogan came closest, winning the Masters, U.S. and British Opens in 1953 but passing up the PGA. Others, including Nicklaus and Arnold Palmer, have won two.

Students of the game say there is no telling how many championships Jones might have won had he not retired at such an early age. Hogan was 35 before he won the first of his four U.S. Opens. Nicklaus, who substantially had two careers, won the Masters at age 41.

Jones also had two careers—seven years of want as a teenage phenomenon before his seven years of plenty.

Born Robert Tyre Jones II, son of a well-to-do Atlanta lawyer and named for his grandfather, he grew up in a country club atmosphere, getting his first baptism in the sport by following his parents around the East Lake course.

Jones practicing to defend his U.S. Open title in Minneapolis in 1930. The competition began on July 10.

In 1930, Bob scored the first and only Grand Slam in golf history, winning the U.S. and British Amateur, and the U.S. and British Open championships.

After acquiring his first golf club at age five, little Bobby built a hand-made course on the family's front lawn and he and friends played for hours.

Bobby was six when he won his first tournament—a six-hole event for neighborhood kids at a birthday party. At nine, he won a junior tournament at the Atlanta Athletic Club, and at 13 he captured two club championships and two invitation events against some of the South's top amateurs.

Bobby was only 14 when he played in his first National Amateur Championship at the Merion (Pennsylvania) Cricket Club. Spectators were awed by the smooth swing of the husky youngster who led first day qualifying and won two matches before blowing up. The press criticized his ungovernable temper.

He lost in the final of the 1919 U.S. Amateur. In his National Open debut in 1920, he was in contention until he blew himself

out of it in the final round. That same year he won the qualifying medal in the National Amateur but lost to Francis Ouimet in the semifinals.

In 1922, having lost his baby fat and developed into a handsome, trim man, Jones made his first trip to England, helping the United States beat the British in their Walker Cup matches. However, he lost in the fourth round of the British Amateur at Holylake and picked up in disgust in the third round of the British Open.

By this time, the young American was getting a lot of attention throughout the world. A favorite almost every time he teed up the ball, he continually found a way to lose.

"That Jones boy," they said, "Great talent but can't go in the clutch."

During his so-called seven years of famine, a Biblical reference, Jones played in 11 major tournaments, often as the favor-

By 1941, Jones had seen his best days on the course. Here, he tees off during the Masters tournament. He finished far down the list with 307. Craig Wood won with 280.

ite, and won none. He acknowledged that he had begun to wonder if he ever could win a big one.

In 1923, the tide turned. Playing in the National Open over the Inwood course on Long Island, Jones tied Bobby Cruickshank after 72 holes, then defeated the little Scottish pro in a dramatic playoff.

Thus began his seven years of plenty. During that period, he amassed 13 national titles—five U.S. Amateurs, four U.S. Opens, three British Opens and one British Amateur. In the last nine years of his career, he played in 12 Open championships, nine American and three British, and finished first or second in 11 of them. Jones considered the latter feat superior to his Grand Slam, which the world followed with feverish interest and for which he will be forever known.

The 1930 sweep began with the British Amateur, where Jones beat Roger Wethered in the final 7 and 6, continued in the British Open and U.S. Open, and culminated with the U.S. Amateur at Merion, outside Philadelphia.

Still a young man at 28, he announced his retirement from competitive golf. He and his financier friend, Cliff Roberts, collaborated on building a course in Augusta, Georgia, where he would play each spring with friends. Thus the Masters was born.

Jones, the soft-spoken Southern gentleman who was the epitome of the amateur spirit, refused to turn pro. He continued to play informally until stricken with a paralyzing spinal ailment which led to his death in 1971.

BILLIE JEAN KING

The Court Crusader

In the mid-1970s, an informal survey was made of tennis players and followers of the game on this theoretical question: If one were facing a highly pressured situation with a crucial point that probably would determine victory or defeat, who would you most prefer to play that point?

Of all the great players, male and female, considered in this hypothesis, one name dominated: Billie Jean King.

This bouncy, tomboyish daughter of a California fireman left a legacy of grit and determination, of an unbreakable will and tenacity not fully reflected in the scores of her court triumphs carved in the record books.

She wasn't the storybook idea of a female superstar. She was a chubby, girl-next-door type with 140 pounds distributed over a 5-foot-6 frame with short-cropped hair, harlequin spectacles and a face full of freckles.

If she had chosen baseball instead of tennis (and she always

Billie Jean King shows the trophy she won as the women's singles champion at the 1971 U.S. Open at Forest Hills. Billie downed Rosemary Casals 3-6, 6-3, 7-6 in the finals. At right is the men's titleholder, Stan Smith.

King's greatest triumph came in the "Battle of the Sexes" against feisty Bobby Riggs in the Houston Astrodome on Sept. 20, 1973. Billie shellacked Bobby, 6-4,6-3,6-3. Here, King stretches to return a smash by Riggs.

regretted that gender had made this impossible), she would have resembled Ty Cobb or Pete Rose in style of play. If she had been a boxer, she would have been like a little Dempsey.

She played the game with a dynamic gusto, scurrying around the court, leaping, bouncing, rushing the net. She didn't know what it was to temporize. She attacked every ball as if it were a mission. As she battled for points, she glowered and screamed at herself:

"Keep your eye on the ball, stupid!"

"You've got the touch of an ox. Think, think, think!"

She left a lasting impression on the game with not only her racket but her tongue. She was the Susan B. Anthony of her day, in the forefront of the feminist movement, an early crusader for open tennis and equal prize money for women players.

She and Rosemary Casals once walked out of their final match in a Pacific Southwest tournament, run by Jack Kramer, in protest of unequal pay. She threatened to lead a boycott of Wimbledon unless ladies' purses were raised to the level of the men's. Most of these inequities were changed.

She helped organize the women's pro circuit, and with husband Larry King, was co-founder and chief sponsor of Team Tennis, an inter-city project. She helped form both the Wom-en's Tennis Association and the Women's Sports Federation. She published a magazine, "WomenSports."

Billie Jean, although both knees carried scars of repeated operations, was ranked No. 1 in the world four times and seven times in the United States. She became the darling of Wimbledon, where on July 7, 1979, she won her 20th title—a record for both men and women—by capturing the women's doubles with Martina Navratilova. She won six Wimbledon singles titles and four American crowns.

Her greatest triumph, however—the one for which she probably will be most remembered—came in the "Battle of the Sexes" against feisty Bobby Riggs in the Houston Astrodome on September 20, 1973.

Riggs, a 55-year-old former Wimbledon and U.S. champion who had turned con man in his later years, taunted Billie Jean for her strong feminist views and insisted that even an old, run-down codger like he could beat the best of the women players. Billie Jean spurned his challenge until Bobby finally inveigled Margaret Court to meet him on Mother's Day in a remote California resort and then shamed the nervous Australian with a straight set victory.

That was more than Billie Jean could take. She threw down

the gauntlet. The match struck a national chord. The buildup was tremendous. They set up training camps, which were covered like a big heavyweight title fight. The slick news magazines featured Bobby on their covers, surrounded by a bevy of Hollywood starlets, and revived tales of Riggs' hustling days. While Bobby gulped vitamin pills and soaked up the fanfare, Billie Jean trained with a passion.

In a circus setting with all the trimmings, the largest crowd ever to see a tennis match—30,472—jammed into the Astrodome to watch a cold-eyed, tight-lipped King gag the obstreperous court jester with a 6-4, 6-3, 6-3 shellacking.

Born Billie Jean Moffitt on November 22, 1943, King grew up in a sports atmosphere. Her father played baseball and basketball. Her mother was a crack swimmer. A younger brother, Randy, was good enough to pitch for the San Francisco Giants. So Billie Jean wound up with a $9 racket because her father was determined that she not be a tomboy.

As a kid, Billie Jean played football and baseball with the boys. At firemens' picnics, she was always one of the first chosen for softball games. She was a natural athlete.

Besides her successes at Wimbledon and Forest Hills, she won national singles titles in Australia, France and Italy. She captured 29 Virginia Slims tour events and became the first woman to win $1 million in prize money.

She fared better at Wimbledon than at home, playing 100 matches on the storied English grass, winning nine doubles and five mixed doubles titles besides her six singles crowns.

"I love Wimbledon," she said. "It is a tournament for players. Forest Hills is a tournament for officials."

The bouncy Californian always was as free-swinging with her rhetoric as with her slashing topspin shots.

Discussing President Ford's Commission on Olympic Sports, she said, "Our sports system is a colossal joke. Amateur athletics stink."

On professionalism: "If a person wants to dedicate himself to sport, he should get paid. People relate to it."

She chided the establishment for its stuffy traditions such as all-white attire and complete silence during play.

"You picture people sipping mint juleps under an umbrella," she said. "Tennis must get away from that country club atmosphere. In basketball and football, the players cuss like sailors. At tennis matches, you can't breathe."

Still in reasonably good form in 1978, Billie Jean engages Martina Navratilova in the finals of the Virginia Slims of Houston tournament. King won the first set, 6-1, but Martina took the next two and the match, 6-2, 6-2.

JACK KRAMER

Refined the Serve-and-Volley Game

He didn't win five straight Wimbledon men's singles titles as did Sweden's Bjorn Borg. He never went two full years without losing a single competitive match as in the case of Don Budge. He didn't hit the ball as hard as Ivan Lendl or control it with the magical touch of a Rod Laver.

Yet wherever tennis is played, whenever devotees of the game gather to talk of the great and review the remarkable growth of the sport, one name inevitably rises to the top.

The name is Jack Kramer, "Big Jake." They still call him "The King."

A World War, a chronic back ailment and a radical evolution of the game prevented John A. Kramer from amassing the statistical successes of Big Bill Tilden, Fred Perry, Budge, Laver and Borg.

Nevertheless, he proved himself the best of his day. He won the big ones—The U.S. and Wimbledon Championships—and he helped break Australia's stranglehold on the Davis Cup.

He is credited with the refinement—if not the actual introduction—of the modern serve-and-volley game. After his amateur career, he emerged as the premier professional promoter and ultimately the one person most responsible for breaking down the hypocritical barriers to permit open tennis. He became everybody's choice for "tennis czar."

The role of a strong tennis commissioner never materialized. Petty jealousies and rivalries in the ruling bodies were too prevalent. Kramer, nevertheless, emerged as one of the powerful influences in the developing sport.

Kramer was born August 1, 1921 in Las Vegas, Nevada, son of a railroad engineer. His ambition was to be a major league baseball player. At the age of seven he owned half a dozen bats, seven gloves and a bucketful of balls. He played baseball, football and basketball on the corner lots—never tennis.

One day he came home from a particularly rough football skirmish, his nose broken, a few ribs cracked and blood streaming down his chin. His parents were shaken.

"This can't go on," his mother said. "Why don't you get in something less brutal?"

"Like tennis," said his concerned father.

"Tennis!" snorted young Jack. "That's a sissy game."

Jack Kramer in action against Jaroslav Drobny in a 1946 men's singles match at Wimbledon. Jack did not win the title that year. However, the following year he wiped out his old rival, Tom Brown, in 45 minutes in one of the shortest finals in history.

However, when the family moved from Las Vegas to San Bernardino, California, there happened to be a public tennis court across the street. In a short time, Jack had a $5 racket and a feel for a new game.

His father enrolled the youngster, then 13, in a class conducted by a professional, Dick Skeen. Later, as happened to most Southern Californians who showed any promise in the game, Jack fell under the tutelage of Perry Jones, director of the Los Angeles Tennis Club.

Kramer's progress was swift. At age 15, he defeated Alice Marble, then rated the best woman player in the world. The same year, 1936, he won the national boys' title. Two years later he captured the national interscholastic crown. Jones felt Kramer was good enough to take a crack at the national championship at Forest Hills.

It proved a misadventure, one of several that seemed destined to plague him throughout his career. Jack ate too many hot dogs, got an upset stomach and lost in the first round. Nevertheless, he attracted the attention of the Davis Cup selectors and the next year was named to the U.S. squad.

At 18, the youngest man ever to play in the Challenge Round, Kramer teamed with Joe Hunt in the doubles against Australia's veteran Adrian Quist and John Bromwich at the Merion Cricket Club. The youngsters lost as did Bobby Riggs and Frank Parker in singles, allowing the Cup to go Down Under where it remained for the duration of World War II.

Kramer teamed with Ted Schroeder to capture the national men's doubles crown in 1940 and again in 1941 and with Sarah Palfrey Cooke for the mixed doubles title in the latter year. Ailments thwarted his early bids in singles.

In 1942, having won 10 straight tournaments, he was stricken with appendicitis on the eve of the National Championships. In 1943, he gained the finals but, weakened by an attack of ptomaine poisoning, lost to his friend, Joe Hunt.

Kramer entered military service as a member of the U.S. Coast Guard and made five landings during the Pacific phase of World War II. He was mustered out a lieutenant in January, 1946. His tennis fortunes skyrocketed.

He swept to the first of his two U.S. singles titles in September and three months later joined Schroeder in crushing the Australians, 5-0, to return the Davis Cup to America. At Wimbledon in 1947, with King George watching from the Royal Box, he wiped out his old rival, Tom Brown, in 45 minutes for one of the shortest finals in history.

Then his ears began buzzing with the clang of cash registers. He turned professional, defeating Bobby Riggs, 69 matches to 20, in their cross-country tour. Boyishly good-looking, he was a natural gate attraction. Riggs took over as promoter of the tour shortly afterward and matched Kramer with a new court standout, Pancho Gonzales, whom Kramer smothered 96-27.

In 1952, entering his 30s and bothered by a bad back, Jack decided to become the entrepreneur instead of the star of the show. He bought the tour from Riggs and vaulted into the position of the world's No. 1 tennis promoter.

He could destroy a nation's Davis Cup team with the stroke of a pen—and he often did as he signed players to pro contracts. He tossed $100,000 contracts around the way some people did quarter tips.

This brought him into conflict with the establishment, but the game's hierarchy ultimately saw the light and embraced open tennis. They embraced "Big Jake" as well.

Kramer playing in a professional match in Madison Square Garden in 1953. Just about that time he bought the pro tour from Bobby Riggs and vaulted into the position of the world's No. 1 tennis promoter.

ROD LAVER

Tennis' First Millionaire

In 1938 when America's Don Budge was sweeping the Australian, French, Wimbledon and U.S. championships for an unprecedented tennis Grand Slam, a cattle rancher and his wife in remote Queensland, Australia, celebrated the birth of their third son. The boy, like Budge, had a shock of red hair. But who in his wildest fancies could imagine that the infant would grow up not only to match the American's role as the world's best player but also would duplicate the coveted Grand Slam?

The Aussie redhead, born Rodney George Laver, later nicknamed "The Rocket," not only repeated the sweep of the four biggest crowns in the game but did it twice, first as an amateur and later as a professional. That put him one up on Budge. Furthermore, many astute observers of the time, the 1960s, went so far as to hail him perhaps as the greatest tennis player who ever lived.

To look at him, one would not have thought it possible. Laver was a puny, skinny kid with a sunken chest, long nose and bandy legs. Even when he grew to maturity, playing before royalty, a king of his own court, he lacked the looks and the demeanor of a great sports champion. He stood five feet, eight inches and weighed less than 150 pounds—the antithesis of Budge, a robust six-footer.

He was shy and unassuming. Only when he took a racket in his left hand—a left forearm inches bigger around than his right and wrists of steel—did the Herculean image emerge.

He was no stylist. He was light and quick in movements, unleashing sudden bombardments of shots, heavy with spin, that neutralized his opponents. He didn't have a cannonball service but relied on a high-bounding drive that he could spin in the corners or down the line.

He was spectacularly aggressive, usually catching the ball on the rise and whacking it across the net for repeated winners. Perhaps no other player attacked as relentlessly or effectively. Against such rivals as Ken Rosewall and Pancho Gonzales, he never temporized. He grabbed the net advantage quickly and volleyed with a swordsman's fury. He turned tennis into a new game.

Young Laver emerged at a time when Australia, as big as the

Many astute tennis observers hailed Laver as the greatest player of all time. In this photo, taken in 1960, he is playing in a second round match at Wimbledon. A year later, he won the men's singles crown there for the first time.

United States in size but with a population only a little larger than New York, was at its zenith as a tennis power. From 1956 through 1971, Aussies won 13 of 16 Wimbledon men's singles titles and 12 American crowns while dominating the Davis Cup under a wily old captain named Harry Hopman, who personally took Laver under his wing.

The first time Hopman laid eyes on Laver, he blinked and remarked, "My, he's a little one. We're going to have to do something about that sunken chest." Actually, Rod's father, a tennis enthusiast, had more confidence in two older sons, Trevor and Bob. But Charlie Hollis, a coach in Laver's hometown of Rockhampton, favored Rod from the beginning.

"Trevor's got beautiful strokes," Hollis told the father. "They're better than Rodney's, but he's got an explosive temper like you. Rodney's like his mother, quiet and determined. He'll make it."

Rod began playing at age 10, using his mother's racket, on the family's lighted court in the backyard. He hung around Hollis' tennis shop, stringing rackets, and absorbing the coach's wisdom.

When Laver was 18, Hopman took time off from his other duties to chaperone Rod and another promising junior, Bob Mark, on a five months world tour, financed by Australian millionaire Arthur Drysdale. At 19, Laver was named a sixth member of the Davis Cup team.

Americans first became aware of Laver's potential in 1960 when, at Forest Hills, he gained both the men's singles and doubles final in the U.S. Championships. He lost in the singles final to Neale Fraser.

The flashy lefthander won his first major crown—the Aus-

Laver captured four Wimbledon crowns, three Australian, two French, two U.S. plus Italian and German singles championships. He also won numerous titles in doubles and mixed doubles.

The unassuming Australian holds his Cup high after winning the 1969 U.S. Open men's singles by defeating countryman Tony Roche, 7-9, 6-1, 6-2, 6-2.

tralian—in 1960. He won Wimbledon in 1961 but lost in the finals of the Australian and U.S. championships. They served as tuneups for his Grand Slam years.

Laver began his 1962 campaign by beating a fellow Queenslander and chief rival, Roy Emerson, in the Australian final. The two crossed rackets again in Paris, Rod winning a five-setter for the second leg of his Slam. At Wimbledon, seeded No. 1 and nervous, he fell behind Spain's Manuel Santana 9-11, 1-5 in the quarter-finals but survived and beat fellow Aussie Marty Mulligan for the title. Only the U.S. remained.

Laver recalled that Budge called him aside prior to the Forest Hills tournament and advised, "Play the game the way you can, don't worry about the Slam."

"It made me more nervous," Laver said, but he persevered,

beating Emerson for the second Grand Slam ever achieved in tennis.

Rod turned professional in 1963, signing a $100,000 contract for three years of one-night stands. He started shakily, losing his Australian debuts to Lew Hoad and Ken Rosewall. But in 1966 and 1967 he compiled the best won-lost record on the pro tour and reestablished himself as the game's undisputed No. 1, solidified when he repeated his Grand Slam in 1969 as a pro, a year after the game had gone open.

His trophy cache included four Wimbledon crowns, three Australian, two French, two U.S. plus Italian, and German singles championships and numerous titles in doubles and mixed doubles.

He retired to California as tennis' first millionaire.

156

SUZANNE LENGLEN

France's Phenomenon

It is hard to visualize Suzanne Lenglen, the graceful, floating court vision of the 1920s in her high silk stockings and calf-length skirts, trying to match her delicate strokes against the riveting serve and volley power of Billie Jean King or Martina Navratilova.

Yet in a poll in the early 1980s, with the aggressively over-powering styles of the modern players fresh in their minds, the world's tennis writers and commentators voted the talented but tormented French mademoiselle the greatest woman tennis player of all-time.

Certainly no other court figure in history exerted such influence on her times. For more than a decade she was the darling of the sports world. Thousands packed arenas just for the privilege of seeing her strike a ball. She was a Wimbledon favorite. She was fawned over by royalty. Her exploits were front page news on every continent.

She was a complex and tragic figure. Pushed by doting parents, she gave the impression of being a prima donna. She demanded limousines for transportation when other players rode trains. She had her costumes made by top designers who fought for the privilege of dressing her without charge. She often sulked and sometimes petulantly pulled out of a match, disappointing huge crowds.

Yet on the court, while the epitome of grace and style, she was a relentless killer. Tense and high-strung, she resented every point scored against her, never giving an inch.

Born in 1899, Suzanne grew up in Nice, daughter of humble and provincial parents who early saw her tennis potential and were determined to mold her into a world tennis champion.

Small and sallow-complexioned as a girl, she was forced to practice hours upon hours on hard courts. She was denied a normal childhood.

Literally she became so precisioned in her shot-making that she could put the ball on a dime. Her father would place a coin—a franc, presumably—on the court and have Suzanne practice hitting it. She became so adept that she sometimes hit five in a row.

Mama and Papa Lenglen were never satisfied. They stood on the sidelines, constantly yelling criticism.

"Stupid girl! Keep your eye on the ball!"

"Move, move, move!"

Certainly this stern discipline paid dividends, yet it ultimately had a devastating effect on her health and psyche. She didn't live a happy life. She was plagued by chronic illnesses and died prematurely at age 39 of pernicious anemia. But she left an indelible mark.

She won the ladies' singles title in the first Wimbledon in which she played at age 20 in 1919 and went on to capture six Wimbledon and six French championships in the space of seven

In a poll taken in the early 1980s, the world's tennis writers and commentators voted Lenglen the greatest woman tennis player of all time.

years as well as 13 doubles and mixed doubles crowns. She captivated Europe but shunned America.

Recurring ailments and bitter experiences spoiled Suzanne's first voyage to the United States in 1921 and the venture, a source of conflict between her parents, discouraged the French star and her family from challenging America's champions on U.S. turf. This provoked scathing criticism by the American press.

Suzanne's popularity in Britain and Europe, however, mushroomed. Fans loved her—her artistry of movement and racket control, her fiery temperament and her risque attire—the low-cut dresses, sleeveless blouses and shocking calf-length skirts that revolutionized women's court styles.

She had beaten Molla Mallory, the veteran American champion, easily in the French Hard Court Championships in the spring of 1921. This brought an outcry for Suzanne to come to America and face Molla on the latter's turf.

After considerable family debate, the Lenglens accepted a plan for a series of charity matches between Lenglen and Mallory in America with a stopover at Forest Hills. But the frail Suzanne became ill on her first ocean voyage, defaulted to Mallory in the second round of the U.S. Championships after a coughing spasm and five days later cancelled the charity tour on doctor's orders.

The American press intensified its criticism but was unable to shake the French woman's popularity and prestige.

In 1923, America's Mallory, having won the seventh of her eight U.S. titles the year before, sailed confidently to England to settle the issue of No. 1 on Wimbledon's Center Court. Meeting in the final, Lenglen swept to a 6-2, 6-0 victory. Later in Nice, Suzanne scored a devastating 6-0, 6-0 victory over the U.S. champion while losing a total of only 18 points.

By this time a new figure was surfacing on the American scene—a stoical, racket-swinging machine in a sailor blouse, white-pleated skirt and green-lined eyeshade named Helen Wills, christened by the American press as "Little Miss Poker Face."

Succeeding Molla Mallory as ladies' champion in 1923, the first of her seven U.S. titles, this unflappable Californian began a long chase of the French phenomenon. But their paths didn't cross. When Helen played at Wimbledon, Suzanne was out with another illness. Suzanne refused to cross the Atlantic again.

Frustrated, Helen issued a statement that she would play Lenglen anywhere at any time. After long negotiations, it was arranged that the two would meet at the Carlton Club in Cannes, France in February, 1926.

Special grandstands were built to accommodate 3,000 spectators. People poured into the French Riviera from all over the world. Lenglen won 6-3, 8-6, the only match between two of the game's most magnetic personalities.

Lenglen and Henri Cochet, another French great, give a demonstration of their talents at the Salon of Beauty court in Paris on June 27, 1936.

SUGAR RAY LEONARD

How Sweet It Was

Sugar Ray Leonard's name can now be mentioned in the same breath with Sugar Ray Robinson's without choking on a single syllable.

Leonard won that intangible but not invisible honor with his slashing, stabbing and sidestepping 12-round victory over the seemingly invincible Marvin Hagler on April 6, 1987, in Las Vegas. Ray erased all doubt that he could not handle a bald bomber like Hagler, the one-time undisputed middleweight king before the boxing bureaucrats left him with only the WBC crown, which Leonard took from him.

It also gave Leonard almost equivalent stature with the silken Robinson, usually rated by most boxing people as the greatest in history on a pound-for-pound basis. Both Sugar Rays won both the welterweight and middleweight championships, two of the toughest crowns to capture. Both fought with stylish textbook technique, speed, a head-snapping jab, crushing combinations and those twin trademarks of the champion, brains and heart.

Leonard, bright, personable and with a sizable ego, has tasted all the great moments boxing has to offer. The first was his Olympic gold medal in the light-welterweight class in Montreal in 1976. Ray was not the household name he was destined to become later. A slim 80-pound girl named Nadia Comaneci stole the show and the hearts of the world with her dazzling display of gymnastics.

Three years later, on Nov. 30, 1979, Ray saw his name in headlines after he took the WBC welterweight title by knocking out Wilfred Benitez in the 15th round. That started the ballyhoo bongos going for a showdown between Leonard and Roberto Duran, the Panamanian billed as having fists of stone and a chin to match. In June of 1980 Roberto scored a controversial 15-round victory over Ray.

Ray seethed over his first professional loss and five months later got his chance to regain the crown. In what was virtually a "Bloodless Battle of New Orleans" he posted an eighth-round knockout over Duran, who made some kind of inept ring history by quitting with the classic line, "No Mas." Translation: No more. For that one night, at least, Leonard destroyed Duran's will to fight.

Ray felt like a king of the ring and was. But even kings have

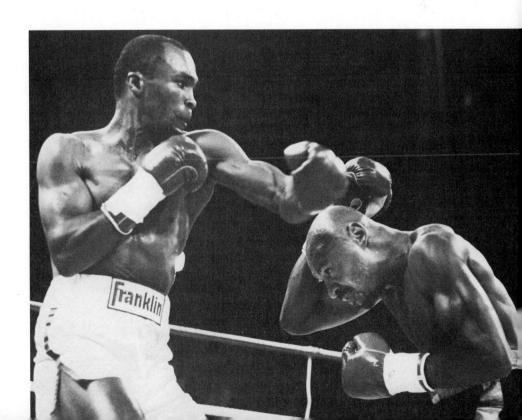

Slashing, stabbing and sidestepping, Leonard scored an upset triumph over the seemingly invincible Marvin Hagler on April 6, 1987 and wrested the WBC middleweight title from the Brockton, Mass. fighter.

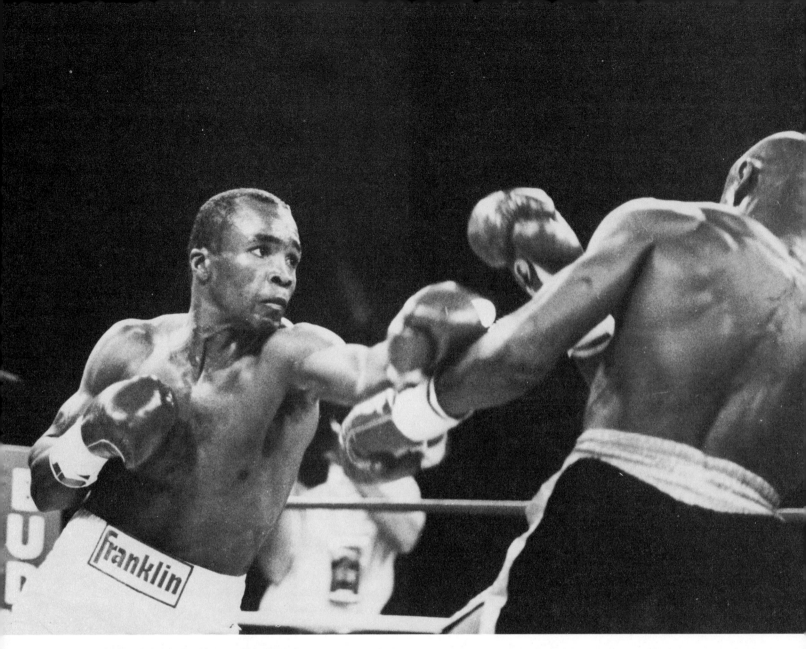

Sugar Ray goes on the attack against Marvelous Marvin in the opening round of their April 6, 1987 championship match. Leonard, a 3-1 underdog, won on a split decision.

problems. Some were lying in ambush. In the summer of 1981, while training for the Thomas Hearns bout designed to crown an undisputed welter champ, Ray was accidentally elbowed in the left eye by a sparmate. It hurt but he shook it off and continued working out. But the seed of later trouble had been planted. He had warmed up for Hearns with a 10-round knockout of Larry Bond in a WBC title defense and had taken the WBA junior-middleweight crown by stopping Ayub Kalule in nine.

The Hearns bout on Sept. 16, 1981, was a classic...Ray's science versus Hearns' slug, slug, slug. The scientist prevailed. Ray was too quick and slick and despite Hearns' jawbreaking power,

Ray wore him out and sent the "Hit Man" to dreamland in the 14th round.

Early in 1982, Leonard knocked out Bruce Finch in three rounds in a title defense. But a short time later, he made the chilling discovery that vision in his left eye was blurred. He had surgery for a partially detached retina. Then, after much soul-searching and at the wish of his wife, Juanita, Ray announced his retirement in November.

He sat out all of 1983, living the good life with Juanita and their two sons, and began a second career as a television boxing color commentator. But Ray became a haunted man. Haunted by a brutal middleweight, Marvin Hagler, considered unbeatable.

Ray didn't think so. He began to dream of a fight with Hagler which would not only bring big money but would settle the question of which man was number one. He launched a comeback in 1984 and, while training, encountered a problem with his right eye. That brought on preventive surgery to guard against another detached retina.

He went through a bout with a virtual unknown named Kevin Howard on May 11, 1984, and for the first time looked bad. Howard actually put Ray on the floor. Ray got up and finished off Howard in the ninth round. Ring cynics shook their heads. The Sugar Man had gone sour.

Ray did not fight in either 1985 or 1986. There were his eyes to think about. He was enjoying life with his family. He was working as a TV commentator. But there was always Hagler, leaping from headline to headline with his powerful punch and relentless fury. Time and again Leonard said to co-workers or friends: "I can beat him." Few people believed him.

Leonard began to train. Toward the end of 1986 he signed for a multi-million dollar fight with Hagler on the 6th of April in

1987. Ray's training tempo quickened. He had a lot of ring rust to shake. Observers thought at times he looked like the swift sharpshooter of old. Others thought he had slowed. Theories were advanced that by building himself close to the middle-weight limit of 160 pounds from 147, he had sacrificed speed for poundage.

Ray had medical clearance from his eye specialists but prophets of doom were heard to say—and write—that he was gambling his sight for money—a guarantee of $11 million—and ego, the desire to prove he was the best there was.

Hagler, who had not lost a fight in 11 years, was a pronounced favorite for the bout, about 3-1, man-to-man. Most ring handicappers thought Marv would win. Ray didn't. He proved he was right—the hard way—he whipped Hagler in the ring.

He made Hagler chase him but slowed Marv from time to time with blazing rallies. He taunted Marv, who lacks Leonard's nimble brain. The crowd kept cheering for "Sugar Ray," which delighted and encouraged Leonard and infuriated Hag-

Leonard, then undisputed world welterweight king, smashes the face of Thomas Hearns during their 1981 title bout in Las Vegas. Ray won on a technical knockout in the 14th round.

Sugar Ray, bright and personable, has tasted all the great moments boxing has to offer. The first was an Olympic gold medal in 1976. In 1979, he took the WBC welterweight crown by knocking out Wilfred Benitez. This photo was taken in June, 1980.

ler, who frequently looked like a bull charging a matador's cape. Ray was so pumped up that on several occasions the referee had to wave him back for leaving his corner before the bell.

Hagler, who had been guaranteed $12 million for the bout, had planned to pin Ray against the ropes and destroy him. But it was not to be. In the 12th and last round, backed against the ropes, Ray exploded with a dozen or more punches to escape.

It was a split decision. Judges JoJo Guerra and Dave Moretti scored it for Leonard. Judge Lou Fillippi had Hagler in front. One significant note: There were four rounds when all three men scored for Leonard and only one in which they agreed on Hagler.

The verdict over Hagler left Leonard with a career record of 34 victories and one loss.

JOHNNY LONGDEN

First Rider To Score 6,000 Victories

When the great Eddie Arcaro quit riding at the age of 46 after accumulating 4,779 winners in 31 years, Johnny Longden said: "Why quit so young? Once you get off horses, you're just a bowlegged little man walking around."

Longden was 59 and crippled with injuries after almost 40 years as a jockey when he decided to retire in 1966, ending the longest riding career in horse racing history with 6,032 winners.

Longden was small, even for a jockey, at 4-foot-10, but he had a strong upper body and powerful arms, a 15½ inch neck and a desire to win.

He guided Count Fleet to the 1943 Triple Crown with easy triumphs in the Kentucky Derby, Preakness and Belmont Stakes. By 1956, when he was 46, Longden broke the world record by riding his 4,871th winner. He became the first rider to post 6,000 victories and concluded his career in the spring of '66 by riding George Royal to a pulsating, upset win in the San Juan Capistrano Handicap at Santa Anita.

It was the final ride of Longden's career, but he didn't become "just a bowlegged little man walking around."

He turned to training horses, and saddled Majestic Prince, winner of the 1969 Kentucky Derby. Before Longden, no one had ever rode and trained a Kentucky Derby winner.

Few athletes reached Hall of Fame status after starting so slowly.

Longden was born in Wakefield, England in 1907, but was raised in the coal-mining towns of Alberta, Canada. He was 14 when he went to work in the mines as a "grease pig." He greased the coal cars that ran along the tracks in the tunnels for which he was paid $2.50 a day.

His last winner! On March 12, 1966 Longden, at age 59 and almost 40 years as a jockey, wound up his career by winning the feature race at Santa Anita aboard George Royal (10).

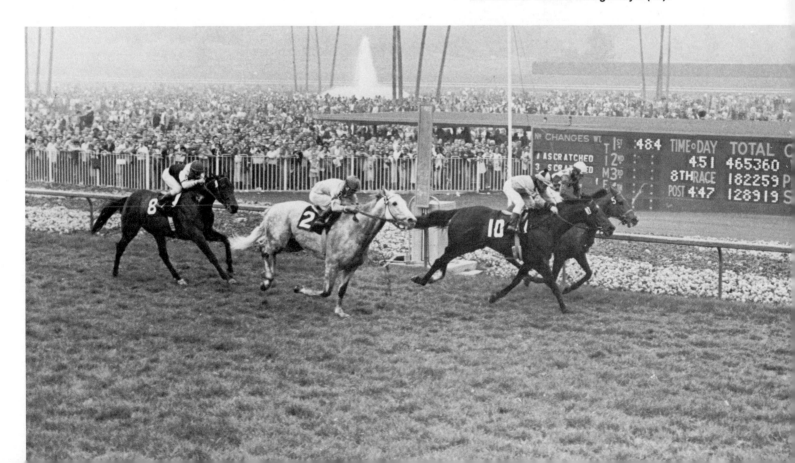

Longden rode 6,032 winners. He was small, even for a jockey, at 4-foot-10, but he had a strong upper body, powerful arms and a 15½-inch neck. He suffered numerous serious injuries.

"It just made me want to get out and do some good," Longden recalled. He tried many odd jobs.

He made money riding horses Roman style at county fairs—steering two horses by standing atop their backs, one leg on each horse. He was once traded for a broken-down horse during his early days as a rider in Calgary.

Longden eventually wound up in Salt Lake City in the fall of 1927 and rode his first official winner, a gelding named Hugo K. Asher. It was the only win for Longden in 16 rides that year.

He won 11 races in 1928, 26 in 1929 and finally gave indications of his potential by winning 72 in 1930 and 113 the following year.

Longden mastered the tricks of the trade—jabbing his whip into the sides of rival horses and bumping other horses off stride. He earned the nickname "The Pumper" for his ability to pump a horse down the stretch.

He led the nation in winners with 236 in 1938, with 316 in 1947 and with 319 in 1948. In 1943 and 1945, he was the leader in stakes money won.

Longden came under the strict discipline of trainer Sleepy Armstrong.

"I didn't know any of the horsemen and I couldn't get any mounts," Longden said. "Frankly, I didn't know anything about race riding and didn't even know my way around the track. Sleepy Armstrong taught me how to ride races, and he gave me my first chance."

Armstrong insisted that riders get the horses out of the gate as quickly as possible. Longden became a master of breaking fast at the start of the race. His pairing with Count Fleet was a match made in heaven.

Count Fleet reached the winner's circle 16 times in 1942 and 1943. The son of Reigh Count won the Derby by three lengths, the Preakness by eight lengths and the Belmont Stakes by 30— all in front-running fashion.

"I never saw a horse before, or since, that was his equal," Longden said. "We never really knew how fast he was."

Longden was involved in so many spills that he lost count. His right leg was broken five times. His backbone was fractured. One foot was partially crushed. His collarbone was broken twice. His ribs were broken or splintered six times. He suffered from rheumatoid arthritis in both hands and knees.

Longden's worst spill came at Arlington Downs in Texas during the brief time that racing was legal there. He was involved in a five-horse spill and was unconscious 13 days and paralyzed from the waist down for three months.

Longden's last day as a rider was announced far in advance at Santa Anita. The fans who used to boo him on the occasions he didn't bring home a winner were there to cheer him.

This was a Saturday and it troubled him when he saw Monday's entries didn't have his name listed alongside any horses.

He had four mounts on that final day. Chicalero, the favorite, won the fourth race with Longden aboard. Photographers busily snapped his picture in the winner's circle, anticipating that it would be his last win.

"I had the feeling that maybe, just maybe, Chicalero was not my last one," Longden said. He failed to win with his next two mounts, including finishing third with Gamin, a 42-1 shot, in the seventh race.

The average age of the eight other riders in the featured race was 29, less than half the years of Longden.

George Royal was 8-1 and the fifth choice in the field for the San Juan Capistrano, a 1¾-mile race.

George Royal, a come-from-behind runner, was dead last at the start and Longden gradually took him past horses. With Longden pumping, George Royal was second turning for home.

Soon he was nose and nose with Plaque, ridden by Bobby Ussery, through the stretch run.

It was difficult to tell which horse won. The stewards decided it was George Royal by a nose.

"Fantastic," Longden said. "Wasn't it fantastic?"

Longden rides to victory aboard St. Vincent in the Washington's Birthday Handicap at Santa Anita in 1957. He won by four and one-half lengths.

JOE LOUIS

The Destructive Brown Bomber

He was a shuffling, unschooled product of America's slave and ghetto conclaves, born in a sharecropper's shack in Alabama and thrust onto the assembly lines in teeming Detroit—a man people would least imagine could become one of the greatest heavyweight boxing champions of all time and help change the social conscience of a nation.

Joe Louis had all the credentials—a lithe, panther-like figure, 6 feet, 2 inches and 200 pounds, with fists of devastating power. But he was black and, when he emerged as a raw but exciting fighter in the mid-1930s, the country was not ready to accept a black man as its heavyweight king.

The Jim Crow laws were prevalent throughout the South, where Louis was born. Black people could not drink water from a public fountain, eat in the best restaurants or go to the main schools in town. They had to ride in the back of buses and say, "Yes, suh" to their white benefactors.

Black baseball players were barred from playing in the major leagues. Pro football was lily white. The colleges had not yet learned to capitalize on the speed and agility of these young off-springs of slaves imported from Africa. Blacks could carry the clubs but couldn't play in the pro golf tournaments. The all-white rule in tennis also applied to the people wearing the attire. A black jockey hadn't had a mount in the Kentucky Derby since the early part of the century.

There hadn't been a black heavyweight contender since Jack Johnson, who hammered his way to the title just after the turn of the century, then offended the public with his arrogance and flaunting of white women.

Louis was different. Born Joe Louis Barrow on May 13, 1914, son of a sharecropper and the seventh of eight children, he was 12 when his family moved to Detroit, where he dropped out of school to take a job in a Ford plant. He boxed as an amateur, winning AAU and Golden Gloves titles while dropping the name "Barrow."

Although shy, he attracted the eyes of the pros and fell into the hands of two affluent black men connected with the rackets, Julian Black and John Roxborough. They immediately began fashioning him to fit society's mold.

Joe Louis walks away, revenged for his defeat of two years before, at the hands of Nazi Germany's Max Schmeling, the man prone in the ring. Schmeling's handlers threw in the towel after 2 minutes, 4 seconds of the first round. The referee is Arthur Donovan. The date: June 22, 1938.

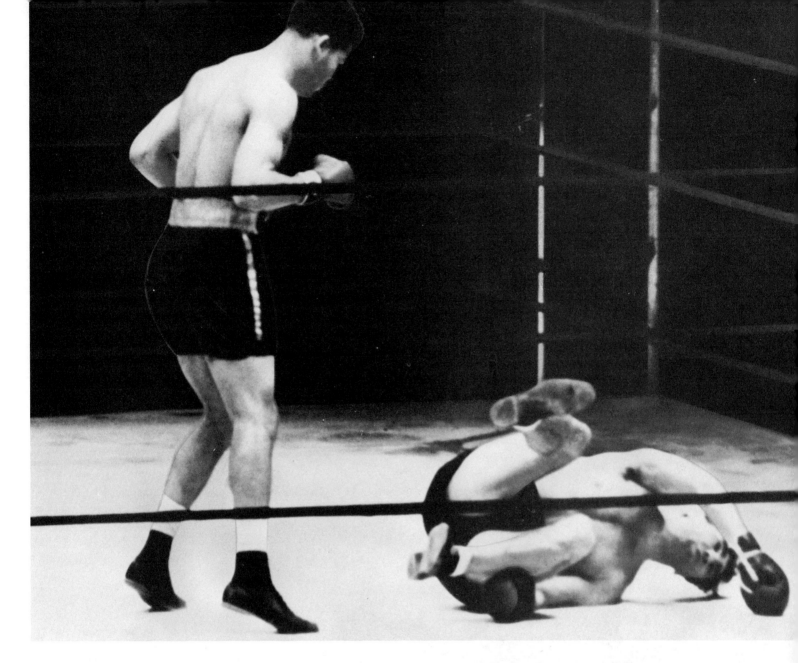

"After you beat a white opponent, don't smile," they said.

"Never have your picture taken with a white woman."

In his 17 years as a professional, 12 as the heavyweight champion, Louis posted a 68-3 record with 54 knockouts.

Louis' two most dramatic fights were against a beetle-browed German named Max Schmeling. Hitler was just beginning to make waves with his military aggressiveness and Nazi philosophy. Louis was 22, a threat to one of sports' proudest titles. Ironically, the first fight, June 19, 1936, was more black vs. white than Uncle Sam vs. Nazism.

Louis was heavily favored, but he was inadequately prepared and overconfident. He built an early lead, but Schmeling surprised him with a right to the jaw in the fourth round that sent him to the canvas. Dazed, Louis rose and hung on until the 12th round when he was dropped again and counted out.

In many places, the South mainly, people danced in the streets. Women named new-born babies for the German victor. "What we thought was tremendous calm" one columnist wrote of Louis, "was nothing more than lack of fire and spirit."

Louis was shamed by the defeat. But he resumed his quest for the heavyweight crown and gained it by knocking out 35-year-old Jim Braddock in the eighth round in Chicago's Comiskey Park on June 27, 1937. "I won't be happy 'til I get that Schmelin'," he told his handlers.

The opportunity came June 22, 1938, by which time Hitler was spouting Aryan supremacy and threatening to conquer the world. Seventy thousand fans crammed Yankee Stadium in New York. When the bell rang, the seething Louis leaped out like a raging bull, fists flying. Two minutes and four seconds later, Schmeling lay on the canvas in a battered, bleeding heap.

above:

Billy Conn goes down and out as champion Joe Louis follows through with a haymaker in the eighth round of their return championship match in 1946. Five years earlier, Conn was leading Louis on points before being knocked out in the 13th round.

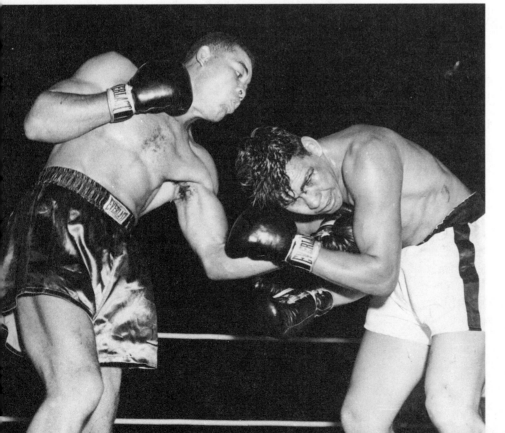

left:

Embarking on a comeback, Louis outpoints Argentina's Cesar Brion in San Francisco on Aug. 2, 1951. Here, Joe lands a left to Brion's ribs in the third round of their 10-round fight.

The American nation celebrated wildly. The black warrior from Alabama had crushed the Nazi monster. Blacks throughout the country found in their hero a new pride and hope which might some day lead them out of their wilderness.

Boxing writers reached for new hyperbole and clichés. Joe Louis: the "Brown Bomber," "Dark Destroyer," "Sepia Slasher."

He lived up to all of his nicknames. A classic, stand-up fighter with a left jab that shot out like a cobra's tongue, he stalked his foes like a jungle cat, backed them into a corner of the ring after which he unleashed a series of short, jolting blows. Then he would step back nonchalantly and watch his victim fall.

It happened often. Of the three opponents who were able to go the distance with him after he became champion—Tommy Farr, Arturo Godoy and Jersey Joe Walcott—Godoy and Walcott were stopped in rematches. Walcott and Billy Conn gave the champ the most trouble but Conn, who led for 12 rounds in 1941 before being knocked out, was kayoed in eight in a rematch after World War II.

The Brown Bomber volunteered and spent almost four years' service in the Army during the war. A gentle, easy-going man, he further endeared himself to the American public by risking his title in a Navy Relief bout against Buddy Baer in 1942, sacrificing money he badly needed to offset the back tax pressures of the IRS.

Louis reportedly earned $5 million during his career and squandered it all on golf course wagering and alimony to former wives. He twice married and divorced his first wife, Marva Trotter, followed with Rose Morgan and finally Martha Malone, a Los Angeles attorney who mothered his adopted children and nursed him in his final days as a public relations representative for Caesars Palace in Las Vegas.

He died of a massive heart attack April 11, 1981.

The comeback is over! A washed-up Louis winces from a right to the head delivered by Rocky Marciano during the fifth round of their Madison Square Garden bout on Oct. 26, 1951. Joe lost by a TKO in 2:36 of the eighth round.

MICKEY MANTLE

The Most Powerful Switch-Hitter

The New York Yankees realized early that to maintain the tradition of "The House That Ruth Built," it was necessary that Yankee Stadium should always try to have a Ruthian personality—a ballplayer who could hit with power and fire the imagination of the fans.

They found such a commodity in Joe DiMaggio, who moved into Babe Ruth's void in 1936 and kept the Bronx baseball tem- ple rocking for more than a dozen years with a potent bat and a quiet dignity that turned him into an idol. But, entering the second half of the century, the son of an immigrant Italian fish-

Mantle hits his 49th home run of the 1961 season in the first inning against Detroit. The blow came with Roger Maris on base. Mickey wound up the campaign with 54 homers while Maris smashed a record-breaking 61.

erman began showing signs of wear and there was concern who could step into his shoes.

The answer lay in a sleepy, little town in the northeastern corner of Oklahoma—known as "Indian country"—where a doting father was carefully fashioning a son for baseball stardom. Elvin "Mutt" Mantle named his eldest son "Mickey" after one of his baseball heroes, Mickey Cochrane of the Detroit Tigers. He put a baseball in the infant's crib and, by the time the youngster was two, had him in the backyard swinging a bat from both sides of the plate.

Born in Spavinaw and reared in Commerce, Oklahoma, Mickey Mantle pulled on his Yankee pinstripes for the first time in 1951, a raw-boned kid of 19, just out of high school, blond, physically attractive, with switch-hitting power and amazing speed. He had arrived, not unknown but in the wake of a tremendous buildup campaign, as a possible successor to Ruth and DiMaggio.

He had been given rave notices by Scout Tom Greenwade,

who had first seen him in an Oklahoma sandlot game and couldn't wait to get his name on a contract ($1,100 bonus).

"He's got it in his body to be great," rasped Manager Casey Stengel, the first time he saw Mickey at bat.

"When he went to the batting cage and started hitting home runs lefthanded and righthanded, players would just stop and watch and the crowd would go wild," said Ralph Houk, another Yankee manager.

Mantle wasn't all that resounding a success off the field. He was basically shy. Because of his rural background, he seemed awed and inhibited by the pressures and the bright lights of the big time. Fans didn't take to him immediately and, stand-offish and quick-tempered, he alienated the press.

This situation soon improved as Mantle matured and began

Teammate Yogi Berra congratulates Mantle as he crosses home plate after hitting a 565-foot home run, the longest ever in Washington's old Griffith Stadium. The blast, on April 17, 1953, came off Chuck Stobbs with Mickey batting righthanded.

hitting baseballs over the fences at tape-measure distances. He became a hero. In the dramatic chase for Babe Ruth's record of 60 home runs in a season in 1961, most fans pulled for Mantle over his teammate, Roger Maris, who subsequently broke the mark with 61 while Mickey hit 54.

Mickey, although plagued by a childhood bone disease (osteomyelitis) and fragile knees compounded by a fall in the 1951 World Series, became the greatest switch-hitter in baseball history. He hit 536 home runs—373 lefthanded, 163 right-handed—a record 18 in the World Series, more than Ruth or Yogi Berra, including a grand slammer in the 1953 Series. He hit 266 home runs in the Stadium.

He was three times the Most Valuable Player in the American League. He played in 20 All-Star games, in all in which he was eligible, and competed in 12 World Series. Besides his 18

home runs in the Series, he scored 42 runs, had 40 runs batted in, 40 walks and 123 total bases.

Five feet, 10 inches tall, Mantle was a lean 170-pounder when he came to the Yankees after a year with the Class C Independence, Kansas, club and another with the Class D Joplin, Missouri, team where he batted .383. But he filled out to a solid 200 pounds, all muscle and speed.

He was a natural home run hitter but one of harnessed power rather than the seemingly effortless swing and lazy arc that marked Babe Ruth's style. As a lefthanded hitter, Mickey feasted on low pitches while as a righthander he hit waist-high rockets into the stands or out of the park. Although he began his pro career as a shortstop, he became an excellent centerfielder, covering Yankee Stadium's cavernous "Death Valley," making dramatic running catches, rarely committing an error and utilizing a strong throwing arm. The baseball fraternity still buzzes with talk about the catch of a Gil Hodges drive which he made in the 1956 World Series against the Dodgers that saved Don Larsen's perfect game.

He was the fastest man in baseball until leg injuries began taking their toll. He was clocked at 3.1 seconds getting down to first base. He was one of the most successful drag bunters in the game.

The respect opposing pitchers had for Mantle's prowess is reflected in the number of walks he received—1,734. He led the league in walks five times. In 1957, with 173 hits and 146 walks, he was on base more than 50 per cent of the time.

While his 536 home runs place him among baseball's Top Ten in that category, Mickey was renowned less for the number of his homers than for their distance. No one in the game ever hit as many balls so far. He originated the "tape measure homer."

Two especially should have been marked for The Guinness Book of Records. In Washington's old Griffith Stadium in 1953, batting righthanded, he hit a shot which soared over the stands and caromed off a billboard in centerfield. It was measured at 565 feet. Some 10 years later, batting lefthanded, Mickey almost put one out of Yankee Stadium—a feat never achieved—by bouncing a shot off the facade in right field.

Mantle's greatest year probably was 1956 when he won the Triple Crown, beating out Ted Williams with a batting average of .353, blasting 52 homers and knocking in 130 runs.

Mantle's number "7" was retired in 1965 and he was inducted into baseball's Hall of Fame with buddy Whitey Ford in 1974.

Al Kaline of the Detroit Tigers, a Hall of Famer himself, once was chided by a youngster who told him, "You're not half as good as Mickey Mantle," to which Kaline replied:

"Son, nobody is half as good as Mickey Mantle."

The Yankee slugger connects for his 500th career home run on May 15, 1967 in Yankee Stadium. The victim was Baltimore reliever Stu Miller and the homer proved decisive in a 6-5 Yankee victory.

ROCKY MARCIANO

The Brockton Blockbuster

Down through the years one of the most hotly contested arguments is that involving heavyweight boxing champions. Who was the greatest of them all—the swarming Dempsey, the Dark Destroyer, Joe Louis; rugged Rocky Marciano or the float-like-a-butterfly-sting-like-a-bee kid, Muhammad Ali?

It is a debate without ending because there is no way to bring the eras together. Or is there? An ingenious entrepreneur of the 1960s sought to solve the problem through modern science. The records, styles and techniques of the great champions were fed into a computer for an imaginary film series and the intricate machine produced the two finalists, Ali and Marciano, with Marciano winning by a knockout in the 13th round.

A lot of hardened, experienced fight observers would not argue with the result. The "Brockton Blockbuster," as the stumpy New England pulverizer was called, left a brief but imposing legacy that brooks little dispute.

Marciano knocked out an aging Joe Louis to set up a title victory over tough Jersey Joe Walcott in 1952 at age 28, defended the crown six times and retired in the spring of 1956 while at the peak of his career. As a professional he won 49 straight fights, 43 by knockout, never lost and was knocked off his feet only twice—once by Walcott and later in his career by Archie Moore. Both indignities were properly avenged by knockouts. Of his title defenses, only Ezzard Charles managed to last 15 rounds but fell in a return bout.

Marciano was hardly the Hollywood version of a boxing hero. At 5 feet, 11 inches in height and 185 pounds, he was one of the lightest and shortest of all heavyweight champions and his reach was the shortest, only 68 inches.

Normally this would be a distinct handicap in a sport where arm length holds such importance as both an offensive and defensive weapon. Yet it didn't bother Rocky, a swarming, brawling gladiator willing to take half a dozen punches to deliver one.

Heavyweight champ Rocky Marciano lands a hard right to the mouth of challenger Ezzard Charles in their return fight on Sept. 17, 1954. Rocky, who had outpointed Ezzard in 15 rounds three months earlier, knocked him out in the eighth round this time.

Marshall Smith, writing in Life Magazine in 1952, marvelled at Rocky's calm, relaxed composure before big fights, remarking that he was "nervous as a fire hydrant."

He also cited what other fight journalists learned at the time, writing, "Marciano is a real live edition of the comic strip character, Joe Palooka—unassuming, clean living, a humble guy with a heart of gold who uses his God-given strength to slay ogres and flatten city slickers."

There was an unusual, contradictory skein in Rocky's character that mixed compassion with brutality, turning him into a bull with a marshmallow heart. Every time he knocked out an opponent he felt so sorry he wanted to apologize.

"When he defeated me, I think it hurt him more than it did me," said Joe Louis after Marciano sent him into permanent retirement with an eighth round knockout October 26, 1951. Walcott said, "He was a man of courage inside the ring. Outside, he was kind and gentle."

Rocky was born Sept. 1, 1923 in a white clapboard house on the unfashionable west side of Brockton, Massachusetts, the oldest of seven children of an immigrant Italian couple named Marchegiano. Papa worked in a shoe factory. Mamma was a

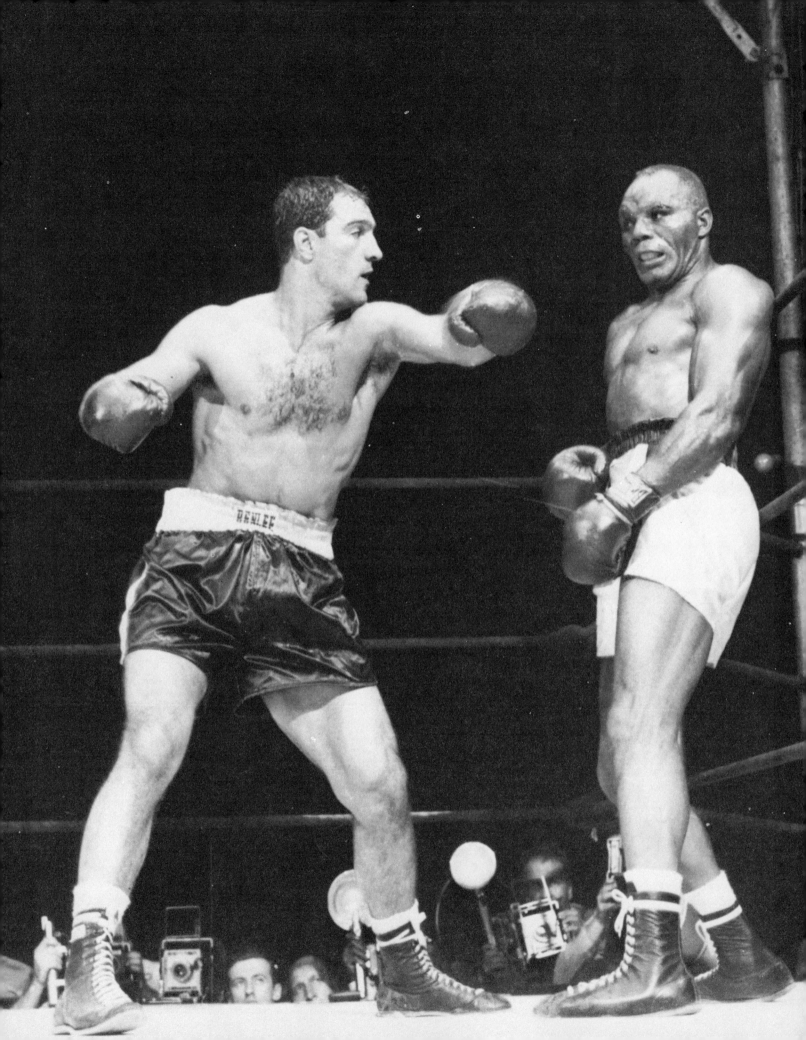

opposite:

Marciano swings, but does not land as Walcott is backed against the ropes in the early going of their Sept. 23, 1952 championship match. This one was one of the most dramatic and exciting bouts in ring history. A 13th round knockout won the crown for the Brockton Blockbuster.

A badly mutilated aircraft lies in a dry creek bed in Newton, Iowa after carrying former heavyweight titleholder Rocky Marciano and two others to their deaths on Aug. 31, 1969.

robust woman, weighing 195 pounds. The boy was christened Rocco Francis. The last name later was changed to Marciano.

At two years of age, little Rocco almost died of pneumonia. It was the strong will of his mother that pulled him through. When Rocco came home from elementary school one day, crying after being beaten up by a bigger kid, an uncle built a punching bag in the backyard. Soon kids left Rocco alone. He had to quit school at 15 to help pay family expenses.

Since his home faced a local playground, Marciano became adept at both football and baseball. He preferred baseball and once even tried out as a catcher for the Chicago Cubs. While he could hit well, he didn't have a good throwing arm. So he concentrated on boxing.

This was a pastime he took up as a private in the army at Fort Lewis, Washington, to escape ditch-digging and KP duty. Upon leaving the service in 1946, Rocco—now Rocky—worked on a construction gang and fought amateur bouts in Brockton,

Mary Ann, the 16-year-old daughter of former champion Rocky Marciano, places a portrait of her father on top of his casket on Sept. 5, 1969, five days after he was killed in a plane crash.

Boston, Lowell and other close-by areas. It was in 1948 that he was ushered into the office of Al Weill, a longtime New York fight promoter and manager. Weill, skeptical of Rocky's awkwardness, needed to see only one punch to sign him up. It was a merger made in heaven.

Marciano began his pro career on March 17, 1947, and ran up a string of 15 consecutive knockouts, nine of them in the first round, before facing a genuine contender. He beat the previously undefeated Roland LaStarza, in New York's Madison Square Garden March 24, 1950. He followed with 10 more victories, highlighted by a sixth-round knockout of Seattle's "Bully Boy," Rex Layne.

He continued to impress ringsiders with the fury and decisiveness of his whirlwind attack, crushing Harry (Kid) Matthews in two rounds to earn a crack at the heavyweight title. The bout with the 38-year-old Walcott was staged in Philadelphia September 23, 1952.

The tough Walcott floored Marciano in the first round but Rocky leaped up at the count of four and it was a bruising, bloody slugfest until he caught the champion on the jaw with a right and knocked him out in 43 seconds of the 13th round.

After six title defenses and career earnings of $1.7 million, the Brockton Blockbuster announced his retirement April 27, 1956 at age 33, saying he wished to spend more time with his family—wife Barbara, a hometown sweetheart, and daughter. A son was born later.

Marciano engaged in several business enterprises and was active in civic work. In 1969, flying home to celebrate his 36th birthday with his family, he died in the crash of a private plane.

BOB MATHIAS

The Decathlon's Schoolboy Phenom

He could have been the model for those soft-cover Frank Merriwell books that our fathers and grandfathers read with such relish as kids—the genuine American hero; young, handsome, talented, too good to be true.

Robert Bruce Mathias of Tulare, Calif., was all of those things and no star in the galaxy appeared too distant for his reach. He was a football star at Stanford University, all-around track athlete, winner of the demanding Olympic decathlon at age 19, repeater four years later, two and a half years in the Marine Corps, motion picture and TV celebrity, finally U.S. Congress-

High schooler Bob Mathias of Tulare, Calif. hurled the discus 144 feet, 4 inches enroute to capturing the decathlon gold medal during the 1948 London Olympic Games.

man and whisperings in the back rooms: Presidential material? Maybe. Certainly he had all the ingredients.

Then came Watergate.

President Richard Nixon, caught up in a web of White House political shenanigans and found guilty of a cover-up, was forced out of office. Many Republicans—including Mathias—went down the drain with him.

"I was not personally involved," Mathias said later. "But I was a Republican and, like Mr. Nixon, was from California. They remandered my district. As a result of the scandal, there was great apathy among Republicans. They didn't turn out for anybody."

Mathias' political balloon burst, but nothing could destroy the impact the young Californian made in winning consecu-tive Olympic gold medals for the decathlon in 1948 and 1952 in the toughest, most rigorous event in the Games.

When Mathias returned home from Helsinki in 1952, he got a reception matched only by that tendered the great Jesse Owens in 1936. Track historians hailed his feat as comparable to the all-around brilliance of Jim Thorpe. Mathias was named The Associated Press' "Male Athlete of the Year" in 1952.

The decathlon is the most gruelling of all Olympic sports and, in the minds of most observers, is the barometer for choosing the world's greatest all-around athlete. It consists of four running events—the 100, 400 and 1,500 meters plus the 110-meter hurdles and six field contests—the javelin, discus, shot put, pole vault, broad jump and high jump.

It is the Olympics' ultimate test of speed, strength, special-

Mathias, shown here putting the shot, soared to a world record score of 7,887 points as he won the decathlon event for the second straight time at the 1952 Olympics in Helsinki, Finland.

An all-around track athlete, a football star at Stanford, a Marine, a motion picture and TV celebrity, Mathias also served as a Congressman for eight years. This photo was taken in 1982.

ized skills and endurance. Endurance is a major factor because the competition covers two days, starting early with eliminations and finishing usually under the arc lights late in the evening of the final day.

At the London Olympics in 1948, scant attention was given to the tall, lean, 19-year-old kid from California. These were the first Games since 1936 because of the intervention of World War II and, while there had been few opportunities for comparison, Mathias was going against older, more experienced athletes.

While he had scored consistently well on the first day, Mathias said the crucial test came with the high jump on the second day. "The bar was put at 5 feet, 10 inches. I missed my first two tries. I knew if I didn't make it on the third jump I might be eliminated.

"Then I heard a big cheer go up from the stands, 'Come on, Tulare!' I looked over there and saw a big group from back home. I got so inspired I made it."

When time came for the 1,500 meter run, the climactic event of the 10-sport grind, darkness had spread over the stadium and most of the spectators had gone home. The stadium had no lights and officials had to use flashlights to illuminate the track.

"It was eerie," Mathias said. "When I finished, I was dead tired and went over and flopped on the infield. When friends came up to me and said, 'Bob, you won!', I couldn't appreciate it. All I could think of was a nice, hot bath."

Mathias captured the decathlon gold medal with a score of 7,139. London newspapers, as well as those back in the United States, heralded the feat as the feature of the Games. He became the "Schoolboy Phenom."

Four years later, now 6 feet, 3 inches tall and 200 pounds, Mathias soared to a new world record score of 7,887. Again he came home to a hero's welcome, besieged by promoters seeking to capitalize on his fame and sex appeal.

Mathias had been a fullback on Stanford's football team, once returning a kick 94 yards for a touchdown against Southern California and playing against Illinois in the Rose Bowl. But he quit college after two years, charging football was too much business and no longer a sport. He was drafted by the Washington Redskins but chose instead to join the Marine Corps.

He starred in five movies, including his film biography "The Bob Mathias Story" and a movie on the revival of the Modern Olympic Games called "It Happened in Athens." He also did a television series. He married his childhood sweetheart and had three daughters. He served eight years in Congress. He later became a stalwart of the U.S. Olympic Committee.

WILLIE MAYS

The Dynamic "Say Hey Kid"

A ball is hit to deep centerfield and almost at the crack of the bat Willie Mays sets out in pursuit, scampering like a flushed-out rabbit. His cap flies off his head. He wheels simultaneously as the ball reaches near the end of its parabola, cups his hands below his chest and cradles the pellet as he might a fragile baby.

The crowd screams in delight. "Say Hey, Willie!"

Later he comes to bat and, with hysteria in the stands heightening, with one mighty swing propels the ball out of the park.

"Oh, you Willie!" Another deafening roar.

Such, in thumbnail, is the baseball profile of the man many diamond historians rate, if not actually the greatest all-around player who ever pulled on a uniform, certainly worthy of ranking with such giants as Babe Ruth, Ty Cobb and Hank Aaron for consideration in that insolvable debate.

When he was inducted into the Baseball Hall of Fame, after a sparkling 22-year career with the New York and San Francisco Giants and the New York Mets, Willie was asked who was the best baseball player he ever saw.

"Me," Willie replied without a second thought.

He wasn't being cocky, simply naively honest. It was an assessment shared by baseball buffs, teammates and rivals.

"He could do everything," said his first major league manager, Leo Durocher. "Joe DiMaggio is the only other player I've seen who could do it all. Willie was a natural."

"When it comes down to needing a run," said Walt Alston, longtime manager of the Dodgers, "Willie is the greatest."

There was always a small boy quality about the superb black athlete out of Alabama. He radiated energy and desire. He acted as if he couldn't wait to get onto the field and, once there, to

Putting all his power into his swing, Willie Mays wallops a tremendous triple to right center that won the first All-Star game of 1959 for the National League over the American League, 5-4.

play with a contradictory mixture of fierce pride and schoolboy enthusiasm. He loved to put on a show.

Once explaining how he kept losing his hat while running down fly balls in the outfield, he said, "Early in my career, my cap came off while I was chasing a ball. The crowd went wild. So I always kept my cap loose to please the crowd."

Actress Tallulah Bankhead, an admirer, wrote, "Willie does everything with a flourish...He has the spectacular...a theatrical quality. In the terms of my trade, he lifts the mortgage five minutes before the curtain falls."

Mays was the ultimate ballplayer. He hit for both percentage and power. He ran the bases as daringly as a Pepper Martin or Jackie Robinson. Flawless in the field, he had a fine arm, good instincts and rarely made a mental error.

He hit 660 home runs, batted .302 for his career and had 1,903 runs batted in. He played in four World Series and was a participant in all All-Star Games from 1954 through 1973. He was named the NL's most valuable player in 1954 and 1956. In 1981, baseball author-historian Maury Allen ranked baseball's all-time top 100 and placed Mays on top, saying: "If not for two years in service, Mays would have outdistanced Babe Ruth in career homers...was the best, most exciting, No. 1."

Willie was born May 6, 1931 in Westfield, Alabama, a mill town just outside Birmingham, and given the little boy name of Willie (not William) Howard Mays, Jr. He grew up in the neighboring town of Fairfield where he starred in several sports in high school and played sandlot baseball with his father, a former outfielder in the pro Negro League. Papa played centerfield, Willie left field.

Mays joined the Birmingham Black Barons of the Negro National League when he was just 17 and it was there in the spring of 1950 that he was spotted by Giants' scout Eddie Montague and signed a contract for $5,000. Willie stayed with the Black Barons until he finished high school, however, and then reported to Trenton in the Class B Interstate League.

At Trenton, he batted .353 in 81 games—"It was like playing in the Little League after the Negro League," he said—and earned promotion the next spring to the Minneapolis Millers of the Triple A American Association.

That stop was brief. In New York, the Giants were struggling early in the 1951 season. In Minneapolis, Mays was hitting .477. Willie was summoned to the Polo Grounds, given number 24

Mays follows through after connecting for his fourth homer of the game against the Braves in Milwaukee on April 30, 1961. His feat tied a record held by nine other major leaguers for hitting four home runs in a single game.

The "Say Hey Kid" singles to center for the New York Mets in the 12th inning of a 1973 World Series game against the Oakland A's. The hit drove in a run and moved the Mets to a four-run inning and a 10-7 triumph.

and thrust onto the field—a raw kid just turned 20, making his debut in the majors four years after Jackie Robinson had pierced the color line.

"They said I was scared and nervous," Willie said. "It was not true. My father worked in the steel mills and later as a railroad porter. I never had it bad. And the crowds didn't bother me. I was used to crowds in the Negro League."

Willie opened his major league career in Philadelphia and got off to an inauspicious start, hitless in his first 12 times at bat, and was becoming discouraged until the team returned to New York for a series with the Boston Braves. Facing all-star lefthander, Warren Spahn, he poled the first pitch over the left field roof for a home run.

He became an immediate idol of the fans. They called him the "Say Hey Kid" because that was the way he greeted people whose names he didn't remember. His rookie season was climaxed with the Giants' dramatic playoff victory over the Dodgers for the National League pennant and a losing effort against the New York Yankees in the 1951 World Series. He was named his league's rookie of the year.

Willie missed most of the 1952 season and all of 1953 because of military service, but returned in 1954 to share in the Giants' World Series victory over the favored Cleveland Indians, marked by his unforgettable, running catch of a Vic Wertz shot which the Indians said "broke our backs." Mays was the league's most valuable player and the Associated Press' Athlete of the Year.

He accompanied the Giants in their move to San Francisco but was never appreciated as in New York. He was traded to the New York Mets in 1972, retiring June 15, 1973 at age 42.

Willie left with a profitable real estate investment business, public relations jobs with an Atlantic City casino and two other firms, condos in New York, Birmingham, Tampa and Reno and eight cars all bearing "Say Hey" plates.

GEORGE MIKAN

Basketball's First Big Man

Before there was a Wilt Chamberlain or a Kareem Abdul-Jabbar, there was George Mikan and, because of him, basketball took on a new dimension.

It ceased to be primarily a game of speed and sleight-of-hand passing, slick geometric designs to work the ball into position until a team's sharpshooter could take aim at the hoop.

The old peach basket pastime of Dr. James Naismith, with Mikan the opening wedge, evolved into a game of strength and muscle. Forget the subtleties. Plant your big man under the basket, work the ball as quickly as possible into his hands and—bang!—with the dunk or the hookshot—deliver the knockout punch.

Not only did Mikan open the door to the big men, he helped stimulate new fan interest for both the colleges and the professional National Basketball Association. Once a floundering stepbrother to football, college basketball saw its NCAA Final Four—the national championship—develop into a sports attraction taking its place alongside football's Super Bowl and baseball's World Series as one of the year's premier extravaganzas. The pros went big time.

Meanwhile, Mikan became a reluctant revolutionary in this revitalization program. He couldn't help being big. He resented what he felt was the curse of being different—looked upon, he was convinced, as an "awkward monster"—and happily would have passed on his mantle.

In his playing prime, Mikan stood 6 feet, 10½ inches and weighed 245 pounds. That would not have created a stir in the 1970s and 1980s when teams were flooded with beanstalks of seven feet and over, but he certainly stood out among the quick, darting dribblers of the World War II and immediate post-war era.

In fact, because of his size, he was rejected for a scholarship at Notre Dame. "Your height is a fine asset and you've got the spirit," George Keogan, the Notre Dame coach, told him, "but you're hopelessly clumsy."

This only exacerbated the self-consciousness that had eaten away at big George's soul throughout his youth.

The son of Joe and Minnie Mikan, who ran a restaurant and bar in Joliet, Illinois, George had grown to 5-9 by the time he was eight years old and reached 6-0 at age 11.

"I remember how I used to stoop all the time to make myself look shorter," he said. "I became round-shouldered, ungainly and so filled with bitterness that my height nearly wrecked my life."

Poignantly he explained how winning a marbles tournament had given him one of his greatest thrills and that his primary ambition had been not to play basketball in Madison Square Garden but to give a piano recital in Carnegie Hall. "I foolishly let myself be laughed out of it," he said.

Mikan played virtually no basketball in high school, shifting from Joliet Catholic High to Quigley Prep, a seminary in Chicago where he even considered becoming a priest. It was while playing for a Catholic Youth Organization team in 1942 that his

Mikan (99) of the Minneapolis Lakers of the Basketball Association of America grabs a rebound in a 1949 game against the Washington Capitols. Also up for the ball is Herman Schaefer (10), a guard. At right is forward Jim Pollard. The Lakers won the game, 84-79, as Mikan finished with 48 points.

coach encouraged him to try and get into Notre Dame. Then came the rebuff.

Ray Meyer, who was Notre Dame's assistant coach, urged Mikan to try another college. Mikan did, and was accepted at DePaul. Ironically, Meyer, in the meantime, had left Notre Dame to become head coach at DePaul.

Meyer, who became one of college basketball's most respected and enduring coaches at DePaul, recognized Mikan's potential and decided to capitalize on it. He put his giant pupil through a demanding training regimen, teaching him quickness, pivoting, passing and shooting techniques.

The individual attention paid rich dividends.

At DePaul, Mikan won All-America honors in 1944, 1945 and 1946 and helped lead Meyer's team to the national college championship in 1945. He led the nation in scoring that year and in 1946, and thrilled a Madison Square Garden crowd in New York by scoring 53 points against Rhode Island.

By this time, he had become an accomplished all-around player. He moved well, had good coordination and developed a fine hook shot. He learned to keep his resentment in check when hostile fans started harassing him because of his size.

Upon graduation from college, Mikan had the luxury of choosing between the established National Basketball League and the new Basketball Association of America. He elected to play with the Chicago Gears of the older league, signing a contract for $12,000 a year—a princely sum at the time.

He played only a half season for the Gears, averaging 16.5 points. When the Gears folded at the end of the season, he joined the Minneapolis Lakers, and in his first full season as a pro in 1948-49, led the Lakers to the BAA championship. He was the league's leading scorer with a 28.3 average.

The next year, the feuding pro leagues merged into the National Basketball Association and Mikan continued to be the league's greatest gate attraction. He led the Lakers to five league titles in six seasons and won three scoring crowns. He retired after the 1953-54 campaign, but essayed a brief and unsuccessful comeback in 1955-56, before quitting for good with a career total of 11,764 points, 1,932 for a single season, and a career average of 22.6, all league records.

Without their big, bespectacled driving force, the Lakers went into a decline. Mikan took over as coach in 1957, but resigned when the club lost 30 of its first 39 games. In 1960, the team moved to Los Angeles. Mikan served two years as commissioner of the ill-fated American Basketball Association before settling down to practice law in Minneapolis.

He could always cherish the memory of the marquee sign over Madison Square Garden: "Mikan vs. Knicks."

HELEN WILLS MOODY

"Little Miss Poker Face"

Helen Wills Moody could have been a great author, a great painter or a great designer. She could have been royalty—a real-life queen sitting upon an ivory throne. In a way, she was all of these—brilliant, complex, stately, enigmatic—and no one would ever question her claim to royalty.

She was truly a queen. Her crown was a green-lined eye-shade, her robe a middy blouse and pleated skirt, her scepter a tightly-strung wooden tennis racket. Her realm reached from the lush grass courts of Wimbledon and Forest Hills, New York, to the asphalt surfaces of California and the red clay of Roland Garros in Paris.

She was Queen Helen. During her prime, no one raised a voice to dispute it.

This serene, introspective daughter of a California country doctor dominated the courts from 1923, when she won the first of her seven United States ladies' singles championships at age 17, until 1938, when she crushed her keenest rival, Helen Jacobs, 6-4, 6-0, for the last of her eight Wimbledon crowns.

With that, she said goodbye to competitive tennis, leaving the sports world to ponder whether it was fire or ice that lurked behind that mystic facade that never showed a flick of emotion on the court, never glared at an errant linesman, and never changed expression regardless of the course of the match, good or bad.

In a mad age when sports heroes were given colorful nicknames, Helen was dubbed "Little Miss Poker Face."

Helen Wills Moody winding up the American part of her preparation for another try at a Wimbledon championship. She captured eight women's singles titles at Wimbledon.

Her impassiveness, her frigid reserve, her penchant for complete privacy resulted in mixed reviews on both sides of the Atlantic. The sassy British press was the most critical, but those who knew her found only good qualities.

William Lyon Phelps, a well-known writer of the period, insisted that Helen's lack of expression during a match did not connote grimness or tension but meant she was "calm, placid, showed only equanimity."

W.O. McGeehan of the New York Herald Tribune wrote: "She plays her game with silent, deadly earnestness. That is the way to win games but it does not please galleries."

Helen Wills was born in October 1905, in Berkeley, California. Her father, who drove a buggy to visit patients in the country, was a fair player. On Helen's 14th birthday, he bought her a junior racket and enrolled her in a junior program under teacher William "Pop" Fuller.

Less than a year after taking up the game, Helen was good enough to be sent to the U.S. Junior Championships at Forest Hills where, at age 15, she won the title for girls 18 years and under. She remained in the East to play the grass court circuit and got a look at two women who were to play an important role in her career—the longtime U.S. ladies' singles champion, Molla Mallory, and the sensational Suzanne Lenglen of France, the talk of Europe.

The next year, Helen returned to Forest Hills and, awing galleries with her unflappable demeanor and shotmaking precision, faced Mallory in the women's singles final. It was immaterial that the California teen-ager won only four games, for she was to return the next year at age 17 and reverse the outcome. She crushed the sturdy Norwegian native, 6-2, 6-1, and launched a reign that included seven national singles titles—one less than Mallory's cache—over nine years.

When Helen made her first trip overseas for the Wightman Cup matches and Wimbledon in 1924, Europe was abuzz with the speculation: Could this new American girl beat Suzanne?

The paths of these two female headliners never had crossed. Suzanne, graceful and exciting but frail and moody, had limited her U.S. excursions. She had been accused of ducking the young American phenom. Helen did not disguise her determination to get Suzanne in her sights. In 1926, upon learning Suzanne was playing in the French Riviera, she abruptly headed for Paris to pursue her art studies.

An enterprising promoter arranged a match at the Carlton Club in Cannes, an implausible setting. The event created worldwide excitement. Tension was electric.

Lenglen, leaping and flowing like a ballerina, won the first set 6-3. Helen, coldly methodical, battled her way to set point in the second set, but Suzanne rallied to win 8-6 for the match. It was their only meeting.

Helen's star lost none of its lustre. She proceeded to win three French titles, and in 1927 became the first American woman in 20 years to capture Wimbledon, starting a dominance that included eight singles titles over the next 11 years.

Her hold on the American crown remained secure until 1933 when, as Mrs. Frederick Moody, she came up against a younger Bay Area rival, Helen Jacobs, who won the title which Mrs.

Queen Helen dominated the courts from 1923, when she won the first of her seven United States ladies singles championship, until 1938.

Moody had passed up the year before. Jacobs was hailed as the natural heir apparent.

Meeting on the stadium court at Forest Hills, Jacobs won the first set 8-6. The older Helen rallied to take the second 6-3. When Jacobs broke Moody a second time for 3-0 lead in the third, the crowd was stunned to see Queen Helen stride to the sidelines, tell the umpire she couldn't continue, put on her sweater and, without a word to her opponent, walk away.

The scene was shocking. The press was sharply critical. Long afterward, Moody explained that she had injured her back gardening and had become dizzy on the court. Five years later, she avenged the loss, beating Jacobs easily in the final for her eighth Wimbledon crown.

She divorced Moody in 1937, married and later divorced socialite Aiden Roark, settling down in Carmel, California, to pursue her loves of writing and painting. She wrote five mystery novels, and her oil paintings and sketchings were displayed in galleries in New York and Europe.

STAN MUSIAL

The Cards' "Mr. Nice Guy"

Stan Musial's legacy in baseball can be capsuled in two words: sock and smile. Or, if one chose to carry the alliteration further, it could be power and personality, grandeur and grace, clout and class.

If his lengthy era in the major leagues could be likened to a graduation class, Stanley Frank Musial undoubtedly would have received cascades of votes as the most talented and most successful but would have been a runaway winner as the most popular.

He was the all-time "Mr. Nice Guy" in a sport that has bred many heroes but limited genuine gentlemen. This relaxed, outgoing athlete from the coal-mining town of Donora, Penn-

left:

Musial swung from a unique coiled, crouching stance and seemed to snap like an unleashed spring. Opposing pitchers compared his swing to a cobra strike.

opposite:

These sequence photos show Stan the Man connecting for a double off Moe Drabowsky in the sixth inning at Wrigley Field in Chicago on May 13, 1958. It was the 3,000th major league hit of the St. Louis Cardinal star's outstanding career.

*Musial displays powerful swing during 1962
exhibition game in Tampa, Fla. against the
Cincinnati Reds. The catcher is Darrell Johnson.*

sylvania, became as well-known for his ever-present smile and friendly handshake as for his batting records in the 22 years as a member of the St. Louis Cardinals.

He never raised a ruckus. He mingled with fans, was never too busy to sign an autograph and was great with kids. He was so respected by rival teams that they never badgered him from the bench.

Newspapermen loved him. No matter how busy, he never turned down an interview after which he would politely ask: "Got enough, fellow? If not, just let me know."

It was natural that historians of the period would compare him in performance and style with the great Ted Williams of the Boston Red Sox in the rival American League.

They were contemporaries but, playing in different leagues, their only confrontations came in spring training, All-Star games, and in the 1946 World Series. They were the greatest lefthanded batsmen of their day—many contend two of the top three of all-time, bracketing them in the same breath with the incomparable Babe Ruth.

Unlike Musial, Williams, who was the last major leaguer to bat over .400 with his .406 season average in 1941, was a sullen, withdrawn man who seemed mad at the world. He resisted invasion of his privacy, feuded with Boston fans and the press and occasionally expressed his hostility with obscene gestures.

But no one questioned the purity of his upright swing and his batting prowess. The "Splendid Splinter," as they called him because of his tall and lean physique, had such remarkable eyesight, they said, that he could read the signature of the American League president as the ball sped over the plate.

The same powers were attributed to Musial, three inches shorter and 30 pounds lighter at 6 feet and 175 pounds, who swung from a unique coiled, crouching stance and seemed to snap like an unleashed spring. Opposing pitchers compared his swing to a cobra strike.

There was a legend that Musial was so precise he concentrated on hitting only the top half of the baseball.

Musial scoffed at this later. "It was just a joke," he said. "I told it to a reporter when I was in the Navy and it stuck." He insisted he had no mystical formulas for hitting.

"I try not to think of anything and to keep my mind clear," he said one time. "I used a 34-ounce bat. I could tell a bat's weight just by picking it up. I could pick up the ball right away after it left the pitcher's hand. Concentration is very important. I knew what the pitch was going to be when it was halfway to the plate."

Stan the Man, as he became popularly known, compiled a remarkable record during his 22 years as an outfielder and first baseman for the Cardinals, starting in 1941. He had a career batting average of .331. He set a National League record of 3,630 hits which stood for two decades before being broken by Pete Rose. He hit 475 home runs and set records in extra base hits, runs and other categories.

He won the National League batting championship seven times and three times was the league's Most Valuable Player. Starting in 1941 when he batted .426 for 12 games as a rookie, he had a streak of 17 straight seasons in which he batted .300 or over. He soared over the mark an 18th time in 1962 with an average of .330, at the age of 41, but slumped to .255 the following season and retired.

Dodger pitcher Preacher Roe once bragged he had found the secret to pitching to The Man. "I throw him four wide ones and then try to pick him off first," Roe said.

Johnny Antonelli of the Giants credited him with having a sixth sense. "Some guys say he can tell what you throw from your windup and body motion. It's unbelievable."

Musial began his professional baseball career by signing a Class D contract with the Cards for $325. He started out as a pitcher but, as in the case of Babe Ruth, was too good a hitter to be used every four or five days. The Cards brought him up briefly in 1941 and immediately made him an outfielder.

He developed rapidly. In 1942, actually his rookie year, he batted .315 and helped the Cardinals overtake the Dodgers for the National League pennant and go on to win the World Series. In his sophomore year, Stan was league batting champion with .357. Later, he was used as both an outfielder and a first baseman, proving himself more than capable in all departments of play.

After retiring, Musial remained in St. Louis, serving the club in various capacities. He and his wife reared three daughters. He opened a popular restaurant, became director of a bank and involved himself in various charitable activities.

Once when the Cardinals were experiencing hard times, Frank Lane, the club's crusty general manager, was asked if he might trade Musial. "Trade Musial?," Lane snapped. "Hell, he's part of this town. You might as well trade the Mississippi."

The Slugging Grandfather. Batting for the first time since becoming a grandfather for the first time on Sept. 10, 1963. Stan homers in the first inning against the Chicago Cubs. Musial retired at the end of that season at 42 years of age.

BRONKO NAGURSKI

Like A Runaway Freight Train

Legendary tales generally get embellished with years of telling and re-telling but football die-hards in the Middle West insist these stories are absolutely true in the case of Bronko Nagurski.

One is that Doc Spears, the coach at the University of Minnesota, driving along a country road on a recruiting mission, stopped to ask directions of a big kid who was plowing a field without a horse just outside International Falls, Minn. The kid responded by picking up the plow in one hand and pointing the way.

That, so the story goes, is how Bronko wound up pursuing an education and football career at Minnesota and ultimately becoming the devastating fullback who led the Chicago Bears to the first championship of the modern pro era in 1933.

The other is that the "Bronk," in a game at Chicago's Wrigley Field where the end zone was only nine yards deep, once scored a winning touchdown by stampeding over two opponents, leaving one unconscious and the other with a broken shoulder. Then, unable to curb his momentum, he collided with a goal post and crashed into a brick wall.

Picking himself up, Nagurski said, "That last guy hit pretty hard."

They say that years afterward, if one looked hard enough, he could still see the crack in the wall. "I've seen it," said Fran Tarkenton, a quarterback whose deeds thrilled pro fans in a later era.

Nagurski, of tough Ukrainian stock, was a massive man, 6 feet, 2 inches tall and 225 pounds heavy in an age of 175-pound tackles. He was rock-hard, all muscle and bone without an ounce of fat. His collar size was 19 inches. The ring he received for induction as a charter member into pro football's Hall of Fame in 1963 was size 19½.

Many legitimate observers contend he may have been the greatest football player of all time, surpassing the great Jim Thorpe, named to that honor in a national poll of sports writers by The Associated Press, and the sensational Red Grange, "The Galloping Ghost," at one time his teammate on the Bears.

Bronko, showing his versatility, passed for two touchdowns in Chicago's 23-21 triumph over the Giants in the first NFL title game.

"He was a star end, a star tackle and a crushing fullback who could pass," wrote Grantland Rice, patron saint of the sports writing fraternity. "I believe 11 Nagurskis could beat 11 Granges or 11 Thorpes."

All-time great Ernie Nevers, said, "Tackling Bronko was like trying to stop a freight train going downhill."

"Running into him was like running into an electric shock," said Grange.

Nagurski was a 60-minute player, performing both on offense

Nagurski, with ball, cuts through center in 1937 game to gain eight yards against the Washington Redskins. "Running into him was like running into an electric shock," said Red Grange, another football immortal, who also played for the Bears.

The "Bronk" from International Falls, Minn. was an outstanding tackle at the University of Minnesota before becoming a devastating NFL fullback for Chicago.

On Sept. 7, 1963, Nagurski poses with bust after he was enshrined by the Pro Football Hall of Fame during dedication ceremonies in Canton, Ohio.

and defense in those pre-platoon days. In one single college game he played end, tackle, guard, halfback and fullback. Spears said he could have been an All-America at any position.

Nagurski's ancestors had migrated from the Ukraine to the village of Rainy River, Canada, where Bronko was born, one of five children. He was four when his family moved across the river to International Falls, a village of about 6,000 residents accustomed to long, icy winters and brief summers of fishing and hunting. Residents found pride in the village's designation, "The Ice Box of the Nation."

Bronko's given name was Bronislau. His pals couldn't pronounce it so at an early age he became Bronko. It turned out to be a fitting nickname. His parents ran a mom-and-pop store. They also had a small farm.

Upon his graduation from college, Bronko was signed in 1930 by Bears' owner George Halas, one of the founding fathers of the National Football League, for $5,000. Halas called him one of the most remarkable physical specimens he had ever seen.

"A lot of men have passed in front of me but none with a build like that man," the boss of the Bears said.

Bronko recalled later that Halas didn't put his money where his mouth was.

"Even though I had a good year, my salary was cut to $4,500 my second year and the year after that to $3,700 where it stayed for a number of years," he said.

Those were Depression years and pro football was a strug-gling enterprise. Nagurski threatened to retire in 1937, so Halas reluctantly relented and raised his salary to $5,000. After seven years, Bronko was where he had started.

"When I asked for $6,000 in 1938, they turned me down," Nagurski related. "I went home figuring they'd call me, but they never did. Not until five years later."

He rejoined the Bears for one more season in 1943 at the age of 35 and helped them win a third championship. Then he retired, returning to the family's modest home on Rainy Lake, just up the Rainy River from International Falls, to resume a normal life with his wife, the former Eileen Kane, and their six children and four grandchildren.

He did some professional wrestling around county fairs. He bought a service station and pumped gas for a few years, then in 1970 settled down to a life of relative ease where four generations of Nagurskis had found peace and security.

He treasured his lifestyle and rejected invitations to travel. For years he never visited a stadium. His weight ballooned to almost 300 pounds but, even after reaching age 75, he remained active and solid as a rock. He kept up with football and other sports on television.

He also became one of the modern game's most severe critics.

"I think there is less enjoyment now," he said. "The quarterback always handles the ball. The games always seem the same. Only the names and numbers change—and the platoons. Remember, we played with only 18 men."

JOE NAMATH

A Genius and a Rascal

"**B**roadway Joe." was his nickname, football his game and the world his oyster.

Joe Namath was half-hero and half-scoundrel. He was a genius and a rascal. Born and reared in a broken home in the steel mill district of Beaver Falls, Pennsylvania, he parlayed an incisive mind, a rare charisma and a rifle throwing arm into a life of riches and fame. He finished his pro career with 1,886 completions in 3,762 attempts (.501) for 27,663 yards and 173 touchdowns passes.

He opened the locks on professional football's tightly guarded coffers when he signed for an up-to-then unimaginable annual sum of $427,000 with the New York Jets of the maverick American Football League. This development unleashed a salary boom—and it was largely his presence that resulted in the National Football League being forced to wed and grudgingly give credibility to "the other league."

Then, as if that wasn't enough, the cocky, young quarterback, after openly predicting the outcome, went out in Miami's Orange Bowl Stadium and led the 17-point underdog Jets to an astonishing 16-7 victory over the NFL's Baltimore Colts in Super Bowl III in January, 1969.

They laughed when Broadway Joe proclaimed "We're gonna win. I personally guarantee it."

If there was ever any question of the legitimacy of the American Football League or of Namath's prowess as a football quarterback and field general, it was swiftly shattered that historic Sunday afternoon.

New York gave him a hero's welcome. He immediately became sports' "Cover Boy," a national idol.

Joe was prepared to partake fully of his new, glamorous role. He checked into an apartment on New York's fashionable East Side, replete with a llama-skin rug. He drove to practice in a green Lincoln convertible. He dated and casually discarded a bevy of pageant beauties and Hollywood starlets.

While the story of his rise from a mill town to a position of affluence and front-page notoriety appeared more suitable for Horatio Alger, he nevertheless became the focus for the tabloid gossip columns and the racy magazines sold in supermarkets. He regularly frequented the popular discos and, in the tradition, danced all night.

"Boats. Planes. Cars. Clothes. Blondes. Brunettes. Redheads. All so pretty. I love them all," he was quoted in one pub-

left:

Namath finished his pro career with 1,886 completions in 3,762 attempts for a .501 average. He passed for 27,663 yards and accumulated 173 touchdown aerials.

opposite:

After openly predicting the outcome, Namath went out and led the 17-point underdog Jets to a 16-7 triumph over Baltimore in Super Bowl III. Here, Colts' huge Bubba Smith tries to block Joe's pass in Jan. 12, 1969 upset in Miami.

lication. With his long Roman nose and sleepy eyes, he was called "the sexiest man in sports."

Namath's lifestyle and outsized salary didn't set well at first with his more obscure teammates. But when he began throwing touchdown passes, these problems evaporated.

His boss, Sonny Werblin, who signed his fat contract, chided him for wearing sweaters and leather coats to the theater and other events. Werblin said he should wear a jacket and tie and be "an inspiration." Namath blamed it all on the media and never changed.

He developed a bitter adversarial relationship with the press, complaining of invasion of privacy. Much in the fashion of Frank Sinatra, he brooded and shunned reporters.

At the height of his national popularity, after one of his many brilliant performances, he would return to his corner locker and sit in silence while reporters swarmed around other players. He didn't want to talk to them.

In 1969 Namath opened a New York night club called "Bachelors III," one of several he hoped to franchise around the

country. Pete Rozelle, commissioner of the National Football League, saying the saloon was frequented by "undesirable characters," ordered him to sell the place. Joe resisted, saying he would quit football first. He later relented.

Joe's unfettered behavior had early roots. The youngest of five children in a broken home, he recalled that he was a "con man" in his youth. He admitted that he collected junk to sell, then stole it back to resell. He also stole pop bottles for deposit money.

None of this, however, affected his natural talent for football. Paul "Bear" Bryant, who coached him at the University of Alabama and once suspended him for violating team rules, called him, "the greatest athlete I have ever coached."

Troubled by bad knees and other injuries, Namath may not have been the greatest quarterback statistically of all-time but few will question that in his prime he had no peer as a clutch player and field general.

Although his fragile knees were held together by braces and taped gauze, he often avoided sacks by the quickness of his release. Football recalls no quarterback with a faster trigger. Also he possessed a rare faculty for reading enemy defenses and picking them to pieces as one might spinning ducks in a shooting gallery.

Namath had one of his several knee operations before join-

Keeping a watchful eye on rushing defenders, Broadway Joe puts the ball right into the middle of running back Bill Mathis during surprise Super Bowl III victory over Baltimore.

In June, 1969, Namath announced that he was retiring from football because of pressure from NFL Commissioner Pete Rozelle to dispose of his night club, Bachelors III. Joe later sold his interest in the club and returned to the Jets.

ing the Jets for his rookie season and, protected by Head Coach Weeb Ewbank, didn't get to start until midway of the campaign. Even then, he was the 1965 Rookie of the Year and the Most Valuable Player in the AFL's All-Star game.

Honors and injuries continued to pile up in the succeeding years. He led the league in passing in 1966 and, in 1967, set a pro record for yardage with 4,007 yards. After undergoing another knee operation in 1968, he was named the AFL's Most Valuable Player.

In October, 1970, after his sensational Super Bowl III per-

formance, he suffered a broken right wrist and missed all but five games of the season. He busted up his left knee again in an exhibition game in 1971, and was sidelined for 19 games.

Although success on the field began to fade, Joe's extracurricular activities continued to boom. He made three movies, joined Mickey Mantle in a travel agency venture and hawked pantyhose, bed sheets and cologne on TV.

Namath went Hollywood physically in 1977 when he moved to the Los Angeles Rams. He played one year with them, and retired.

MARTINA NAVRATILOVA

Wimbledon's Perennial Power

Martina Navratilova immediately fell in love with the United States during her first visit there early in 1973. It took much longer for Americans to warm up to Martina Navratilova.

"My first impression of Americans was how friendly they were," she wrote in her autobiography. "I still like that openness about Americans... You can be honest and be yourself with Americans. I always felt I could be me, the real Martina, from the first time I came to the States."

It was during that trip, in Akron, Ohio, that her first-round opponent was "America's Sweetheart," Chris Evert, almost two years her senior. That was the beginning of the longest rivalry in professional tennis, an almost unparalleled rivalry that has helped put both on the list of the sport's all-time stars.

Born Oct. 18, 1956, in Prague, Czechoslovakia, Martina Subertova was raised near the village of Spindleruv Mlyn in a ski lodge some 1,200 meters high in the Krkonose Mountains, where her father, Miroslav Subert, was a ski instructor. Later, after her parents divorced, she and her mother moved to Revnice, where she began playing tennis, a sport in which her maternal grandmother had excelled.

It was there, at the municipal tennis club, that Martina met Miroslav Navratil, who eventually became her stepfather. She later changed her name to his, adding the feminine ending 'ova,' becoming Martina Navratilova.

Most Americans heard about Navratilova the first time in September 1975 when, during the U.S. Open Championships, she defected to the United States. At the time, however, she was ranked No. 5 in the world and seeded third in the women's singles in the Forest Hills, N.Y. tournament.

By then, she already had won two Grand Slam titles, teaming with fellow Czechoslovak Ivan Molina to win the French Open mixed doubles title in 1974 and with Chris Evert to capture the 1975 French Open women's doubles. And she had led Czechoslovakia to victory in the 1975 Federation Cup.

But, consumed with her love of American fast food, especially hamburgers and milkshakes, Navratilova gained weight and became known as the "Great Wide Hope." Still, the talent was there as she displayed flashes of brilliance in her aggressive serve-and-volley style.

Her first coach in Prague was George Parma, a former Czechoslovak Davis Cup player. He not only worked on her game but gave her advice.

"Work hard, Martina. Compete wherever you have the chance. Get to see the world. Sports is one way you'll be able to travel," he told her.

Top-seeded Martina Navratilova is about to backhand the ball to Chris Evert Lloyd during the final of the 1986 French Open. Martina lost this one in three sets.

"He would tell me to set my sights on becoming a good European player—maybe, just maybe, in the top ten in the world," Navratilova wrote. "Meantime, my father was telling people I was going to be a Wimbledon champion some day and I wasn't about to disagree with him."

That day came in 1978, when she defeated Chris Evert in the final. She went on to win eight Wimbledon singles crowns, including an unprecedented six straight, the most recent in 1987. In 1980, she had a bad year, although she was part of the winning women's doubles teams at the U.S. Open and the Australian Open. She dropped to No. 3 in the world, behind Chris Evert Lloyd and Tracy Austin.

The following year was her most disappointing. After winning the Avon Championships at New York's Madison Square Garden against Andrea Jaeger, she appeared ready to capture her first U.S. Open singles title. It was not to be, however, as Tracy Austin fought back after dropping the first set to defeat Navratilova. It was especially disheartening because she had received her U.S. citizenship shortly before the tournament.

Her tears of defeat, however, were wiped away when the crowd at Flushing Meadow gave her a standing ovation following the

match. She was, at last, accepted by American fans, and later that year she won her first Australian Open women's singles crown.

But in December, at the season-ending Toyota Championships in East Rutherford, N.J., she again lost to Austin after winning the first set. And the following March came another major disappointment, as she was upset by West Germany's Sylvia Hanika in the final of the Avon Championships.

It was time for Navratilova to devote her every moment to tennis. She hired a full-time coach, went on a special diet, and began a physical training regimen, including lifting weights.

It paid off immediately, as she won the French Open women's singles crown for the first time, captured her third Wimbledon singles title and began her domination of women's tennis.

In 1982, she won 90 matches while losing only three times and earning nearly $1.5 million. The next year, she was nearly

perfect, posting an 86-1 record, her only loss coming in an upset to young Kathy Horvath in the fourth round of the French Open. Again she earned more than $1.4 million.

She also began putting together record-breaking streaks in 1983.

Beginning with Wimbledon in 1983 and lasting through the 1984 U.S. Open, Navratilova won six consecutive Grand Slam singles crowns. And she teamed with Pam Shriver to win eight consecutive Grand Slam women's doubles titles, beginning with Wimbledon in 1983 and extending through the 1985 French Open. The two also set a remarkable record, winning 109 consecutive doubles matches, from April 1983 until July 1985.

When she lost to Hana Mandlikova in early 1984, it snapped a 54-match singles winning streak, only one shy of Chris Evert Lloyd's record 55 straight. Navratilova's next defeat came against Helena Sukova of Czechoslovakia in the semifinals of the 1984 Australian Open, halting a consecutive match winning streak of 74. She also had a 58-match string stopped by Mandlikova in the Australian Open final in 1987.

But she did team with Shriver to win the Australian Open women's doubles in January 1987, giving her a total of 43 Grand Slam titles, second on the all-time list to Australia's Margaret Smith Court, who won 66.

Only Chris Evert has won more matches in her career than Navratilova. But nobody comes close to her record from 1981-1986, when she won 427 matches and lost only 14.

She has earned more than $11 million in her career, more than any tennis player, male or female. She holds the record for highest earnings in one year, $2,173,556, set in 1984, and her 125 tournament titles is second only to Chris Evert.

Yet her greatest thrill came while playing for the United States in July 1986, when she returned to Czechoslovakia for the first time since her defection and led the American team to the Federation Cup title as overflow crowds cheered her every move. Martina had discovered that she could go home again.

BYRON NELSON

The Texan With a Textbook Swing

Bob Jones had his Grand Slam, Ben Hogan his professional Little Slam, Arnold Palmer his Army and Jack Nicklaus his remarkable cache of 20 major championships. But no one ever played the caliber of golf that Byron Nelson did over a two-year period during the mid-1940s.

Sports analysts insist that no one ever will. It is unimaginable in the context of the modern game.

Lord Byron, as the press respectfully referred to him at the time, a tall Texan with a textbook swing, won 27 tour tournaments, 19 during the 1945 season, 11 in a row. He was the leading money winner with $35,005 in 1944, with a stroke average of 69.67 for 85 rounds, and in 1945 with $52,511, averaging 68.33 for 120 rounds.

The latter average has stood challenges by such greats as Hogan, Palmer, Nicklaus, Sam Snead and Tom Watson in Vardon Trophy (best stroke average) compilations over the ensuing four decades.

To properly assess his money winnings, it's necessary to recall that a tournament's total purse during that period was $10,000, with the winner getting $1,500. It's been calculated that if Nelson's big year of 1945 could have been transposed to modern times, his earnings would have exceeded $2 million.

His 19 victories, 11 in a row, have been compared with Joe DiMaggio's seemingly unbreakable 56-game hitting streak and Lou Gehrig's 2,130 consecutive games in baseball.

Unfortunately, Nelson's fairway blitz never received the public recognition it deserved because it occurred when World War II was winding down and many of the country's leading golfers, Hogan and Snead particularly, were in military uniforms.

Overlooked was the fact that golfers, as in the case of other leading athletes, were in special services and continued to perform in order to sell war bonds. Snead was released from the Navy prior to the 1945 season and Hogan showed up in an Army lieutenant's uniform to play in numerous tour events. Nelson, 4-F because of a blood disorder, had to face his sternest rivals.

In addition, he had to play the same courses which, if anything, were more difficult—scruffy and poorly manicured. On the greens, players could not clean the ball or repair ball marks. Scores stand as a testament to Nelson's greatness.

Nelson had a classic one-piece, upright swing, reminiscent of England's great Harry Vardon. Few men were better at hitting woods or long irons off the fairway—low trajectory shots that carried at least 200 yards. Hogan said no one was better with the wedge.

Nelson and Hogan, two ex-caddies out of Fort Worth, Texas, born six months apart, were rivals since they were kids, two champions of the same age who paradoxically played in two different eras. Nelson retired in 1946 at age 34. Hogan was to win the first of his four U.S. Opens a year later.

Nelson was born February 4, 1912, in Waxahachie, Texas, but

Lord Byron, as golf writers referred to him, blasts out of a sand trap during the 1939 National Open Championship. He won the title in a playoff.

Nelson watches intently as his tee shot hits the green of the 160-yard third hole in the third round of a Tam O'Shanter Open Tournament in Chicago. In 1945, he won 19 tournaments, including 11 in a row.

his family moved to Fort Worth, where Byron began caddying at the Glen Garden Club alongside another youngster named Ben Hogan. The two were 14 when they met in a club caddie tournament with Nelson the victor—a result that was to be repeated later under more meaningful conditions.

At 18, Nelson won the Southwest Amateur, then turned professional two years later. His first tour ventures a failure, he took a club job first in Texarkana and later at Ridgewood, New Jersey. He quickly attracted attention in the East by winning the New Jersey Open in 1935 and the Metropolitan New York Open in 1936.

This success earned him an invitation to the 1937 Masters. There, a rank outsider, he picked up six shots on front-running Ralph Guldahl on the finishing holes to earn the first of his two green jackets. The second came with a playoff victory over Hogan in 1942.

Nelson won the U.S. Open in 1939 at Philadelphia, beating Craig Wood and Denny Shute in a double playoff after Sam Snead had blown to an eight on the final hole. In 1946, he tied for first but lost in a playoff to Lloyd Mangrum.

He defeated Snead in the final of the 1940 PGA, then a match-play event, and won another PGA title in 1945 with a 4 and 3 victory over Sam Byrd, the former New York Yankees'

outfielder. He was PGA runner-up three times, twice losing extra hole matches, and was twice second in the Masters.

During the War, the tour was dominated by Nelson and Harold (Jug) McSpaden, who were dubbed the "Gold Dust Twins." But the titanic twosome became a lonesome onesome once Nelson got rolling in 1944.

He began his 1945 sweep in the Miami Four-Ball with McSpaden, moved across the South and Atlantic Coast like a brush fire, won the Chicago Victory National Open, the PGA, the rich Tam O'Shanter Open and the Canadian Open before returning to the South where his streak was broken by an amateur, Fred Haas, at Memphis, Tennessee.

Nelson played another year, winning six events in 1946, then retired to devote himself to his wife, Louise, and their cattle ranch at Roanoke, Texas. "It was pressure, not my health," the quiet man said. "I got tired of it all."

He made sporadic appearances—in the Crosby, which he won in 1951, and his beloved Masters. He did golf commentary for ABC-TV. He had a tour tournament named for him in Dallas. And his latter years were spent sharing his expertise with prominent players who sought his advice—Tony Lema, Ken Venturi, Tom Watson and others.

JACK NICKLAUS

The Golden Bear With a Golden Touch

In 1962 a fat kid out of Ohio, playing his second year as a pro, shook up the golf world, first by tying and then beating in a playoff the idolized Arnold Palmer for the U.S. Open Championship.

The charismatic Palmer, a fast-walking, belt-tugging, go-for-broke attacker, was at the height of his game and popularity. With the aid of television, he had made the sport a universal attraction, becoming a heart-throb for women and a hero to their husbands.

Everybody knew the kid, Jack Nicklaus, blond and beefy, was a comer but he had no right to challenge the man they called "The Charger."

In the Open playoff, over the Oakmont Club outside Pittsburgh, "Arnie's Army," defending its idol, taunted big Jack almost every step of the way.

"Miss it, Fatso!" they yelled as Nicklaus stood over a crucial putt.

"Get lost, Whalebone!"

Palmer, embarrassed at such a show of poor sportsmanship, several times stopped and pleaded for his supporters to show more restraint.

Unshaken, Nicklaus proceeded to shoot a 71 in the playoff to win by two strokes. It marked the passing of an era, and no one recognized that milestone more than Palmer himself.

"That was it," Arnie commented later. "If I could have stopped that big dude out there, I might have held him off for five years. But he just took off."

That Nicklaus did.

In the ensuing years Nicklaus set records that defied belief. He completely dominated the game for the next two decades, piling up a total of 71 tour victories, 20 major championships and close to $5 million in official earnings while pursuing in later years broad-based business enterprises that grossed around $400 million a year.

He scored multiple triumphs in the four blue ribbon tournaments that comprise the professional Grand Slam, winning six Masters, four U.S. Opens, three British Opens and five American PGAs, added to two earlier victories in the U.S. Amateur.

While wild thousands scrambled for vantage positions at Augusta and millions watched on TV, Jack captured his sixth Masters in 1986 at age 46. It was one of sports' most miraculous achievements of the generation. He set scoring records, which still stand, in both the Masters and U.S. Open and fell only one stroke short of the British record when he lost an historic head-to-head struggle to Tom Watson's 268 at Turnberry, Scotland, in 1977.

Nicklaus captured his sixth Masters championship in 1986 at the age of 46. Here he hits from the sand in the second round of the '86 competition at Augusta, Ga.

Follow the ball in these five consecutive frames from a sequence camera and you can see Jack Nicklaus sinking a 23-foot putt on the 18th hole at the Baltusrol Golf Club in Springfield, N.J. in 1967. The putt gave Jack a 65 in the final round and a U.S. Open record total of 275. Watching at right is Arnold Palmer, who placed second.

Nicklaus hits from the rough on the No. 1 fairway before a large gallery of hometown fans in Columbus, Ohio during the third round of the 1964 PGA championship.

After Jack shot a record 271 at the Masters in 1965, going one stretch of 28 holes without a bogey and having only one three-putt green, an ailing Bob Jones, who watched on a TV screen in his white cottage, commented:

"Palmer and (Gary) Player played superbly, but Nicklaus played a game with which I am not familiar."

Besides his 71 tour triumphs, Nicklaus had 51 second places or ties and 33 thirds or ties. He was runnerup in the British Open seven times and three times in each of the U.S. Open, Masters and PGA. His victories around the world totaled 89, including six Australian Opens.

Jack Nicklaus was moving the ball almost from the day he was born—January 21, 1940 in Columbus, Ohio, the son of a prosperous and sports-minded pharmacist. Jack was 10 when his dad, Charlie, took him to the Scioto Club and put a set of clubs in the boy's hands. They played nine holes. Jack shot 51, the highest nine he ever had. By age 12, the boy was beating adults.

Jack won the Ohio Open at age 16, beating established pros, and then set off on a brilliant amateur career, qualifying for seven National Amateur tournaments, winning two—in 1959 and 1961. As an amateur, he finished second to Palmer in the U.S. Open at Denver in 1960, then competed in the World Amateur Team Championship at Merion (Pennsylvania) where his 72-hole score of 272 was 15 shots lower than that of Ben Hogan in winning the U.S. Open over the same course.

By this time, the golf world was hailing Nicklaus as "another Bobby Jones" and traditionalists in the game were hoping that Jack would remain an amateur and thus launch a pro-amateur rivalry such as marked the Bobby Jones-Walter Hagen confrontations decades before.

Jones, shortly before his death, wrote a personal letter to Nicklaus and his father urging that he remain an amateur, pointing out the great contribution for golf generally and assuring Jack of financial security in the business world. Long an admirer of Jones, Nicklaus wrestled over the decision and finally decided in 1962 to take the professional route.

"My reasoning was," Jack explained, "that if I intended to make golf my career, and I did, I should pursue it in the arena where the best golf is played—the tour."

The then husky Ohio State graduate got off to a slow start, failing to become an overnight sensation. The U.S. Open win over Palmer at Merion was his first tour triumph. His career took off but not without some interruptions.

One of Jack's big problems was his ballooning weight. At 5 feet, 11 inches, he let his weight get up to 225 pounds. He was especially heavy around the hips and thighs.

"I'm from a German family," Jack explained. "We like to eat. I find I play better at around 200 or 210."

While he was playing once in Australia, a sports writer from that country looked at him on the green and commented, "Look at that Nicklaus—just a big 'Golden Bear.'" It was a name that stuck. He had his blond hair cut in crew-cut style. This plus his weight gave him an appearance that elicited such uncomplimentary nicknames as "Blob-o," "Whaleman" and "Ohio Fats" from some indiscreet sports writers.

Deeply offended by such treatment and fearing he was becoming complacent, Nicklaus underwent a strict diet in the early 1970s, dropped to a lean 180 pounds and let his hair grow to the popular length at the time. The change was dramatic. He was hardly recognized as the old Nicklaus. Wives and teeny-boppers began to swoon over him. Jack thus became not only the greatest golfer in the world but one of the most admired.

An astute businessman, Nicklaus set up a corporation called "Golden Bear Inc." and became involved in golf course design and construction plus services, real estate development, equipment manufacture, TV commercials and licensing of products. He oversaw an umbrella of 13 different companies each with its own officers.

Wall Street writers called him "the richest man in sports." But the world will remember him not for his balance sheet but for skills and temperament that made him the most successful golfer who ever lived.

PAAVO NURMI

The Flying Finn

It was a dank and drizzly late summer day in Helsinki, Finland, but the vast Olympic Stadium throbbed with fanfare and pageantry as thousands of spectators awaited the climactic lighting of the torch for the 1952 Olympic Games.

Old Avery Brundage, president of the International Olympic Committee, had made a terse speech. The flag of the five rings had been raised, and the smartly-clad athletes of competing nations stood at soldier-like rest in the infield.

Suddenly, through a portal, emerged a figure carrying the flame overhead. He was a stringy little man with knobby knees and a bald head, but he ran with an easy grace that was immediately recognizable.

The huge crowd gasped at first, then broke into a roar as Finland's greatest sports hero, Paavo Nurmi, circled the track, sped up six flights of steps and put the torch to the cauldron. The athletes broke ranks.

After a quarter of a century, the Flying Finn, 55, perhaps the greatest distance runner who ever lived, was thrilling Olympic galleries again. For the proud Finns, it was a page out of history, a dramatic exercise in nostalgia.

To many, it might have seemed as if the nude Nurmi statue which stood outside the stadium as a memorial, had suddenly become flesh and blood, because the dour, reclusive racing machine, with an antipathy for crowds and public attention, had virtually hidden himself from the world in the intervening years.

Nurmi dominated distance running as no one ever did, challenged perhaps only by Emil Zatopek's sweep of the 5,000 and 10,000 meters and the marathon in the Helsinki Games. But whereas the Czechoslovakian's feat was packaged into a single Olympiad, Nurmi's conquests were spread over most of two decades.

He competed in three Olympics—1920, 1924 and 1928—and accumulated 10 gold medals, unmatched in track and field annals—seven individual and three in team events. He might have added to his total had he not been barred from the 1932 Games at Los Angeles by the International Olympic Committee for alleged expense account irregularities in a German meet three years earlier.

In those days, the IOC enforced a strict, if unrealistic, amateur code, as the great American Indian athlete, Jim Thorpe, learned to his dismay when stripped of his 1912 medals for playing semi-pro baseball.

Nurmi set world records for distances from 2,000 meters to 20,000 meters. His mark for six miles lasted 18 years; for 10

Nurmi (1) competed in three Olympics—1920, 1924 and 1928—and accumulated 10 gold medals—seven individual and three in team events.

The once-Flying Finn sprints around the track at the Olympic Stadium in Helsinki with the Olympic flame during the opening ceremony of the 1952 Games.

miles 17 years, and for the mile eight years. In the 1924 Olympics, he set world records in two events—the 1,500 and 5,000 meters—in the space of an hour, a test of endurance that astounded track observers.

Contemporaries recalled that he wasn't friendly or outgoing, but was sullen and grim, rarely laughing. They attributed his cold personality to his disadvantaged youth.

He was born in Abo, Finland, on June 13, 1897. His father died when he was 12. His mother had to work and he ran errands and later got a job in a foundry to help support his mother, brother and two sisters. He reportedly became a vegetarian, not by choice but because there was no meat.

At an early age, he came under the influence of a former Olympic champion, Hannes Kolehmainen. Young Nurmi ran as much as 50 miles a week, usually alone, sometimes racing against streetcars. Drawn into military service with the outbreak of World War I, he would get up before daybreak and run for miles along icy country roads, rushing back in time for reveille. Legend is that he could run 15 kilometers (9.3 miles) in less than an hour in full military gear.

He wasn't a classic runner. He had a huge chest for such a relatively small man and he sometimes ran with both arms dangling at his side or with a stop watch in one hand close to his chest. He ran on his toes with long strides.

He competed in his first Olympics at Antwerp in 1920, finishing second to France's Joseph Guillemot in the 5,000 meters but winning a gold in the 10,000.

Nurmi's greatest glory was reserved for the 1924 Games in Paris, where the Finns charged organizers had scheduled the 1,500-meter and 5,000-meter events within an hour of each other to thwart their champion. The so-called "Peerless Paavo" was undeterred. He won both in world record time.

He also won gold medals in the cross country and 3,000-meter team races. He was denied a chance to run in the 10,000 meters, but that was an honor that could not be denied him in 1928 at Amsterdam, when at age 31 he repeated his triumph of eight years earlier.

Nurmi, who had made a successful tour of the United States in 1925, was deeply disappointed when he was denied a shot at the marathon in the Los Angeles Games in 1932.

"If I did something wrong," he said of the IOC ban, "why did they wait three years to take action?"

Nurmi won his last race in the Finnish national championships in 1933, capturing the 1,500 meters, then drifted into retirement. His earnings from his American tour and from other amateur expenses enabled him to launch a business career. He became a contractor and opened a haberdashery in Helsinki, where one could get an autographed tie for a princely price.

He had a brief marriage in the 1930s but it ended in divorce. Friends said Paavo's wife disapproved of her husband's stretching the feet of their infant son to condition him to become a runner.

Actually, Nurmi made few friends. He wasn't very sociable. He refused interviews and public appearances. He died in 1973 at age 76, still seething, they say, over the Olympic Committee's action in barring him from the 1932 Games.

209

AL OERTER

Iron Man of the Discus Throw

To win one gold medal in the Olympic Games is a dream of athletes the world over. To win two is a heady, unbelievable experience and to win more than that sometimes defies imagination. But to win four gold medals in a single event in four consecutive Olympics and, 16 years later, to have aimed for a fifth at age 47 constitutes one of the athletic miracles of the age.

It is the legacy of a relentlessly determined giant of a man from New York's suburban Long Island named Al Oerter. His story is one for the medical journals. His feat of winning the discus competition, always as the underdog, in the 1956, 1960, 1964 and 1968 Games is one unmatched in the event's modern history dating back to 1896.

More than that, Oerter tossed his discuses into a corner of the closet after his fourth gold medal in Mexico City in order to rear two growing daughters and didn't touch them during the period of the 1972 Games in Munich and 1976 Games in Montreal.

"My younger daughter, Gabrielle, was seven and my older one, Chrystiana, was nine when I won at Mexico City," he said. "When I got back, they were asking questions. If I had neglected them, I would have regretted it all my life."

But as the two girls grew to adulthood, Oerter became more restless with his life. The thrill of competition began beckoning again.

A 20-year-old collegian out of the University of Kansas, Oerter won the first of his four Olympic gold medals in Melbourne in 1956 when he tossed the discus 184 feet, 10 inches, a world record.

After emerging as the winner again in Rome in 1960, Al is flanked on the podium by two other Americans, Richard Cochran (left), the bronze medal winner, and Richard Babka, who placed second.

"I tried reading," he said. "I jogged. I played tennis. But mainly I became lethargic. I even let my garden go to pot. I needed motivation. So I decided: A comeback."

During his temporary retirement, Oerter had grown soft in the body as well as in competitive urge. His weight dropped from the massive 295 pounds his 6-foot-4 frame carried at Mexico City to 220. His marriage fell apart, contributing to his restlessness.

Working as a communications manager for a computer firm in Bethpage, N.Y., he adopted an abbreviated schedule to allow for a rigid training routine. He engaged in a weights program, working up to 700 pounds on deep knee bends. He gained weight and strength. His discus throws began reaching internationally accepted distances.

"I don't believe the human body starts to deteriorate," he said. "If you start believing all that nonsense your capabilities start to leave you. You might as well get in a rocking chair."

He set his sights on the gold medal at the Moscow Olympics in 1980. He worked tirelessly. In an Amateur Athletic Union meet in Westfield, New Jersey, he threw the discus 219 feet, 10 inches with a slightly favoring wind—below the world record but more than seven feet better than his personal best.

He believed he was ready to challenge Wolfgang Schmidt, East Germany's world record holder at 233 feet, 5¼ inches, and America's Mac Wilkins, whose best was 232-6. Then came the United States' boycott of the Moscow Games.

It dashed his hopes for a fifth gold over a period of 24 years. But he refused to give up. He merely accelerated his training for the Los Angeles Games in 1984 only to bow to Father Time.

In retrospect, here had been a man who was in position to win gold medals in seven Olympics. Oerter easily qualifies as the "Iron Man" of the international event.

He was just a strapping 20-year-old collegian out of the University of Kansas when he made the long trip to Melbourne with the U.S. team in 1956, unheralded and unnoticed. He upset the world record holder, Fortune Gordien, with a toss of 184 feet, 10 inches, a world record.

He was similarly an underdog in Rome in 1960 and Tokyo in 1964, overshadowed by teammates with better records but he won again. Then came 1968.

"In Mexico City, I wasn't given a chance," Oerter recalled. "I was 31. I had ballooned to 295 pounds. I had to beat a younger teammate, Jay Silvester, fresh from a world record toss of 225 feet, 4 inches. Nobody gave me a show except myself."

On one of his first efforts, Oerter threw the discus 212 feet, 6½ inches, farthest he had thrown it in his life. Then he let Silvester and others fire at it. Psyched out, none challenged the new Olympic mark.

"I don't know why, but something special always happens to me in the Olympics," the four-time champion said. "I think it was because I managed to relax, conserve my energy and not press too much."

Oerter attributed his athletic longevity to two things—heredity and the proper mental attitude.

Although he held world records at various times, he held none going into any of the four Olympics in which he competed and never was conceded much chance of winning. Yet he won all four in Olympic record distances.

Oerter said psychological warfare and gamesmanship always have been accepted practices among Olympic competitors and he had not been averse to it himself—"not malevolent, you understand, just clean competitiveness."

"I enjoyed being overlooked," he added. "Most of the other guys were tense. I never let myself give in to pressure. My own strategy was to try to get off my best throw in my first attempt and establish a position. Then I would relax and work on my techniques. I left the mental battle to the other guys."

Payton Jordan, track and field coach of the 1968 U.S. team, had another assessment."

"Oerter," Payton said, "is all heart and guts."

211

BOBBY ORR

The Grace of a Ballet Dancer

Prior to the 1970 National Hockey League's Stanley Cup final, St. Louis Coach Scotty Bowman was asked how he planned to stop Boston's Bobby Orr.

"We practiced covering Bobby Orr for six hours today, but the only trouble is, we don't have a Bobby Orr to practice against," he said.

And, neither did any other NHL team, because Orr was unique.

The Bruins swept Bowman's Blues, 4-0, in the best-of-seven series, with the 22-year-old Orr scoring an overtime goal in Game 4 for Boston's first NHL championship since 1941.

It was May 10, 1970. The Bruins led the series 3-0 and the score was 3-3, about 30 seconds into overtime.

"I passed the puck to (Derek) Sanderson," said Ed Westfall, who started the game-winning rush up ice. "The puck went into the corner and Bobby (Orr) went streaking in from someplace in center ice. When he went in, I stayed back to cover his spot on the blue line. Then the puck came out from Sanderson (to Orr) and—bang!—it's in the net."

The Bruins were champions, led by the best defenseman who ever played the game.

Two years later, the Bruins won the Stanley Cup again, this

Orr was named winner of the Norris Trophy as the NHL's best defenseman eight consecutive times and captured the Hart Trophy as the league's Most Valuable Player three times.

The 22-year-old Orr flies through the air after scoring the winning goal in sudden death overtime in the final game of Boston's Stanley Cup series against St. Louis in 1970. The goal enabled the Bruins to return the Cup to Boston for the first time in 29 years.

time in six games over the New York Rangers. Orr played the series on a swollen left knee, but as one Ranger said: "Orr is better on one and a half legs than most people on two."

Although he was reserved off the ice, on the ice, Orr gave the big, bad Bruins color. He had the grace of a ballet dancer, a blond whirling dervish who electrified crowds with his rink-long dashes—unusual for a defenseman.

With Orr were teammates every bit as flamboyant as baseball's Gas House Gang of the 1930s; in fact, the Bruins became known as the Ice House Gang.

Orr was the equivalent on ice to a playmaking guard in basketball. His supporting cast included: Sanderson, a free spirit; John "Chief" Bucyk and John McKenzie, who scored and checked with equal verve; and sad-eyed, wise-cracking Phil Esposito, who cruised the slot waiting for an Orr pass from the blue line.

Orr was just 18 when he joined the Bruins from the Ontario Hockey Association for the 1966-67 season. He had 13 goals

and 28 assists, won the NHL's Calder Trophy as Rookie of the Year and was named to the second All-Star team.

When the Rangers' Harry Howell was voted the Norris Trophy as the league's top defenseman the same year, he said he was glad "because I've got a feeling from now on it's going to belong to Bobby Orr."

Howell knew what he was talking about.

From 1968 through 1975, Orr won eight consecutive Norris trophies. In 1970, '71 and '72, he won the Hart Trophy as the league's Most Valuable Player.

In 1969-70, Orr became the first defenseman to capture the NHL scoring title, with 33 goals and 87 assists. He won another

213

After playing on two bad knees for Boston, Bobby underwent surgery and joined the Chicago Blackhawks in 1976. Here, he carries the puck for Chicago behind the net in a 1977 game against the New York Islanders. He retired shortly thereafter.

scoring crown in 1974-75, with 46 goals and 89 assists. And his 102 assists in 1970-71 set a league record.

Following the 1975-76 season, the Bruins and Orr—then playing on two bad knees—parted over money, and he signed with Chicago.

"I didn't feel Bobby would ever wear another uniform after playing so many years for the Bruins," Boston General Manager Harry Sinden said. "But it was a matter, perhaps, of us not knowing how he felt about the situation and him not knowing the situation here. I would say it was just as sad for Bobby... because he did love Boston and the Bruins...as it was for me. I just didn't ever think he'd do it."

But Orr did leave. After those wonderful years in Boston, he left the city he loved with some bitterness, and signed with the Blackhawks.

Chicago was starving for a hockey attraction after Bobby Hull left for the World Hockey Association.

Orr did what he could in the time he had left, but his knees couldn't stand the stress.

Sinden was well aware that Orr's left knee was ravaged by surgery.

"What happened with Orr was two cartilages rubbed each other away," Sinden said. "The body replaces this with new cartilage, but it's very inferior and it's never as strong as the original. Eventually, he had nothing there but bone on bone."

At the age of 30, and after playing 20 games with the 1976-77 Blackhawks, Orr underwent a final operation and stayed off skates for more than a year to give the knee the rest and time needed to recuperate.

But Orr's knee didn't heal properly.

"He told me one time when he was 21 or 22 that he didn't think he'd play past 30," Sinden said. "His goal was to play until he was 30 and accomplish...the Stanley Cup was foremost in his mind."

Orr accomplished that and much, much more.

On the night of Jan. 9, 1979, Orr's No. 4 was retired and raised to the rafters of Boston Garden.

"He was a hero," Boston Mayor Kevin White said. "He's a legend."

JESSE OWENS

Star of Hitler's Nazi Olympics

Jesse Owens, a black man in a white man's world, started life in an Alabama cabbage patch, endured the indignities of a Jim Crow society yet went on to become America's most celebrated Olympian and most fluent defender of his country's democracy.

In a world torn by racial ugliness and hate, he maintained a tremendous calm and sobering influence. His cache of Olympic gold medals was outshone only by a spirit of understanding that never wavered.

"I live here. It's all I know and all I have," he once said when called upon to join his race's protests against social injustice. "My job is not to complain but to try to make things better."

Jesse Owens takes baton from Frank Wykoff on the last 100-yard lap of the 400-yard relay during dual meet between U.S. and Great Britain in 1936. Jesse led off the U.S. team that captured the gold medal in the 1936 Olympics in Berlin.

Owens jumps 26 feet, 5⅝ inches in the 1936 Olympics, breaking the former Olympic record by more than a foot. This photo was taken just as Jesse hit the ground. Jesse won four gold medals all told.

Owens shattered Adolf Hitler's claim of a superior Aryan race by winning four gold medals in the 1936 Nazi Olympics in Berlin. No previous athlete had won more than three.

When Hitler abruptly gathered his swastika-adorned entourage and left the royal box before Owens could complete the final event of his unprecedented sweep—a gesture which the foreign press interpreted as an outright snub—Owens refused to join the chorus of condemnation.

"It was all right with me," the American speedster said later. "I didn't go to Berlin to shake hands with him anyway."

Although treated shabbily by his countrymen after returning home a hero—forced to race against horses, lead a band and do one-night stands to keep his head above water, he never displayed resentment. He took to the road, made about 200 speeches a year—all of an uplift, patriotic nature—and caught the attention of the establishment.

He became a national public relations counselor for six firms. In 1972, he moved from his home in Chicago to a sprawling ranch in Paradise Valley, Arizona. The U.S. Olympic Committee gave him an important post as a director and liaison between the committee and the athletes. It was a move that saved the Olympic Committee unending embarrassment.

In the 1968 Olympics in Mexico City—a turbulent period in American life with Martin Luther King heading up marches in Alabama, blacks destroying property in places such as San Francisco, Detroit and Cleveland and the nation sitting on a powder keg—it remained for Jesse Owens to cool the fevers of black athletes.

These black athletes, forming the bulk of the U.S. team, were on the verge of a wholesale walkout after sprinters Tommie Smith and John Carlos were suspended for staging a black fist salute on the victory stand. The gesture, which would have wrecked the American effort, was avoided when Owens thrust himself into the picture. The athletes had such high regard for Owens that they refused to go against his wishes.

"I told Tommie and John that I could understand their actions," Owens explained. "I told them they should fight their battle on the battlefield. This was the wrong one."

Owens grew up in a small cotton-growing community in Oakville, Ala., one of nine children of a sharecropper. His memories weren't pleasant ones.

"There were no towns to go to," he recalled. "The nearest cotton gin was 10 miles away. I learned to read and write in a one-room school where I could go only when it wasn't cotton-picking time. I was picking cotton when I was seven years old. My quota was 100 pounds a day. We caught hell and at the end of the year we still owed the boss money. We had to buy everything at the company store."

His father packed up the family and moved to Cleveland when Jesse was nine. Jesse went to school at Bolton School in Lakewood, Ohio, which had other famous alumni in Bob Hope and the great quarterback Benny Friedman. The youngster showed a fierce dedication to learn as well as physical attributes.

"I could run," he said, "run very fast. After all, in Alabama, all we kids had to do was run, so we ran." He earned a scholarship to Ohio State University.

"On campus, there was no segregation," Owens recalled. "But off campus there was no good restaurant or place I could go with friends. I got used to riding the back of the bus."

On the cinder track, however, everybody was equal but the running wizard from Alabama's cotton fields was more equal than the rest.

Although he failed to make the Olympic team in 1932, Owens was not to be denied after a spectacular one-man show in a Big Ten Conference track and field meet at the University of Michigan in Ann Arbor on a sultry afternoon May 25, 1935. In the space of less than an hour, he tied the world record in the 100-yard dash and shattered world marks in the long jump, 220-yard dash and 220-low hurdles.

First, the sleek black runner streaked to the 100-yard dash victory in 9.4 seconds, matching Frank Wykoff's world mark. Ten minutes later he soared 26 feet, 8¼ inches in the long jump. Almost immediately afterward he won the 220-yard dash in 20.3 seconds. He had a 26 minute rest before running the 220 low hurdles in 22.6 seconds.

"I had hurt my back two weeks before in a fall at the fraternity house," Owens recalled. "Before the warmup, I couldn't even jog because my back was so stiff. I wondered if I would be able to compete at all."

Owens dons the victor's oak-leaf crown during presentation of gold medal at Berlin following his triumphant long jump. On right is Lutz Long of Germany, who placed second and on left is Tajiman of Japan, the third-place finisher.

Jesse is the fellow with the broad grin as Manhattanites feted returning 1936 American Olympic stars with a Broadway ticker tape parade.

In the Olympics Jesse won the 200-meter sprint in 20.7 seconds, breaking a 21-second barrier that had lasted 36 years and setting a record that stood for 20 years. He won the long jump with 26 feet, 5⅜ inches, a foot farther than anyone had leaped in the Olympics before. The mark stood for 24 years. Owens also won the 100 meter dash and led the 400-meter relay, both in world record times.

As his long day neared an end in Berlin's Olympic Stadium, Jesse noted that Hitler, who had personally honored German winners, began making his exit.

"The Storm Troopers were standing shoulder to shoulder like an iron fence and then came the roar from 100,000 throats in that stiff-armed salute, 'Heil, Hitler!' 'Heil, Hitler!'" Owens said. "It was frightening but I was too engrossed in what I had to do. I never once felt I was insulted."

Jesse Owens died of cancer at the age of 66 on March 31, 1980, but his feats, carved on the concrete wall of the Berlin Stadium, will stand for a long time to come.

SATCHEL PAIGE

The Incomparable Ageless Wonder

The story is—and veteran California Bay Area sports writers swear by it—that in 1935 when New York Yankees' scouts were looking over a young hotshot named Joe DiMaggio, they conceived a wild plot to put him to the supreme test. How would he do against top-flight pitching?

They contacted old Satchel Paige, who was in the area, proposing a game against the club with which DiMaggio was playing off-season exhibitions. With only catcher Ebel Brooks as a nucleus, Paige filled out his roster with high school kids and local semi-pro players.

In his first two times at bat against the fabled Negro League star, DiMaggio struck out, and fouled out to the catcher. On his fourth appearance, he hit a hopper which Paige, who had fanned 15 in 10 innings, lost in the shadows.

A scout promptly dispatched this wire to the Yankees: "DiMaggio all we hoped he'd be. Hit Satch one for four."

There are more legends than documented facts surrounding the lanky, spindly-legged black right-hander because he spent virtually all of his productive years in the ugly shadows of the Jim Crow era when blacks were barred from playing in the major leagues and no records were kept of his feats.

He was approaching 50 when the establishment finally let him run out his string with brief stints with the Cleveland Indians, St. Louis Browns and Kansas City Athletics. Even then, he continued to dazzle.

While there are no records to prove it, Satchel Paige indisputably—subscribed to by black and white baseball men of three generations—was the greatest pitcher of all time.

Paige was 42 years old in 1948 when Bill Veeck signed him for the Cleveland Indians. Here, he relieves Bob Feller in the sixth inning of a game that year against the New York Yankees.

The year is 1965. The fellow on the left, just signed by the Kansas City A's, is 59-year-old Satchel Paige. Sitting on his lap is another pitcher, 19-year-old prospect Jim (Catfish) Hunter, named earlier this year to Baseball's Hall of Fame.

A veritable beanpole—6 feet, 3½ inches and only 140 pounds of gristle when he started, a shuffling, easy-going prototype of the movies' Stepin Fetchit, Paige is estimated to have pitched in 2,500 games, winning about 2,000. His no-hitters were figured at between 50 and 100.

He often pitched 125 games a year, frequently working five to seven days a week. In one month in 1935, he pitched 29 days in a row against top-flight hitters, suffering only one loss. He pitched in the Negro League, which produced such future major leaguers as Jackie Robinson and Roy Campanella, and in the off-season tested his skills against major league all-stars in exhibitions.

He once outpitched Dizzy Dean 1-0 in 13 innings, and in 1947 he went against Cleveland's fireballing Bob Feller, striking out 16 batters in an 8-0 victory that earned him a chance with the Indians.

In his career, he reportedly traveled close to a million miles. He was not simply a ballplayer but a showman, who for 20 years worked solo in a uniform with "Satchel" across the shirt. "Have Arm—Will Travel" was his credo. He advertised himself as "The World's Greatest Pitcher—Guaranteed to Strike out the First Nine Men." He often earned as much as $35,000 a year—a fortune.

Joe DiMaggio called him "the best pitcher I ever faced—and the fastest." Slugger Hack Wilson said that when Paige's fastball came to the plate "it looked like a pea." Paige once fanned Rogers Hornsby, the greatest right-hand hitter in the game, five times.

Many observers insisted that the gangling black phenom threw the fastest ball ever to leave a pitcher's hand—there were no speed guns in his day. It got faster as Paige added some 40 pounds to his frail frame. His longtime battery mate, Josh Gibson, said Paige's fastball not only was blinding but had a snap at the end that made it almost disappear, and he also had a cunning curve and precision control.

The Baseball Encyclopedia records that Leroy Robert Paige

was born July 7, 1906, in Mobile, Alabama. His father was a gardener. His mother, Tula, said Leroy was the sixth of her eight children and was born in 1903. This only compounded the mystery surrounding his age.

Paige was a gawky six-footer by the time he was 12. He played hookey from school, got in gang fights on the street and wound up in a reform school. He said he learned much of his pitching accuracy throwing rocks through windows.

Getting out of reform school at 16, Paige got a job as a redcap at a Mobile train station, where he ingeniously devised, with a pole and ropes, a means of carrying 10 to 20 bags at a time. "There goes Leroy—looking like a satchel tree," a friend remarked. Thus the name he'd never lose.

Paige began playing sandlot ball. A year after leaving reform school, he was discovered by a Pullman porter from Chattanooga and recommended to Alex Herman, owner of the Chattanooga Lookouts of the Negro Professional League. Herman signed him for $50 a month, the money to be sent home.

The Negro League was a ragtag enterprise without central organization. Teams and players moved from city to city, a barnstorming show for a pittance in receipts.

In addition to the Lookouts, Paige played at various times with the Birmingham Black Barons, the Nashville Elite Giants, the Kansas City Monarchs, the New Orleans Pelicans and the Pittsburgh Crawfords. With the Crawfords, Paige was teamed with Gibson, a great hitting catcher who joined him in baseball's Black Hall of Fame, a special category. Paige became such a drawing card he struck out on his own.

With Bismarck, North Dakota, in 1934, he pitched 29 games in a month and won 104 of 105 games for the year.

He was 41—or 44—when Jackie Robinson broke the color barrier with the Brooklyn Dodgers in 1947. In 1948, Bill Veeck signed him for the Cleveland Indians and he drew crowds totaling 150,000 for his first two starts. He followed Veeck to the St. Louis Browns in 1951, pitching three years. At age 59, he pitched three innings of one game for the Kansas City A's.

He died June 8, 1982, his ageless right arm an unsolved mystery to gerontologists—but not to Paige. "The more I pitched," he said, "the more my arm got stronger."

It's 1971 and Paige stands alongside the plaque showing him to be a member of Baseball's Hall of Fame at Cooperstown, N.Y. He was named to the shrine earlier that year.

ARNOLD PALMER

Charismatic Leader of "Arnie's Army"

Arnold Palmer won only one U.S. Open and failed to capture another top prize of his trade, the PGA Championship, yet no other individual had greater impact on the fabulous growth of golf.

In the 1950s and early 1960s when this onetime rather snobbish sport spilled out of the fashionable country clubs and into the parlors of every day society, it was Palmer, the charismatic, belt-tugging, fast-walking charger who greased the track for the transition.

Network television was just burgeoning into a giant, hungry monster which had to be fed constantly to keep the cash registers clanging. The golf tour was seen as an appealing morsel for the sports fan. The Saturday and Sunday afternoon channels became choked with live and taped golf competitions, replacing the usual fare of cowboys and Indians. The whole family watched.

It was a situation that called for a Ruthian figure, a heroic symbol such as major league baseball found in the great Babe Ruth after the credibility of the sport had been threatened by the Black Sox Scandal of 1919.

Palmer was it—the catalyst of his time. He burst upon the scene as a natural hero—the rugged, strong-faced son of a greenskeeper from the small steel town of Latrobe, Pennsylvania, about 30 miles from Pittsburgh. A sturdy 165 pounds, he was built like a middleweight fighter with powerful, tapering shoulders, hands like ham hocks and arms like pistons.

To go with the physical assets he had a boyish, nut-brown face that ran the gamut of changing expressions. While concentrating, his brow became furrowed and his jaw tightened, a cigarette at times dangling from his lips, a habit later discarded.

His mannerisms titillated the galleries and enthralled housewives and the teen-age set, who formed the major segment of what became familiarly known as "Arnie's Army."

In the midst of a tense match, he often would stop and, his nose wrinkling, stare skyward at a passing airplane. When he rolled in a long birdie putt—too often for the comfort of his adversaries but always to the delight of his worshipful legions—his face would break into a broad grin.

He carried on a running conversation with the gallery. When he was on one of his characteristic rolls, he was inclined to increase his walking pace as if eager to step in for the kill.

"With this man, it's let it go or blow it, all or nothing," said Palmer's longtime caddie at the Masters Tournament, Nathaniel "Iron Man" Avery. "He don't know what it is to play safe. When he makes one of his charges, he just tugs at his glove, jerks on his trousers and starts walking fast and tells me, 'The game is on.'"

The veteran Gene Sarazen said Arnie was most dangerous when he appeared on the ropes, "ready to be counted out."

"He is fantastic," said contemporary Jimmy Demaret. "He just seems to will the ball into the hole."

During Palmer's heyday, the period between 1956 and 1964 when he won four Masters crowns, Arnie's Army was co-ed with no age limitations. Young ladies wore sweaters with "Arnie

Arnold Palmer, who had the greatest impact on the fabulous growth of golf, tees off on the 15th hole in the July, 1955 St. Paul Open tournament.

Housewives and the teenage set formed the major segment of "Arnie's Army." Note the "Go Arnie" sign here on the 12th green at the Houston Champions International golf tournament in May, 1967.

baby" crocheted across the chest. Other fans flaunted signs which said, "I am a member of Arnie's Army." The Army had its own air corps. Often, when Arnie was on the course, small, private planes would fly overhead, trailing streamers which said, "Go, Arnie, Go!"

Such flagrant displays of partisanship were often distracting to Palmer's rivals and an embarrassment to Palmer himself. Often galleries would break and start running to the next tee after Arnie holed out even though his playing partners were still on the green with putts remaining.

Although he won only one U.S. Open, Palmer tied for the title on three other occasions only to lose in playoffs and was also runner-up a fourth time. Meanwhile, he was racking up a total of 61 tour victories, including his four Masters; capturing consecutive British Open crowns in 1961 and 1962 and making frustrating runs at the PGA, which mysteriously escaped him although he finished second three times.

Arnie was given his first set of clubs by his father, Milfred "Deac" Palmer, when he was four, and began caddying and working in the caddie shop of the nine-hole Latrobe course when he was 11. He shot a 71 and won a tournament when he was in the seventh grade. He attended Wake Forest University, spent three years in the Coast Guard and began playing golf regularly while working as a manufacturer's agent in Cleveland.

He won the National Amateur in 1954 and, shortly afterward while playing in an amateur tournament in Pennsylvania, met Winnie Walzer, to whom he proposed a week later. The two planned to spend their honeymoon in England while Arnie played with the U.S. Walker Cup team. Instead, Arnie and Winnie decided to hit the pro tour. With $600 borrowed from Palmer's dad, the two set out in a second-hand house trailer.

After the PGA's six-month probationary period, Palmer began collecting prize money almost immediately. He won his first tournament in 1955, two in 1956, four in 1957, virtually

Still a highlight of the gallery, Palmer engages in a practice session for the 1986 Masters tournament. Altogether, Arnie won four Masters crowns.

doubling his prize money each year. He was the leading money winner in 1958 with $42,608 after capturing his first Masters.

He became the game's first millionaire.

His greatest year was 1960 when he won the Masters, rallied with a stunning 65 to capture his only U.S. Open at Denver, then went to ancient St. Andrews where he had the British Open virtually clinched before a rainstorm hit, allowing Australian Kel Nagle to edge ahead by a stroke.

Palmer was golf's first conglomerate. He set up his own company which manufactured golf clubs, balls, shirts, slacks, shoes and gloves. He headed 11 clothing companies with branches in Australia, Japan and Europe. He was the largest stockholder in a chain of putting courses. He owned a printing company, insurance agency, investment firm and several golf courses.

He became the outstanding sports personality of his day. He was President Eisenhower's favorite golf partner. He wrote instructional articles, appeared in several TV skits, cut records and endorsed dozens of items.

Most of which he probably would have swapped for one PGA trophy.

WALTER PAYTON

A Standout, Durable Record-Breaker

Walter Payton is certainly one for the books.

In his college days at Jackson State, when he ran, kicked field goals and extra points, and passed, Payton broke into the NCAA record books with 66 touchdowns and 464 career points.

As a professional with the Chicago Bears, he continued to break records by the yard. In 1984, his 10th year in the National Football League, Payton surpassed Jim Brown's all-time rushing record of 12,312 yards. And in 1986, he became the first player in NFL history to amass 20,000 all-purpose yards.

En route to those magnificent statistical achievements, Payton generally became recognized as the game's quintessential halfback: He could run or receive with equal ability, and even throw the ball when the situation demanded.

Considering Payton's style as a punishing runner, and the pounding he took from opposing players, his longevity alone was remarkable.

"It's amazing," said former Bears' running great Gale Sayers, whose career was cut short by a knee injury. "It's as if the

Chicago Bears' great Walter Payton carries the ball for a six-yard gain in the second quarter of a 1984 game against Tampa Bay. The Bears won, 34-14.

man upstairs said, 'Walter, I'm going to make you a football player. And for as long as you want to play, you can play.'"

Payton's durability has been almost as much of a story as his statistical accomplishments. In his first 12 years in the league, he missed only one game, and that was in his rookie season, 1975.

"He follows the old gladiator code," Brown said.

Before the 1983 season, Payton had surgery on both knees, yet toughed it out for the entire year. Despite damaged knees, he rushed for 1,421 yards.

"He ran stiff-legged all year," Bears' Coach Mike Ditka recalled, "and he ran for more than 1,400 yards. The doctors wondered how he did it on those knees."

Whether plunging through a hole in the line, cutting outside or squirming forward with tacklers draped all over him, Payton may well be the hardest back to bring down in the NFL.

"I don't know if there's a way to stop him," said Bart Starr, the former quarterback and coach of the Green Bay Packers. "I haven't seen anyone in the league do a good job of it. You just try to contain him. You don't reach and grab and arm-tackle him."

Payton also set the NFL record for most rushing yards in a game, 275, against the Minnesota Vikings on December 29, 1977, and at one point won five straight National Conference rushing titles, including the 1977 season when he gained 1,852 yards, third-best in league history. At that point, Payton was the best running back in football, and he later was voted to the all-NFL team of the 1970s.

A self-effacing player who continually gives credit to the offensive line for his exploits, Payton not only is a good runner, but a good blocker. In short, Payton plays bigger and stronger than he looks. He is actually 5-foot-10½ and about 200 pounds.

"To me," former Bears Coach Jack Pardee said, "he's a big man without great height. He's big in every sense—bone structure, muscle structure. He's got great leg strength and back strength. He has fine agility and is light on his feet."

On the field, Payton inflicts as much punishment as he receives from tacklers.

"If you want to play a long time," Payton said, "you have to protect yourself. You can't always keep accepting the blows."

Having watched Payton reintroduce the wicked straight-arm to a new generation of safeties and cornerbacks, one teammate observed: "It's like a recoilless rifle. There are a number of defensive backs in the league with fewer neck vertebrae because of it."

Payton first attracted the attention of the pros with his accomplishments at Jackson State, where he earned the nickname "Sweetness," for his sweet moves on the football field.

Looking for a centerpiece in their efforts to rebuild, the Bears picked Payton on the first round of the 1975 draft, the fourth player chosen overall.

After an inauspicious rookie year in which he gained only 679 yards rushing, Payton broke loose for 1,390 yards in his second NFL season. Except for the strike-shortened 1982 campaign, 1,000-yard seasons became an annual occurrence for him after that.

Carrying him along, as much as anything, was a boyish enthusiasm for the game that he never lost. After tackles, Payton hops up and rushes back to the huddle. During timeouts, he leads the stadium in cheers. When he puts the ball down after he is tackled, he inches it ahead a little—a practice he figures has gained him about 100 extra yards in his career.

And when friends describe Payton, they invariably compare him with a kid who in some ways never has grown up—despite various business interests that have made him successful away from football.

"He's always snapping towels and lighting cherry bombs," said Bob Avellini, a former Bears' quarterback. "In a meeting when everybody's half-asleep, he'll give out an inhuman scream just for the heck of it."

The playful Payton also once astounded onlookers by leap-frogging over the head of 6-4 Brad Ecklund, the Bears' defensive line coach. Another time, he walked 50 yards on his hands across a football field while teammates stared with open-mouthed amazement.

Someone suggested that Payton was football's answer to Pete Rose and he liked the analogy.

"I'd like to be remembered like that, somebody who stands for hard work and total effort," Payton said. "I want to do everything perfectly on the field—pass blocking, running a dummy route, carrying out a fake, all of it."

To many, Payton has come closer to that sublime ideal than anyone in football.

In 1984, his 10th year in the NFL, Payton surpassed Jim Brown's career rushing record of 12,312 yards. Here, Payton is honored for his achievement by receiving a medal of honor at Chicago City Hall. Brown (left) was given a key to the city.

PELE

The World's Most Famous Athlete

To the world he was simply "Pele." Single names always have been sufficient to connote greatness. Caesar. Michelangelo. Garbo. In his field, there was none greater than Edson Arantes do Nascimento, the poor kid from a remote Brazilian village who became the most celebrated figure in the world's most popular sport—the sport known as football or "futbol," but called soccer in America.

If a universal poll were taken to determine the greatest athlete of the century, the honor almost certainly would fall on the slender shoulders of the leaping, dashing, ball-kicking wizard known as Pele, "The Black Pearl."

Soccer, a game requiring extraordinary coordination, finesse and skill, never gained major league status among Americans, weaned on baseball and converted to the violence of gridiron football. But you can find kids kicking soccer balls in vacant lots from Brisbane to Bangladesh, Madagascar to Madrid.

Everywhere, their hero is Pele.

Relatively slight at 5 feet, 8 inches and 160 pounds, he was a veritable Houdini on the field—gliding along the green pitch, feinting, dribbling, legs moving like a marionette as if controlled by invisible strings, and smashing the ball into the net with bow-and-arrow accuracy.

He was lionized by fans and world leaders.

His recognition factor in the capitals of foreign lands matched, if it didn't actually exceed, that of former heavyweight boxing champion Muhammad Ali. He stopped traffic on the boulevards. Fans tore at his jersey and shorts for souvenirs. He was mobbed by admirers at every game.

It's said that when he visited Biafra, a civil war there was suspended for two days. Similarly, political disputes in Khartoum and Algiers were put in abeyance while he performed. In Spain, they cancelled bullfights rather than compete with Pele's appearance on television.

Pele was born in the small Brazilian village of Tres Coracoes. His father, whose nickname was Dondinho, played on the town's soccer team. Later, the father got a better job and moved the family to Bauru, a larger city.

Young Edson, who hadn't yet been given the name Pele, idolized his father and hoped to follow in his footsteps. He had to quit school at the age of 10 because of poor grades and clashes

Before retiring from Brazil's national team in 1971, Pele, "the Black Pearl," scored 1,086 goals during his 16-year career. Four years later, he signed to play for the New York Cosmos of the North American Soccer League.

with his classmates. The townspeople got accustomed to seeing him practicing on the streets with a makeshift ball made of a stocking stuffed with rags.

Pele was only 11 when a friend of his father, a former Sao Paulo player named Waldemar de Brito, gave him a chance to play with the Bauru team, which was strictly small time. Yet de Brito was convinced the kid was destined to play with the sport's elite.

Failing to get his old club, Sao Paulo, to take a look at his protege, de Brito finally prevailed on another friend with the Santos team to give the sensational youngster a tryout. The Santos coach, Louis Alonzo Perez, agreed reluctantly and, over the objections of his superiors, hired Pele on a trial basis for $75 a month.

That seemed like a fortune to the 15-year-old Pele who, like his father, had been playing for $4.50 a game.

The youth was awed by his new surroundings and suddenly found his confidence shaken, although he continued to play hard and started to gain recognition from his older teammates.

"I was scared of failing," Pele recalled.

"He was just an errand boy for the older players at first," the Santos coach said. "He would buy soda for them—and things like that. Then, before they knew it, they were looking up to him."

Pele is carried off the field in a driving rain by members of the New York Cosmos and Santos of Brazil after he completed a 1977 exhibition game in which he played for both teams. He's waving the Brazilian and United States flags in Giants Stadium in New Jersey. The game was announced as Pele's last of his brilliant career.

Pele moved from the junior team to the regular squad, and at age 16 became a regular on the Santos Football Club. His salary was raised to $600 a month. The club rewarded the Santos coach with a $1,000 bonus.

Pele led Santos to league championships in his first six seasons. He played more than 1,000 games for the team, averaging a goal a game. In the low-scoring game of soccer, 1,000 career goals are considered the equivalent of 1,000 home runs in baseball.

He helped Brazil to three World Cup championships—like the Olympics, staged every four years—in 1958, 1962 and 1970, although he was injured during the 1962 tournament.

Pele scored his 1,000th goal on November 19, 1969, in Rio de Janeiro's National Stadium, an event given precedence in many newspapers over the lunar landing of Apollo 12.

Twenty months later, on July 18, 1971, having scored his 1,086th goal earlier at Sao Paulo, Pele made his final interna-tional appearance against Yugoslavia in Belgrade. The spectacle was televised throughout Europe and South America.

Pele played a half, then trotted around the field in tears, waving his jersey to the crowd as the band played the Brazilian national anthem. The 130,000 spectators went wild.

Having been married early in his career to Rosemarie Cholby, Pele had secured a sound financial business base with endorsements and other enterprises reportedly netting him $1.5 million a year. He had an office staff of 20.

Still, there was one last hurrah.

In 1975, he signed a $4.7 million contract with Warner Communications to play three years and do promotional work for the New York Cosmos of the North American Soccer League. The signing at the swank 21 Club in New York almost turned into a riot.

"You can tell the world," Pele said, "soccer has finally come to America."

WILLIE PEP

"The Greatest Boxer I Ever Saw"

Willie Pep, perhaps the most brilliant featherweight champion in ring history, could beat anybody in the world his weight with two exceptions: A tall, bony jaw-bender named Sandy Saddler and, sadly, a guy named Willie Pep.

Pep fought Saddler four times for the 126-pound crown and lost three of them, all by a knockout. He outpointed Sandy once in a fight that rattled the rafters at the old Madison Square Garden and is still listed high in the annals of boxing for its 15 rounds of legal mayhem. That fight, on Feb. 11, 1949, was probably Pep's peak as a boxer.

Willie was called his own worst enemy and worked at it. He made a lot of money but spent even more. His financial mistakes forced him to keep fighting long after he should have quit the ring. At the time of his last pro bout, a losing six-rounder to somebody named Calvin Woodland in 1966, Pep was 43.

Before he encountered the human meat-grinder that was Saddler, Pep lost only one bout in a string of 136. He began his career with 62 victories in a row, lost an over-the-weight fight to the awkwardly skillful Sammy Angott, a two-time lightweight champ, and then ran off 73 wins in succession.

Born Guglielmo Papoleo in September, 1942, in Middletown, Conn., he gravitated to the ring at an early age and was a star amateur in the late 1930s. Willie turned pro in 1940, changing his name to the Americanized version. At 18, he already was a classic boxer with fast hands, magnificent legs, a sharpening ring brain and a warrior's heart.

By November, 1942, after 55 straight victories, he was given a shot at Chalky Wright's featherweight crown. He was barely 20. Wright was a battle-tested toughie with skill and a solid punch. But, in the fight, also at Madison Square Garden, Pep poured it on, stabbing jabs, vicious crosses, utilizing speed and then more speed, to win the decision. At 20 he was the youngest champion in four decades.

Ring historians have listed Pep as a superior boxer. He was,
but not the Fancy Dan kind. Willie was closer to being an alley fighter. He punched equally hard with both hands. He was dangerous when hurt. His philosophy was... "Hit the other guy as often as you can but don't let him hit you."

Angelo Dundee, who later trained Muhammad Ali, called Pep the greatest boxer he ever saw. Not trained. Saw. Pep himself summed up his talents this way: "I was strictly a boxer but, boy, could I box. When I got hit, I was sometimes hurt. But I won a lot more fights than I lost. And I fought a lot of times, once or twice a month, for a number of years."

The record book lists the unnerving total of 241 bouts for Pep. He knocked out 65 opponents and won 164 decisions. There was one draw and he dropped a decision five times. He was knocked out on six occasions. Willie was elected to the Boxing Hall of Fame in 1963.

He first took on Saddler in October, 1948, and lost his championship on a four-round knockout. Willie looked weary, surprisingly so for someone only 26 years of age. For the first time he felt the lash of criticism. There even were suggestions that he should retire. Pep bristled and made plans to win back both his title and reputation.

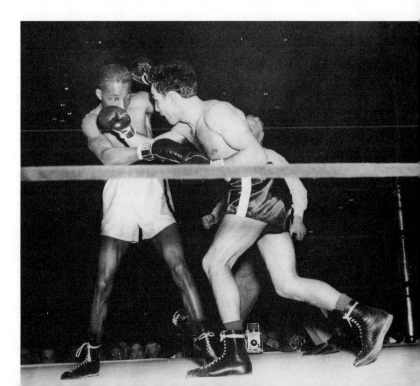

Pep connects with a right to the face of champion Sandy Saddler in the first round of their 15-round featherweight return title bout in Madison Square Garden on Feb. 11, 1949. Pep regained the crown he had lost to Sandy by scoring a unanimous decision.

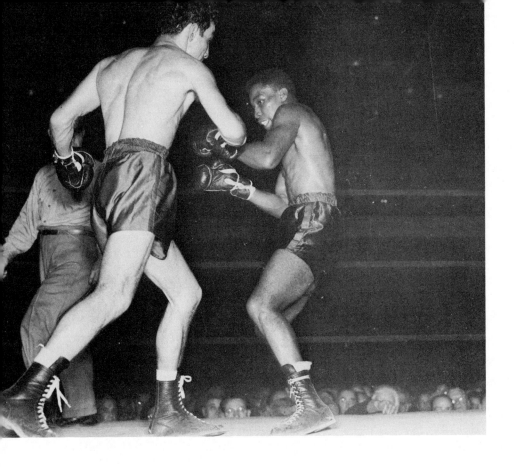

After the contract for a return bout was signed, Pep, grim and silent, trained with the dedication of a Spartan seeking revenge for an affront. "I know there aren't going to be many more chances if I miss this one," he told Manager Lou Viscusi. "But I won't miss it."

Every seat was filled at the Garden and they were standing all around the rear rows when Pep and Saddler slid between the ropes. The referee was Eddie Joseph. The ensuing 15 rounds were right out of Sylvester Stallone's movie ring classic, Rocky, but there was one difference. Pep and Saddler were using live ammunition. Slashing, punishing gloves were their weapons. There were no doubles, no stunt men, no fake punches, no ketchup substituting for blood.

Pep took an early lead over Saddler, who at 5-11, was more than five inches taller than wily Willie. Pep moved constantly, flicked jabs to earn points, and had Saddler wondering where he would turn up next. Sandy located him in the fourth round and nailed Pep with three hard lefts, thud, thud, thud. Willie must have been hurt but his eyes didn't show it. He ducked under Sandy's long arms and escaped to the center of the ring.

In the middle rounds, Pep popped Sandy with a couple of surprise right leads and shook him up. But mostly it was hit-and-run, Willie on those dancer's legs and Sandy trying to catch him. In the 10th round, Sandy caught Willie with a pistol right hand and turned him wobbly. He also opened cuts on Pep's face and at the end of the round, Willie's corner wanted to know if he wanted the fight stopped. Pep's eyes blazed: "No."

Willie found new life in the 11th and 12th and had Sandy dizzy with his quick shots to the face and artful dodging. They were Pep's rounds big. Saddler came out for the 13th raging and went after a knockout. Pep was hurt but not groggy. A thin line of blood ran down his face. But he stayed on his feet.

In the 15th and final round, Saddler again went on to hunt for a finisher. For half the round it seemed he might get it. But Pep again reached deep for some hidden reserve. He stood in mid-ring and his punches forced the amazed Saddler to retreat. Pep simply took the ring away from Sandy.

At the final bell, the noise could be heard back in Willie's hometown of Hartford, Conn. Referee Joseph gave him the decision, 10 rounds to five. Judge Frank Forbes had it 9-5-1. Judge Jack O'Sullivan scored it 9-6. The verdict was unanimous for Pep. Willie was so battered from Sandy's fists he needed 11 stitches in his face. But he had the featherweight title again.

But nothing was ever the same for Pep after that. He lost to Saddler on an eight-round K.O. in 1950 and went out the same way in nine rounds in 1951. Things went from bad to worse and ultimately to worst for the once great fighter. He was accused of being somewhere between lackluster and inept in some of his fights. He even got a suspension from the august body, then the boxing seat of power, known as the New York Boxing Commission.

Looking back at the end of his career, Pep mused: "I guess everybody would like to know what happened to all the big money I made. So would I. I have so much scar tissue I look as though I'm wearing blinders. But boxing was my business. And I think I was pretty good at it."

On balance, Pep was more than good. He was great.

RICHARD PETTY

Stock Car Racing's Best

One can usually tell what part of the racetrack Richard Petty is in. Just look for the swarm of people that almost constantly surrounds him.

The "King" of NASCAR stock car racing for more than a quarter of a century holds court most of the time when he is at his place of business.

He isn't hard to spot. He usually is wearing a feathered cowboy hat, sunglasses and snakeskin cowboy boots, and smoking a long, thin cigar.

If he isn't signing autographs and talking to fans, Petty is telling stories to the media or talking with other racing people about the sport he has loved since he began helping his father, Lee, in the formative days of NASCAR.

The rest of the time, the tall, slim racing veteran helps work on his car, and even that normally uninspiring chore usually draws people who simply want to bask in the presence of royalty.

Lee Petty was a NASCAR champion and winner of 54 races, but his eldest son has far surpassed not only him, but everyone else in the sport.

The native of Level Cross, N.C., has won seven championships, seven Daytona 500s and, most amazing, a total of 200 races, almost double the amount accumulated by the runner-up, David Pearson.

"I've had some good luck during my career," "King Richard" said. "I had the good fortune to grow up with the sport and have my daddy to watch and learn from. Then I raced with some of the greats and they taught me a lot. And maybe I taught them a few things, too."

Petty, who was crew chief for his father for several years—one of the youngest crew chiefs ever—finally got behind the wheel of a NASCAR stock car in 1959. But he didn't win for the first time until 1960.

"After I drove a few races, I began to wonder if I wouldn't be better off taking care of daddy's cars," Petty said. "I found out real quick how much I didn't know about driving a race car,

even after watching daddy for so long. But I found out quickly that I enjoyed it. And I learned from just about everybody."

He learned well enough that in 1960, at the age of 22, he won his first three races. It could have been four.

Early that season, still winless and admittedly beginning to wonder if he ever would win, Petty got his car "hooked up" at the old Lakewood Speedway in Atlanta, one of the many dirt tracks of that era that no longer exists.

"I was just flying that day," he recalled. "All of a sudden, I was running out front. Funny thing, with all the traffic and the

Sweet victory. Petty, the king of NASCAR, kisses the trophy he received for winning the 1974 Daytona 500 at the Daytona Speedway. The triumph marked the fifth time he had won the event.

Another Daytona success. Petty in car #43 gets the checkered flag as he wins the 21st annual Daytona 500 in 1979. Darrell Waltrip in car #88 came in second.

dust, it didn't seem a lot different than being behind, but I knew the difference and I liked it.

"When I got the checkered (flag), I didn't know what to think. It was a great feeling. Then, just when they were going to hand me the trophy, somebody came up and said, 'There's a protest.' Turned out that daddy, who was second, protested that I cut across the grass in one turn, which everybody did.

"They (NASCAR) decided for him, and daddy got the win and the trophy. People usually tell that story to show how competitive our family is. But, there was a lot better reason.

"I was disappointed, but daddy explained it to me later. NASCAR wanted to get some of the guys to buy new cars and not keep running the same old ones year after year. They paid more for winning in a new car. Daddy was in a new car and I was driving our old one, so by him winning, we got more money for first place, and I still got second-place money.

"Besides, daddy said I'd probably win some more races later."

By 1967, Lee was retired and Richard, with brother Maurice as his crew chief and first cousin Dale Inman the team manager, was the dominant figure in the new and growing sport.

Petty won 27 races that year, a single-season record that is unlikely ever to be challenged, much less broken. In fact, he finished in the top ten, 39 times in 48 starts that season.

He won 21 in 1971, and, in 1973, after the schedule had been shortened to about 30 races a year, he set the modern standard of 13 victories in 30 starts.

"It's always been hard to win," Petty said. "But, now, there's so much good equipment and so many good teams, that it's tough to dominate like we did in '67."

His landmark 200th victory came on July 4, 1984, in the Firecracker 400 at Daytona Beach, Fla. Among the more than 100,000 spectators was President Ronald Reagan.

For Petty, who had just turned 46, it was a gratifying and fulfilling moment.

"Each time you win a race, you start thinking about the next one—if you'll get it, when you'll get it. The 200th though, was so special that I thought about it and enjoyed it for a while."

The car he drove to that victory now is on display at the Smithsonian Institution in Washington, D.C., an honor that delights Petty, who still can't resist joking about it.

"The next thing they'll put in the Smithsonian is me, after I retire."

JACQUES PLANTE

The Masked Gambler

The truly inspired, innovative athlete is one who leaves a lasting impact on his sport. In Jacques Plante's case, he left a legacy for which every hockey goaltender—from the NHL to midget leagues at the local rink—is thankful. He was the first to wear a facemask in a game.

"Jacques Plante meant as much to hockey as any man," said Emile Francis, a former goalie who became a coach and general manager in the National Hockey League. "He revolutionized the way to play goal and he knew what the future would be when he came up with the mask."

For much of the 1950s and early '60s, Plante was the game's premier goalie. But his accomplishments—seven Vezina Trophies for lowest goals-allowed average, including an unprecedented five straight while leading the Montreal Canadiens to Stanley Cup championships from 1956 through 1960; six NHL titles; a lifetime 2.38 goals-against mark; 82 shutouts—only tell part of the story.

Certainly Plante would have made the Hockey Hall of Fame on his statistics alone. When he entered the Hall in 1978, however, the numbers became somewhat obscured. For Plante will be remembered as the goalie who brought a new, gambling style to the crease—and areas beyond. And, of course, for developing the facemask, which has become a standard piece of every goalie's equipment.

Plante joined the Canadiens in 1953, making his NHL debut in a playoff game at Chicago.

"I was so nervous, I couldn't tie my skates," said the native of Shawinigan Falls, Quebec, who once played for 50 cents a game in an industrial league. "I was shaking before the game and I wondered if the other players thought there was something wrong with me."

They found nothing wrong with his goaltending, as Plante blanked the Blackhawks 3-0 in Game 6 of the semifinals. The

Canadiens won the next game to take the series, then beat Boston in five games to win the championship. Plante started only one game of the finals, a 4-1 loss, but, by the next season, he had supplanted Gerry McNeil as Montreal's No. 1 goalie.

Plante's early years as a regular in Montreal were remarkably successful, although his wandering style of goaltending wasn't readily accepted by the public.

"One of the amateur teams I played for was so bad I had to always chase the puck behind the cage," he explained.

Coach Toe Blake tolerated Plante's sojourns from the crease

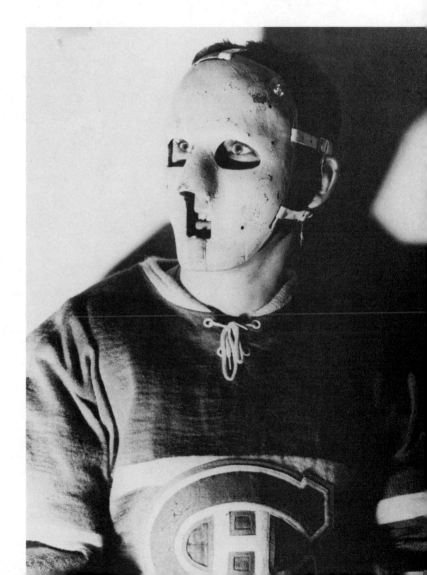

Plante, pictured here in 1960 wearing a Montreal Canadiens' uniform, introduced the face mask for goalies on Nov. 1, 1959 after suffering facial injuries in an NHL game against the Rangers in New York's Madison Square Garden.

to clear pucks because "Jacques was so good at it, it was like having a third defenseman on the ice."

But the fans often shouted at Plante to return to the net or "reveille-toi!" (Wake Up!) when he allowed a goal because he was out of the net.

Plante never took well to such criticism. When he injured a knee in 1960 and the five-time champions lost several games because of spotty goaltending, Plante was enraged by the reaction of the not-so-faithful Montreal Forum crowd.

"After seven years, all they see are my saves... not my work,"

Playing for the Rangers in a 1964 game against Toronto, Plante leaves his goal crease to clear the puck. "The mask never hindered me," the legendary netminder insisted. "It was made for me to see the puck from all angles."

he said. "I play pro hockey. I know what it is like. But most of them, they played school hockey. They do not know."

What the fans did not know until Nov. 1, 1959, was that Plante was working on a plastic mask to use in games. He had designed a rudimentary one which he used in practice.

"It did not hinder me at all," Plante said. "It was made to allow me to see the puck from all angles. There is enough open room around the eyes and mouth and nose for breathing, and it gives the goalie protection from getting hurt badly in the face."

Stitches in the face were as much a part of a goalie's apparatus as his catching glove and blocker. Soon after that night of Nov. 1, 1959 in New York's Madison Square Garden, the face-mask would be found in every goalie's equipment bag.

Early in the first period, the Rangers' Andy Bathgate, one of hockey's hardest shooters, fired a backhander that caught Plante

on the nose. Plante was taken to the dressing room and stitched up, and Blake asked if he was ready to return to the ice.

"I said OK, if I could wear the mask," Plante said. "What could Blake do?"

Nothing except allow Plante to return to the net. The Canadiens won 3-1, and Plante had secured his place in history.

Plante was traded from Montreal to the Rangers in 1963, but he didn't like New York and retired 1½ years later to work for a Canadian brewery.

"It was fine for a while," he recalled. "But I was only 36, which is not old for a goalie."

In 1968, the St. Louis Blues, an expansion team which had lost in the Stanley Cup finals to the Canadiens the previous spring, persuaded Plante to return and team with Glenn Hall, another Hall of Fame goalie. Together, they won the Vezina Trophy and Plante had a 1.96 goals-against average in 37 appearances.

"Playing with Glenn was a treat for me," Plante said.

After two years with the Blues, Plante went to Toronto for three seasons and spent his final active years playing goal for Boston and then Edmonton of the World Hockey Association.

Later, he became a goaltending coach, and his books on the art of goaltending are part of every serious goalie's library.

How good was Plante? Since 1955, he was the only goalie to win the Hart Trophy as the NHL's Most Valuable Player. And, when he died of cancer in February 1986, the descriptions of him inevitably included one phrase:

"Legendary goaltender."

GARY PLAYER

The "Black Knight" of South Africa

Gary Player was the middle man in the celebrated triumvirate of golf's "Big Three," packaged and marketed by the ingenious entrepreneur, Mark McCormack, to grub for gold on the multimillion-dollar circuit. He was six years younger than Arnold Palmer and five years older than Jack Nicklaus, a link that forged a steel chain of fairway dominance from the late 1950s through the early 1980s.

He provided the international flavor to the famous trio—an undersized South African with powerful shoulders and arms who maintained a rigid discipline of diet and physical fitness routines to stay abreast of his two more muscular and more famous contemporaries.

McCormack built his world-girdling personal management company—the International Management Group—on an old golfing pal, Palmer, and ultimately added Player and Nicklaus as their fortunes increased. Nicklaus broke away to handle his own affairs.

Player felt slighted performing in the shadow of the charismatic, go-for-broke Arnie, the "Charger," one of sport's all-time heroes, and Nicklaus, the game's most prolific collector of major championships. He continually reminded the media that he must be considered in any vote on the greatest living golfer.

He had his credentials. He wasn't content, as are most players, to confine himself to the rich PGA tour. He was golf's Gulliver. He played—and won—all over the world.

No one—not Palmer, not Nicklaus—could match his record of international triumphs. Playing on four and sometimes five continents a year, he amassed a total of 128 titles, including 13 South African and seven Australian Open championships. He became the first foreigner to win the Masters in 1961 and added two more Masters titles, in 1974 and 1978.

He won the British Open three times and captured the U.S. Open in 1965, donating his first prize of $25,000 to the U.S. Golf Association for junior development but stipulating that $5,000 go to the cancer fund. He became one of only four players to have won all of the four major titles (the U.S. and British Opens, Masters and PGA). The others were Gene Sarazen, Ben Hogan and Nicklaus.

Player won the Suntory Match Play Tournament, a rigorous test against the world's best, five times; the World Series of Golf three times, and twice was individual titlist in the World Cup.

He carried a commuter card for air trips across the Atlantic. He fought time zones, jet lag, harassment because of his country's apartheid policies, and often golf writers chiding over his

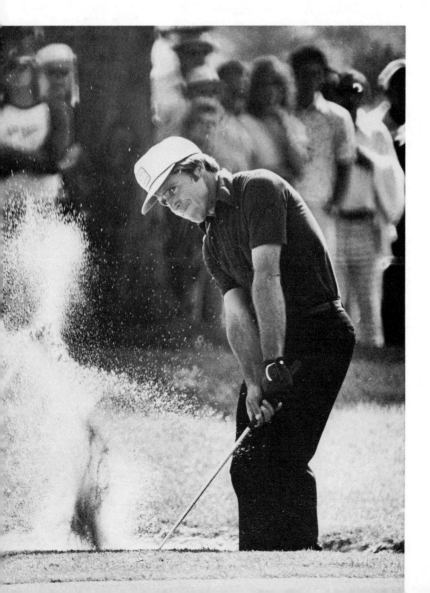

The "Black Knight" keeps his eye on the ball as he blasts from the trap during the 1979 Tournament of Champions in Carlsbad, California.

Player, practicing for the 1979 PGA championship, watches a putt glide to the cup. He became one of only four players to have won all the four major titles—the PGA, the U.S. and British Opens and the Masters.

many fetishes. But he faced every obstacle with a gentlemanly grace that made him a favorite of fans and fellow players. He was one of the original inductees into the World Golf Hall of Fame at Pinehurst, North Carolina.

Perhaps his closest friend on the tour was Nicklaus, who named a son after Gary.

A small man, 5 feet, 6 inches and 150 pounds, Player sought to compensate for his physical shortcomings through hours of strength-building exercises and psychological stimuli. For a long period, he wore complete black attire—cap, shirt, slacks and shoes. "It gives me strength," he said.

He went on a raisin binge. Signing a contract with a raisin company, he had raisins by the gross delivered to the locker room and shared them with his pals and the press. After losing the contract, he switched to bananas, and they poured in by the bunches. "Raisins rot your guts," Gary would say in a petulant jab at his former sponsors.

He might shoot an 80, then tell the press, "I never hit the ball better in my life."

He was careful not to offend his local guests by criticizing their golf course. But in his dispatches to the Argus newspapers back home, he might say, "The course stinks."

Player, called the "Black Knight," was an intense, deliberate competitor cut from the same swatch as Ben Hogan without the latter's dour, icy coldness.

Long an admirer of Hogan, Gary, experiencing a slump, once phoned the fabled "Wee Ice Mon" in Fort Worth, Texas, to ask how he might correct his problem.

"Who do you work for?" Hogan asked. "Dunlop," Gary replied. "Then call Mr. Dunlop," Hogan, manufacturer of his own clubs, snapped, and hung up.

Player was born November 1, 1935, in Johannesburg. His father was a strapping six-footer who worked in the gold mines. His mother died of cancer when Gary was eight.

In school, Gary lettered in rugby and cricket, ran the hurdles in track and was a crack swimmer. He also hung around the Virginia Park golf course, where he met Vivienne Verway, the pro's daughter, his future wife and mother of his six children.

Player became Verway's assistant at 16, and at 18 turned professional, making the South African tour on his father's borrowed money. He received an invitation to the Masters in 1957 and played in the U.S. Open in 1958.

Gary's first major victory came in the British Open in 1959.

In the 1961 Masters, he got the green jacket when Palmer took a double bogey on the final hole.

Playing in the 1969 PGA Championship at Dayton, Ohio, Gary was badgered by anti-apartheid demonstrators throughout his round. Once, as he moved from green to tee, a spectator tossed a cup of ice in his face.

Stunned, Player looked at the offender and asked, "What have I ever done to you, sir?"

Passionately patriotic, Gary never tried to apologize for his country's policies nor did he defend them. Instead, he invited Lee Elder, America's best-known black golfer, to South Africa as his personal guest and, in the United States, insisted on having a black caddie, Rabbit Dyer.

WILLIS REED

The Ultimate Team Player

Willis Reed was once asked, "What would you want written about you as a ballplayer after your playing days are over?" His answer was simple.

"If just one thing was to be written about me, I'd like it to be, 'Willis Reed gave 100 percent of what he had all the time,'" he said.

"They don't have to write that I was the greatest ballplayer in the world," Reed said. "When a man gives 100 percent as a ballplayer and as a man, there's nothing else that can be asked of him. And he must be considered successful in his own eyes and those of others."

Unquestionably, Reed was a successful player—a self-made player. He did not have the natural skills of a great athlete, but through determination and hard work, he became an out-

standing athlete—good enough to earn a place in the Basketball Hall of Fame at Springfield, Massachusetts.

Reed reached his greatest heights as a player during his 10-year career in the National Basketball Association with the New York Knicks, from the 1964-65 season until the 1973-74 season, when painful knee injuries forced him to retire at the age of 31. He stepped down reluctantly, doing so only when he realized he would never be able to again perform up to his own standards.

When he retired, he got his wish: It was written that he had given 100 percent effort.

The most memorable example of that came on May 8, 1970, in the seventh and deciding game of the NBA championship series between the Knicks and the Los Angeles Lakers.

The first four games were split, each team winning one in the other city. The fifth game, in New York's Madison Square Garden, seemed to belong to the Lakers. They opened a big lead, then watched Reed leave the game with a severely bruised hip. But the Knicks rallied to win 107-100.

The still ailing Reed sat out Game 6 at Los Angeles, and the Lakers trounced the Knicks 135-113, behind Wilt Chamberlain's 45 points and 27 rebounds and Jerry West's 33 points and 13 assists. When the teams returned to New York for Game 7, it did not appear that Reed would be able to play. When he was not with the team during the pregame warmup, the sellout crowd of 19,500 expected the worst.

Suddenly, moments before the start of the game, a cheer began to ripple through the crowd. Everyone focused on the tunnel that leads from the locker room area under the stands onto the court.

There, walking slowly, dragging his right leg, was Reed. By the time the Knicks' 6-foot-10, 240-pound center stepped onto the court, the roar of the crowd was deafening.

His leg bandaged and shot with painkiller, the hobbling Reed managed to hit his first two shots—the Knicks' first two field goals—over the shocked Chamberlain. Those were the only points that Reed was to score during the game, in 27 minutes,

Reed (19) and Dave DeBusschere, both of the New York Knicks, vie with Boston's Dave Cowens for possession of a rebound during NBA game in Nov. 1972.

Slipping between Boston Celtics, Reed grabs the ball during 1973 playoff game in Boston Garden. At left is the Celtics' Paul Silas.

but he had provided the inspiration that the Knicks needed to beat the Lakers 113-99 for their first NBA championship.

Although Walt Frazier had helped account for 74 Knicks' points with 36 points and 19 assists, the courageous Reed was named the winner of the Most Valuable Player Award for the championship series. It capped a season in which he also had been chosen the MVP in the NBA All-Star Game and for the regular season—making him the only player in league history to win all three awards in the same season.

Teammate Cazzie Russell marveled at the clutch performance of the Knicks' captain in the decisive seventh game against the Lakers.

"The captain showed us something that night," Russell said. "He showed us he has a lot of guts. His mere presence, the way he kept going—it made us play harder."

Reed enjoyed another outstanding season in 1970-71, but his 1971-72 season was limited to 11 games because of excruciat-

ing pain in his knees and legs. Determinedly, he came back in 1972-73 and led the Knicks to another NBA championship, earning MVP honors again. But after playing only 19 games in the 1973-74 season, Reed's ravaged legs no longer could stand the pounding, and he had to quit.

He had averaged 18.7 points and 12.9 rebounds per game for his career, played on two championship teams and in six All-Star Games, but more important than the cold statistics was his character. Reed was a player who measured success in terms of victories, not points scored.

And his pride was most impressive.

That pride was instilled in him by his parents, his teachers and his coaches while Reed was growing up in rural Louisiana.

Reed was born June 25, 1942, in Hico, Louisiana, but he grew up in nearby Bernice, where he attended segregated West Side High.

"I remember when I was young, out in the fields picking cot-

The most memorable example of Reed's courage was exhibited on May 8, 1970 when, despite a severe leg injury, he helped the Knicks beat Los Angeles in the deciding game of the championship final. Here, in 1976, he holds his uniform with number 19 on it which was retired during pre-game ceremonies. Former teammate Walt Frazier is at the left.

ton," Reed wrote in his book, "A Will to Win." "I wanted to pick enough cotton to earn four dollars a day. Most of the time I couldn't make that much money because I just couldn't weigh-in that much cotton. Then I got to the point where I was able to take on the more strenuous job of hauling hay.

"I had to work hard, but I could earn five dollars a day hauling hay. I was so proud that I could work at the same job as my father, make the same amount of money he did, even overtime if I wanted... I received plenty of encouragement from my mother and father."

Reed's hard work toward his basketball career began in high school, where Coach Lendon Stone helped mold his values. "Coach Stone was a dominant force in my life... and more than just athletics," Reed wrote.

From West Side High, Reed went to Grambling, where under the guidance of Coach Fred Hobdy, he led the Tigers to a 110-17 record in four years, as well as three Southwestern Athletic Conference titles and an NAIA championship. Reed also was selected a Little All-American three times and scored 2,335 points.

He then was selected on the second round of the 1964 draft by the Knicks. He became their starting center, the team's only representative in the All-Star Game and the NBA's Rookie of the Year. It was the start of a brilliant NBA playing career, but when Reed's playing days ended, his relationship with the Knicks did not.

He coached the team to a 43-39 record and a playoff berth in the 1977-78 season, but was fired after 14 games of the 1978-79 season because of disagreements with management. He spent the next five years in business, buying real estate on the Ivory Coast and in New York, and a restaurant in Washington, D.C., then returned to basketball in 1980 as a part-time assistant at St. John's. He then coached at Creighton University from 1981-85, compiling a 52-65 record, and became an assistant coach with the NBA's Atlanta Hawks and Sacramento Kings.

Reed will hardly be remembered for his coaching. His playing days, however, will long be remembered. He was a players' player, a man who made the most of his ability and could be counted upon to do his job every game. He always gave 100 percent.

MAURICE RICHARD

...And the Rocket's Red Glare

One of the many accepted axioms in hockey for nearly 30 years was that there was no place on the ice for the unorthodox. Except, perhaps, in the net.

To place a left-handed shooter on right wing was as preposterous an idea in the 1940s as for a goaltender to wear a mask...until "The Rocket" launched himself into the Montreal Canadiens' lineup and toward the Hall of Fame.

Maurice Richard earned that nickname early in his career. He was "The Rocket" for many reasons—his skating speed; his ability to explode from a standing start; his strength and relentlessness. When Richard moved in on a target, usually the puck and, then, the enemy goal, there was no stopping him.

"'The Rocket' was the perfect description for Maurice," said Toe Blake, a teammate of Richard's and later his coach with the Canadiens. "When he would take off, nothing got in his way that could stop him."

"What I remember most about Rocket was his eyes," recalled goalie Glenn Hall. "When he came flying toward you with the puck on his stick, his eyes were all lit up, flashing and gleaming like a pinball machine. It was terrifying."

Just the thought of taking on Richard had to be terrifying for opponents. His intensity was matched by an explosive temper which often got him into trouble. He always fought back and, sometimes, was the instigator, although Richard usually felt he was the victim.

That fiery temperament spurred Richard to previously unattained heights. While players such as Bobby Hull, Phil Esposito, Mike Bossy and Wayne Gretzky made 50-goal seasons commonplace, Richard was the first player to reach the half-century figure. When he did it in 1944-45, it was in a 50-game season compared to 80 nowadays.

Richard scored 544 goals in his 18-year career. He did so without the benefit of a curved stick blade or a ripping slapshot. He did it playing the off wing. He did it in an era when a 70-point season was considered outstanding.

And he did it in the pressurized atmosphere of Montreal, where hockey is a religion and anything but a Stanley Cup-winning season is unsatisfactory.

"We were supposed to win all of the time," he said. "When we did not win, it was a tragedy to many fans. They did not rec-

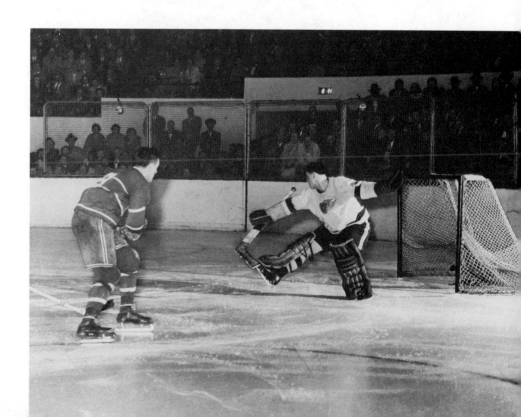

The puck's in the net as the Rocket blasts one past Detroit Red Wing goalie Terry Sawchuk in the third overtime period of a 1951 playoff game to give the Montreal Canadiens a 1-0 victory.

ognize how hard we tried, that we were beaten by better teams or that we maybe had injuries. All they knew was win, win, win."

Led by Richard, the Canadiens did win. Eight times, Richard was on a Cup winner, including his final five seasons, 1956 through 1960.

He also led the NHL in goals five times, although he never won a point-scoring championship.

Richard overcame a series of severe injuries just prior to joining the Canadiens in the 1942-43 season. And he broke an ankle in the 16th game of his rookie season. By the next year, however, Richard was an established NHL star. By 1944-45, he was on his way to becoming a legend.

The first indication that Richard could be unstoppable came in the 1944 playoffs, against archrival Toronto. In Game 2 of the opening round, Richard scored five goals, including three in a period. The Canadiens won, 5-1, and, in the traditional post-game stars selection, Richard was picked as the first, second and third star of the game.

"I had only six or seven shots on goal all game," he said, seeming somewhat amazed at what he had done. "Every goal was scored in a different way."

Richard could do that. His blistering speed would get him breakaways, on which he was deadly. His strength and determination made him difficult to dislodge from the slot. His wrist

"When Rocket came flying toward you with the puck on his stick," recalled Chicago goalie Glenn Hall, "his eyes were all lit up, flashing and gleaming like a pinball machine. It was terrifying."

shot, perhaps the best the game has ever seen, put shots into spots no wider than the puck itself. His innate sense for being where the puck would wind up placed him on a higher level than the normal player.

The 1944-45 season was Richard's best, and the most dominant any player would have for another generation. It was the year he scored 50 in 50, a feat that impressed even Richard.

"There were games when I felt everything I shot would go in," he said. "On some nights, if I touched the puck, I knew I would score. I think it was a year you can never expect to have and you will never forget having."

Although his scoring feats marked his career, Richard drew the most headlines for an incident in 1955 which severely tested the security of NHL President Clarence Campbell and the power of the Canadiens' front office.

Montreal was trying to beat out Detroit for first place and Richard was ahead in the race for the point-scoring title. In the final week of the season, a fight between Boston's Hal Laycoe and Richard broke out and Richard was cut. He went wild and, in the ensuing attack on Laycoe, Richard slugged linesman Cliff Thompson.

Campbell didn't take long to mete out punishment. Richard was suspended for the rest of the regular season (three games) and the entire playoffs.

Richard never stopped seething about it. The Canadiens applied every kind of pressure to get the president to lighten the sentence. Nothing worked.

When Campbell attended the Montreal Forum for the Canadiens' next game, fans threw things at him, swore at him in two languages, and one spectator actually got close enough to Campbell to punch him.

A tear-gas bomb was exploded in the Forum after the first period and the building was evacuated. Campbell ruled it a Canadiens' forfeit. It took an appeal on the radio by Richard to calm down the public.

Richard continued his explosive play and similarly dynamic behavior until 1960. As a measure of his achievements, he made the Hall of Fame only nine months after his retirement. The usual waiting period is three years.

OSCAR ROBERTSON

"He Could Beat You All By Himself"

In today's basketball parlance, achieving a "triple-double" has become the epitome of all-around prowess.

Only a handful of players each season are able to accomplish the feat of reaching double figures in points, rebounds and assists in one game. Earvin "Magic" Johnson of the Los Angeles Lakers had a total of 72 "triple-doubles" in his first seven years in the NBA, an average of 10 a season, to easily become the best at putting together an outstanding all-around game.

But if "triple-double" figures had been kept during the 1960s, there was no doubt that Oscar Robertson would be the league's all-time leader.

Robertson, a legend as a high school player in Indianapolis and a college star at Cincinnati, arrived in the NBA in 1960 and became one of its greatest guards.

He was named to the all-time All-NBA team in a poll of sports editors of the nation's 100 largest newspapers, receiving more votes than any player except Wilt Chamberlain.

In Robertson's first four seasons with the NBA's Cincinnati Royals, he averaged 30.2 points, 10.7 rebounds and 10.4 assists—"triple-double" figures—in 309 games.

The 6-foot-4 Robertson, known as "The Big O," went on to average 25 points, 9.5 assists and 7.5 rebounds during his 14-year NBA career, which included 12 All-Star appearances (he was the all-time leading scorer in All-Star games). He also was the NBA's Most Valuable Player in 1964 and led the league in assists six times.

"There is nothing he can't do," former Boston Celtics Coach and General Manager Red Auerbach said of Robertson. "No one comes close to him or has the ability to break open a game like Oscar. He's so great he scares me. He can beat you all by himself and usually does."

Richie Guerin, who played against Robertson, called him "a man that most people consider the best all-around basketball player in the last 20 years. He meant so much to a team."

Robertson was his harshest critic.

"All passes aren't good passes just because the ball reaches the teammate you intend it for," he said. "Playmaking is getting the ball to the man so he is in a position to take his best shot."

For all his impressive statistics, an NBA championship eluded Robertson for 10 years with the Royals. Then he was traded to the Milwaukee Bucks in 1970 and joined with Kareem Abdul-Jabbar, then known as Lew Alcindor, to win an NBA title in 1971.

The Big O turns the corner past a Phoenix Sun defender in April, 1971 NBA game. Those lanky legs at the left belong to Robertson's Milwaukee teammate Lew Alcindor, now known as Kareem Abdul-Jabbar.

With the Cincinnati Royals in 1961, Robertson looks apprehensively over his shoulder as Jerry West of the L.A. Lakers adjusts his balance with a hand on his back.

Oscar (12) broke the major college record for field goals here with the 957th of his career with the University of Cincinnati in Feb. 1960. Note how Robertson is aiding his cause by stiff-arming Wichita's Gene Wiley in the face.

Robertson also was active in the fledgling NBA players union, serving as its president for one term. During his presidency, he filed a suit in 1970 challenging the reserve clause that tied players to their teams. The suit led to the Robertson settlement in 1976 that refined college draft rules and brought about free agency.

As NBA salaries escalated during the 1980s, Robertson was amazed at the effect his suit had on the sport.

"I have to admit, the situation's gotten out of hand," Robertson said. "Why should an owner pay a player $1 million when he's only worth $100,000? Then the fans are misled. They get down on a player because they expect him to play like a million dollars and he's not worth it."

But Robertson said he didn't begrudge today's athletes their large salaries.

"Athletes make big money, but so do movie stars and the presidents of auto companies," he said. "Don't direct your animosity at athletes; look at society as a whole. The salary structure has risen in pro basketball because the owners are impatient and they're willing to pay whatever it costs to win."

Robertson, who made $33,333 in his rookie season, said players during his day were taken advantage of by NBA owners. "There were a lot of things the owners did that weren't considered All-American," he said. "A lot of guys were blackballed.

If owners didn't like the way you dressed, the car you drove, anything, they could keep you from playing. Believe me, it happened."

He said that "owners had things their way for a long time, but now the players want their share of the money. The owners say 'Be patient,' but the players aren't settling for that anymore."

For a time, Robertson often was mentioned when coaching vacancies came up, but his sometimes rebellious nature probably turned off NBA owners.

"If I'm going to coach, I would want to run the whole show," Robertson said. "I'd want to control draft choices, trades, all of that. It only seems fair, since good players make the coach.

"If it's a situation I could live with and the money was right, I'd be interested. If I got the right offer, I would coach. but New York, for example, would be tough. In New York, I wouldn't have the time I'd need to build a winner.

"Owners want a winner. When they don't get it, they tend to blame the coach."

JACKIE ROBINSON

Breaker of the Color Line

During the 1972 World Series between the Cincinnati Reds and Oakland A's, Jackie Robinson, scheduled to throw out the first ball, was approached by a youngster as he waited in the catacombs of Cincinnati's Riverfront Stadium.

"Will you please give me your autograph," the boy said timidly, offering a clean baseball.

The sturdily-built black man, with gray flecks creeping from his thick, close-cropped dark hair, took the ball, stared at it a few moments and replied apologetically:

"Son, I don't know—I can hardly see the ball." He laboriously scrawled his name and limped away.

Two weeks later—stricken with diabetes, a heart condition and failing sight—one of the true all-time giants of baseball was dead at the age of 53.

Dead yet imperishable, he left an imprint on the game and on society that will prevail long after many greater deeds performed on the diamond are forgotten. He played a major part in restoring a nation's conscience. He broke the color line.

Jackie Robinson's plaque in the Hall of Fame in Cooperstown, New York, unveiled in 1962, told of no majestic feats to compare with the multiple home runs of Babe Ruth and Hank Aaron, the .406 batting average of Ted Williams or the 100-plus base thefts of Maury Wills, Lou Brock and Rickey Henderson. He made his contributions on the field—a fine athlete, tough, competitive, productive—but he will be most remembered for the character he showed under extreme duress.

Jackie's Hall of Fame inscription is terse, cold and reveals only a small fraction of the man and his life. It reads:

"Jack Roosevelt Robinson: Brooklyn, N.L. 1947 to 1956. Leading NL batter in 1949. Holds fielding mark for second

Summoned to Brooklyn's Ebbets Field, Robinson was lectured by Dodgers' General Manager Branch Rickey on the responsibilities of the first black man to crash the longtime big league barrier. The 1987 season was dedicated to Robinson, who made his debut in the majors 40 years earlier.

Robinson playing his first game in organized baseball with the Montreal Royals in a game in Jersey City, N.J. on April 18, 1946. Here he slides safely into third base. Jackie collected four hits, including a home run, as Montreal won, 14-1.

basemen playing in 150 or more games with .992. Led in stolen bases in 1947 and 1949. Most Valuable Player in 1949. Lifetime batting average .311. Joint record holder for most double plays by second baseman, 137, in 1951. Led second basemen in double plays 1949-50-51-52."

There wasn't much room to tell how this black man, born in the Jim Crow South, suffered through the indignities of racial bias; continued to stand up to abuse from players and fans after being thrust into the role of the first black man in modern times to play baseball in the major leagues; lost a son first to drugs and then to a terrible automobile accident and finally battled debilitating ailments until his untimely death on October 24, 1972.

Jackie was born January 31, 1919, in a rural area near Cairo, Georgia, the son of a sharecropper and the grandson of a slave. He was six months old when his father deserted his mother, who bundled her six children onto a train and headed for California. Settling in a frame house in Pasadena, the mother worked as a maid to keep her children in food and clothes. Jackie recalled that she instilled them with a sense of pride.

Jackie related in his autobiography, "Wait 'Til Next Year," that at the age of eight he was taunted by a neighbor girl who yelled at him, "Nigger, nigger, nigger," and at 14 almost being arrested for wading in the Pasadena City Reservoir, which was closed to blacks. A sheriff arrived, drew his gun and ordered him out of the water, mumbling behind his .38, "Looka here, niggers in my drinking water."

Such incidents, Robinson recalled, left deep personal scars as did an event in World War II, while assigned as an infantry lieutenant to Fort Hood, Texas. He was arrested after refusing an order to sit in the back of a bus. The court martial dismissed the complaint.

Jackie had to endure fewer indignities in junior college and at the University of California at Los Angeles where he starred in basketball, football and track as well as baseball. He coached briefly in Austin, Texas, and in 1945 signed to play baseball with the black Kansas City Monarchs with the idea of later getting into physical education.

It was while with the Monarchs that he came to the attention of scouts hired by General Manager Branch Rickey of the Brooklyn Dodgers, who was intent on getting major league baseball integrated. Summoned to Ebbets Field, Robinson was lectured for three hours by Rickey on the responsibilities of the first black man to crash the longtime barrier—"don't respond

In his second major league season in 1948, Robby is shown stealing home as part of a triple steal against the Boston Braves. The Braves' catcher is Bill Salkeld. The batter is Billy Cox, Brooklyn's third baseman.

to insults from fans or players, don't talk back to umpires, don't go to parties or frequent night clubs."

Robinson signed a contract for a $3,500 bonus and a salary of $600 a month to be paid by the Dodgers' triple-A farm club, the Montreal Royals of the International League. Jackie was sworn to secrecy because months would pass before baseball executives, although voting 15-1 against integration, were commanded by Commissioner A.B. "Happy" Chandler to open their rosters to black players. "This is America," Chandler bellowed.

The admission of a black player into organized baseball was greeted with both skepticism and hostility. Proud and a fierce competitor by nature, Robinson eased the transition by following Rickey's advice to keep his cool and by producing on the field. He batted .340 at Montreal, had a .985 fielding average and led the Royals to victory over Louisville in the Little World Series. Jeers turned to cheers in Montreal.

However, new perils greeted his entrance into the majors with the Dodgers in 1947. Dixie Walker, an Alabaman, asked Rickey to trade him. The St. Louis Cardinals threatened to strike. In the locker room, Robinson had to hang his clothes on a nail instead of in a locker. He was booed by fans and even sent death threats. For a long time, he didn't mingle with other players.

It didn't take long for almost everybody to forget the color of Jackie's skin. Pigeon-toed but quick and pirate-bold; he was a threat every time he got on base. He stole home 19 times. He was a great clutch hitter, fine fielder and relentless competitor. He retired in 1956 to spend his final few years as a successful executive and family man in Connecticut.

SUGAR RAY ROBINSON

"Pound For Pound, the Greatest"

Legend has it that back in the late 1930s a sportswriter, impressed after watching a scrawny, 19-year-old black kid polish off an opponent in a small fight arena in upstate New York, turned to the youth's handler at ringside and remarked:

"That's a sweet boy you have there."

"Yeah," replied Manager George Gainford, "sweet as sugar."

The sportswriter pounced on the phrase for his morning newspaper column and thus was born one of the most familiar and electrifying names in the annals of boxing.

Sugar Ray Robinson went on to become one of the most celebrated figures in the game, a classic boxer-puncher who rode a roller coaster to championships in two weight divisions and almost a third and to two fortunes squandered by high living.

From 1940 through 1965, he established a remarkable record of 202 professional fights, winning 175. He reigned as welterweight titleholder for four years, was five times winner and loser of the middleweight crown and barely missed making boxing history by losing a hard fought lightheavyweight title bout against Joey Maxim in 1952.

In his first 12 years, when at his peak, he lost to only two foes—Jake LaMotta, whom he beat on five other occasions, and Randy Turpin, whom he knocked out in a return meeting.

In an age when heavyweights were the glamour figures and dominated public attention, Sugar Ray was acclaimed "pound for pound, the greatest fighter who ever lived."

The phrase became one of the sport's most enduring cliches but, as the years passed, no one emerged seriously to dispute it.

A onetime street dancer, Robinson combined artistry and speed with bone-rattling power. Oldtimers compared him with George Dixon, Joe Gans and Benny Leonard. Latter day critics said Sugar Ray was the inspiration of Muhammad Ali's "float like a butterfly, sting like a bee" routine.

A superb ring tactician, Robinson used Leonard's technique of rocking into range, unleashing a salvo of blows and then rocking back again. He had a flicking rat-tat-tat left which set his opponent up for a crunching left hook or right cross. Contemporaries marveled at his vast repertoire of moves.

After being floored in a welterweight title bout, Tommy Bell

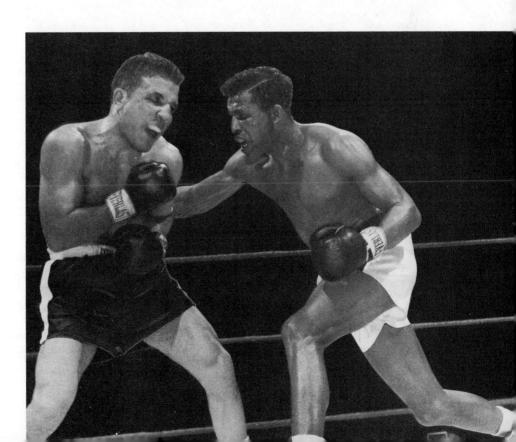

The "Raging Bull" is hurting! Challenger Ray Robinson lands a hard right to the midsection of Jake LaMotta in their middleweight title fight in Feb. 1951. Sugar Ray captured the crown on a 13th-round TKO.

His fists still cocked, Robinson glances toward reeling Randy Turpin of Britain as referee Ruby Goldstein nudges him toward a neutral corner in the 10th round of their Sept. 1951 title fight. Seconds later, the bout was stopped, enabling Ray to regain the championship.

said, "He came at me with two punches, a right and a left. I don't know which hit me. I didn't feel hurt but when I started to move, my legs wouldn't go with me and I fell over on my head."

Although a fierce gladiator who constantly pressed in for the kill when he had a foe in trouble, Sugar Ray professed in later years that he never really had a love for ring combat. He got his greatest kicks out of the high jinx that accompanied the role of ring idol.

Quite possibly this lust for high living was a reaction to his grim and spartan background.

Robinson was born Walker Smith May 3, 1920 in Detroit's tough, so-called "Black Bottom" district but found himself in New York's Harlem at an early age after his mother was deserted by his father. He acknowledged that he ran with a street gang, danced for nickels and pennies on the sidewalks of New York's

Times Square and shot craps all night with other gang members in the back alleys.

Befriended by a priest, he began working out in a neighborhood gym where he caught the eye of Gainford. It was Gainford who pulled a stray card out of his pocket when "Smitty," as Ray was then called, showed up for an amateur fight without credentials. The name was that of another obscure fighter, Ray Robinson. The name stuck.

Robinson was brought along carefully by Gainford. He even fought an aging Henry Armstrong, carrying the old, legendary fighter for 10 rounds. He won his first pro title—the 147-pound championship—in 1946, beating Tommy Bell. He defended the title only four times before moving into the middleweight division, where he produced his greatest fights.

Meanwhile, he was burning the candle at both ends. Frequently he would stay up until 4 a.m. at the Cotton Club, swinging with friends. He drove a bright red Cadillac. They said his closets housed 1,000 suits. He toured Europe with a dozen or more courtiers including a harem of interracial beauties, a valet, hair dresser and even a court jester. A family could have lived a year on his champagne bills.

Although his purses never compared with the exorbitant guarantees of the 1970s and 1980s, Sugar Ray never lacked for a cash flow. He owned a string of apartment buildings on New York's Seventh Avenue and operated several variety shops. He was a landlord who needed a bevy of secretaries to handle his interests.

He actually had two careers. The first, starting in 1940, ended June 25, 1952 when he was overcome by heat prostration in the 13th round of a lightheavyweight title challenge against Maxim.

Broke, having dissipated more than $4 million, his marriage dissolved, he announced his retirement the following December and began a career as a tap dancer, booked into nightclubs for $15,000 a week. When this venture dulled, he essayed a ring comeback in 1954, regaining some of his old magic and recapturing the middleweight title from Bobo Olson. He earned good purses in bouts with Gene Fullmer, Carmen Basilio and Paul Pender, losing, regaining and then losing again the middleweight title. He earned more than $1.5 million, which subsequently evaporated.

Then, by his own admission, he saw the light. He remarried, settled in Los Angeles, reactivated the Ray Robinson Foundation and threw all his energies into working with kids and church groups.

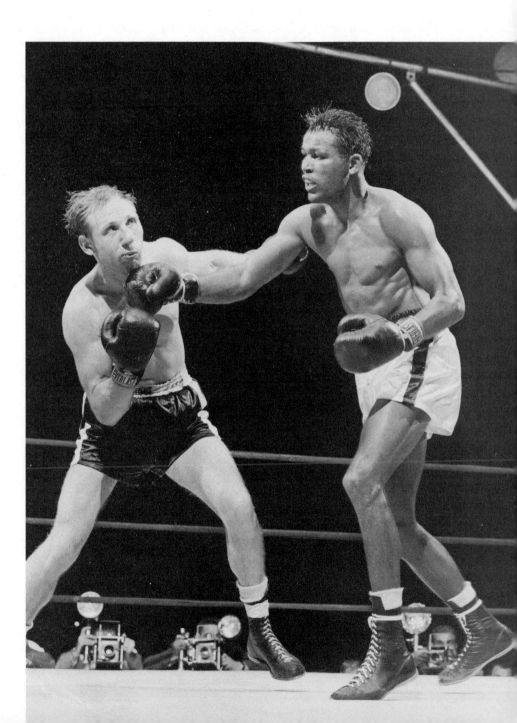

Sugar Ray bounces a right off the jaw of Charley Fusari in the 15th round of their welterweight title bout in Jersey City, N.J. on Aug. 9, 1950. Robinson retained the crown.

PETE ROSE

The Hustling "Hit" Man

When Ty Cobb put away his sabre-sharp spikes in 1928, baseball men shook their heads and said the sport would never see another like him—a fierce, fiery competitor, all grit and gristle, who turned every game into a battlefield for a quarter of a century and survived to set records that defied imagination. Who, in a softening society, they asked, would ever again rack up 12 batting titles, get more than 4,000 hits and score 2,225 runs?

Near duplicates—but not quite—emerged later in the forms of the Cardinals' Enos Slaughter, a slashing, baserunning hot-head, and the black Jackie Robinson of the Dodgers, who played with a passion born of a racial crusade, yet suffered from a shortened career.

Everybody had to wait for the rugged, bandy-legged son of a Cincinnati bank clerk and part-time semipro football player to grow up and prove that no goal—no matter how lofty—was unattainable to one willing to scrap and scramble, eat dirt and endure endless bumps and bruises to fulfill a destiny.

That was Harry "Pete" Rose's kid, Pete, who spent a career seeking to live up to the expectations of a father who died before his time. On the field, young Pete was a Ty Cobb reincarnate but only in the intensity and aggressiveness of his play. In character, he was the antithesis. Whereas Cobb was egotistical, arrogant, mean and detested, Rose was as much a fighter but personable, obliging and respected by all.

Pete Rose never looked like a big league superstar. He didn't have the graceful style of a Joe DiMaggio, the awesome power of a Mickey Mantle or the theatrical flair of a Willie Mays. At 5-foot-11 and 195 pounds he gave the impression of being stumpy. He wasn't exceptionally fast. He wasn't remarkably deft. He was described as having only average baseball skills. Early in his career, he appeared to be just another journeyman ball player.

What Pete may have lacked in natural talent he more than made up with hustle and heart. Few men, if any, in this American pastime ever played with greater zeal and more raw guts.

left:

On Sept. 11, 1985, Rose watches his record-breaking hit fly toward left field in Cincinnati in a game against San Diego. The shot enabled Pete to break Ty Cobb's major league career record of 4,191 safeties.

opposite:

Pistol Pete slams into American League catcher Ray Fosse to score the winning run for the National League in the 1970 All-Star game.

A switch-hitter, Rose, with the Montreal Expos in 1984, pounds out his 4,000th career hit while batting right-handed against Philadelphia lefty Jerry Koosman.

The years he persevered over most of three decades and the all-time records that he sent cascading into the books were testimony to his durability and greatness.

Moving into the mid-1980s, a brilliant career behind him and managerial responsibilities ahead, Pete kept figure filberts busy rewriting baseball's record books. Some of the oldest and most cherished batting marks, many fashioned by the relentless Cobb, fell to his busy bat.

First he overtook Stan Musial's National League record of 3,630 hits, then set out in pursuit of Ty Cobb's sacrosanct 4,191, once believed out of reach of mortal man. He topped it in Cincinnati's Riverfront Stadium on the evening of September 11,

1985, after weeks of wild fanfare. But this was just salad dressing. He had plenty of meat and potatoes to go with so rich a menu.

At age 45, coming off his worst season in 1986 during which he batted only .219 in 237 times at bat, Rose removed himself from the club's protected list so that a younger player could take his spot. However, Pete had accumulated many noteworthy standards.

He set all-time major league records for most games played (3,562), most at bats (14,053), most singles (3,215), most total bases by a switch-hitter (5,752), most seasons with 200 or more hits (10), most seasons with 100 or more hits (23), most seasons with 600 or more at bats (17) and most seasons playing 150 or more games (17). Through the 1986 campaign, he had 4,256 hits.

Attesting to his versatility, he became the only major league player in history to play more than 500 games at five different positions—first base, second and third, left field and right field. He established himself as the game's "winningest player," participating in more than 1,900 winning games.

He played in four World Series with the Cincinnati Reds, winning two, and was the league's most valuable player in 1973 and World Series MVP in 1975. He set numerous National League marks such as consecutive years played, most career runs, career doubles and longest consecutive hitting streak, 44 games, set in 1978.

His statistics became mind-boggling.

Peter Edward Rose was born April 14, 1941, in Cincinnati. His father was a semi-pro football player who got Pete to play on the same team. He signed with the Cincinnati Reds in 1960 at age 19, played minor league ball with Geneva (New York), Tampa and Macon (Georgia) before joining the parent club in 1963 and winning National League Rookie of the Year honors.

Pete batted .273 his first year in the majors, then fell off to .269 the next year. "I had some doubts about whether I could hit big league pitching," he said.

With some hard work on his batting stroke, he raised his average to .312 and went nine straight seasons, 14 of the next 15, batting better than .300. He averaged .381 in seven championship series, the last two with Philadelphia. He played in 16 All-Star games, starting at five positions.

Never overpaid as a Red, Rose opted for free agency after the 1978 season and signed a $4 million contract to play five years for the Philadelphia Phillies. He moved to Montreal in 1984, playing only part of a season before returning to Cincinnati as player-manager on August 16, 1984.

As a skipper, he was as obsessive and demanding on his players as he always had been on himself and the club's immediate improvement reflected the results.

"He's not like the rest of us," said Sparky Anderson, Pete's old boss at Cincinnati, who later managed Detroit. "He thinks and lives baseball day and night. He is baseball."

Previously honored as the 1970s Athlete of the Decade, Rose saw his career reach a climax when he chased and finally overtook Ty Cobb's hit record. He became "Cover Boy" of the slick magazines, guest of dozens of TV talk shows, object of a book and one of the hottest commercial properties in the game.

"All I am," he said, "is a young American boy who knew what he could do... and did it for a long, long time."

A Pete Rose trademark! Advancing from first base on Joe Morgan's single in the ninth inning of the seventh game of the 1975 World Series, Pete dives head first into third. The defender is Boston's Rico Petrocelli. The Reds won the game, 4-3.

WILMA RUDOLPH

A Symphony of Speed and Grace

They made a movie of Wilma Rudolph's life and, if one were not cognizant of the true story, one would believe it was padded with the fiction and sentimental, tear-jerking stuff for which Hollywood is known. In Wilma's case, no such puffery was necessary. It was her life as she lived it and the most imaginative script writer would find it difficult to exaggerate.

It was a story that had all the ingredients of high drama—a black girl, daughter of a struggling handyman, born in the South, the 20th of 22 children, stricken with paralyzing ill-nesses at the age of four, apparently doomed to be a cripple, yet one who fought back to become the greatest American woman runner ever to compete in the Olympic Games.

"I am basically lazy," she insisted. "When I am home, I plant myself in front of the television set and watch the soap operas. I get all involved. I cry and I worry with the continuing problems of the cast."

One could hardly believe that.

Conquering her early deformity as she grew up in her native

Wilma captured three gold medals in the 1960 Olympic Games in Rome—the 100 and 200 meters and for the 400-meter relay.

Clarksville, Tenn., she went on to become a fine high school athlete, qualify for the 1956 Melbourne Olympics at age 15, returned four years later in Rome to sweep to three gold medals—the 100 and 200 meters and 400-meter relay—and seal her niche in the Olympic Hall of Fame.

Later wed to a high school sweetheart, Robert Eldridge, and mother of four children, it seemed plausible that the "lazy" Wilma would settle down to a soft domestic life.

Not so.

She taught high school, modeled, worked as a Hollywood publicist, served as an analyst on the faculty of a university, lectured, campaigned as a fund-raiser and did television commentary.

She became very active in the Women's Sports Foundation, lobbied for Title IX (the law requiring equal treatment for women in college sports), and became the driving force in the establishment of the $1.5 million Track and Field Hall of Fame in Charleston, S.C.

Her madcap schedule intensified after the divorce from her husband in the mid-1970s, with her children growing into adulthood. She served as a consultant on the movie of her life, "Wilma," produced by Bud Greenspan, did a cross-country tour for a bakery sponsoring the 20th Century Fox filming of the 1980 Olympics and maintained a busy travel schedule promoting causes for underprivileged children.

Wilma was four years old when she was stricken with scarlet fever and double pneumonia.

"For a long time I didn't see any improvement," she wrote later in her autobiography. "My leg was crooked and I had to wear a brace... I learned how to fake normal walk so that people would think there was nothing wrong." Soon she was walking normally—a miracle, the doctors said—and participating in sports.

Tall for her age, she became a star basketball player in high school, once scoring 49 points which still stands as a record for the school. With long legs and innate speed, she became a natural for track.

She was only 15 and weighed 89 pounds when she won a berth on the U.S. women's track and field team for the 1956 Olympic Games in Melbourne.

Wilma said she took the long trip to Australia confident that she would win a gold medal. She was disappointed when she had to share a bronze medal for third in the 400-meter relay. Yet she was enthralled to see Australia's Betty Cuthbert score victories in three events—the 100, 200 and 400.

261

"I was determined," she said. "that four years from then... I was going to win a gold medal or two for the United States."

Reaching her 16th birthday during the Melbourne Games, Wilma returned home, finished high school and enrolled at Tennessee State in Nashville where she profited from the teaching of Ed Temple, a well-known and respected track and field coach who later was to be named coach of the 1960 U.S. Olympic team.

Wilma acknowledged that, unlike her attitude at Melbourne, she was uncertain and nervous in Rome. Her insecurity was increased when she accidentally stepped in a hole and twisted her ankle in the opening heat of the 100 meters—her first event.

Although the pain from her ankle injury was severe, Wilma won the 100-meter dash in 11 seconds flat, an Olympic record. By the time the 200 meters came around, she was already the darling of the Romans.

A lithe, beautiful lady, six feet tall, floated over the track like a fawn with long, graceful strides, and the sun bouncing off her copper skin. There were some major disappointments on the American men's track and field team and Wilma emerged as the queen of the show.

She won the 200 meters in 24 seconds flat and captured her third gold in the 400 meter relay. She had reached her goal. But there was agony mixed with her joy of triumph.

Wilma said she had been so tense she was unable to sleep at night. As a result, she frequently took a nap in the locker room while waiting to be called to the track.

She also cried.

"When I saw all those reporters and microphones," she said, "I burst into tears. I couldn't face them."

As promoter of the Wilma Rudolph Foundation for underprivileged kids, the statuesque Tennessean soon lost her timidity and became a favorite the world over.

Yet she was incensed when a Communist paper in Rome wrote in 1969 that, because she was a Negro, she was living in poverty and had to hock her gold medals to make ends meet.

"I flew to Rome to refute the charges," she said. "I have never lived in poverty. I am far from wealthy but I am rich in freedom and opportunities."

With their medals around their necks, Rudolph, the winner, goes into three-way handshake with silver and bronze medal winners in women's 100-meter dash at 1960 Olympics in Rome. At left is Britain's Dorothy Hyman, the runnerup, and at right is Italy's Giuseppina Leone, who ran third.

BILL RUSSELL

"Best Defensive Player of All Time"

When Boston picked Bill Russell, a two-time college All-America and Olympic gold medalist, in the first round of the National Basketball Association draft in 1956, many of the game's most astute critics, including Philadelphia owner Eddie Gottlieb, said wily coach Red Auerbach of the Celtics had pulled a boner.

"Russell wasn't a scorer in college," warned Gottlieb. "People say he can't shoot and can't score. What good is he?"

Auerbach apparently saw in his gangling, 6-foot-10 rookie what his peers had failed to observe—intangibles that were to be reflected and vastly instrumental in the Celtics' phenomenal success over the next two decades.

Sitting in his office preparing to present a $24,000 contract, Auerbach reminded Russell of the negative appraisals. "Everyone says you can't shoot well enough to play with the pros," he said. "Does that bother you?"

Russell, who told of the incident years afterward, replied, "Yeah, I'm a little concerned about it."

"Okay, I'll make a deal with you," Auerbach said. "I promise as long as you play here, whenever we discuss contracts, we will never talk about statistics."

According to both men, they never did. In 1980—with the feats of Wilt Chamberlain, Kareem Abdul-Jabbar, Julius Erving, Elgin Baylor and other stars fresh in mind—the nation's basketball writers voted Russell "Greatest Player in the History of the NBA."

Russell couldn't stuff the ball through the hoop with the ease of seven-footers such as Chamberlain and Jabbar. He couldn't fly through the air as did Erving nor exhibit the ball-handling legerdemain of a slick Bob Cousy. What he could do—and did better than anyone else—was to keep the opposition from doing all those things he couldn't do. He was the great equalizer, generally regarded as the "best defensive player of all time."

He blocked shots. He exercised ball control. He turned defense into an exact science and revolutionized the game. John Havlicek, a Celtics' teammate, said he had seen Russell block a shot, gain control of the ball, feed it to one of his forwards and then follow the fast-break to the other end of the floor ready to grab a rebound.

Against Philadelphia in 1957, Russell had 32 rebounds in a half, an NBA record. He was the NBA all-time playoff leader in rebounds. He also set the league record for rebounds in the championship series—40 against St. Louis in 1960, repeated against Los Angeles in 1962.

Big Bill Russell, voted by the nation's basketball writers in 1980 as the "Greatest Player in the History of the NBA," jumps higher than the basket during this 1961 game against Detroit. Defending for the Pistons are Gene Shue (21) and George Lee (12).

His defensive genius was credited with leading the Celtics to 11 NBA championships in the 13 years he played, eight in a row and the latter two times in 1968 and 1969 as player-coach. He was the NBA's Most Valuable Player five times and played in 11 All-Star games. Chosen in 1966, he had the distinction of being the first black coach in the NBA. He was elected to the Basketball Hall of Fame in 1974.

Born February 12, 1934 in Monroe, Louisiana, William Felton Russell moved with his family to Oakland, California, when he was nine years old. He attended McClymonds High School where as a 6-foot-2, 128-pound sophomore he was so awkward coaches paid no attention to him on the basketball floor. Eventually he added seven inches and 100 pounds to his muscular frame and improved enough to get a scholarship at the University of San Francisco, a small Jesuit school.

Russell and a teammate, K.C. Jones, who followed him to the Celtics and subsequently also became the team's head coach, led San Francisco to No. 1 in the college rankings in 1955-56 and were stars in the United States' gold medal victory in the 1956 Olympics at Melbourne, Australia. Bill was the No. 1 college player his final year.

It had been a struggle and Bill was the first to acknowledge it. "Basketball didn't come easy to me," he said. "Defense is not an innate talent or luck. You have to work years to perfect it. I should epitomize the American dream for I came from long odds."

A striking figure, 6 feet, 10 inches tall and 220 pounds, the goateed Russell was almost immediately tossed into a personal conflict with the awesome 7-foot-1, 275-pound Wilt Chamberlain when the latter entered the NBA in 1959. It was offense vs. defense, differing styles, a clash of strong personalities, a natural rivalry which delighted fans.

Sparks were bound to fly—and they did.

Basketball writers drew comparisons. Contemporaries passed judgment, one of them, Jerry West, saying, "I think Wilt is a better all-around player but, for one game, I'd rather have Russell."

Chamberlain managed to outscore Russell in their personal confrontations but it was usually Russell's team which came out on top. In the 10 years Russell and Chamberlain stalked each other, the Celtics won the NBA championship nine times and held an 84-57 edge over Wilt's Philadelphia, San Francisco and Los Angeles teams.

This was frustrating for the hulking Wilt the Stilt, who rationalized: "I outscored him (Russell) in head-to-head meetings 440-212, outrebounded him 333-161 and even blocked more of his shots than he did of mine."

Russell countered: "Only the first year against Wilt was a challenge. Then it became clear that he was great—but I was better."

One of Russell's teammates, Satch Sanders, insisted: "Look, it's simple. Russell made the talent around him better. Chamberlain didn't. When Russell was on the floor the game was in the bag."

Retiring after the 1969 season, Russell signed a lucrative contract with the telephone company, lectured on college campuses, did TV commentary and commercials and, in 1973, returned briefly as coach and GM of Seattle's NBA team. Last April, he was named coach of the NBA's Sacramento Kings.

"I have achieved the absolute in my fields," he said.

opposite:

The rebound king, Russell, shows how it's done in this 1963 game against the New York Knicks. In the contest, Bill shattered the league's career rebound record, adding 19 to bring his total to 11,041.

right:

Russell embraces his former coach, Red Auerbach, on Jan. 5, 1985 during a pre-game ceremony at Boston Garden where Auerbach was honored for his achievements as the Celtics' coach, general manager and president. Russell, also a former Boston coach, was named coach last April of the NBA's Sacramento Kings.

BABE RUTH

Savior of Baseball

In an era of flamboyant prose and graphic nicknames for sports heroes, they called him "Bambino," "The Sultan of Swat," "The King of Clout," "The Savior of Baseball,"—a superfluous exercise since one word would have been enough.

Simply the "Babe."

He was hardly the textbook figure for an athletic idol. He was 6 feet, 2 inches tall and weighed variously between 215 and 250 pounds, with most of the avoirdupois concentrated in a mammoth belly that hung like bouncing jelly over his belt line.

He had a round, boyish face with a bulbous nose and, when he took up a bat which looked like a toothpick in his beefy hands and sent the ball on a lazy arc into the stands, he toured the bases with mincing, girlish steps on matchstick thin legs.

Off the diamond, he was a big, overgrown kid, a glutton who gorged himself on beer and hotdogs, who flouted club rules and indulged heavily in the good life of wine, women and song.

Truly a king with earthly, human tastes.

Few will deny that Babe Ruth remains the most magical name in American sports—a name that is still spoken with reverence in such foreign countries as Japan and Britain, while names of other great performers are forgotten.

Baseball men will tell you he was the greatest all-around player of all-time—a brilliant pitcher before becoming a home run-hitting outfielder, a man without a technical flaw.

More than that, the Babe was credited with saving baseball at a time the game had lost public confidence because of the 1919 "Black Sox Scandal," in which some members of the Chicago White Sox were suspended for allegedly throwing the World Series against the Cincinnati Reds.

A young star named George Herman Ruth was just emerging as a slugger with the Boston Red Sox. A winning lefthanded pitcher, the beefy kid had just been turned into an outfielder that year and hit an all-time record of 29 home runs. Sold to the New York Yankees in 1920, the Babe, profiting from the introduction of a livelier ball, electrified the nation by hitting 54 home runs. The scandal was soon forgotten and baseball was launched on an unprecedented era of prosperity and home run fever.

Turnstiles hummed and cash registers jingled as fans rushed to the ball parks to see the pot-bellied slugger slam baseballs out of the park, and he obliged—714 career home runs. He drove in a record 2,217 runs and compiled a lifetime batting average of .342.

The Babe's home run marks—including the 60 he hit for a

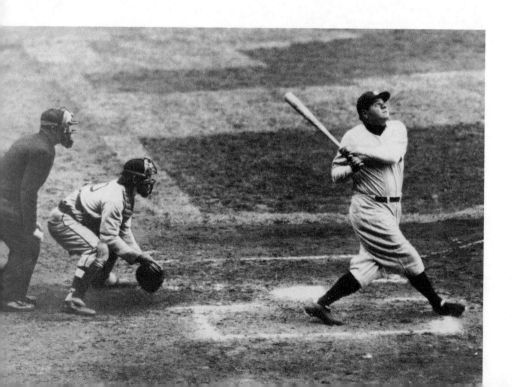

Turnstiles hummed and cash registers jingled as fans rushed to the ball parks to see Ruth, the pot-bellied slugger, slam baseballs out of the park.

With a mighty swing, the Bambino blasts his record 60th home run of 1927 into the seats at Yankee Stadium. The victim was Washington pitcher Tom Zachary.

season high in 1927—became so sacred that many baseball fans were extremely upset when the Yankees' Roger Maris came along to hit 61 in 1961 and the Braves' Hank Aaron soared past the Babe's career total, hitting his 715th on April 8, 1974 in Atlanta.

In fact, the Babe's record of 60 home runs in one season was so sacrosanct that baseball was constrained to attach an asterisk to Maris' feat in 1961, specifying that it was attained over a longer (162 instead of 154) game schedule. The sports' hierarchy didn't see fit to treat subsequent other records—and they were many—with the same disdain.

It emphasized Ruth's shadow over the entire game.

George Herman Ruth was born in 1895 on the Baltimore waterfront to parents who died when he was very young. An unwanted waif, he wound up in St. Mary's Industrial School where a Catholic priest got him interested in baseball. The kid started out as a left-handed catcher but shifted to the pitcher's role. It was at St. Mary's that he caught the eye of Jack Dunn, owner of the minor league Baltimore Orioles, who signed him for $600 in 1914.

Historians say this also was the origin of the Babe's nickname. The youngster, 19 and timid, clung so closely to the boss' heels that players would say, "There goes Jack and his new babe."

In 1914, Ruth became a pitcher for the Boston Red Sox and helped pitch them to a pennant in 1918. "He was as good as any left-handed pitcher I ever saw," said Ed Barrow, manager of the Red Sox and later general manager of the Yankees.

Here the home run king is wearing his famed No. 3 uniform for the last time as he is honored at Yankee Stadium in June, 1948. Two months later he was dead of lung cancer.

Ruth was so impressive on the mound that he graduated to the Boston Red Sox just before the end of the year. He won two of his three decisions and, beginning in 1915, he reeled off winning seasons of 18, 23 and 24 games. He beat the Brooklyn Dodgers in the 1916 World Series. He faced the great Walter Johnson eight times and won six, three of them by 1-0 scores. Once he struck out the Detroit Tigers' Bobby Veach, Sam Crawford and Ty Cobb with the bases loaded.

Overall, he had a career pitching record of 94 victories and 46 defeats, a 2.28 earned run average, a 3-0 record and an ERA of 0.87 in the World Series with a record of 29⅔ consecutive scoreless innings that endured for 40 years.

Ed Barrow, manager of the Red Sox and later general manager of the Yankees, called Ruth "as good as any left-handed pitcher I ever saw," yet it was he who decided that the Babe would be more valuable with a bat in his hand playing every day and converted him into an outfielder.

In 1920, the Red Sox, in financial difficulty, sold the Babe to the New York Yankees for $125,000 and a $350,000 mortgage on Boston's Fenway Park—a price that seemed exorbitant at the time but proved to be a steal. The Babe responded with his 54 home runs. It changed the face of the game.

Previously it had been a game of pitching and finesse, managers strategically squeezing out one and two runs at a time. Ruth turned it into a power exercise that produced runs in clusters.

A new dynasty was born. The Yankees moved out of the shadow of the New York Giants in the Polo Grounds in 1923 and into Yankee Stadium, their own concrete palace in the Bronx. The "Bronx Bombers" became a national fetish.

Ruth led or tied for the American League home run crown in 10 of his 14 years with the Yankees. He hit better than .300 in six World Series, twice belted three home runs in a single Series game and set a Series batting mark of .625 in 1928.

His most famous blow was struck in the 1932 World Series against the Chicago Cubs when he took his stance at the plate, pointed to a centerfield spot and then hit a home run to the bleacher section to which he had gestured. The incident became a source of debate among those on hand.

Chagrined that he never was given a chance to manage the Yankees, Ruth asked for his release in 1935, joining the Boston Braves. He batted only .181 but hit six home runs, three in one game. Shortly afterward he retired. He died Aug. 16, 1948 of lung cancer.

GENE SARAZEN

Maker of Golf's "Miracle Shot"

It was near the end of a crisp spring day in Augusta, Georgia, in 1935, that the committee of the Augusta National Club was gathered upstairs in the Colonial clubhouse measuring Craig Wood for the green jacket that goes to the Masters golf champion.

Wood had finished with a score of 282 and none of the handful of laggers still on the course had a ghost of a chance to catch him.

Suddenly, a runner burst into the room, screaming excitedly:

"Mr. Sarazen got a three on fifteen! Mr. Sarazen got a three on fifteen!"

It was before the age of sophisticated electronic communication. News of progress in a golf tournament depended on runners just as they did in ancient Greece.

Everybody was skeptical.

"Impossible," said Alan Gould of The Associated Press. "Hey, kid, go out and recheck it." Grantland Rice, Bill Richardson and other sports writers of the time refused to accept it.

Finally it was confirmed. Gene Sarazen, playing the final holes and needing three birdies on the four tough finishing holes to tie, had laced a 220-yard spoon shot into the hole for a double eagle on the 485-yard 15th hole.

It became golf's "miracle shot"—the most talked about in the game's history. It projected Gene into a tie with Wood for the title which he won by five shots in the playoff.

The double eagle—which technically is one shot better than a hole-in-one—became the badge of international recognition for the bouncy ex-caddie from New York's suburbs although he carved a career that placed him solidly among the game's immortals.

He won two U.S. Open Championships, 10 years apart, 1922-1932; tied for another in 1940, losing a playoff to Lawson Little, and missed by a stroke in 1934. He won the Professional Golfers Association title three times—1922, 1923 and 1933—when that tournament was a hazardous and gruelling match play grind, and was a runner-up in 1930.

He also won the British Open, thus joining the very select and exclusive society of players to have won all four of the major crowns. The only others have been Ben Hogan, Gary Player and Jack Nicklaus.

Gene Sarazen was an anachronism. His career was a link spanning four distinct eras, from Harry Vardon to Nicklaus. While lacking in formal education, he was possessed with a

The smooth-stroking Sarazen chips out of the rough on his way to winning the British Open in 1932. His most sensational drive, however, was the "miracle shot," a double eagle that enabled him to score a come-from-behind victory in the 1935 Masters.

sharp, incisive mind that was constantly pouring out revolutionary ideas to improve the game—enlarge the cups to six inches in diameter, streamline courses to put a greater premium on finesse, and force faster play. Yet while other golfers changed to slacks and short-sleeved shirts, he stuck to the style of the 1920s, knickers and turtleneck sweaters.

He was an innovator. Putting, he insisted, played a too important part in the sport with half the strokes of a round used on the greens. Thus the cups should be enlarged. He proposed courses be streamlined to half their size, enabling businessmen to get in a full 18 holes after office hours. He conceived and popularized the sand wedge, which became one of the most vital clubs in the bag.

He carried on a lifelong campaign against slow, methodical play, the habit of studying every shot meticulously and standing frozen over a three-foot putt. He practiced what he preached.

He was one of the game's fastest practitioners. It was his habit to walk up to his ball, give the situation a hurried look and then hit his shot, moving briskly to the next assignment. In 1947, he and George Fazio played a round in the Masters in one hour, 57 minutes, a record.

He was a pirate-bold, cocky player, called feisty by some of

Two of the all-time greats, Sarazen (right) and Walter Hagen pose before competing in a June, 1939 tournament in Toledo, Ohio.

his opponents. This rare trait did not escape one of his keenest rivals, the great Bob Jones.

"Sarazen has ever been the impatient, headlong player who went for everything in the hope of feeling the timely touch of inspiration," Jones once said. "When he is in the right mood, he is probably the greatest scorer in the game."

Sarazen rallied from four shots back in the final round to win his first National Open crown in 1922. Ten years later, he won the British Open at Sandwich, England, with a record score of 283, 13 under par. He returned home to stage one of the most sensational scoring streaks in history to add the U.S. Open title.

Eight shots back with 28 holes to play, the saucy squire blistered the remaining holes in 100 strokes—"the finest competitive exhibition on record," Bob Jones said—to sweep to the 1932 Open crown at New York's Fresh Meadow Club.

Sarazen, whose family name was Saraceni, was born in a two-family house in the workingmen's district of Harrison, New York, February 27, 1902, son of an Italian carpenter.

He started caddying at age eight, bringing home 45 cents a day. He quit school at 15 to become a carpenter's assistant and, after his family moved to Bridgeport, Connecticut, got a job in a pro shop. He took to golf naturally.

He was only 20 when he won both the U.S. Open and PGA crowns in 1922 and defeated Walter Hagen in a 72-hole match for the World's Unofficial Professional Championship. He was 39 when he tied Lawson Little for the U.S. Open title in 1940, losing the playoff by three strokes.

It was Sarazen's last serious bid for a major crown although he remained active well past his 80th birthday—a living monument to the game he loved and mastered.

TERRY SAWCHUK

The Temperamental "Mr. Zero"

Most of hockey's great players are measured by the number of goals they scored or set up, or the championships they won. The best defensemen are remembered for their ability to hold off the most potent attackers.

And the goalies?

Some became known for weird antics, others for their fearlessness. One invented the mask that no goaltender would be caught without anymore.

Terry Sawchuk is remembered for his 103 career shutouts, easily the most by any NHL goalie. And for his 21 seasons and 971 games, marks that, in today's coast-to-cast, high-speed game don't figure to be approached.

Sawchuk also was known for his injuries. He had more than 400 stitches in his face; three elbow operations, in which 66 bone chips had to be removed; a broken right arm that did not heal properly and left him with a right arm that was inches shorter than the left; punctured lungs; ruptured discs; severed hand tendons; and, in 1957, when he contracted mononucleosis, it temporarily drove him from the game in which he tried so hard to excel.

Sawchuk also is recalled for the mysterious circumstances in which he died. As a 40-year-old reserve with the New York Rangers, Sawchuk died of abdominal injuries in 1970 after what

he described as "horse play" with his teammate and friend, Ron Stewart.

For Sawchuk, playing goal was a mission. As a 10-year-old in Winnipeg, his older brother Mike developed a heart murmur and died. Terry carried on in Mike's stead, determined to make good in the sport his brother loved.

"It always seemed like Terry was looking to prove something," said Emile Francis, a former goalie who was the general manager and coach of the Rangers when Sawchuk died. "He was one of the most nervous players I've ever met. Everything seemed to bother him."

Gordie Howe, a teammate of Sawchuk's on some of the Detroit Red Wings' best teams, recalls that the goalie "always let you know when you messed up. He was not the kind of player you could let down without hearing about it."

Al Arbour, the coach of four Stanley Cup champions with the New York Islanders and a former defenseman in front of Sawchuk, said, "If you ever hit Sawchuk in the head during practice, that was it. He'd leave."

Sawchuk, the perfectionist in approach, was nearly that in the crease. He won the Vezina Trophy as the league's stingiest goalie four times. His lifetime goals-against average was 2.52, and for five consecutive years, he posted an average below 2.00.

Sawchuk, a long-time star for the Detroit Red Wings, looks to his left after stopping a shot fired by Tod Sloan (11) of the Toronto Maple Leafs in 1958 game.

Terry posted a record 103 NHL career shutouts. He played for 21 big league seasons and participated in 971 games. Three times he had 12 shutouts in one season.

"He was always flopping around on the ice and I guess somebody thought he looked like an octopus," Red Wings' spokesman Bill Jamieson said.

Surprisingly, Sawchuk was traded to Boston for the 1955-56 season. His tense demeanor unnerved many teammates in Detroit and his terse reactions to the media did not make him any more popular. Even though he was at his peak—or perhaps because he was at the top of his game and had the most trade value—Sawchuk went to Boston in a nine-player deal.

Sawchuk's two-year stay in Boston was miserable. He did not make the playoffs for the first time, was in a losing situation for the first time as a pro, and, understandably given his nature, his nerves became more jangled than ever.

In the middle of the 1956-57 season, he suffered mononucleosis, a strength-sapping blood disease. The usual recovery period is about six months. Sawchuk tried to come back in 12 days.

"It was a very serious mistake for me because I was much too weak to play well or help the team," he said. "All I did was make it worse."

He suffered a nervous breakdown while recuperating and missed the remainder of the season. And his feud with the Boston writers reached a zenith.

"Those Boston writers called me everything in the book, including a quitter," he said. "It was so bad I threatened to sue four newspapers for libel. I didn't go through with it, though. I guess those guys have to make a living, too."

The Red Wings, realizing the mistake they had made in trading Sawchuk, and gambling that he would recover from his physical and mental woes and be more comfortable back in Detroit, reacquired him for left wing John Bucyk on June 10, 1957. Bucyk went on to become the NHL's No. 4 all-time scorer.

And Sawchuk was superb in the Red Wings' net for seven more seasons.

"He was the same when he came back," Howe recalled. "He was a great goalie and a winner, and he was very difficult for people to get along with off the ice."

Sawchuk eventually wound up with Toronto, playing for another championship team in 1966-67, then Los Angeles, back to Detroit for one season, before finishing his career with the Rangers.

Sawchuk was as unorthodox as Montreal goalie Jacques Plante, the first to wear a facemask in a game. Sawchuk's crouching style—once described as resembling a near-sighted man peering into a tunnel for a runaway train bearing down upon him—and superior quickness made him look unusual. But it was effective enough that he gained immediate entrance into the Hall of Fame after his death.

Three times he had 12 shutouts in one season, once he had 11, twice he collected nine. He earned the nickname "Mr. Zero."

After winning Rookie of the Year honors in 1950-51, Sawchuk won all eight of his postseason appearances the following year, four of them shutouts, in leading the Red Wings to the NHL title. He also led Detroit to Stanley Cup crowns in 1954 and 1955.

And he was the inspiration of an unusual tradition in the Detroit Olympia. A dead octopus—or several of them, depending on the significance of the game—would be thrown onto the ice in front of Sawchuk before a game.

WILLIE SHOEMAKER

Ageless Sultan of the Saddle

Fifty-four years after his 2½ pound frail body was placed in a shoebox and shoved into an oven to keep it alive, Willie Shoemaker nursed a 17-1 shot, a colt named Ferdinand, to victory in the 1986 Kentucky Derby.

It was one of sport's most memorable achievements. It would have been an historic feat no matter who was in the saddle, but, coming as it did from the gifted hands of the world's greatest jockey at such an advanced athletic age, the feat took on miracle proportions. The sports world was awed and delighted.

The victory put a crown of gold on a 37-year career that saw the pint-sized Texan ride more horses, win more races, capture more stake purses and earn more prize money than any jockey who ever lived. As the sport moved through the 1980s, Shoemaker had climbed aboard close to 35,000 mounts, scored more than 8,000 victories, including more than 800 in stakes events, and won close to $100 million in prize money.

With his artistry and perseverance, he had long since passed Johnny Longden's record of 6,032 career victories and Eddie Arcaro's long-standing total of 554 stakes triumphs, which had earned Arcaro the proud title of "King of the Stakes Riders." With no more worlds to conquer, the "Shoe" still was winning in a sport which was his consuming passion.

Shoemaker considered Arcaro his toughest rival and envied his two sweeps of horse racing's Triple Crown events (the Kentucky Derby, Preakness and Belmont Stakes) with Whirlaway and Citation, the only prize to escape him. "He was terrific," Shoemaker said of Arcaro. "I think he beat me more than I beat him." They had some great duels.

Shoemaker needed no excuses for his own record in Triple Crown events. He won the Kentucky Derby four times, with Swaps, Tomy Lee, Lucky Debonair and Ferdinand; two Preakness Stakes with Candy Sports and Damascus, and five Belmont Stakes, with Gallant Man, Sword Dancer, Jaipur, Damascus and Avatar.

Then there was his notorious blunder in the 1957 Derby when, seemingly cruising to victory aboard Gallant Man, he mistook the sixteenth pole for the finish line, stood up in the stirrups and allowed Iron Liege to win by a nose.

Jockey Willie Shoemaker rides Ferdinand to the winner's circle after they won the 1986 Kentucky Derby. Willie was 54 years old at the time and Ferdinand was a 17-1 shot. It was Shoemaker's fourth Derby victory.

"An error like that would have destroyed most men," Arcaro said. "Only a guy like Willie could have survived it. He's a tough son-of-a-gun."

That toughness was tested from the day of his birth and throughout a career that saw him labeled at first "too small to be a jockey," suffer two life-threatening accidents during the late 1960s, undergo marital problems, and temporarily lose some of his competitive drive after being lured into the fast lane of California celebrity life.

He came close to retirement during the mid-1970s, telling his agent, Harry Silbert, "I'm tired. I've had it."

Billy Lee Shoemaker was born August 19, 1931, in a rural community near Fabens, Texas, son of a cotton mill hand. He was so tiny at birth—little more than the weight of a loaf of bread—that the doctor said he wouldn't live through the night. But his grandmother turned the kitchen oven into an incubator and kept him warm—and alive.

His parents divorced, and his father, fired by the mill, moved to California. Shoemaker spent most of his youth on the sheep and cattle farm of his grandparents near Winters, Texas, where he nearly drowned in a water tank and fell in love with horses. When he was 10, he and brother Lonnie joined his father in California, where, staying away from school, he got a job on a thoroughbred farm in Puente.

Shoemaker galloped horses at Hollywood Park and Del Mar, never getting a chance to race because of his small size. At Golden Gate Fields on March 19, 1949, the scrawny 17-year-old got his first mount, riding an old mare named Waxahachie in a six-furlong race and finishing fifth. Shoemaker recalled that Longden had cut him off coming out of the gate.

In his first full year, Shoemaker had 219 winners. The next year, he tied for first with 388 winners. In 1953, he set a record of 485 victories in one year. He was on his way. He became known as "Silent Shoe," because of his unemotional, reserved and almost deferential personality.

"I could talk," Shoemaker said. "But it's best to listen."

Shoemaker was a naturally small man—4-feet-11 and 95 pounds, small hands, small feet, 1½ boot size—but he was a giant in the saddle. He was gentle and intelligent. He sat still and let the horse run. "Like a computer," one track official said. Arcaro said Shoemaker could ride a horse with silken threads for reins.

Amazer, a 3-year-old filly, crosses the finish line with Willie Shoemaker up, to win the $150,000 Yellow Ribbon Stakes at Santa Anita in November, 1978.

Shoemaker (right) is in excellent company as he joins Eddie Arcaro (left) and Johnny Longden in placing their footprints in cement as they are inducted into the Walk of Fame at Hollywood Park in June, 1979. Longden's arm is in a sling as he recuperates from shoulder surgery. At the time, the three all-time greats had combined to ride more than 18,000 winners.

Shoemaker and Arcaro met in their most dramatic duel in the 1955 Kentucky Derby. Shoemaker rode Swaps, the pride of the West, to victory over heavily-favored Nashua, the big horse of the East, who later won the Preakness and Belmont.

Shoemaker avoided serious injury until January 1968, when his mount, Bell Bush, fell and accidentally kicked him, cracking a bone in his leg. A rod had to be inserted and Shoemaker was out of action for 13 months. Fifteen months later, he was thrown against a hedge at Hollywood Park when his mount flipped over backward, leaving him with a crushed pelvis, torn bladder and nerve damage in the legs. He defied predictions that he would never ride again.

Lifestyle almost succeeded where accidents failed in keeping him off the tracks. Shoemaker's first marriage to Virginia McLaughlin, when he was 18, lasted 11 years. His next wife was Babbs Bayer, a Texan whose social interests led Shoemaker to neglect his riding in the early 1970s. They were divorced in March 1978, and shortly afterward Shoemaker married a 27-year-old sportswoman and longtime friend, Cindy Barnes.

It proved to be a tonic for a brand new career.

O.J. SIMPSON

"The Juice" Was Loose

In the 1970s American television viewers got accustomed to seeing a lithe figure of a man with a big "32" on the back of his uniform weaving his way through frustrated tacklers on the pro football field. During the 1980s, they saw him in a three-piece business suit dashing madly across the lobby of an airport.

Whether he cradled a pigskin football or an alligator attache case in the crook of his arms, O.J. Simpson came across as a running man. He ran his way to the Heisman Trophy as a tailback at the University of Southern California and then started pursuing Jim Brown's records in the National Football League. He seemed to never stop running.

Even after hanging up his helmet after 11 seasons in the NFL, acclaimed as one of the greatest ball-carriers ever, he hardly broke stride, challenging Brown's success as a movie actor and other sports idols in an age of excess commercialism as the most marketed athlete of his time.

He had the credentials for greatness in both fields. A handsome figure at 6-foot-2 and 212 pounds, with a strong face and skin like burnished copper, he brought a pleasant, warm personality to his athletic skills.

George Allen, former coach of the Los Angeles Rams and Washington Redskins, in his book "Pro Footballs' 100 Greatest Players," rated Simpson second only to the incomparable Jim Brown in his list of all-time great runners, placing him above Gale Sayers, Bronko Nagurski and Walter Payton. He called O.J. the "best late-game running back I ever saw."

Allen said that while O.J. was a workhorse he lacked the durability of Brown which hurt his effectiveness in later years. "Simpson achieved what he did with a lot less help than Brown," the former coach added. "O.J. was a world class sprinter... He picked holes as well as anyone... He wasn't a power back but he could knife through a line for a few yards when you needed them and often break into the open."

Simpson became the first back in NFL history to rush for more than 2,000 yards in a season, racking up 2,003 yards in 1973 to shatter the record of 1,863 set by Brown 10 years earlier. O.J.'s mark survived 11 years, broken in turn by the Los Angeles Rams' Eric Dickerson in 1984 with 2,105.

Playing almost his entire career with one of the poorest teams in professional football, the Buffalo Bills, who never reached further than one NFL playoff game, O.J. squirmed and wove his way to 11,236 rushing yards in his nine seasons with the Bills

The first to reach 2,000! O.J. Simpson (32) begins his seven-yard run in the fourth quarter in the Dec. 1973 game against the New York Jets which gave him a season total of 2,003 yards—the first in NFL history to rush for more than 2,000 yards.

The Juice (32) finds a hole as he runs past Denver linebacker Tom Jackson (57) in Buffalo's 1977 game against the Denver Broncos.

and final two with the San Francisco 49ers. He rushed for 61 touchdowns, the longest 94 yards, and scored 14 more as a pass receiver, one covering 64 yards.

Born July 7, 1947, in San Francisco, O.J. grew up in a ghetto neighborhood called Porreo Hills with a brother and two sisters, reared by their mother, a hospital worker. He was street tough, ran with a gang, often skipped school and was constantly flirting with trouble.

"We were always smoking, shooting craps and getting called into the dean's office," he said.

Christened Orenthal James Simpson, it is easy to understand how O.J. got to be called by his initials and later in life nicknamed "Orange Juice" or simply "The Juice." At Buffalo,

the offensive line proudly dubbed itself "The Electric Company." "We turn on the juice," a mate said.

O.J.'s lifestyle got turned around when he joined a local Community Club, dedicated to helping street kids. He was a 5-10, 160-pound tackle, the biggest player on his high school team, and when he got ready to go to college he found his grades too poor to enter a four-year institution.

He got a summer job in Las Vegas and entered City College

of San Francisco where he became the most celebrated junior college player in the country, averaging 9.9 yards a carry as a running back and scoring 26 touchdowns. Southern California won a scramble for his services.

At USC, O.J. set 13 school rushing records, led the NCAA in rushing and made All-America both of his final years climaxed with his winning the Heisman Trophy. As a crack sprinter, he shared USC's world record (38.6) in the 440-yard relay in 1967. He was named College Athlete of the Decade (1960s).

First pick in the 1969 NFL draft, he was plucked by the lowly Bills and paid $100,000 a year. His reputation and his sensational ball-carrying ability injected new life into the Buffalo franchise. The city's old, 46,000-seat War Memorial Stadium couldn't hold the surging crowds and it had to be replaced by the modern Rich Stadium, seating 80,000.

O.J.'s running style was said to be a cross between that of Jim Brown and Gale Sayers. Not as big nor as strong as Brown, he couldn't bull over would-be tacklers but powerful legs made him hard to bring down. He had the quickness and instincts without the breakaway qualities of Sayers. Some old-timers said he was better than Red Grange.

Simpson had six 200-yard rushing games in his career, his best day against Detroit at Pontiac Stadium in 1976 when he rushed for 273 yards, a mark later broken by Payton. He led the league in rushing four times but regretted that he fell short of Jim Brown's career record of 12,312 yards.

"My one ambition," he once said, "was to be able to walk down the street, have people point at me and say, 'There goes the best ball-carrier in the world.'"

He settled for the more durable label, "Nice Guy."

"He's a better person than he is a football player, if that's possible," said Bills' owner Ralph Wilson. Honored in 1973 for breaking Jim Brown's season rushing record, O.J. insisted that his offensive line share in the ceremonies.

Retiring in 1979 after a rash of injuries, Simpson, a father of three, found himself swamped with duties as a TV network broadcaster; a movie career that included top-rated films with such stars as Richard Burton, Paul Newman and William Holden; commitments as active spokesman for a dozen or more major companies and numerous charity drives at both state and national levels. A runner to the end.

O.J. (right) and Joe Namath stand in front of the Pro Football Hall of Fame in Canton, Ohio in Aug. 1985, the day before their official induction in the sports shrine.

SAM SNEAD

The Slamming Mountaineer

It is one of the regrettable ironies of sports that golf annals will always record Sam Snead as the remarkable talent who never won the United States Open Championship.

This rugged, long-hitting Virginia hillbilly enthralled galleries for half a century with a swing as smooth as molasses pouring over a stack of flapjacks and as explosive as a cannon shot. He won more than 100 tournaments throughout the world, 84 on the Professional Golfers Association tour. He won more tour events than Arnold Palmer and Jack Nicklaus.

He played in the era of such giants as Ben Hogan, Byron Nelson, Lloyd Mangrum and Jimmy Demaret, beating them more often than he lost. Fellow professionals rated him as the finest striker of the ball who ever lived.

Yet it was his fate to carry the negative tag: He couldn't win the Open.

An amazing athlete, he seemed to defy the aging process. Long after many of his contemporaries, including Hogan and Nelson, had retired, Sam continued to tee it up with the Palmers and Nicklauses and even the so-called young lions. They all would stop, watch and admire when he prepared to swing. He became one of the game's irrefutable legends.

He shot his age many times. When the day's round was complete, even after he had moved past age 70, Snead would entertain fellow players in the locker room by doing a complete flip from a standing start or kicking the top of a door frame. His body was so limber it seemed to lack bones.

If Snead felt that fate dealt him a bad hand in his pursuit of the National Open—he had a chance to win a half-dozen of them only to be thwarted by some bizarre incident—he never allowed his frustration to surface. He took a philosophical attitude.

"It gives you an eerie feeling sometimes," he acknowledged in the sunset of his career. "I've won tournaments I had no business winning and I've had tournaments snatched right out of my hands when by all rights they should have been mine. It's almost as if your name is written on a tournament before it starts."

Snead couldn't complain much. He was the victor in lot of prestigious tournaments even if the Open continued to elude him. He won three Masters, between 1949 and 1954, and was runner-up twice. He won three PGA titles in tough match play competition and was a finalist on two other occasions. He won the British Open in 1946 in his first try.

He was the tour's leading money winner in 1938, 1949 and 1950 and the Vardon Trophy winner (lowest scoring average) in 1938, 1949, 1950 and 1955. Seven times he was a member of the U.S. Ryder Cup team, compiling a 9-2 record.

In the U.S. Open, he tied for the title in 1947 only to lose the playoff to Lew Worsham. Both were within near tap-in range

Snead was one of only two American golfers to win the British Open between 1934 and 1953. He won at historic St. Andrews in 1946. Photo shows him driving from the 12th tee.

on the final green. When Sam prepared to putt out, Worsham interrupted, demanding a measurement. Rattled, Sam missed from 30½ inches. Worsham sank from 30.

Snead's first disappointment came in 1937 when he was a raw rookie of 25. Playing brilliantly over the tough Oakland Hills Club in Birmingham, Michigan, he had the Open title apparently clinched when Ralph Guldahl charged home with a closing record 69 to win by two strokes.

Two years later at Philadelphia's Spring Mill course, Sam came to the par five, 558-yard final hole needing only five to win the title and a bogey six to tie. He skied to an eight in one of the biggest collapses in golf history. He barely missed winning the 1949 and 1953 Opens—finishing second to Ben Hogan in the latter after hitting his tee shot out of bounds at the start of the final round.

Snead was born May 27, 1912 on a cow and chicken farm in Ashwood, Virginia, a few miles from Hot Springs. His mother and father were both hardy mountain folk. He had four brothers and a sister, all good athletes.

Sam was a fast and shifty halfback in football. He was a good baseball pitcher. In basketball, he usually scored more points than the entire opposition combined.

He shagged balls for older brother, Homer, in a pasture near the family home. He was seven years old when he cut a swamp maple limb with a knot at the end and fashioned his first primitive golf stick. He swung it for hours at a time and practiced accuracy by belting rocks at fence posts 125 yards away. He later fashioned his own golf course in the farmyard, sinking tomato cans for holes.

Although offered several college scholarships, Snead chose to skip higher education for a career in golf. He got a job caddying at the fashionable Homestead Hotel in Hot Springs, became an assistant pro and later was lured to the Greenbrier Hotel in White Sulphur Springs, West Virginia, where he became the resident pro. It was a famous old resort frequented by presidents, industrial tycoons and financial barons.

After winning several regional tournaments in the mid-1930s, firing a 61 in one tournament and beating top players in exhibitions, Snead was given a stake by club members and sent out on the tour. There he attracted the interest of Fred Corcoran, the PGA tournament manager and promotional genius who handled such prominent athletes as Babe Didrikson Zaharias, Ted Williams and Stan Musial.

Giving him the name of "Slammin' Sammy," Corcoran promoted the colorful, long-hitting mountaineer for all he was worth and soon Snead was the hottest commodity on the circuit. Fans came out by the thousands just to see the magic swing.

Sam never disappointed. At age 50, he led the Masters with four holes to play before losing his putting touch. He won six PGA Seniors, five World Seniors and, with Don January, the Legends title in 1982.

He was the game's all-time leading money winner until Arnold Palmer came along to found the "Millionaire's Club."

Snead hits one of the first shots as he and Gene Sarazen, honorary starters, get the 1986 Masters tournament underway.

MARK SPITZ

Conqueror of the Water World

He was tall, slim, dark with a dashing mustache—and he could swim like a fish. For one minuscule moment in time—seven days in the late summer of 1972 in the Olympic pool at Munich, Germany—he proved himself the greatest swimmer of all time. Then, like a chameleon, he was supposed to shed his old skin and take on a new image to become Johnny Weissmuller, Errol Flynn and Clark Gable all wrapped into one neat, marketable package.

Mark Spitz fulfilled his destiny when he swept to seven swimming gold medals, including three for relays, all in world record time. It was perhaps the most astounding individual feat ever in the Olympic Games. Yet, having conquered the water world, he found himself ill equipped to measure up to the expectations of his fans and commercial advisers.

Despite all his medals with their attendant glory and his physical assets, he turned into a major disappointment. All the multi-million-dollar efforts to make him a public idol collapsed almost immediately. His fame faded.

"I was a porpoise out of water," the handsome Californian said poignantly afterward. "All my life I had done little except concentrate on my swimming. I was determined to be the best in the world. I never learned how to relate to my friends and the public."

Spitz, cocky and often arrogant, was always at loggerheads with his teammates. Some found him immature—a characteristic which he openly acknowledged. A close friend said he was a hypochondriac, a complainer, and a worrier.

Spitz had the misfortune to compete in what is possibly the most snobbish, clannish and insensitive sport in the Olympic Games. A historian once commented that the only way you could tell swimmers apart was to throw them in the water and see what stroke they swam. Spitz concentrated on the freestyle and butterfly.

Born February 10, 1950 of well-to-do parents in Modesto, California, he grew up in the shadow of Don Schollander, the blond and popular Yale man who won four gold medals in Tokyo in 1964 and a gold and silver in Mexico City in 1968.

In the tradition of the sport—that swimmers reach their peaks as teen-agers and are over-the-hill before they can vote—Spitz and Schollander, the latter four years older, were of two different eras although their paths crossed in Mexico City.

Spitz was 18, just arriving on the launching pad for his meteoric career. Schollander was an "old man" of 22, still basking in the limelight of his four golds in the previous Games and the highly respected dean of the U.S. team.

Spitz had been a national champion in high school and had been lured by a scholarship to Indiana University, an institution renowned for its water program. He quickly alienated his Olympic teammates by brashly predicting that he expected to win six gold medals at Mexico City. The result was that he soon found himself "frozen out" by veteran members of the squad.

Spitz's life was made miserable for the six weeks the team spent in a training camp in Colorado Springs, Colorado, prior to the Games. Mark was moved out of the main dormitory into

HIS 7TH GOLD MEDAL. *Mark Spitz is seen in the butterfly part of the 400-meter medley relay won by the American team during the 1972 Olympic Games in Munich.*

Superswimmer Spitz (center) poses with runnerup Jerry Heidenreich of Dallas (left) and bronze medal winner Vladimir Bure (right) of the Soviet Union after receiving his sixth gold medal for his triumph in the 100-meter freestyle event at the Munich Olympics.

a small room of his own. The older members stuck together and, when they elected to speak to Spitz, who was Jewish, it was often to make fun of him. They aimed anti-Semitic remarks at him and scoffed at his grandiose goals.

A teammate, Gary Hall, acknowledged that there was a group scheme to shake Spitz's confidence. "He was really susceptible. You could psych him out," Hall said. Other team members admitted sheepishly later that Mark had been given a bad deal.

Instead of winning six gold medals, Spitz captured a disappointing two, both in the freestyle relays. He finished third in the 100-meter freestyle and second in the 100-meter butterfly, failing to qualify for the medley relay. Schollander had to settle for second in the 200-meter freestyle and a share of a single gold in the 800 freestyle relay.

Mexico City proved a disheartening experience for Spitz, who later confessed that he thought he might never compete in another Olympics.

"I told myself," he said, "that even if I never go to another Olympics I could still say 30 years from now 'Well, I got two golds, a silver and a bronze. I didn't win any individual events, but I held 35 world records. That isn't all that bad.'"

Dreams don't die that easily.

Three years after Mexico City, Spitz, having established himself as the world's best swimmer, swept to five gold medals in the Pan American Games. Then he set his sights on Munich, 1972.

They were the "Horror Olympics," scene of the Arab massacre of the Israeli athletes, disqualification of U.S. sprinters for failing to report on time; a pratfall by America's top miler, Jim Ryun, and the first defeat ever for the U.S. basketball team. But there was no denying Spitz his cascade of gold.

A more mature man now, admired by his teammates and hailed by the fans, he reeled off victories night after night, setting one world record after another. He captured the 100 and 200-meter freestyle and butterfly events and helped the Americans win two freestyle and one medley relay.

A few hours after Mark had won his seventh gold, the terrorists moved in, leaving a carnage of death. Because he was Jewish, Spitz was quickly whisked out of the country.

He returned to the United States a genuine hero, his earlier problems forgotten. He signed with one of Hollywood's biggest talent agencies for a reported $6 million. He was groomed for the movies, TV and commercial shots. The ventures all flopped. Critics were brutal, declaring that he was a drab personality with no sex appeal.

"I wasn't an actor and I wasn't an entertainer," he said. "I knew I could make money in other ways. I am not bitter. I reached my goal and went out gracefully."

BART STARR

Lombardi's Unflappable Leader

It was as tough a job as advising Jack Nicklaus on making a winning putt... writing a brief for Edward Bennett Williams in major litigation... or arranging a song for Ol' Blue Eyes, Frank Sinatra.

Bart Starr was the alter ego, calm and efficient, for the five star general among pro football coaches, Vince Lombardi, for nine seasons with the Green Bay Packers. Those were the years, 1959-67, when Green Bay was Titletown, U.S.A., and maybe something more, a gridiron Camelot ruling the realm of the National Football League.

Starr, backed by Lombardi's lashing will on the sidelines, quarterbacked the Packers to six NFL championship games in those nine seasons and the first two Super Bowls. The Pack won five of the six league title tests and romped in Super Bowls I and II. The only loss in a playoff final in those years for the Starr-Lombardi tandem was in 1960 when the Philadelphia Eagles outlasted Green Bay, 17-13, for the league crown. The Packers didn't lose the game as much as they did a race with the clock.

They were battering on the door to the Philadelphia end zone when time ran out.

Bart was the MVP of the first Super Bowl game, a 35-10 put-down of the Kansas City Chiefs, and also of the second game, a 33-14 stomping of the Oakland Raiders. That, by the way, was Lombardi's final game as Green Bay's head coach.

Always a money player, almost with banker-like style, Starr was at his best in the big games. In the six NFL title tilts, he completed a total of 83 passes in 142 attempts for 1,069 yards and 11 touchdowns. He was intercepted just once in the 360 minutes of play. The unflappable Alabama Arrow had one string of 294 consecutive aerials without an interception in regular season competition at the height of his career.

For his full career at Green Bay, 1956-1971, Bart showed these numbers: 1808 successful tosses in 3,149 tries for 23,718 yards and 152 scores. In the first Super Bowl, he hit on 16 of 23 for 250 yards and a pair of touchdowns. The following year he completed 13 of 24 for 202 yards and one score.

Trailing 17-14 with 13 seconds remaining in the 1967 NFL title game, Green Bay had possession on the Dallas one-yard line. A tying field goal attempt seemed to be the correct call. However, the Packers gambled and, here, Starr (15) at left pushes into the end zone for the winning TD.

In this 1967 regular season game, Starr cocks his arm for a pass in a game against the Giants in New York. The Packers won, 48-21.

Starr never played in a title game except for those under Lombardi. But after the 1960 loss to Philly, the Pack racked up five NFL championships in seven years. Those were the seasons of glory in Green Bay. A 37-0 whipping of the Giants in the 1961 championship; a 16-7 decision over New York in 1962; a 23-12 beating of Cleveland and Jimmy Brown in 1965; a 34-27 screamer over Dallas in 1966 and the legendary Ice Bowl Game in 1967.

The "Ice Bowl" was played in Green Bay with the temperature 13 below zero. The Dallas Cowboys and their Doomsday

Defense had a 17-14 lead over the Packers with 13 seconds left and Green Bay in possession on the Cowboy one-yard line. The Packers had one time out left and called it. It seemed obvious when Starr trotted to the sideline to talk to Lombardi that a tying field goal would be the call. It wasn't. Vince and Bart decided on the kind of gamble only a high-rolling crapshooter takes. The play was a quarterback sneak and Starr, head down, pushed into the end zone behind Jerry Kramer and Ken Bowman, who almost planted Jethro Pugh, the Dallas defensive tackle, in the first row of the bleachers. The final score was Green Bay 21, Dallas 17.

The Starr-Lombardi alliance began in 1959, Vince's first year in Green Bay after leaving an assistant's job with the New York Giants. Years later Starr described the relationship as "businesslike," an odd word but perhaps a fitting one. "It was always a comfortable thing," Bart said, "never stilted or uneasy. With each passing year, it became something close to a father-son relationship."

Bart was asked many times what made Lombardi, who died in 1970 while coaching Washington, such a remarkable coach. "He was extremely demanding," Starr said, "because he demanded a great deal of himself. He was extremely knowledgeable about pro football. Under his coaching, I think we were ahead of our time in audibles at the line of scrimmage—which I called—and taking advantage of defenses, which Vince read like the front page of a newspaper."

A quarterback has to do more than take the snap and either hand off to a darting runner or fade to pass. He has to lead and he also has to magically make the other 10 men in the huddle feel that he is in control and they are going to go down the field for a touchdown.

"A lot of people thought Starr was too nice, too much of a quiet gentleman, to run a team," Forrest Gregg, the star offen-

sive tackle of the Pack and a Hall of Famer said. Gregg and Starr reached the pro shrine in Canton, Ohio, the same year, 1977.

"Bart's big thing," Gregg continued, "was knowing what he had to do and how to do it. When he called the play, there were no doubters in the huddle. He had the respect of every player on the team. He was wonderful at calling an audible. He could recognize defenses and make a change in the play at the line of scrimmage so well there were no missed assignments."

Kramer, a free-wheeling guard and an outspoken individualist, commented: "There was a softness to Bart in many ways, a sort of gentle manliness. But there also was an iron-hard spirit."

Bart was 6-1 and 197 pounds. He was, incredibly, a 17th round draft choice in 1956. One reason for that was the fact that his senior year at the University of Alabama, 1955, was the first

Bart (left) poses with Green Bay's legendary head coach, Vince Lombardi. Later, Starr was named to the same position Lombardi held.

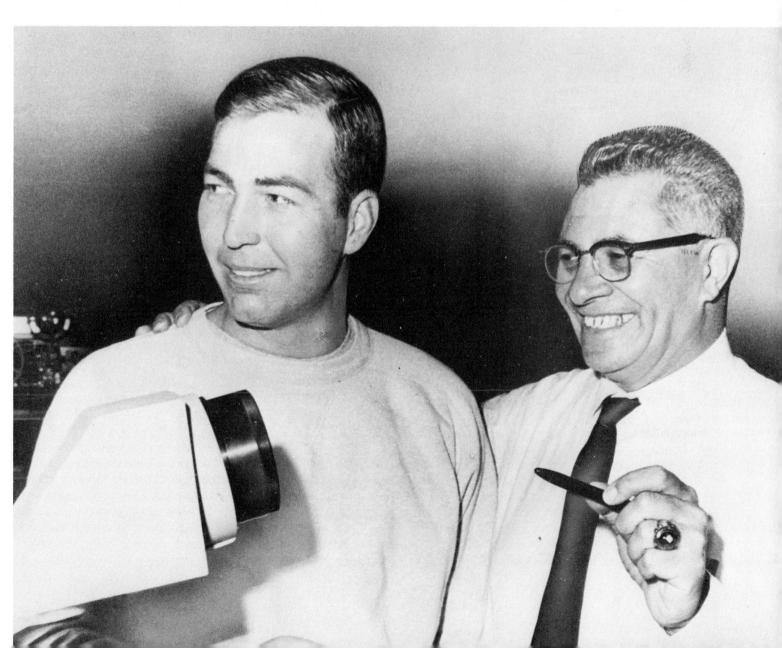

Unable to find a pass receiver, Starr takes off and gains enough ground for a first down in a 1966 game against Detroit. Pursuing Bart is the Lions' Darris Brown.

under a new coach, J.B. Whitworth, who decided to build for the future. Starr was literally shunted aside. Green Bay only drafted him because it thought it had run out of logical choices.

The starting Packer quarterback in Bart's rookie year was tough Tobin Rote. The next year Rote was traded to Detroit, where he helped the Lions win the league crown. It was Starr and the veteran Babe Parilli in 1957 and 1958. The Pack went 3-9 in 1957 and 1-10-1 in '58. Then came Lombardi and the first step on the road to fame and fortune.

After retiring in 1971, Starr coached Green Bay for nine seasons, 1975-1983, and made the playoffs just once, in 1982. He was fired in December, 1983, and a short time later joined the corporate setup of a team without a squad, the Arizona Firebirds, as coach and general manager. Arizona wanted an NFL franchise and three years later was pushing hard for one. If the Firebirds get a chance to fly, Starr will be the man with the job of picking players good enough to compete on the high level of the NFL.

ROGER STAUBACH

The Cowboys' "Mr. Clutch"

Roger Staubach was not as prolific a passer as Fran Tarkenton or Johnny Unitas nor as glamorous as Joe Namath. But for overall proficiency as a football quarterback he had no peer, and no one was better able to rally a team to victory.

When he retired after the 1979 season, following 11 years with the Dallas Cowboys, Staubach carried with him the highest quarterback ranking in the National Football League, topping such greats as Tarkenton, Unitas, Otto Graham, Bart Starr, Namath and Sammy Baugh.

He had the statistics to prove it. But not shown in the cold numbers was his facility for being able to lift the Cowboys from the brink of defeat to victory in the closing stages of a game.

Twenty-three times he brought the Cowboys from behind to win in the final quarter, and 17 of those times he did it in the final two minutes. He was the king of pro football's two-minute drill. He was the game's "Mr. Clutch." A darting, elusive scrambler, as well as a poised passer, he was the master of the big moment—a Reggie Jackson in football pads.

"Roger Staubach was the best passer-runner I ever coached against," said George Allen, former coach of the Los Angeles Rams and Washington Redskins, in his published analysis of pro football's 100 greatest players. "A better runner than Terry Bradshaw and Fran Tarkenton...a great passer."

The National Football League ranks quarterbacks under an intricate system that takes into account passing attempts, completions, yards, touchdowns, interceptions and yardage per attempt. Staubach led the league four times—1971, 1973, 1978 and 1979—and closed his career with these totals: 1,685 completions in 2,958 attempts, a 57 percent completion average, for 22,700 yards and 153 touchdowns.

His completions and yardage fell well below those of Tarkenton and Unitas, each with seven years more service, but when all the categories were fed into the computer, Staubach led all NFL quarterbacks with a rating of 83.5. Tarkenton was fourth, Unitas ninth.

Staubach's total production would have been more impressive had he not chosen the U.S. Naval Academy for his higher education and committed himself to five years of military service before being able to launch his pro career. This was the reason he was virtually ignored in the pro draft and, although the

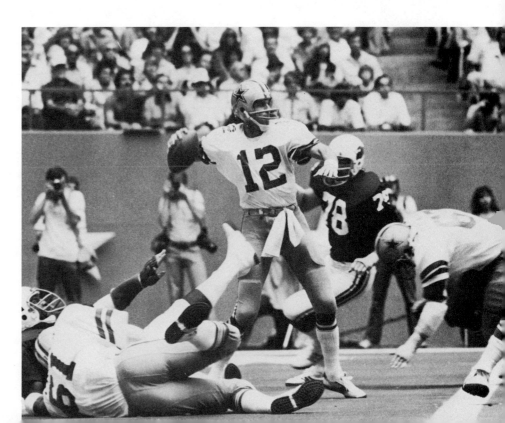

Cowboy quarterback Staubach (12) gets good pass protection from tackle Jim Cooper (61) in this 1979 game against the St. Louis Cardinals.

country's top college player and Heisman Trophy winner in 1963, he was not picked until the 10th round, a gamble by the Cowboys.

The Cowboys long enjoyed the distinction of being "America's Team," and it was coincidental that they should wind up with America's model athlete to call signals and spark their juggernaut. Staubach was a straight arrow—Midwest upbringing, service in Vietnam, clean-cut, patriotic, religious and strong on basic values.

He was born of well-to-do parents on February 5, 1942, in Silverton, Ohio, a suburb of Cincinnati. He showed a proclivity

Roger the Dodger gets ready to run with the ball after failing to locate a receiver. Staubach gained 12 yards on the play in the 1973 game against the Los Angeles Rams.

for sports at an early age and, after being appointed to the Naval Academy, developed into probably the greatest athlete in the academy's history. He won seven letters in football, basketball and baseball, but it was on the football field that he established himself as a national figure.

He was a two-time All-America at Navy, grabbing headlines for his remarkable scrambling ability as much as for his pinpoint passing. He won both the Heisman and Walter Camp trophies as the country's top college player in 1963, his junior year, and the Maxwell Award in 1964.

In 1963, "Roger the Dodger"—as the media called him—completed 66 percent of his passes for 1,474 yards, rushed for 418 yards, engineered a dramatic victory over Army for a 9-1 record, and led the Midshipmen into the Cotton Bowl to play

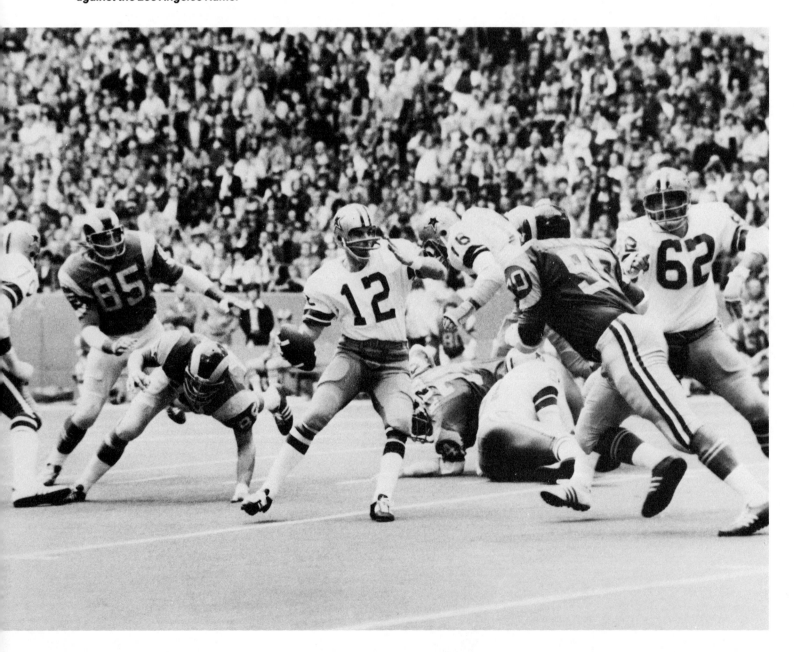

Texas for the national championship. Texas won 28-6, but not before Staubach had dazzled the crowd by completing 21 passes, a bowl record.

Many thought Staubach deserved to repeat as the Heisman winner for his senior year although hobbled by an ankle injury.

Staubach was lean, hungry and anxious when he got out of the Navy and reported to Coach Tom Landry of the Cowboys in 1969 as a 27-year-old rookie. At 6-3 and 202 pounds, he was physically fit and he felt ready. But was Landry?

The answer came quickly in the opening game of the 1969 season against St. Louis. The Cowboys' No. 1 quarterback, Craig Morton, was injured, so Landry had no other choice than to use Staubach.

"I was very nervous," Staubach recalled. "It was not only my first game but I thought it could have been my last."

Dallas' Staubach prepares to throw a pass in the 1972 College All-Star game in Chicago. During his career, Roger brought the Cowboys from behind to win in the final quarter 23 times.

Staubach completed his first of two touchdown passes—"to Lance Rentzel on the run," he remembered—and the Cowboys won, 24-3. Staubach also ran for 140 yards.

"Coach Landry wasn't happy with my scrambling, then or ever," Staubach said. "It was a running feud. I put up with his play-calling and he put up with my scrambling."

Staubach appeared in four Super Bowl games. He considered the first of those games, against the Miami Dolphins in 1972, as one of his greatest and most important. The Cowboys won 24-3, Staubach passing for 119 yards and two touchdowns with no interceptions. He won the game's Most Valuable Player Award.

"It was my 10th game as a starter," he said, "and it erased the tag that the Cowboys couldn't win the big one."

On March 31, 1980, Staubach retired to his suburban home in Dallas with his wife, Marianne, a grammar school sweetheart, their five children and a host of responsibilities—a successful real estate business, television commentary, several charities and numerous civic and religious obligations. A scrambler to the end.

JIM THORPE

The Greatest of Them All

By the sheer enormity and breadth of his exploits and the assessment of sports historians whose job it is to gauge them, Jim Thorpe must be acclaimed indisputably the greatest athlete of all-time.

He should have received a dozen calls from the President and been honored with a reception at the White House. He should have been in more than one Hall of Fame. A statue of him should stand on the city square and he should be memorialized in bronze. Children should read about him in school.

But this remarkable Indian half-breed, master of many sports, was destined to receive the back of the hand from a cruel and insensitive society. His Sac and Fox Indian ancestors were uprooted from their native lands in Iowa by greedy white neighbors. With the aid of blue-coated U.S. troops, they were driven into Kansas and finally herded to an arid, godforsaken territory in Oklahoma.

It was in this grim, hopeless atmosphere that Jim Thorpe was born on May 28, 1888, one of 19 children, son of a half-breed farmer and Indian mother. The father, part Irish, had five wives. The mother, part-French, weighed 200 pounds.

Rare athletic skills saved the youngster from this bleak existence. He got a scholarship to the Carlisle Indian School in Pennsylvania, became an All-America football star, excelled in numerous other sports and made the Olympics.

In the 1912 Olympics in Stockholm, Sweden, Thorpe won gold medals in both the decathlon, a gruelling variety of 10 different specialties, and the pentathlon, five events—regarded the premier tests of versatility and endurance in the entire Games.

Six months afterward, a sportswriter disclosed that Thorpe had received money for playing professional baseball in a small league in North Carolina during summer vacations while at school ($2 a game plus expenses). The austere and hypocritical International Olympic Committee stripped Thorpe of his medals and had his records erased from the Olympic book.

Thorpe went on to play both professional football and major league baseball but the shadow of his Olympic experience never left him. For years, friends and advocates of justice sought to have the medals restored and Thorpe's record cleansed, without effect.

The International Olympic Committee, later headed by the United States' Avery Brundage, refused to yield.

Thorpe's plea was that he was just an innocent Indian kid who was unaware of any wrongdoing. His supporters used the

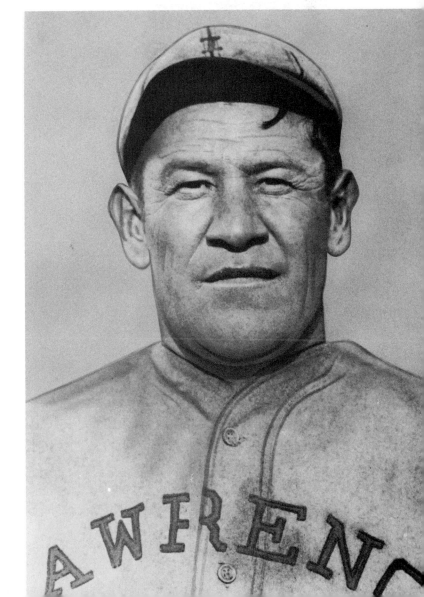

Thorpe was truly a phenomenon, the world's greatest all-around athlete. Football was his first love, but he also played major league baseball for the New York Giants and Cincinnati Reds.

tests of professionalism had to be made within 30 days after the Games. It brought small solace to Thorpe's family and friends. The Olympic hierarchy, however, never restored his records.

After the Olympics, Thorpe had the distinction of playing both major league baseball and pro football at the same time. He earned what could be considered respectable salaries at the time—he had natural drawing power at the gate—but was careless with his money. By the time the 1930s Depression occurred, he was virtually broke, married for a second time with four children to support.

He tried his hand at a variety of jobs—painting and acting, winding up making $4 a day wielding a pick and shovel. When a newspaper photographer caught him doing this menial work, the nation was shocked. Charles Curtis, vice-president of the United States at the time, invited him to sit in the presidential box at the 1932 Olympics in Los Angeles. The crowd gave him a huge ovation.

Thorpe served in the Merchant Marine during World War II and virtually dropped from sight until his death in 1953 at age 65. There was one last splash of glory. In 1951, a poll of sportswriters by The Associated Press named him both "Greatest All-Around Athlete" and "Greatest Football Player" of the first half-century.

He was indeed the athletic marvel of the age.

Thorpe wasn't a big man, by modern standards. He was 5 feet, 11 inches tall and weighed 185 pounds with narrow shoulders and hips but thick thighs and legs and arms like railroad ties. He ran with such an easy gait that he was accused of being lazy. He called it relaxation.

At Carlisle, playing under the legendary Coach Glenn S. "Pop" Warner, he was a brutal runner, averaging close to 10 yards a carry and 16 points a game in a conservative, low-scoring era. The Carlisle Indians were national champions.

Thorpe was the spearhead of the Carlisle team that crushed Army, a power of the time, 27-6, provoking an Army end named Dwight Eisenhower to say, "We could have won if it hadn't been for Thorpe—he's the best I've ever seen."

From Carlisle, the rugged Indian went to the Canton (Ohio) Bulldogs of the American Pro Football Association, forerunner of the National Football League, where his ball-carrying and drop-kicking brought three national crowns.

He played with the New York Giants baseball team, under crusty John McGraw, for six years, 1913-1919, and briefly for Cincinnati, as an outfielder. He finished his career with three years in the minors, hitting over .300. Thorpe was adept at tennis and could shoot in the 70s in golf with practice. His bowling average was over 200. He also excelled in handball, billiards, rowing and gymnastics.

Proving his versatility had no limits, he even won a ballroom dancing contest with a Carlisle co-ed in 1912.

argument that Thorpe's offense was minuscule compared with other flagrant violations of the Olympic amateur code.

"Ignorance of the law is no excuse," crackled Brundage, who was Thorpe's decathlon and pentathlon rival in the Stockholm Games and who some said bore a deep jealousy of the man who beat him.

Thirty-odd years after his death, Thorpe's medals finally were restored, thanks to a Swedish researcher who discovered an escape hatch in the Olympic charter which specified that pro-

BILL TILDEN

The Artistic Court Jouster

William T. Tilden II was a society blueblood from Philadelphia's swank Main Line who fancied himself a Shakespearean actor and author yet found his stage to be the lush grass tennis courts of Germantown, Wimbledon and Forest Hills.

Years after advancing age and chronic injuries forced his retirement in 1933 at age 40, tennis buffs acclaimed him the greatest of all-time.

"A rare genius," said Berkeley Bell, a contemporary.

"No one ever studied the game as he did. No one ever produced a repertoire of spin, speed and variety to compare. An astounding man," added Vincent Richards, his onetime doubles partner.

"The greatest—there can never be another like him," said another American player of the era, J. Gilbert Hall.

They were assessments that found no dispute among the court experts of succeeding generations. In 1969, an international panel of tennis writers, with the heroics of Don Budge, Fred Perry, Jack Kramer and Rod Laver still fresh in their minds, voted Tilden the "Greatest Player of All-Time." Earlier an Associated Press half-century poll placed him alongside Babe Ruth, Jack Dempsey, Bob Jones and Red Grange as the greatest in his particular sport.

They called him "Big Bill," a designation to differentiate him from his sternest rival, "Little Bill" Johnston, a frail, 5-foot-8, 120-pound retriever who wore a ladylike 4½ size shoe.

Tilden was a magnetic figure on or off the court. Six feet, two inches tall with broad, sloping shoulders, a receding hairline and lantern jaw, he moved with a long stride and flowing grace. When he walked onto the Center Court at Wimbledon with his long white flannels, V-neck cable stitch sweater and a half-dozen wooden Top Flight racquets cradled in his arm, one could imagine that occupants of the Royal Box should stand and bow to him instead of the reverse ritual.

"Big Bill" gave every indication that it was indeed he who was tennis royalty, and let no one forget it.

Unlike the bam-bash, serve and volley breed who were to succeed him, he was strictly a backcourt specialist, taunting his opponents with spins, chops and slices that wrecked their rhythm while covering the court like a blanket. With his long legs and arms, there seemed no corner of the court he couldn't reach in one huge bound.

While content to battle with ground strokes, he could go to

Tilden playing at the National championships at Forest Hills in 1930. He won seven U.S. crowns and three Wimbledon men's singles titles.

Although Big Bill preferred the flat drive off both forehand and backhand, he developed spins, chops and slices. More than a mere striker of the ball, he was a tactician.

the net when desirable and his volleys, as the rest of his game, were sharp and deadly. He relied on a big service and forcing service returns.

"You cannot volley the service," he once said. "In any match between the perfect baseline player and the perfect net rusher, I would take the baseliner every time."

While that strategy is deplored by most modern teachers and their go-for-broke proteges, Sweden's Bjorn Borg gave it considerable credence in his five consecutive Wimbledon triumphs, starting in 1976.

Tilden was a perfectionist. After losing to "Little Bill" John-ston in the U.S. Championship finals at Forest Hills in 1919, he went into seclusion at a farm in Connecticut and spent the winter refining his backhand. He spent several hours a day hitting balls against a backboard. When spring appeared, he ended his hibernation and launched one of the most successful tennis careers in history.

Born Feb. 10, 1893 in Germantown, N.Y., he had a racquet thrust in his hand by the time he was big enough to walk. At the exclusive Germantown Cricket Club, he was exposed to some of the country's best players but he matured late. He was 27 years old before he won a major championship and that came after being personally tutored by Mary K. Browne, a national women's champion.

Tilden was the first American to win the men's singles championship at Wimbledon and he added two others, the last in 1930 at the age of 37. He put together a string of six U.S. crowns and added a seventh in 1929. He won seven National Clay Court titles, also the National Indoor and National Hard Court. In Davis Cup play, he won 17 singles matches and lost only five.

He became the stormy petrel of the game, feuding with the tennis establishment and frequently engaged in court antics that delighted rather than offended the galleries. He was puckish, sometimes headstrong and unpredictable. Crowds loved him. He never ceased being an actor.

He always said he got his artistic instincts from his mother, an accomplished violinist. His father was a prominent wool merchant.

Tilden called the tennis fathers "inept and stupid" when they suspended him for writing a tennis article for money. He never berated linesmen and umpires. But once when the crowd began booing him for what it considered a half-hearted effort, he meticulously gathered up his gear and walked off the court without explanation. Another time he staged a sitdown strike on the court until spectators were removed from trees outside the stadium.

Often Tilden, realizing that an opponent was an easy prey, would drop the first two sets purposely. Then when word went out that "Big Bill is in trouble" and spectators began flocking to the court, he would improve his game and run out the match.

It was his private little ploy to create drama.

"Big Bill" never got drama out of his blood. He appeared in several Shakespearean plays on stage as well as in "Dracula," Booth Tarkington's "Clarence," and, in 1942, his own production, "The Nice Harmons." He wrote several tennis books, some fiction, and none very successful.

After turning professional in 1931, Tilden took a tennis show on the road, making one-night stands against hand-picked rivals. When Ellsworth Vines beat him in a head-to-head, cross-country series, Tilden retired in 1933. He died June 5, 1953, at age 60, a bachelor, a broken man still seeking to reclaim some of his old glory on the tennis court or on the stage.

Still active at 58 years of age, Tilden scores first round victory in the International Pro Championships in Cleveland in 1951.

JOHNNY UNITAS

"Like Being in a Huddle With God"

The National Football League is a multi-million dollar operation, rich in scouts, ecstatic press-agentry and sophisticated terminology. But the case of Johnny Unitas makes one suspect that the NFL was not all that accomplished in the mid-1950s.

Nobody wanted Unitas in 1955. However, he eventually became one of the greatest players in the game's history. In 1957, he was named the league's most valuable player—the first of three occasions he was to receive this honor. In 1958, he led his team—the Baltimore Colts—to the league championship, a dramatic 23-17 overtime victory against the New York Giants that has been called "the greatest game ever played."

He also guided the Colts to the 1959 title, a 31-16 triumph over the Giants, and took Baltimore into the 1964 championship game, before losing to the Cleveland Browns 27-0.

In commemoration of the NFL's 50th anniversary, Unitas was voted the greatest quarterback in its history. He also was chosen the Pro Football Athlete of the Decade for the 1960s in a poll of the nation's sportswriters and sports broadcasters.

In his 18-year NFL career—17 years with the Colts, one year with the San Diego Chargers—Unitas completed 2,830 passes for 40,239 yards and 290 touchdowns, including at least one scoring pass in a record 47 consecutive games.

And in 1979, Unitas was inducted into the Pro Football Hall of Fame at Canton, Ohio.

In an emotion-packed ceremony on the steps of the domed shrine, the calm and dignified Unitas told an enthusiastic crowd of several thousand: "A man never gets to this station in life without being helped, aided, shoved, pushed and prodded to do better. I want to be honest with you, the players I played with and the coaches I had...they are directly responsible for my being here. I want you all to remember that. I always will."

It was a typical speech for a man who never was flamboyant, never overly enthusiastic, never boastful...who just did his job thoroughly, efficiently and quietly.

About the only criticism Unitas ever received was a charge that as his fame increased, he became conceited. But Unitas said, "There is a difference between conceit and confidence. A quarterback has to have confidence. Conceit is bragging about yourself. Confidence means you believe you can get the job done. I always believed I could."

And most often, he did.

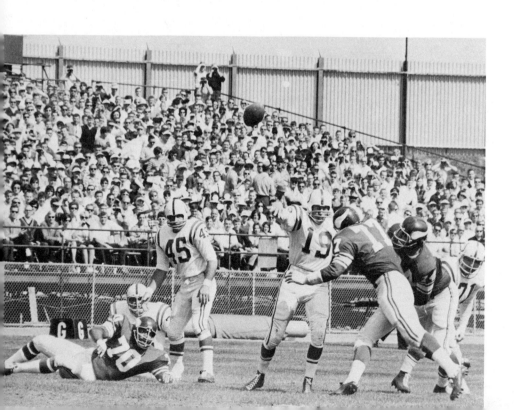

"He had the uncanny instinct for calling the right play at the right time," said Baltimore teammate Raymond Berry about Unitas. Here, Johnny (19) gets away a pass as Minnesota's Gary Larson (77) reaches out to grab him. The Colts won the 1966 game, 38-23.

Sid Luckman, also ranked among pro football's great quarterbacks, said, "Johnny Unitas is the greatest quarterback ever to play the game, better than I was, better than Sammy Baugh, better than anyone."

Raymond Berry, Unitas' teammate on the Colts and later coach of the New England Patriots, said, "What can I tell you about John Unitas? Well, I can tell you about his uncanny instinct for calling the right play at the right time, his icy composure under fire, his fierce competitiveness and his utter disregard for his own personal safety."

"I'm sure no one predicted such greatness for John Unitas in 1955," Berry added.

In 1955, after the Pittsburgh Steelers had selected Unitas on the ninth round of the NFL draft out of the University of Louisville, they cut him late in training camp. Before leaving, Unitas sent a telegram to Paul Brown asking for a tryout with Cleveland. Brown told him the team's quarterbacking positions were filled, but if he still was available to contact him the following year.

If it were not for Brown's encouraging reply, Unitas' football career might have ended then. As it was, he still seriously considered going into teaching. He had graduated from Louisville with a B.S. in physical education and economics.

Meanwhile, a former Louisville teammate, Freddie Zangaro, suggested that Unitas join him on a semi-pro club, the Bloomington Rams. Unitas was hesitant. He was married, with one child and another on the way.

"I didn't want to get busted up to where I wouldn't be able to work," he said, "but I finally decided to give it one year so that I'd be in shape if Paul Brown brought me to camp."

With the Rams, Unitas played on fields in Pittsburgh that were strewn with rocks and shattered glass. And he earned $6 a game!

If nothing else, the experience toughened him up for the NFL, which came calling in 1956. But instead of the Browns who sought his services, it was the Colts.

There are two stories of how Baltimore came to pick up Unitas. In one, General Manager Don Kellett insisted that in going over old waiver lists, he came across Unitas' name. "We had scouted him...and...had him down as a late draft choice if he was still eligible," Kellett said.

The other story, according to Coach Weeb Ewbank, is that "Unitas was signed after we received a letter from a fan—addressed to the club, not to me—telling us there was a player in Bloomington deserving a chance."

"I always accused Johnny of writing it," Ewbank said.

At any rate, Kellett offered Unitas a contract for $7,000. In his workouts with the Colts, Unitas was impressive, and Ewbank kept him as a backup to George Shaw.

But in the fourth game of the season, Shaw suffered a broken left leg, and Unitas was rushed into action. He did not make a very auspicious debut. His first pass was intercepted by Chicago's J.C. Caroline and returned for a touchdown. On the next play from scrimmage, Unitas collided with fullback Alan Ameche on a handoff and fumbled. The Bears recovered and scored again. Again the Colts received, again Unitas botched a handoff and again the Bears scored. The final score was: Chicago 58, Baltimore 27—after Unitas had inherited a 20-14 lead.

Ewbank was not discouraged about Unitas' dismal showing. He excused it by saying that the youngster had not had enough time to work with the first unit, and his timing was off. The following week, Unitas was ready, and he guided the Colts to a 28-21 victory over Green Bay. He also led them to three more victories that season, and finished with the highest completion average ever recorded by a rookie, 55.6 percent. He had become Baltimore's starting quarterback—and held the job for 16 more years.

During that stretch, he had the utmost respect of his teammates.

When Unitas gathered the offensive unit around him to call a play, tight end John Mackey said, "It's like being in a huddle with God."

Another Unitas completion...this one in 1969 game against the Dallas Cowboys. In commemoration of the NFL's 50th anniversary, Unitas was voted the greatest quarterback in its history.

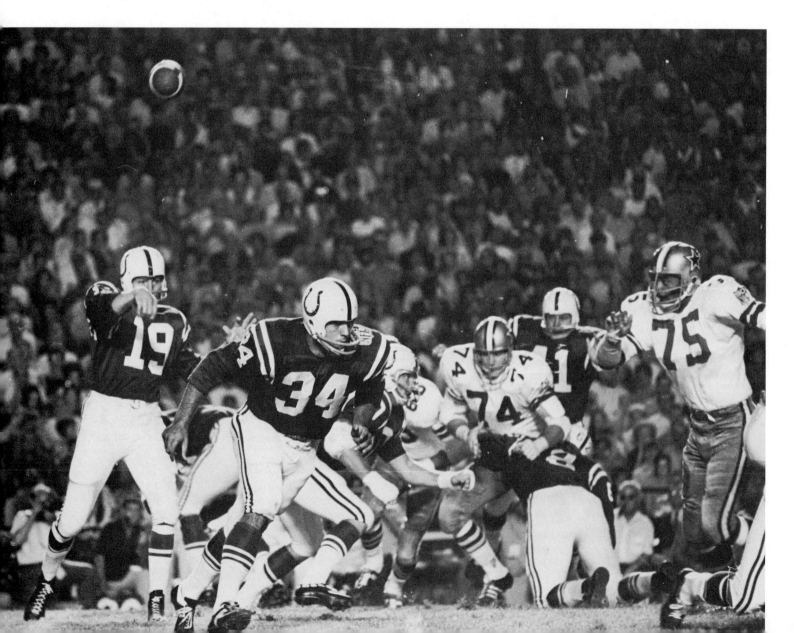

TOM WATSON

The Perennial Golfer of the Year

A young man, freckle-faced with a shock of red hair, and his wife were having breakfast in a Memphis, Tenn. Holiday Inn years ago.

They couldn't help but overhear two middle-aged couples at a nearby table who were busily misdirecting each other about how to get to the golf course for the first round of the Memphis Open.

Hopelessly confused, they asked the young man for help. He quickly sketched a map on a paper napkin, then suggested a prime viewing spot—near the 18th tee—once they found their way to the course.

"Have a nice day at the tournament," he said. "I hope you enjoy it."

"By any chance, are you one of the players?" asked one of the men.

"Yes, I am," said the young man.

"What's your name?"

"Tom Watson."

He was greeted with blank stares.

It was understandable.

At that time, Watson had yet to win a golf tournament. He was just one of the young hopefuls struggling for a career on the PGA Tour. He played where he could, fighting his way through qualifying rounds when he had to and playing in second-tour events when he couldn't make the main tour.

But even at that early stage, Watson was exhibiting some of the characteristics that helped him become one of golf's finest players, the dominant figure in the game at one time.

Chief among those virtues was patience, as illustrated by that scene with the middle-aged couples. He was cheerful, helpful and patient, interrupting his breakfast to be of assistance.

That patience was to be sorely tried only a couple of seasons later. It was necessary for Watson to score a triumph over himself and his emotions before he was able to go on to some heights reached by no other American on the tour.

Watson, a native of Kansas City, joined the PGA Tour in 1971 after receiving a degree in psychology from Stanford.

His amateur career was not distinguished, and, as a young pro, he was subject to all the learning experiences necessary for professional success: he had to learn to qualify into the tournament fields; he had to learn to make the cut and thus insure both a check from the current tournament and a place in the next one; he had to learn to contend; he had to learn to win, and then he had to learn to win the big events.

It wasn't easy.

His first real chance for victory came in the 1974 Hawaiian

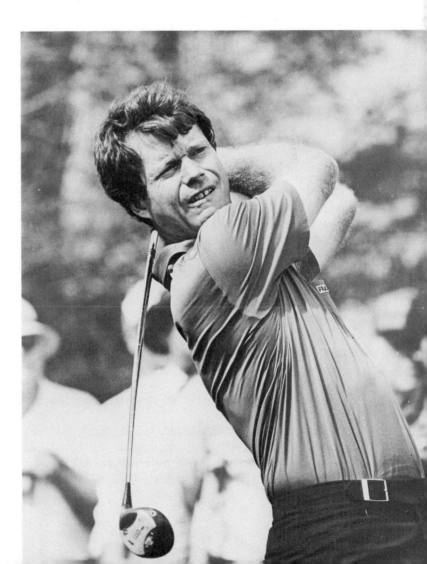

Tom Watson watches his tee shot on the 10th hole of the pro-am round of the 1985 USF&G Golf Classic in New Orleans. The previous year, Tom won a record sixth Player of the Year title and led the American tour in money-winnings.

The magnificent season lifted him into the front rank of golf's great stars. It was the first of four consecutive years in which he led the American tour in money-winnings; the first of four consecutive Player of the Year awards; the first of three consecutive Vardon Trophy awards.

In that four-year period, he won 20 American tournaments, including the Masters, and many foreign events, including two British Opens. He was the world's outstanding player.

Although he dropped out of the No. 1 money-winning spot, he remained the game's leading attraction, enhancing his record with another victory over Nicklaus in the 1981 Masters.

And in 1982, he achieved a lifelong ambition with one of the greatest shots in the history of golf.

Nicklaus was in the scoring tent beside the 18th green at the Pebble Beach Golf Links, signing a card he was certain would account for a record fifth U.S. Open title when a roar from the gallery reverberated along the cliffs and crags overlooking Carmel Bay and, at least momentarily, shocked him out of his customary composure.

Watson, in ankle-deep rough above and behind the 17th green, was facing at least a bogey, with double bogey a distinct possibility. Instead, he chipped the ball into the hole for a birdie that gave him the lead—and, one hole later, the U.S. Open title—and sent him scampering around the green, his putter raised in salute to the grandest moment of his golfing life.

He won a fifth British Open title at Royal Birkdale in 1983, becoming the first American—and only the fifth golfer—to win that title five times.

Watson won a record sixth Player of the Year title and again led the American tour in money-winnings in 1984, but his loss to Seve Ballesteros in the British Open at St. Andrews was the signal for a frustrating, puzzling slump that plagued him for more than two seasons.

Despite the slump, however, he had achieved his primary golfing goal.

"When my career is done, I want to have the respect of my peers," Watson said. "I want to know that they'll be sitting around, talking, years from now, and someone will be able to say, 'You know, that Watson, he was one heckuva player'."

He can be sure of that.

Open. It didn't materialize. He faded in the final round, but left the Hawaiians talking enthusiastically about "The Kid."

It was only the first of many to get away from him.

Although he scored his first triumph in the 1974 Western Open—with wife Linda too nervous to watch the action, sitting cross-legged on the floor of the press room talking to friends— Watson had trouble preserving a lead.

Time after time, he'd put himself in or near the lead, then falter.

Even though he won the 1975 British Open on the windswept moors of Carnoustie in a playoff against Jack Newton, he couldn't escape the stigma of a last-round collapse in the U.S. Open earlier that season.

His name began to be associated with the word "choker."

Despite the enormous frustrations, he patiently bided his time, working on his game, improving his skills, awaiting the time it would all come together.

It did in 1977.

He erased forever the "choker" label in most dramatic fashion, beating Jack Nicklaus in a run down the back nine at Augusta National and claiming his first Masters title.

He won three other American titles that year and capped the season with the victory that established his dominance in the game.

That was at Turnberry, Scotland, where he again beat Nicklaus in one of the greatest golf tournaments ever played. Watson won that British Open by one stroke with a record 268 score, including 65s in the final two rounds.

JOHNNY WEISSMULLER

Tarzan of the Swim Lanes

When Mark Spitz electrified the 1972 Olympic Games in Munich, Germany, by sweeping to an unimaginable seven gold medals in swimming, there was one man who was relatively unimpressed. Living out his days more renowned as the movie Tarzan, 68-year-old Johnny Weissmuller said, "I was better than Spitz. I never lost a race."

Whether or not he was correct on his first premise, which shall forever be a matter of conjecture, he found no dissenters of the latter, which probably was stated more in honest conviction than in idle boast.

Johnny Weissmuller was king of the water in sport's Golden Age of the 1920s, which bred such athletic giants as Babe Ruth, Jim Thorpe, Jack Dempsey, Bill Tilden and Babe Didrikson, all of whom were voted the greatest of their craft over the first half-century in a 1950 poll of the nation's sports writers and broadcasters by The Associated Press.

This strapping, handsome son of struggling Viennese immigrants dominated his sport as none ever did before and none has done since, although changing times, scientific research, diet and new techniques have enabled 15-year-old girls to record faster times in events in which he excelled.

Weissmuller was unbeatable for more than a decade in every distance from 50 yards to half a mile. He won a total of five gold medals in two Olympics, captured 52 national titles and shattered 67 world records in his incredible career. He touched first in every race he ever swam.

Weissmuller competed under primitive conditions compared with later conditions in the sport. When he raced, there were no starting blocks, flip turns or lane ropes. He didn't have the benefit of all the intricate coaching ideas developed in ensuing generations. Yet he was far ahead of all his rivals.

Weissmuller was born June 2, 1904, in Windber, Pennsylvania, in the heart of the coal country. His father worked in the mines. Johnny was a tyke of eight when the family pulled up stakes and moved to Chicago where the elder Weissmuller, a moody and often abusive man, got a job as a saloon keeper and died shortly afterward.

The Weissmullers' modest second-floor, frame apartment

Weissmuller (left) defeated Hawaii's Duke Kahanamoku (right) in the 100-meter men's swimming finals in the 1924 Olympic Games in Paris. Johnny also won the gold in the 400-meter freestyle and shared victory in the 800-meter relay. Four years later, he captured two more Olympic gold medals in Amsterdam.

Johnny beat out more than 100 candidates for the title role in the movie "Tarzan of the Apes," the first of a long-running series of Tarzan motion pictures. His co-star was Maureen O'Sullivan and a featured role was played by Cheetah, a chimpanzee.

was near Fullerton Beach on Lake Michigan and that's where Johnny and a younger brother, Peter, spent their idle hours splashing around in the surf that lashed the shoreline boulders. "It was dangerous but, to a couple of kids like us, very adventurous," Johnny was to recall later. "Swimming just came natural to us."

With his mother struggling to make ends meet, Johnny quit school and took odd jobs to help the family survive. He worked as an errand boy for a while, and later got a job as a bellhop at the Chicago Plaza hotel.

"Your guts get mad when you try to fight poverty and its constant and inevitable companion—ignorance," he said. "I made up my mind to fight my way out of it any way I could."

When Johnny was 16 he was persuaded by a friend to try out for the swimming team at the Illinois Athletic Club. There the youngster, tall and skinny, fell under the influence of a coach, a bulbous, 350-pound man named Bill Bachrach, naturally called "Big Bill." Johnny, wearing a swimming cap to control a head of hair that fell below the nape of his neck, was impressive in a junior meet and, because he showed a lot of natural ability, captured the undivided attention of "Big Bill."

"Stick with me, son," said Bachrach, "and I'll make you a champion." After Weissmuller won a junior 100-yard freestyle in the 1921 Central AAU Championships, Big Bill began hustling well-heeled members of the club by betting them the scrawny kid could swim certain distances in faster time than the world record. With timekeepers and stop watches on hand, Johnny kept padding Big Bill's wallet.

Later in 1921, Weissmuller, at age 17, won the 50-yard freestyle in the National AAU Championships in 23.2 seconds, a fifth of a second off the world mark, and shortly afterward broke the world 150-yard record in 1 minute, 27.4 seconds at Brighton Beach, New York. Still just a kid, he married the first of his five wives, a beach girl named Lorelei.

Johnny had hit bigtime. With Bachrach as tutor, he made a trip to Hawaii for an exhibition and then set his sights on the 1924 Olympics in Paris. He qualified by beating the marks of Hawaii's Duke Kahanamoku, a two-time Olympic champion.

Having beaten the Duke's time, Weissmuller now had to beat the Hawaiian in person in their first confrontation in the 100-meter finals—not just one Kahanamoku but two, since the Duke's younger brother, Sam, also was in the race.

Off winging, Johnny won the 100 meters in 59 seconds flat. He also took the gold in the 400-meter freestyle in 5:04.2 and shared the victory in the 800-meter relay. Four years later, he won Olympic gold medals in the 100-meter freestyle and in the 800-meter relay in Amsterdam.

Johnny toured Europe and returned to find himself much in demand in American cities. It was while in Hollywood that he met the swashbuckling Douglas Fairbanks, Sr., who looked over the swimmer's sleek, muscled 6-foot-3, 195-pound figure and suggested him for a movie part which he had turned down.

The movie was "Tarzan of the Apes," based on the Edgar Rice Burroughs' novel. Johnny beat out more than 100 candidates for the title role in which he co-starred with demure Maureen O'Sullivan as Jane and a chimpanzee named Cheetah.

With his long hair and lithe, muscled physique scantily clad in loin cloth, Weissmuller became an American staple for generations, his long-running series of Tarzan movies repeated later in TV reruns. Meanwhile, he had a succession of wives, including actress Lupe Velez, but children by only his fifth, Maria, who bore him three heirs. He retired to Fort Lauderdale, Florida, site of the International Swimming Hall of Fame, and died January 21, 1984 at the age of 79.

JERRY WEST

The Lakers' "Mr. Clutch"

There are two ways to sum up the brilliance of Jerry West. With a record book—or simply with a nickname.

The record book shows that West was a high school star, a two-time college All-America at West Virginia University, captain of the 1960 U.S. Olympic gold medal-winning team, a 10-time first-team NBA All-Star with the Los Angeles Lakers and a member of the Basketball Hall of Fame.

West's career scoring average of 27.1 points per game is third in NBA history. His 29.1 playoff average is No. 1 all-time. He also was named to four NBA All-Defensive teams in the first five years the award was given.

West's nickname, "Mr. Clutch," best describes his play under pressure.

"Jerry West is by far the greatest clutch player who ever

Jerry West, referred to by the Lakers' president, Bill Sharman, as "the greatest shooter when the game was on the line," attempts to elude Ron Williams of San Francisco and move into scoring position in this 1970 NBA game.

The Lakers' "Mr. Clutch" soars high to score with a one-hander against the Cincinnati Royals on Dec. 11, 1962. Wayne Embry (15) of the Royals waits for the rebound which didn't materialize.

played," said long-time Lakers' broadcaster Chick Hearn. "He made basket after basket to win games."

"He was undoubtedly the greatest shooter when the game was on the line," said Lakers' President Bill Sharman, a Hall of Famer who coached West and the Lakers to the 1972 NBA championship. "Throughout his career, he must have won 40 to 50 games with the last basket."

Ironically, West's most famous shot may have come in a game that the Lakers didn't win.

The Lakers and New York Knicks were tied in the final seconds of regulation play in Game 3 of the 1970 NBA finals when Bill Bradley sank a jumper to give the Knicks an apparent victory.

West took the inbounds pass and let fly from the top of the foul circle in his backcourt...a shot of more than 60 feet. The ball went through the net.

If West had made that shot today, he would have had another game-winner. But in the pre three-point field goal era, all his long-distance shot did was tie the score. The Knicks went on to win in overtime and eventually captured their first NBA crown.

But there were numerous other games in which West's last-second heroics turned a loss into a victory. One of the most famous was the 1972 NBA All-Star Game, played at the Lakers' home arena, the Forum in Inglewood, Calif.

With the score tied at 110 and time running out, West, playing for the West team, took an inbounds pass, dribbled toward the basket and—with New York defensive ace Walt Frazier covering him closely—calmy hit the game-winning basket.

"I definitely wanted him to take that shot," said Sharman, who was coaching the West squad that night. "It was a typical 'Mr. Clutch' type of shot."

"It was total excitement," remembered Hearn, who was calling the game on radio, "because they were playing in the Forum and Jerry was such an idol there."

Despite his heroics, West said he wasn't fond of the "Mr. Clutch" label.

"I really don't like that name," he said late in his career. "I've had some bad games, too, and when I do, when I miss the winning shot or something, people can use it to make fun of me.

"Besides, if you play well for 10 games and then do badly in

West gets set to shoot a free throw during a December, 1970 game in Atlanta. The shot was good and gave West an NBA regular season total career of 20,000 points. He finished his career with 25,192.

the next one, that's the one they're going to remember. You're only as good as your last game."

Still, when the game was on the line, West got the ball.

"I know I play well under pressure," he said. "I don't know why; maybe the challenge stimulates me. I want the ball. I know I can do something positive with it because I've done it before...and I'm proud of it."

Fred Schaus, who coached West at West Virginia and again with the Lakers, said his star guard "had everything—a fine shooting touch, speed, quickness, all the physical assets, plus a tremendous dedication to the game."

One thing that West didn't have, however, was freedom from injuries. Only once, in his rookie season of 1960-61, did he

manage to play every game. By the time age and nagging injuries convinced him to retire after the 1973-74 season, West had piled up a medical dossier including nine broken noses and two broken hands.

West's on-court success has followed him into his post-playing career. He coached the Lakers to three straight playoff berths during the late 1970s, then served as a consultant to the team before being named its general manager in 1982.

But it's as a player that West is best remembered.

"His concern was: No. 1 for basketball, No. 2 for the team and No. 3 for Jerry West," said Hearn. "That's about the highest accolade you can give a player."

TED WILLIAMS

Last of the .400 Hitters

They said his eyesight was so keen he could read the autograph of the American League president on the ball as it sped to the plate. When he served in the military, they said he had the vision of one in 100,000. He almost never swung at a ball an inch out of the strike zone and umpires came to respect his judgment.

If Ted Williams was not the greatest hitter in baseball, he was acknowledged to be the purest—a tall, stringbean of a man with a classic upright, left-handed stance, a long and flowing swing and wrists like bear traps that could uncoil in a lightning instant and propel the ball to distant targets as accurately as a William Tell bow.

Legend is that once in batting practice he wagered he could hit the painted footage figure on an outfield wall. He bounced the ball off the "O."

Playing half his games in Boston's Fenway Park, with its nearby leftfield wall providing favoritism for right-handed hitters, the so-called Splendid Splinter was the only batter in modern times to break the .400 mark. His .406 in 1941 was the first to reach that elusive plateau in the American League since Harry Heilmann in 1923 and the first in the majors since Bill Terry of the New York Giants in 1930.

Despite two tenures of military duty, which took five full seasons out of his career, Williams polled 521 home runs and compiled a lifetime batting average of .344. He led the league six times in batting average and runs scored, four times in home runs and four times in runs batted in.

At 39 years of age, Williams became the oldest player in Major League history to win a batting crown, winning his fifth in 1957. He won it again at 40 in 1958.

He had a lifetime slugging average of .634, second only to Babe Ruth. In this statistic, based on times at bat and total bases, he set a club record with .735 in 1941 and an astronomical .901 in 1953 while playing only 37 games after returning from the service. He hit 13 home runs and batted .407 in that abbreviated stretch.

He also ranked second to Ruth in bases on balls. He had 2,018 walks. Twice he was walked 162 times in a single season, including a streak of 19 straight games in 1941. Pitchers rarely attempted to brush him back or knock him down.

Williams drills a long home run against the New York Yankees in 1952 game. Also observing the Thumper's power are Yankee catcher Ralph Houk and umpire Ed Hurley.

Five times he hit 35 or more home runs in a year. Three times he hit three homers in a single game. He had 17 grand slam and seven pinch-hit home runs, blunting some critics' charges that he couldn't hit in the clutch.

Battling such criticism became the negative and galling aspect to his brilliant 19-year career with the Boston Red Sox, covering four decades. Williams was both a sports idol and anti-hero in a city notorious for its demanding fans and caustic, competitive press.

"I've got the best pair of rabbit ears in all of baseball," the great slugger acknowledged later. "Those fans in the left field stands were vicious. I admit I blew my top."

High-strung and sensitive, he early developed an adversarial relationship with a small and ugly segment of the fans and much of the news media.

He sulked and refused to talk to newsmen, who he felt never gave him a fair shake. In his rookie year he became so angry at being booed for a miscue that he decided never again to tip his cap—a cherished baseball ritual—when the fans gave him an ovation. It was a vow that he never broke—even after the stands exploded in wild acclaim in 1960 when he closed out his career with his 521st and longest home run.

Prodded on why he continued never to tip his cap, Williams wryly replied, "Why should I? Does the pitcher tip his cap when he strikes me out?...Let 'em cheer and let 'em boo. My cap stays on."

In 1950, razzed by the fans for a couple of errors, temperamental Ted responded with a profane gesture, for which he was fined $5,000. "I was out of line," he said later. "When those buzzards poured out the abuse, I blew my cork."

Baseball's complex clouter was born August 30, 1918, in San Diego, California, and given the proud handle of Theodore Samuel Williams, by his mother, a Salvation Army worker who later was deserted by his unstable father.

Ted's religious mother kept him under tight restraint. She refused to let him play on a local team run by a liquor store owner. But he played American Legion, high school and semi-pro baseball, where he showed outstanding promise as both a pitcher and hitter. He batted .586 and .403 in high school, attracting scouts. He joined San Diego in the Pacific Coast League as a pitcher at age 17, earning $150 a month.

It was there that Eddie Collins saw the lean and hungry-looking youngster—then 6-3 and 143 pounds—and recommended him to millionaire Tom Yawkey, owner of the Boston Red Sox, who signed the kid with reluctance in 1938.

At Boston's spring camp "The Kid," as Ted became known, was brash and cocky, antagonizing teammates. So Manager Joe Cronin assigned him to the club's Minneapolis triple-A farm for both seasoning and humbling. The latter didn't take.

Williams still had a chip on his shoulder when he joined the Red Sox in 1939 but there was no way to keep The Kid's big bat

Although the shift packing infielders on the right side of the infield against the lefty-hitting Williams was devised by Cleveland manager Lou Boudreau, the St. Louis Cardinals used it during the 1946 World Series. Note, third baseman Whitey Kurowski shifts to a normal second base position and second baseman Red Schoendienst moves closer to Stan Musial at first. Marty Marion remained at shortstop.

*Williams crosses home plate on Sept. 28, 1960
after hitting his 521st and final major league
homer. Greeting him is the next batter, Boston
catcher Jim Pagliaroni.*

out of the lineup. In his rookie year, Ted batted .327, hit 31 homers and knocked in a league-leading 145 runs.

He grew bigger and stronger, finally reaching 200 pounds, and continued to dominate pitchers. Yet, he never mellowed. He spat at hostile customers and shunned the press.

When Lou Boudreau of the Cleveland Indians devised the "Boudreau Shift," packing fielders on the right side of the field, Williams ignored the challenge and refused to finesse the ball to the left. "I'm paid to hit," he said.

Despite a three-year hitch in World War II as a Marine fighter pilot and a recall for the Korean War, he never lost the symphony and power of his swing. He retired at the end of the 1960 season at age 42, managed the now defunct Washington Senators briefly and finally settled down to his other two loves—Florida fishing and his Jimmy Fund for crippled children.

BABE DIDRIKSON ZAHARIAS

The Phenomenal Wonder Woman

During the 1970s and 1980s tykes and grown people alike were enthralled by the mighty deeds of a fictional character called "Wonder Woman," who could leap over the tallest skyscraper in a bound, choke a lion to death with her bare hands and destroy an evil enemy's army without catching a second breath. Her mighty exploits became a regular diet in the Sunday comics, on Saturday's cartoon dramas and even a prime-time TV series.

Engrossing as were these make-believe heroics, everyone accepted this powerful female character for what she was—a figment of a story-book writer's imagination. No such person ever lived.

But one did—on a smaller and more realistic scale but no less amazing in the breadth of her physical feats. Her name was Mildred "Babe" Didrikson Zaharias, and she truly was the "Wonder Woman" of the age, not colored newsprint or flimsy film but real life flesh and blood.

"The athletic phenomenon of our time, man or woman," wrote Grantland Rice, the nation's most respected sports writer of the period, bridging the two World Wars.

She was the lean, raw-boned daughter of a Norwegian ship's carpenter who settled in Port Arthur, Texas. She was an All-America on a Dallas semipro women's basketball team that won three national titles. She once threw a baseball 296 feet to win a national contest. In an exhibition baseball game, she struck out Joe DiMaggio.

She competed in eight track and field events in the national Olympic trials and won five—the 80-meter hurdles, baseball throw, shot put, long jump and javelin—setting three world records. In the 1932 Olympics in Los Angeles, at age 19, she won gold medals in the hurdles and javelin and should have had a third in the high jump but was disqualified for diving over the bar, a technique later ruled legal.

There was no sport she wouldn't try. She even donned heavy pads and headgear to mix it up with the guys in football. She played tennis, bowled, fenced, skated and became adept at shooting, cycling, billiards and handball.

Later in life, she took up golf at the suggestion of Grantland Rice. The first tournament in which she played she shot a 95. After three lessons, she got her score down to 83. She could belt the ball 250 yards off the tee. She became the world's best woman golfer, winning both the British and U.S. ladies' amateur championships before turning pro to give birth to the ladies' golf tour. She won the U.S. Women's Open three times, the last in 1954 when she was dying of cancer.

In her early years, she even boxed. She signed for a bout with

The Babe, second from right, leads her USA teammate, Evelyne Hall (right) over last hurdle to win the 80-meter hurdles event during the 1932 Olympic Games in Los Angeles.

the brother of heavyweight contender Young Stribling but withdrew with an apology and vow:

"I've decided I want to be a lady now."

In all of her achievements in realms dominated by men, the "Babe," as she became popularly known, fought to maintain her femininity.

Difficult as it was, since she was more comfortable in baggy slacks and sweat shirt, she forced herself to wear frilly dresses, have her hair coiffeured and nails polished at a beauty salon and labor with high heels for formal occasions. She was good with the sewing machine. She could cook. She was proud that she could type 80 to 100 words a minute. She was a graceful ballroom dancer.

She played the harmonica, read good books, beat all her friends in gin rummy and amused herself solving difficult crossword puzzles.

"There's not a crossword puzzle I can't finish in half an hour," she once boasted.

The "Babe" was not unattractive. She had long legs and supple muscles and a strong and expressive face framed by a shock of short, dark hair. She was ebullient, admired and beloved by contemporaries, but as free and unharnessed in her public relations as in her athletic endeavors.

She disdained phoniness and was inclined to talk and act on impulse, without thought of social niceties.

In winning the British Ladies' golf title in 1947, the first

American to do so, she started out by wearing a proper skirt but shifted to what she called her "lucky pants" between rounds, stunning the sensitive British galleries.

When a British journalist asked her how she managed to get so much distance on her drives, she replied:

"I just loosen my girdle and let the ball have it."

Once, playing in stifling heat in a tournament outside Philadelphia, she called a recess in the fairway of the fourth hole, summoned some women to make a circle, removed her slip and tossed it over to her caddie.

Another time, playing an exhibition, a gentleman opponent politely offered her the honor of driving off first.

"You better hit first," she said, "because it's the last time you'll get the honor. And you better bust a good one if you don't want to be outdriven twenty yards by a gal."

The Babe's outgoing personality made her a natural show business commodity on which she capitalized after her Olympic triumphs and augmented following her sensational golf victories. She was much in demand. She played golf exhibitions with such greats as Gene Sarazen. She won a fly-casting contest over Ted Williams. She worked out with the Southern Methodist University football team. In 1947, she signed a $300,000 contract with a movie company.

A year later, she played in a golf tournament as a partner of a burly, 300-pound professional wrestler named George Zaharias, who was advertised as "The Crying Greek from Cripple Creek." It was a disaster. The two headstrong personalities barked at each other all around the course. A few months later they were married.

It was a match made in heaven. The two adored each other. Independently wealthy, Zaharias retired to help take care of the Babe's affairs. Their dream world ended tragically. In 1953, the Babe was diagnosed as having terminal cancer. On September 27, 1956, at the age of 43, she died—the greatest woman athlete the world has known.

Anyone for boxing? In 1933, Babe put on the gloves and worked out at a New York gym to keep in trim while looking for contracts to start a pro career as an athlete. Later, she became the world's best woman golfer.

EMIL ZATOPEK

The Indefatigable Czech

"**Z**a-to-pek! Za-to-Pek."
Like the clackety-clack of the wheels of a rumbling train under a full head of steam, the chant reverberated through Helsinki's spacious Olympic Stadium and seemed to reach into the heavens and fall like thunder on the ears of the world.

It might well have been the theme song of the 1952 Games, the second of the great international sports festivals following the 12-year hiatus of World War II. It was also the first in history to produce the head-to-head confrontation on the athletic field of the two surviving powers—the United States and the Communist giant of the Soviet Union and its satellites.

Emil "The Indefatigable" Zatopek ran under the red colors of Czechoslovakia, a part of the Iron Curtain bloc. But politics and ideologies were forgotten as this balding, reed-thin Czech army officer churned to long distance running feats that never before had been achieved and, according to most track and field authorities, probably will never be duplicated again.

Zatopek swept to victory in three of the most demanding tests in sports—the 5,000 meters, 10,000 meters and the marathon, the latter a footrace covering 26 miles and 385 yards. Finland's fabulous Paavo Nurmi had won the 1,500 and 5,000 meters in 1924 and the 10,000 meters in 1920 and 1928 but to capture all three in a single meet would have defied his own comprehension.

Emil Zapotek was a scrawny man with a seemingly frail frame at 5 feet, 8 inches tall and 145 pounds. As he ran, it appeared he might collapse at any minute, falling prostrate on the track, gasping for breath.

His style was far from classic. As his pounding spikes chewed up the yards, his head bobbed from side to side, his arms flailed the air and his face became contorted as if he were suffering the severest pain.

Red Smith, the famous columnist, who covered the Helsinki Games, wrote that Zatopek ran "like a man with a noose about his neck...on the verge of strangulation...his hatchet face crimson, his tongue lolled out."

No matter. The crowd loved it. And as the inexhaustible Czech moved from event to event, his popularity grew. He became the Games' cult hero and fans by the thousands jammed the stadium to appreciate his awkward brilliance and cheer him on.

Zatopek, son of a laborer and second youngest of eight children, left home at 16 and got a job in a shoe factory. In Communist countries, clubs and factories engage heavily in sports competitions. Emil first ran for the shoe factory. He showed

The straining Zatopek breaks the 5,000 meters Olympic record in the 1952 Games in Helsinki, Finland.

enough speed and dedication to be chosen for special training. He decided to concentrate on distance running.

He ran at night, wearing heavy boots and carrying a flashlight. He initiated his own routine which confounded his coaches. He said he got the idea from the great Nurmi.

"I heard that Paavo Nurmi, in one hour, was able to run four times 400 meters in excellent time," he explained later. "I thought what if I make six times 400 meters, more than Nurmi, and what if I run a short distance, 100 meters, at full speed and then not sit but jog, and do that over and over again."

Trainers scoffed at his regimen but Zatopek continued it. To practice for the 10,000, he would run five times 200 meters, 20 times 400 meters and five times 200 meters. He never sat. He jogged between routines.

Soon he was the best long distance runner in Czechoslovakia. He did what most good Communist athletes do—he joined the army. In the 1948 Olympics in London, the first in 12 years, he won the 10,000 meters going away but finished second in the 5,000, rallying from 30 yards back to lose by two-tenths of a second. He skipped the marathon. In 1949, he broke Viljo Heino's world record in the 10,000 with a clocking of 29 minutes and 28 seconds.

At Helsinki in 1952, Zatopek won the 10,000 meters easily. The Finns took to him naturally. Nurmi had left in them a deep-seated devotion to long distance running. Zatopek said he worried about the 5,000 meters not only because of the stronger field but because the shorter race left him confused on strategy. Should he set the pace or lay back and unleash a kick at the end?

Zatopek relied on instinct and confidence in his staying powers. With 200 meters to go, he trailed Chris Chataway of Britain, Alain Mimoun of France and Herbert Schade of Germany but, with the roar of "Za-to-pek" ringing in his ears, he spurted to win by four meters.

He called it the most rewarding day of his career. He not only had two gold medals but his wife, Dana, added another for the family cabinet by winning the javelin. In addition, it convinced Zatopek he should also try for the marathon, a race he had never won, and a shot at the "impossible triple slam" of distance running.

Helsinki was beside itself. The big stadium was jammed with chanting fans. Zatopek didn't disappoint. Running a strategic race, he burst into the arena amid a deafening roar, his face grimacing, head bobbing and arms flying. He set an Olympic record.

Zatopek became a national hero. He was a colonel in the army. He received all the government gratuities lavished on sports heroes—home, car, the works. The honeymoon was short-lived.

A liberal and supreme patriot, he openly criticized the USSR's stranglehold on his homeland.

He argued that, to survive, Communism must give its adherents "air to breathe."

He was stripped of his rank. He was reduced to menial jobs such as cleaning toilets. He and Dana lived for a while in a trailer before moving to a modest home in the country. But no one could destroy the legend of the indefatigable Czech.